Lenny Lipton is also the author of
Lipton on Filmmaking
The Super 8 Book
Foundations of the Stereoscopic Cinema

INDEPENDENT FILMMAKING

REVISED EDITION

LENNY LIPTON

Introduction by
Stan Brakhage

with Video for the Filmmaker

A FIRESIDE BOOK
Published by Simon & Schuster, Inc.
NEW YORK

Simon & Schuster Building
Rockefeller Center
1230 Avenue of the Americas
New York, New York 10020
FIRESIDE and colophon are registered trademarks of Simon & Schuster, Inc.
Manufactured in the United States of America
Printed and bound by Fairfield Graphics
3 5 7 9 10 8 6 4
Library of Congress Cataloging in Publication Data
Lipton, Lenny
Independent filmmaking.
"A Fireside book."
Includes index.
1. Cinematography. I. Title.
TR850.L62   1983   778.5'3   83-475
ISBN 0-671-46258-X

This book is dedicated to Diane Julie,
and to the memory of
Uncle Bill, who has joined
the Buddhas.

Contents

Author's Preface
to the Revised Edition

For some time now people have been asking me to revise *Independent Filmmaking*. I remember one film instructor who shook his head and clicked his tongue and told me I'd better hurry up and get the job done. Now, after having sold some 100,000 copies, *Independent Filmmaking* begins its second decade in print in a completely revised and updated edition.

There have already been a number of corrected printings, updating the text on a more or less minimal basis. But this edition represents a much broader effort at changing the existing text, and as the reader will see for himself, or herself, I've added a chapter, *Video for the Filmmaker*. This chapter is not primarily designed for people who want to work directly in video. It aims to orient filmmakers to the possibilities of video, and the technical means whereby film and video may be successfully interfaced. This material supplements rather than replaces anything in the revised body of the text.

For the past several years I have been deeply involved in video, and the word *deeply* is to be taken literally. My organization, Stereographics Corp., designed and built what is to my knowledge the first good quality NTSC-compatible stereoscopic television system. But there isn't anything about stereoscopic video herein, since the subject is too esoteric for most readers of this book. Those who are interested in three-dimensional video might obtain a copy of *Foundations of the Stereoscopic Cinema*, published by Van Nostrand Reinhold in 1982.

That film instructor I alluded to earlier wasn't quite on the mark. It is true that a number of changes in motion picture technology have taken place, but few of them are genuinely earthshaking. Ninety to ninety-five percent of what was written here more than ten years ago is as good today as it was then. New cameras have arrived on the scene, but the old ones are as good as ever. Film stock of greatly improved characteristics has been introduced. Most important, the 16mm filmmaker has fast, good quality negative materials with which to work. In fact, this switch from reversal to negative is undoubtedly the most significant trend in recent years.

Nevertheless, film technology has remained basically the same. Looked at through a microscope, the statement doesn't stand up, but given a reasonable perspective, I think it's correct. Film technology was very well advanced when I wrote the original version of *Independent Filmmaking*. Thus, changes have been minimal, or I could even characterize them as superficial. Given the wisdom granted by hindsight, *predictable* may be a better word.

Video technology, on the other hand, is newer. Video recording is only three decades old and many video formats have come and gone, whereas the original 35mm format designed by Edison and Eastman is still with us, virtually unchanged. One basic difference is that film emulsions can be improved without any need to invent a new film format, which would require new film cameras. For example, the cameras which were used to shoot features at the studios in black and white in the forties were simply loaded with new films from Ansco and Eastman in the fifties to enable them to shoot color.

Such is not the case for video. New tape formats or methods for encoding better quality signals require substantial changes to the video infrastructure, most notably to video tape recorders. In addition, new types of light-sensitive camera pickup devices have led to improvements, not to mention the rapid advances in solid state circuitry, which have vastly simplified the innards of all video equipment. And the changes continue, at an accelerated pace.

No book could possibly keep up with the state of the video art. The monthly magazines devoted to video are barely equal to the task. Therefore, I have tried to skirt the problem by sticking to fundamentals, to more basic principles, which hopefully will withstand the test of time, or a few years at least, so that the information I am imparting will remain useful in book form.

Point Richmond, California   *August 1982*

Introduction

Every filmmaker is independent at heart, as surely as each human
being is alone, finally, in every activity that has any personal
meaning — thus this is a handbook for every filmmaker, whether he
is a beginner or an experienced one. I realize that is as suspicious
a statement as those extravagant claims made for snake oil by the
19th century 'drummers'; but this book is really that kind of a
miracle that, say, aspirin is; and it does manage to solve most technical headaches, whether they be those of a 'know-nothing' amateur or those of a 'know-too-much' professional.

The so-called 'professional's' worst handicap, in making
anything, is that his knowledge sets into him and concretizes all his
thought, thus blocking him from creative adventure. The main
attempt, in the writing of this book, is to get most of this technically complex, constantly changing, sprawling subject between
'covers' in a language clearly understandable and even fun to read,
so that beginners can have a good beginning and more experienced
filmmakers can have a text wherewith they may 'shake up' and 'refocus' all their personal knowledge of the medium, and 'fill-in' the
often missing links (such as, say 'lab talk') which connect one area
of this subject matter with another.

I was never a 'fan' of Lenny Lipton's weekly column in *The
Berkeley Barb;* and, in fact, I came to quarrelsome words with him,
once, about what I took to be the sloppy rhetoric of his writing style
therein; I mention this because I want to assure all those who may
have shared my view of his newspaper style, that it does *not* infect
this text. His playful explosiveness of language is held in absolute
balance by the technical nature of this book and the intensity which
he accorded to the task of writing it. This book is obviously a labor
of love; and it prompted all the many aspects of Mr Lipton's nature:
the filmmaker; the technical perfectionist; the teacher; the 'barbed'
wit; the journalist; and, perhaps most of all, the film appreciator.
His language is brimful of joy, herein; but it never 'spills over' or,
in any way, distracts from the technical information it constantly
imparts at the center of all pleasurable reading.

I began filmmaking coincident with the publication of
Raymond Spottiswoode's *Film and Its Techniques;* and it was the
only guide in the maze of machinery I'd then entered which was of
any use to me whatsoever. Yet its influence on my early endeavors
was a mixed blessing: for the general assumption of that book is
that the filmmaker reader is contemplating a commercial career;
and its sense of the term 'independence' terminates in the idea that
the filmmaker may create a small film business of himself as a

'freelance' photographer, etc. Most of Mr Spottiswoode's book was, therefore, of no use to me, either as beginning filmmaker or latter-day perfectionist; and much of it had to be 'argued with,' while reading it, to prevent its commercial assumptions from infecting any creative filmmaking that might be coming out of me. Still, in the twenty-some intervening years, I've recommended it to hundreds of students and beginning amateurs and hopeful artists, having no better text to offer. What a relief, then, that there is now, herein Mr Lipton's book, the antidote to the clutch of commerce upon all technical information. What a relief to have, at last, the first book I can fully recommend to any filmmaker, whether he's thinking of himself as artist or hoping for a Hollywooden career.

It has been my experience, from earning a living often as a commercial filmmaker, that the success of even a professional *is* absolutely dependent upon his sense of himself as intrinsically independent: commerce, for him, is a means to an end; and, while its limitations may trap him creatively in the end, the meantime of his rise to commercial recognition is, almost always, conditioned by his independence of attitude within a job limitation. Gertrude Stein wrote that there are only two kinds of people: 'independent dependents' and 'dependent independents.' I think this book is written for both of these possibilities. I stress this point, as introduction, because I think Mr Lipton takes his ability, naturally, for granted: whereas 'the reader,' whoever he may be, will find this the *most* crucial question when imagining himself as filmmaker. I wish to encourage him to take full advantage of this happily open and unprejudiced text to focus his sense of himself in preparation for any making he may consider.

My other book recommendation (these last twenty years) as an opposite alternative to Mr Spottiswoode's, has been the *American Cinematographer Manual* (mentioned by Mr Lipton throughout this book): this is strictly a pocket reference manual, revised and published anew every several years. It is filled with data sheets, highly technical descriptions of materials and equipment and advertisements. If Spottiswoode's book assumes the filmmaker is going commercial, the *American Cinematographer Manual* assumes he's 'arrived': it is written for professionals and it is as puzzling to amateurs as would be a set of Don Juan's seduction techniques to both young lovers and happily married couples . . . which is to say the *American Cinematographer Manual* contains useful information for anybody, but in an *un*emotional, almost humanly inaccessible, form.

Independent Filmmaking

However, unless Mr Lipton's book is revised every several years, he cannot hope, herein his *Independent Filmmaking,* to entirely replace the *American Cinematographer Manual* — though he has gone a long way toward relieving the beginner of such extra-reference necessity. I especially appreciate the fact that the illustrations in Mr Lipton's book, along with their careful captions, act as immediate reference, and/or 'memory aid,' adequate to the working needs of most filmmakers: Mr Lipton's selection of handbook pictures, tech sheets, etc, coupled with the main body of the text, make this two books in one: and the illustrations (even if not kept up-to-date through constant revision) will at least train the beginning filmmaker so that he can read the current professional jargon of commerce, manufacturer's specification 'info,' etc, and such data as is collected in professional reference works.

I think I have now fulfilled, what I take to be, my main obligation as 'introducer' of this book — *i.e.* I've encouraged appreciation of it: I so much wish I'd had such a book as this when I began filmmaking that my tendency is to lavish praise on Lenny Lipton to the extreme of everyone's embarrassment; but, you see, it is a book I've wanted for almost twenty years; and, now that it's in my hands at last, I see Mr Lipton has written it so fully that it is still of use *to me* — rather than, simply, something I might recommend to students, etc — I am, naturally, very happily astonished and grateful.

I also think it proper to introduce it according to these happy feelings because it has been my experience that people can most readily learn from any person, or object, they are most receptive of/open to. Trust is the best leverage of thoughtfulness and usability of whatever means! I would hate to think any reader took this book 'for granted' and read it with that contempt which prevents the mind from such basic openness as is absolutely necessary for the process of learning.

I take it that my secondary responsibility (and perhaps the most important one) is to give some insight of the particularities of Mr Lipton's text, so that the reader can take full advantage of the 'personality' of this book at the very beginning of his reading; before introducing a person I valued, I would naturally state his background and give at least some indication of what *now* to expect from him: I will, therefore, attempt to give such a human introduction as that to such a humanly usable book as this is.

From the very beginning, you can expect Mr Lipton to supply information, on all levels, within the milieu of history and with direct relation, in terms of technique, to the future: his speculations about the future extend, in his last chapter, to the description of machinery which may make his book obsolete; and his eye on the past gives the reader constant perspective on the development of the whole film technology (as well as provocation through such asides as: 'The speed originally chosen by Edison was 40 frames per second.' I call this bit of information historical 'news' of the highest order — now that post-Edison fps speeds have risen gradually from 12 fps up to 32 fps as audiences have proved the eye is quicker than the claw of the camera or projector).

But the main excitement, for the reader, should be that Mr Lipton (for all his past and future perspective) is presently personal in his writing. He is a filmmaker himself, currently working (such a rare quality to have in a writer!); and he is, additionally, *interested* in *others* thus working (peppers his text, from beginning to end, with reference to independent filmmakers alive and kicking— kicking against all such blocks as unproductive thought has created in this medium, against all such stagnant 'idealism' most technical writers trip us up with, critics trip us up with); yet, while being very personal in *his* descriptive criticisms, he never becomes 'pushy' about one or another piece of equipment, nor 'cranky' about his own work habits in discussing comparative methods (I, for instance, would praise the Bell & Howell 70-DR for its sturdiness and condemn the comparative fragility of Bolex 16mm cameras: Mr Lipton implies this distinction without becoming a 'crank' on the subject — thus leaves the reader free to choose his camera according to the assets of each piece of equipment — what each can accomplish — thus according to positive personal need). Mr Lipton has immediate use of his book in mind; and he is not afraid to add any bias of his thought in this milieu of grace: 'I would like to offer this *personal* warning...' (my emphasis) and/or: 'It has been my experience,' etc '... from my limited experience' and so forth; take advantage of this, Reader: for he has been exceedingly careful with respect to You!

Right in chapter 1, we find Mr Lipton asking: 'What do we mean by quality?' and answering himself '... quality is entirely relative to purpose'; all of which would sound philosophical were it not for the facts of the main body of the text which are presented in such a way as to give any filmmaker maximum *personal* choice. His sympathies are certainly with the independent filmmaker, in the freest sense of this term: he starts, right off the bat, with '... traditional concepts of *best* quality or *good* quality... is, in fact, damaging to creative expression' and whole sections of

Independent Filmmaking

chapter 5 are almost an insistence on freedom from Hollywood trappings: yet he evokes the names and spells out the techniques of Stanley Kubrick, Alfred Hitchcock, etc, when these are useful: his use of Hitchcock, in the last chapter of this book, apropo the question 'to script or not to script' states the choice as well as I've ever heard or read it.

The opening (Film Forms an Image) of chapter 2, *The Film,* is a model of clear explanation of the chemical nature of this, the most basic material of the medium; and this is easily understandable by the beginner *and* of interest, as memorable writing, to the professional: but the following passage (The Qualities of Film) will mostly 'stump' the beginner — of necessity: Mr Lipton has wisely chosen to aim this passage of writing at the advanced filmmaker with certain simplistic asides ('A film speed of about 50 would serve under most outdoor conditions...' etc) to carry the beginner along — and this approach is instinctively right, in my opinion; it has been my experience as a beginner, once, and teacher, after, that such matters as ASA ratings, and the other particularities of film speed, f stop, etc, are incomprehensible to those who haven't worked them; and it is, in my opinion, damaging to entangle the filmmaker beginner with systems of numbers which cannot be remembered — far better for him to over- and underexpose a lot of film, or even use electric eye cameras, etc, than to try to master abstract systems before photographing. As Introducer of this book, I'd like to encourage beginning filmmakers to read swiftly through such difficult technical passages and concentrate upon the few lines therein comprehensible, saving the rest to return to later; for the wonder of this book *is* that it will serve filmmakers at any stage of development; and the 'price' of that wonder is that the beginner will have to skim quickly through some, to him, incomprehensible technicalities while the more advanced filmmaker will have to skip quickly over simplicities which would otherwise bore him. As Mr Lipton says, 'I realize that many readers will find this information either totally incomprehensible, or if you have a background in such things, very sketchy'; the point *is* — and beautifully thus — the 'info' is *in* there, this book.

Mr Lipton makes his prose style memorable throughout— particularly where it counts, as for instance he 'pins' any comparative number discussion on doubling or halving that number ('In general, negative processed as reversal roughly doubles in speed') and centers his discourse at this point, as he does, say, in chapter 7, thus locating his description of the scientific nature of sound upon the doubling or halving of frequency to lower or raise a note one octave (his prose leans, throughout the book, upon this kind of memory peg) and as, for another instance, he describes 'low contrast' as 'flat,' and 'high contrast' as 'snappy' (as well as 'contrasty') as if it were film flapping in the breeze of the language itself (or as if, as is so, it were the ultimate 'highest' contrast).

I realize it sounds as if I were making a literary review of this book; but I mention Mr Lipton's prose style to encourage readers to use such careful arrangements of language for memory's sake— rather than to just read over those memory aids as if they could carry the book in their coat pocket during filmmaking. The great value of many passages in this book is that the language is memorable: and Mr Lipton is not afraid to repeat technical statements again and again, varying his language slightly, to aid memory, nor to draw upon whatever metaphor will best stick in the mind— comparing, for instance, a retrofocus lens to using binoculars backwards, tri-pack color to comic strip color technique and/or pointillist painting. His passage on Color Balance and Color Temperature is a perfect 'turn' of cosmic speculation, which all scientific engineering is premised upon, into usable information—for instance, his description of the sun as a blue-white poker and of any electric lamp as a lower heated yellow-orange poker, and, for other instances, his descriptions of basic optics, basic acoustics, basic *anything* in this book: my favorite is the discourse on 'Polarization,' one of the best examples of science 'pop' I've yet read.

Mr. Lipton goes from the sublime (which he makes usable) to the ridiculous (which he dignifies) again and again. He takes such laboratory terms as 'Sharpness' and 'Acutence,' in film resolution, and 'Modulation-transfer function and curves,' and even such lab jargon as 'go-to' and makes it all memorable enough so that you can 'talk turkey' to the technicians who'll be processing your film and making your print; and, not content with this, he gives some good psychological insight (in chapters 8 and 9) apropos talking to the engineer, the sound recording engineer and/or talking to the lab man and, even, advice on establishing credit with the lab, taking film expenses off your income tax, etc—what more could you ask? He gives you advice that can save you thousands of dollars and, also, isn't above encouraging you to store batteries in the refrigerator to make them last longer. In short, he runs the gamut. And I suppose the point of my mentioning this is that I very much want to encourage you to *take* his advice: my twenty years experience of filmmaking backs up 90 percent of such advice in this book.

Independent Filmmaking

Here is where I disagree with him: I believe that magnetic striping *does* cause wear on film, inasmuch as the material flakes off and collects in the projector gate; he says that there is very seldom a wrongly manufactured film sprocket problem, whereas it has been my experience that the less expensive regular 8mm films are often so poorly sprocketed they will not even pass through some cameras; I've used *both* extension tubes and front mounted close-up lenses for close focus on telephoto lens, and he says I / you can't; he doesn't often enough, nor strongly enough, state the absolute difference between still photography and motion picture making— though he does touch on the subject in Indoor Lighting in chapter 5, and he does give us a nice quote on the subject in chapter 3: 'The kind of composition that works in film could often be considered noncomposition in terms of still photography'; but the matter is far more serious, to my mind, than that — it is, in fact, that still photography and motion picture photography are polar opposite techniques, all the more confusing inasmuch as they each share certain equipment and must be practiced as opposites from the beginning. (I have become terrified by, and groan audibly at, the happy student who announces to me, as his teacher, that he has mastered 'stills' and is now, therefore, ready for 'movies': I have learned, from years of painful teaching experience, that he will have to *un*learn, and 'take arms against,' everything he has 'mastered' in still photography.)

My final nit-pic of Mr Lipton's book is with the gist of his attitude throughout the chapter on splicing, chapter 6: everybody has an Achilles' heel and I'm afraid Mr Lipton's weakness is the splice. He bravely sees this subject through and does a good job; under the circumstances his technical information is as accurate as ever. I therefore urge you to read this chapter as carefully as all the others, more carefully, perhaps; but I urge you also to see through him, his weakness in the matter, while reading. He starts this chapter with a declaration of complete dissatisfaction with *all* splicing methods developed thus far, then later advises the reader to consult his 'horoscope' (as he lapses more and more into humor, a happy blessing, under the circumstances). I think the key to this trouble, and that of many other filmmakers (for his splice-crankiness is, alas, rather standard among filmmakers these days) is that it is *not* a simple subject but, rather, the heart of the matter of filmmaking. Oh, I know, Mr Lipton (and others) will insist that 'splicing' means simply putting two pieces of film together — that the term refers only to a mechanical process; I say, *no!* — emphatically — I say that until a man is excited about the mechanics of putting two pieces of film together, and thrilled by his own 'sweat' in the matter, he'll never make a connection as meaningful as that expected of any village blacksmith.

After all, Mr Lipton has managed elsewhere in this book, to excite us terrifically about such seemingly mechanical matters as film stock numbers; why, once he begins describing 16mm film stocks, the text essentially would become a reference work except that the excitement about these materials keeps the reader as thrilled about stock numbers as he would be about licence plates of getaway cars in a detective story; and Mr Lipton is as personal about cameras as to differentiate whether they're better for left-handed or right-handed people; as humanly beautiful, describing film colors, as to take it right down to one of the most immediately important facts in the matter: will it, any given film stock, reproduce 'skin tones of both black and white people'; well, I'd like to be as immediately relevant, and absolutely human, about the splice: the creative soul bends there, stretches, breaks even and/or transforms itself *right* there in midst of the exactitude of holding two pieces of film together in creative process.

Okay, I hope (above) to have counterbalanced what I take to be Mr Lipton's weakness. One *can* sidestep the splice issue by foregoing all editing process in filmmaking: but then (as I take it) the mechanical involvement with the camera must be equal (at least), in each shot change instant, to that editing table sweat which fusses every filmmaker who refuses to take it (as all else) *on* as a *joy!* I must mention that I think Mr Lipton's weak 'heel,' in this matter, also leads him into praising the tape splice in an unqualified manner: *viz, my* experience is that the tape splice streaks, in time, and tends, thus, to leave long black glue marks along the surface of the film; it is also very visible (especially in 8mm); it does also easily come apart; many labs will not even accept it.

That takes care of all the notes I marked 'criticism' while reading this book; and *look* how few criticisms I have, considering the very large size of this book! Each person who reads it, in the spirit in which is was made, will have his criticisms — most different from mine, no doubt — for the spirit of the book engenders activity and involvement on a working level, and it encourages extreme individuality: and it is a beauty.

Stan Brakhage

Independent Filmmaking

The Format

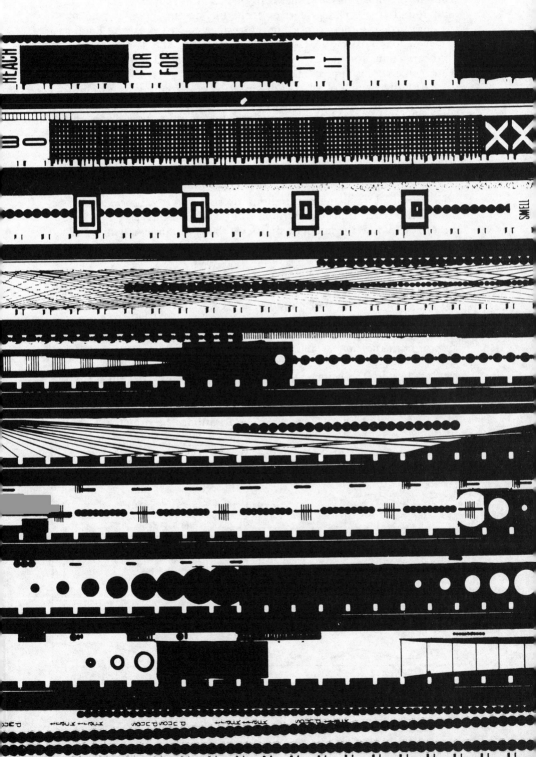

The word *format,* often used interchangeably with gauge, refers specifically to the film's physical makeup: that is, its size, perforations, image
and sound track. Gauge derives from the measurement of the film's
width. Format is a less confusing term, since, as in the case of 8mm and
super 8, it is possible to have two formats with the same gauge. The
numbers 8mm, 16mm and so on, designate the actual width of the film.
One inch contains approximately 25 millimeters.

Although much of what is discussed here can apply to all film formats, the ones specifically referred to are 8mm (double 8 or standard 8),
super 8-single 8 and 16mm, since they are the most available, economically feasible and widely used by present independent filmmakers. Although the formats differ, their similarities are more profound than their
differences.

Common to All Formats

Picture, sound track and perforations are common to all formats. Movie
film is a flexible transparent ribbon of successive images that's hardly
necessary to describe in detail since everybody is familiar with it. What
will be explained is the design of motion picture formats in general,
rather than specific discussions of particular formats.

Beside the photographic images on film, there is a row of *sprocket
holes,* or punched perforations. Although *sprocket wheels* in a camera or
projector engage the perforations and serve to advance the film, the
most important function of the perforations has been described as the
indexing function. The perforations assure the proper positioning of the
film in both the camera and projector. A device, shaped like a hooked
finger and called the *shuttle,* or *claw,* engages the perforation and advances the film the height of one frame, or picture. Assuming that the
perforations are accurately made—have a consistent shape and are the
same distance apart—the camera will expose the image in the same position with relation to each successive perforation. The projector's shuttle

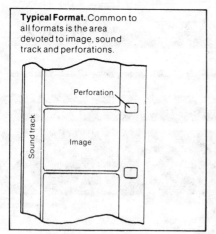

Typical Format. Common to all formats is the area devoted to image, sound track and perforations.

Perforation

Sound track

Image

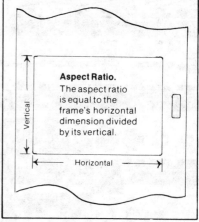

Aspect Ratio. The aspect ratio is equal to the frame's horizontal dimension divided by its vertical.

Vertical

Horizontal

Independent Filmmaking

will also properly register each perforation, and therefore hold each image in the same position.

The 16mm frame illustrated here is a model or typical format showing image area, perforations and sound track. Part of the area is devoted to a sound record, which can be heard, as the image is seen, when played back on a suitable projector. The track may have either a magnetic or photographic (optical) record of sound information. Each of the formats described in this book has all the features of the 16mm frame illustrated: each has perforations, an image area and room for a sound track. The film's width and the manner in which these three functions are proportioned distinguishes each format and determines its characteristics.

Aspect Ratio

All frames are rectangular, and the most generally used proportion is the one established by Thomas Alva Edison for 35mm. The measure of the image area's *rectangularity* is its *aspect ratio*. It is the ratio of the horizontal image dimension to the vertical. A ratio of 1:1 is the ratio of a square. The aspect ratio of 8mm, super 8 and 16mm is 4:3, or more commonly, 1.33:1 (read as one point three three to one).

Choosing a Format

What must you know about formats before you can choose one? Each choice of format requires a supporting system of manufacturing, production and postshooting features or services. Film stock, cameras, projectors, editing equipment and laboratory services must be compatible with or complementary to the chosen format. Formats have a wide price differential, and future print distribution, in fact printmaking itself, is determined by format choice. Both film cost and quality are proportional to the image area. But if the problem were that straightforward, the choice of format, film, equipment and services, in other words, the

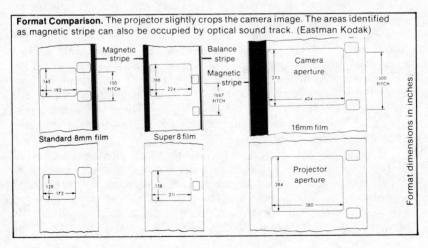

Format Comparison. The projector slightly crops the camera image. The areas identified as magnetic stripe can also be occupied by optical sound track. (Eastman Kodak)

The Format

choice of motion picture system, would be far simpler than it actually is.

A filmmaker might be far better off choosing a particular format because of his temperament and the kind of film he is making, than just the size of his purse. There's nothing wrong with, and as far as I'm concerned there's everything right with, choosing a format for emotional reasons. But this doesn't mean that the filmmaker is reduced to this because he doesn't have enough information to come up with a logical decision. Even after he learns what he needs to know, there are so many ambivalent factors, so many ifs and buts, that the format decision usually tends to be an intuitive one. Therefore this chapter is geared to give you, the independent filmmaker, the information you need. The format choice, rational or not, is up to you.

The Origins of the Formats

16mm

The 16mm format was introduced as a system for amateur use in 1923 by Eastman Kodak in cooperation with Bell & Howell and Victor. These film and equipment manufacturers believed that this new system, less costly than the professionally employed 35mm, would be attractive to the general public. Previously, 17.5mm film, and corresponding equipment, had been offered for amateur use, but Kodak wanted to discourage the use of this gauge which could be cut down, or slit, from combustible 35mm film.

At that time, and as late as the fifties, 35mm theatrical films were shot and printed on cellulose nitrate base film. Cellulose nitrate is both highly combustible and susceptible to rapid deterioration in storage. Kodak's intention was to avoid the hazard of using, and the stringent requirements for projection of, nitrate base film by making the new format available only in safety base—cellulose acetate. Cellulose acetate base film is neither as combustible nor as subject to deterioration as the nitrate variety. If 17.5mm film had become the amateur standard, slit nitrate stock might have been offered for sale. Since 16mm film, however, cannot be cut economically from 35mm stock, this was avoided.

From the beginning 16mm film was marketed as black and white reversal film which can be projected and viewed with a normal image, rather than negative tones. This advantage, it was hoped, would be attractive to the amateur since the actual camera film could be projected without the additional expense and delay of having a print made as the 35mm negative-positive system required. There was some public use of it as a home movie medium, but 16mm proved to be of comparatively little interest to the amateur.

Although 16mm projection equipment was already being used widely in schools, it was not until the Second World War that many people were exposed to 16mm filmmaking and technology. Then, the need for portable equipment to handle training and entertainment films led to the setting up of military standards for 16mm performance. Gradually the virtues of 16mm became more generally known, and, at the same time, 16mm film stock and equipment were substantially improved.

Increased commercial interest in 16mm has led to the development of better equipment and a proliferation of services that have benefited the independent filmmaker. Without the commercial 'spots,' TV news films, training films and 'documentaries,' the creative filmmaker would not have available this relatively high quality and technically sophisticated medium.

Double 8mm

By the early thirties it was believed in Rochester that 16mm film, which had failed to interest enough amateurs to be profitable, could be used in appropriately designed cameras to produce pictures half the height and width of the standard 16mm frame. One half of the film could be exposed in the camera first, and then the second half could be exposed on another pass. This is similar to the scheme used by dual track monaural tape recorders. When the film went into the camera it was 16 millimeters wide, but after processing, the laboratory slit the film in half, and spliced the halves together on a single reel. In this way, because of the height and width reduction, the filmmaker could get not just double, but quadruple (since the height of the frame is also halved) the screen time out of a roll of 16 millimeter wide double 8 film, as it is called.

Cameras and projectors had to be manufactured for the new format, and only slight modification of existing film specifications was necessary (it had to have twice as many perforations). One advantage, from the manufacturer's point of view, was the high degree of compatibility between the manufacture and processing of 16mm and double 8 film. The amateur could be served by a medium of *lesser* quality, but with the advantage of greater economy.

Super 8

Despite growing quality in 8mm film and equipment, slumping sales

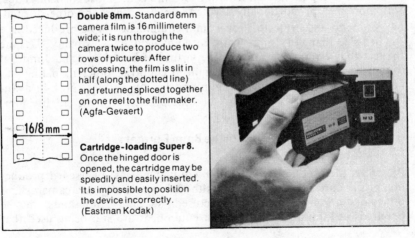

Double 8mm. Standard 8mm camera film is 16 millimeters wide; it is run through the camera twice to produce two rows of pictures. After processing, the film is slit in half (along the dotted line) and returned spliced together on one reel to the filmmaker. (Agfa-Gevaert)

16/8 mm

Cartridge-loading Super 8. Once the hinged door is opened, the cartridge may be speedily and easily inserted. It is impossible to position the device incorrectly. (Eastman Kodak)

The Format

helped encourage Eastman Kodak to seek out yet another new system for amateur use. One problem that had to be solved was the loading of film into the camera. Previously, cartridge loading had been offered by Kodak, with their preloaded reusable metal cartridges, and by the Bell & Howell cameras that accepted cartridges which the filmmaker himself loaded with double 8.

The old Kodak cartridges, which were (and are) offered in both 8mm and 16mm, often jammed and had to be loaded by the factory, after time-consuming and costly inspection, with fresh film. Needed now was a jam-proof, simple-to-load, disposable cartridge of low cost. After several years of research, Kodak offered super 8 format film in Instamatic cartridges in 1965. Super 8, and its Japanese equivalent, single 8, are the two latest additions to the filmmakers' choice in film format.

'The Living Corpse'

In the history of filmmaking, many gauges, or formats, have had their proponents, and it is difficult to describe the fanatical, nay, near-religious zeal of these visionaries and experimenters. However, it's one thing to envision the virtues of a gauge 3.14159 millimeters wide, with a golden rectangle proportion image, and quite another to propagate the necessary manufacturing and distribution capability for it to be shown outside the small circle of friends and family of the 'gauge nut.'

The nickname 'living corpse' has been given to one interesting gauge that, for the most part, is confined to a hearty group of individualistic filmmakers in England and France. Introduced and popularized in Europe by Pathé, 9.5mm was more or less killed off after 8mm's introduction, but some film by 3M and Kodak, and some equipment by Pathé, Heurtier and other European manufacturers is offered.

The image area of 9.5mm is very nearly the same as 16mm, but, obviously, the film is only 9.5 millimeters wide. The perforations in this interesting gauge run down the center of the film between the frames. In terms of carrying picture information, 9.5mm is the most efficient gauge, with more area proportionally devoted to picture than any other format.

Cameras and projectors for 9.5mm equipment can be produced in a smaller size than for 16mm with an equivalent image quality. Despite the fact that 9.5mm has some of the virtues of both 8mm and 16mm, it cannot be considered a viable medium in countries other than England and France because equipment, film and backup services are not available. It's a pity that 9.5mm hasn't become practical for the creative filmmaker, for it has decided advantages.

Qualities of the 8mm Formats

8mm

Presently, the production of super 8 equipment has superseded production of standard 8mm equipment. Although nearly all 8mm cameras and projectors are no longer manufactured, so many thousands, maybe hundreds of thousands, of pieces of equipment are still being used that

8mm film will continue to be manufactured for many years.

The least expensive filmmaking system available is 8mm. It's somewhat less expensive than super 8, and much cheaper than 16mm. Film stock for 8mm is available in a wide range of emulsions, both color and black and white, while the super 8 user is presently comparatively limited in his choices.

Also, 8mm cameras and projectors are relatively inexpensive as well as compact, lightweight and, therefore, highly portable. The usual conservative or *straight* advice for using a movie camera is to mount it on a tripod whenever possible. However, it doesn't make sense to me to take a beautifully lightweight and compact 8mm camera and chain it to the ground. Being able to handhold an 8mm camera easily is part of the joy of the format, as every home movie maker knows.

Not only is there equipment of high quality, but many have a range of automatic features rarely found in 16mm cameras. Many 8mm camera models effectively prevent you from being able to make creative decisions about exposure, but they can free the filmmaker to concentrate on filming. 8mm cameras featuring zoom lenses, automatic exposure control, through-the-lens viewing and focusing, power zoom and other features, can be purchased for about the price of many a good 16mm lens.

I can't honestly recommend 8mm or double 8mm, described next. These formats are truly obsolete and old fashioned.

Double 8mm

This name, sometimes applied to 8mm, derives from the film's size—16 millimeters wide; 8mm is also called *standard,* or normal, 8 to distinguish it from super 8. See how 8mm film is derived from stock 16 millimeters wide. Note that is has twice the number of perforations as the regular 16mm film. Again, after the film has run through the camera, it makes a second pass, exposing a second row of images. After processing, the film is slit and the 8mm halves are joined on a reel.

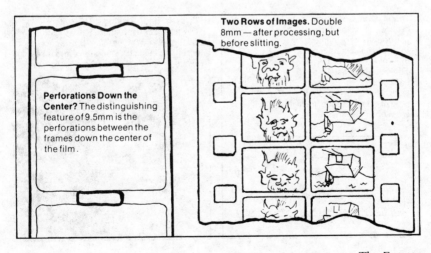

Perforations Down the Center? The distinguishing feature of 9.5mm is the perforations between the frames down the center of the film.

Two Rows of Images. Double 8mm—after processing, but before slitting.

The Format

Ordinarily, 8mm film is supplied in lengths of twenty-five, fifty, one and two hundred feet even though the fifty, two hundred and any longer lengths have to be special ordered from the manufacturer. The majority of 8mm cameras accept a maximum film capacity of twenty-five feet, from which the filmmaker gets fifty feet of processed film. At the silent running speeds of 16 or 18 frames per second (fps), this amounts to about four minutes of screen time; at the sound running speed of 24 fps, 2 minutes and 46 seconds.

However, total spool footage is actually greater than this since some extra film is used as leader to prevent the rest of the roll from being light-struck, or fogged, and to thread the film into the camera. Therefore, the usual length of a twenty-five foot spool is thirty-three feet.

Ordinary 8mm film can be run through a 16mm camera, but not vice versa. Double 8 with twice the number of perforations as 16mm allows the shuttle in a 16mm camera to engage every other perforation. Sixteen millimeter film lacks the necessary perforations for an 8mm mechanism to advance the film through the camera.

You can use unslit double 8 film on a 16mm projector to obtain four images on the screen. If the 8mm camera is held upside-down for the second pass, all four images will be the same side up, even though the second row will have backward motion.

Super 8

Much of what has been said about 8mm equipment is also true for super 8; it is lightweight, easy-to-use, and usually has all the automatic features of 8mm cameras, plus very rapid loading. Super 8's image area is moderately greater than 8mm's, and an improvement in image quality is often quite visible. Super 8 is somewhat more expensive to shoot than 8mm, but a great deal cheaper than 16mm. Film for 8mm and super 8 is supplied in reversal emulsions for either black and white or color.

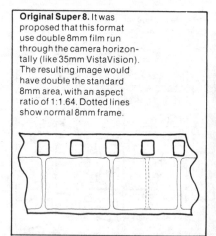

Original Super 8. It was proposed that this format use double 8mm film run through the camera horizontally (like 35mm VistaVision). The resulting image would have double the standard 8mm area, with an aspect ratio of 1:1.64. Dotted lines show normal 8mm frame.

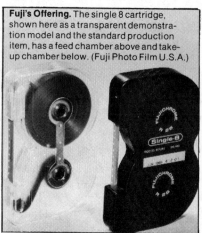

Fuji's Offering. The single 8 cartridge, shown here as a transparent demonstration model and the standard production item, has a feed chamber above and take-up chamber below. (Fuji Photo Film U.S.A.)

Independent Filmmaking

As far as I can determine, super 8 first appeared in the British magazine *Amateur Cine World* in 1954 when it was suggested that 8mm film could be run horizontally rather than vertically through a modified camera. This would double the film area and change the aspect ratio. In its present context, super 8 was first used by columnist Ivan Watson in 1963 when he christened Kodak's then newly proposed format in *Amateur Cine World*.

Super 8-Single 8

Both super 8 and single 8 systems use a quick loading plastic cartridge, but of different designs. The film format within both is identical. When Kodak scientists were publishing the first papers on their new format, Fuji of Japan was planning an 8mm cartridge-loading system of its own. The Kodak papers were discussions and not concrete proposals; they stressed the new format's audio-visual (a-v) applications in education; nothing in the Kodak papers said anything about cartridges for the film. Nevertheless, Fuji must have seen the handwriting on the wall for they changed their plans. Their cartridge was also designed for film 8 millimeters wide—standard single 8 film. Thus, the film wouldn't have to be run through the camera twice. Fuji decided to load their cartridge, based on a design originally used by Agfa, with the new format film, that is, super 8 film. That's why two completely different cartridges are available for the same format film. Fuji decided to call their system— cartridges, film, cameras and projectors—*single 8*. Since the film supplied in both Kodak and Fuji cartridges have the same format dimensions, projectors for super 8 or single 8 are interchangeable.

Double Super 8

One of the biggest attractions of the new format is its incorporation in a cartridge-loading system. Not only is this form easier and quicker to load than 8mm rolls, but the filmmaker can easily replace a cartridge at any time, with a cartridge containing a different kind of film.

Be that as it may, super 8 film is now supplied as *double super 8* on one hundred foot spools. Kodak supplies film in this form, and longer lengths are available on special order. The film is handled just like standard double 8mm. One half of it is exposed on the first pass through the camera, and then the second half on the next pass through the camera. In the laboratory it is slit and mounted on reels. Pathé has adapted its 16mm camera to accommodate this form of double super 8. (The American distributor is Karl Heitz Inc., of New York.) This is the only double super 8 camera currently in manufacture.

Cartridges

The super 8 and single 8 cartridges are not alike even though both hold fifty feet of film and are made of plastic. The Kodak cartridge is squarish and stubby while the Fuji cartridge is thin and tall. The Kodak cartridge is of coaxial design. The feed and take-up chambers are adjacent to each other with their centers along the same axis. The film travels a twisted path between them, through the cartridge and across its built-in pressure plate. The pressure plate is the spring-loaded device which holds the film against the camera aperture plate. The Fuji single 8 cartridge's design is more straightforward. The feed chamber is above the take-up chamber, enabling the film to travel in a straight path. The pressure plate is built into the camera and not the cartridge; it swings into position as the camera-loading chamber door is closed. Although the film is entirely enclosed in the Kodak cartridge, the Fuji has an opening for the camera pressure plate. (The open film path of the Fuji cartridge might allow its use in a single system sound camera, but the Eastman design rules this out.) Both cartridges can key in automatic film speed settings through notches or protrusions which engage the built-in camera feelers. In cameras with automatic electric eye systems, the position of the feelers is used to set the film speed adjustments. The Kodak cartridge, in addition, keys the camera for the color balance of color film.

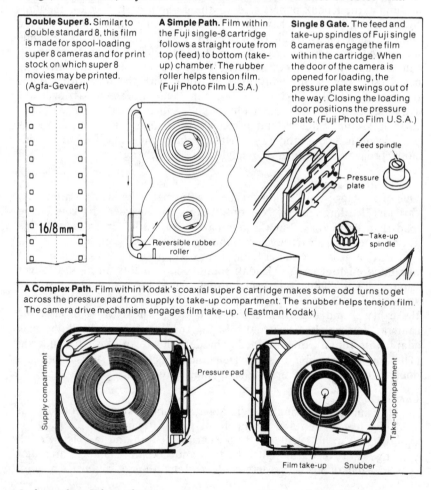

Double Super 8. Similar to double standard 8, this film is made for spool-loading super 8 cameras and for print stock on which super 8 movies may be printed. (Agfa-Gevaert)

16/8 mm

A Simple Path. Film within the Fuji single-8 cartridge follows a straight route from top (feed) to bottom (take-up) chamber. The rubber roller helps tension film. (Fuji Photo Film U.S.A.)

Reversible rubber roller

Single 8 Gate. The feed and take-up spindles of Fuji single 8 cameras engage the film within the cartridge. When the door of the camera is opened for loading, the pressure plate swings out of the way. Closing the loading door positions the pressure plate. (Fuji Photo Film U.S.A.)

Feed spindle

Pressure plate

Take-up spindle

A Complex Path. Film within Kodak's coaxial super 8 cartridge makes some odd turns to get across the pressure pad from supply to take-up compartment. The snubber helps tension film. The camera drive mechanism engages film take-up. (Eastman Kodak)

Supply compartment

Pressure pad

Take-up compartment

Film take-up   Snubber

Independent Filmmaking

Cartridge Quality

Because the exact positioning of the film and pressure plate is crucial, I would suspect that the Fuji cartridge could produce superior pictures. Not only is the pressure plate metal, but being a part of the camera and not the cartridge, its relationship with the aperture and shuttle is fixed. However, despite the fact that the Kodak pressure plate is plastic and part of the cartridge, it also does an excellent job. It is held in final camera position by three raised surface protrusions which contact the aperture plate. Since it takes three points to determine a plane, these projections accurately locate the pressure plate. In effect, the camera positions the pressure plate as well as the film path. All in all, it's only fair to say that both cartridge designs work very effectively.

Image Steadiness

At the time of the introduction of these cartridges it was feared that super 8 films might be unsteady because the design calls for the shuttle

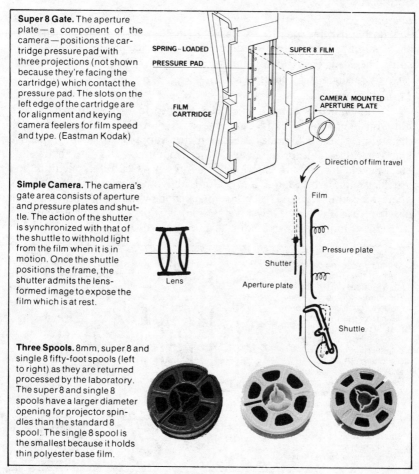

Super 8 Gate. The aperture plate—a component of the camera—positions the cartridge pressure pad with three projections (not shown because they're facing the cartridge) which contact the pressure pad. The slots on the left edge of the cartridge are for alignment and keying camera feelers for film speed and type. (Eastman Kodak)

SPRING-LOADED PRESSURE PAD

SUPER 8 FILM

FILM CARTRIDGE

CAMERA MOUNTED APERTURE PLATE

Direction of film travel

Simple Camera. The camera's gate area consists of aperture and pressure plates and shuttle. The action of the shutter is synchronized with that of the shuttle to withhold light from the film when it is in motion. Once the shuttle positions the frame, the shutter admits the lens-formed image to expose the film which is at rest.

Film

Pressure plate

Shutter

Lens

Aperture plate

Shuttle

Three Spools. 8mm, super 8 and single 8 fifty-foot spools (left to right) as they are returned processed by the laboratory. The super 8 and single 8 spools have a larger diameter opening for projector spindles than the standard 8 spool. The single 8 spool is the smallest because it holds thin polyester base film.

The Format

to engage the film two frames above the exposed frame. The film is thereby pushed through the camera and projector, instead of being pulled as with standard 8mm. The fears proved groundless; film shot with either cartridge can be as steady as, or steadier than, footage shot with and projected by 8mm equipment. The reliably steady image has turned out to be one of super 8's strong points. There are two possible reasons for this: the super 8 image, because it is larger, requires less magnification for the same screen size than standard 8. Also, the position of the shuttle in both camera and projector has been standardized.

If the same sprocket hole is used to register the position of the frame in both camera and projector, the resulting image can be aligned in exactly the same position without bounce or jiggle. In practice, 8mm equipment had no such uniformity. A manufacturer might produce a camera with the shuttle engaging two frames below the aperture, while a second manufacturer could market a projector with a shuttle engaging at the third perforation.

Loading

Both cartridges load very easily even though the Kodak cartridge has a slight advantage in loading because of its totally enclosed film path. The Kodak cartridge seems to be foolproof, but a fool might conceivably misload the Fuji device.

Cartridge Film

Your choice of camera might be reduced to the question of which film you like. Fuji loads its cartridge with Fuji Film, and Kodak with their film. These companies are the major suppliers of their respective film cartridges, although many other manufacturers are marketing film packaged in Kodak cartridges. At present, Fuji offers medium and fast black and white films, and indoor and outdoor color film. Kodak offers medium, fast and very fast black and white film, and slow and fast indoor color film. Only reversal film is supplied in single 8-super 8 cartridges. Fujichrome is about as fine grained as Kodachrome II but

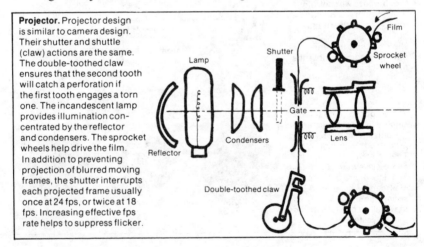

Projector. Projector design is similar to camera design. Their shutter and shuttle (claw) actions are the same. The double-toothed claw ensures that the second tooth will catch a perforation if the first tooth engages a torn one. The incandescent lamp provides illumination concentrated by the reflector and condensers. The sprocket wheels help drive the film. In addition to preventing projection of blurred moving frames, the shutter interrupts each projected frame usually once at 24 fps, or twice at 18 fps. Increasing effective fps rate helps to suppress flicker.

Film
Shutter
Lamp
Sprocket wheel
Gate
Condensers
Lens
Reflector
Double-toothed claw

Independent Filmmaking

produces warmer yellows and reds. Both films have the same sensitivity 33
to light, or speed, E.I. (exposure index) 25 for outdoor work. (See chapter
2, under Film Speed, for an explanation of exposure index.) Fuji supplies
outdoor and indoor balanced color film. Kodak, seeking a 'universal' color
film, supplies Kodachrome only in a tungsten-balanced variety. Shooting
outdoors with this film requires a filter which is usually built into cameras
accepting the Kodak cartridge. Fuji film is slightly less expensive than
Kodak, but Kodak cartridges can be found more readily.

Each manufacturer uses a different base material: Kodak film is
supplied on standard acetate base film. Fuji, in order to get the same
load, fifty feet, into their relatively small feed and take-up chambers,
switched to polyester base film. Polyester film can be roughly one third
the thickness of acetate base film with even superior strength. Until recently it wasn't possible to cement splice polyester; only tape splices
were feasible. Although it is now possible, difficulties with cement splicing polyester have made this procedure relatively uncommon.

In the late seventies Kodak introduced a two-hundred-foot version of
their super 8 cartridge, loaded with sound-striped Kodachrome or fast
Ektachrome film.

Backwinding

The cartridges differ in another important way, which may be the
deciding influence in some filmmakers' choice. Film can be backwound
in the Fuji cartridge, but cannot ordinarily be backwound in the Kodak
cartridge. What is backwinding? After the film has been exposed, it can
be rewound, either by hand, or if the camera's motor allows, by power-
driven reverse. This backwound film can be reexposed for double exposures, dissolves (by combining a fade-in over a fade-out), or for titles
to be superimposed. Film laboratories can produce any of these effects
for the 16mm format, but in 8mm or super 8 they usually must be created
in the camera.

A thin plastic ratchet in the Kodak cartridge feed chamber, serving
to properly tension the film, makes backwinding the film in the cartridge nearly impossible. There are several super 8 cameras which offer
limited backwinding. They can produce dissolves up to 90 frames long.
They accomplish this by stuffing a short length of film into the feed
chamber, while the feed reel itself is held in place by the ratchet.

Although the Fuji single 8 cartridge allows for backwinding, not all
single 8 cameras have this feature. If a single 8 camera lacks a backwind
facility, it is possible to remove the cartridge and manually backwind the
film in the dark.

Cameras

Both 8mm and super 8 cameras (and single 8 cameras) are, in
general, lightweight and easy-to-use. Besides the quick loading capability of super 8, the only major difference in the new equipment so far is
not so much a change, but rather a solidification of a trend that began
with standard 8mm: there are no spring-driven super 8-single 8 machines. All have electric motors and are driven by power cells.

The Format

Projectors

There are a number of fine 8mm and super 8 projectors on the market. The best of the super 8 projectors are compact and lightweight and nearly as bright as some late model 16mm equipment. There are many dual projectors which will show 8mm or super 8 film. Many manufacturers, such as Kodak, Fuji and Eumig, offer 8mm or super 8 magnetic sound projectors. These machines can record as well as reproduce sound.

Printmaking

Prints from 8mm or super 8 original camera film can be made in laboratories in the same format as they were shot, that is an 8mm original to an 8mm print, or super 8 to super 8; a few laboratories will print 8mm to super 8 and vice versa. Quality heavily depends on the camera original. If it is a little underexposed, or even somewhat dense, usually good prints can still be made; but an overexposed, thin original will probably not print very well. Presently, super 8 is not considered a fully

Loading and Unloading. The drop-in and drop-out techniques used with a single 8 cartridge. (Fuji Photo Film U.S.A.)

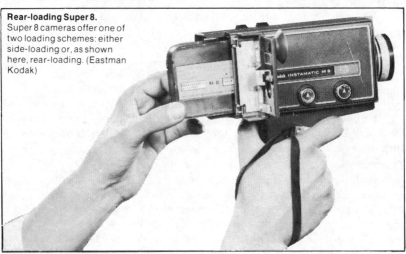

Rear-loading Super 8. Super 8 cameras offer one of two loading schemes: either side-loading or, as shown here, rear-loading. (Eastman Kodak)

Independent Filmmaking

developed professional printmaking system. The expectation that super 8
printing services and quality would approach 16mm has never materialized.

Blowups

Many fine film laboratories offer optical enlargement from 8mm or super 8 to 16mm, faithful to the original. It has been my experience that good 8mm equipment will produce superb 16mm copies, even if an intermediate printing master is used for release printmaking (chapter 9 offers more detail concerning printmaking). To fill the 16mm frame, 8mm must be enlarged 4.5 times; super 8 about 3.5 times. One should expect super 8 to 16mm enlargements to be better than those of 8mm to 16mm, and my experience bears this out. When properly executed, good quality blowups from super 8 to 35mm are possible!

Comparing 8mm and Super 8

Formats

The most obvious difference between 8mm and super 8 is that while both are 8 millimeters wide, the super 8 image is larger. How much larger? The usual answer is half again, if we're considering the projectable image size. However, there is a difference between the area actually projected and the picture area of the film. A small amount of film image is concealed by the projector aperture, the mask surrounding the picture in the projector's optical system. This aperture is designed to crop the picture just slightly to prevent adjacent frames from creeping onto the screen (see the earlier illustration on format comparison).

Although the actual super 8 format picture is only one third larger than the 8mm image, accepted manufacturing standards dictate that it is cropped proportionately less than the 8mm image. For practical purposes, it is fair to say that the super 8 image is 50 percent larger, that is, it has 50 percent more projected area than the 8mm image.

Super 8 perforations are narrower than 8mm perforations, designed so that the image size could be made wider; once it was made wider, the

Super 8-Single 8, Standard 8 Projector. Since the formats are identical, any projector which can show super 8 films can show single 8. This Kodak Instamatic M95 projector will also show standard 8 films. Because the projector is sprocketless, the format change is simplified. The spindles are easily adapted with sleeves, and the shuttle and aperture are altered by turning a lever. (Eastman Kodak)

The Format

picture had to be made taller to retain the standard 1.33:1 aspect ratio. So the perforations had to be placed farther apart. Another way of saying this, is that super 8 perforations have a greater *pitch* (the distance between two perforations) than 8mm perforations. Also, the position of the perforations has been changed so that they are along the side of each frame, not between the frames, as for 8mm.

Because of the greater height of the new format's image, the same running time, at the same number of fps (frames per second), uses more film than regular 8mm—about 10 percent more.

Sound Tracks

Standard 8mm sound track is adjacent to the perforations, while the super 8 track is opposite the perforations. Coating or striping 8mm or super 8 with iron oxide magnetic material converts it into a form of magnetic tape. Magnetic oxide can be coated in the track positions before or after the film is processed. Similarly, the track can be recorded before or after the film is processed.

Since this record stripe is raised above the surface of the film, a balance stripe of the same material is applied to the perforated side so that super 8 film will spool properly on the reel. This balance stripe could be used as a second information track, for stereo sound or for a foreign language version of the film. At present, there are a large number of makes and models of super 8 machines to utilize the balance stripe this way. There is no room on 8mm for such a balance stripe. Often, 16mm magnetic sound track film carries a balance stripe. Both the 8mm and super 8 tracks are 30 mils wide (0.03 inch).

Two reasons account for super 8's potentially superior sound. First, the track is separated from the perforations. Perforations tend to cause depressions, or valleys, in the surface of film; oxide falling into these valleys would be held away from the recording or playback heads resulting in reduced volume for that segment of the track. This cannot

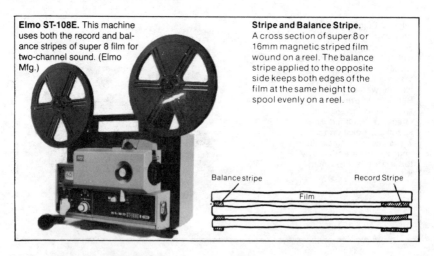

Elmo ST-108E. This machine uses both the record and balance stripes of super 8 film for two-channel sound. (Elmo Mfg.)

Stripe and Balance Stripe. A cross section of super 8 or 16mm magnetic striped film wound on a reel. The balance stripe applied to the opposite side keeps both edges of the film at the same height to spool evenly on a reel.

Balance stripe   Film   Record Stripe

Independent Filmmaking

happen to the super 8 track which is separated from the perforations.
Second, since super 8 uses 10 percent more film for the same running time at the same fps, the linear speed of super 8 is also 10 percent greater than 8mm. Increased speed in magnetic recording and reproduction devices can improve the high frequency or treble range and reduce wow and flutter, or variations in tape speed, which sound like changes in pitch.

Quality

You'd expect super 8 sound and image to be of better quality than 8mm because of its higher linear speed and larger image. Well, how much better? At present, the difference is marginal—just a little better. Similarly, does a 50 percent increase in image size improve image quality? It does, but also marginally. This improvement can best be seen in shots with a lot of detail. Practically speaking, this means that *long shots* in super 8 tend to appear sharper than similar shots in 8mm. However, there is one decided advantage of super 8 over 8mm: its projected image is usually very, very steady. My overall impression is that super 8 projection is noticeably better than standard 8mm.

Is the confusion introduced by this new system worth the trouble? For one thing, 8mm's dimensions were a compromise, based on what was best for 16mm. The perforations are too large for what they have to do: they waste too much area. Super 8 is what 8mm should have been from the beginning. Although the improvements may be marginal, I feel they are justified. The super 8 format is a part of a system that is composed of film, emulsions, cameras, lab services and projectors. As all these aspects of film production are constantly being improved, it would be foolish to saddle them to an inadequate format design.

Compatibility

If only quality improvement were the question, why retain the 8 millimeter wide film size? Why not film 9 or 10 millimeters wide? Keeping the 8 millimeter width retained the compatibility of the same sized formats and directly benefited the independent filmmaker.

The most important area of compatibility is projection. As mentioned earlier, there are many dual gauge 8mm-super 8 projectors (sound and silent). These projectors convert quickly back and forth from 8mm to super 8. In the case of Kodak Instamatic M95, for example, the change is made just by flipping a switch. Because of these machines, people who have worked with standard 8mm can switch to super or single 8, and show their films with the same projector. Also important for workers in both formats is the proliferation of dual gauge editing equipment, viewers and splicers.

16mm

Format

This film, which is, of course, 16 millimeters or ⅝ inch wide, has the largest picture area of the three major formats discussed. Its image has 4.5 times the area of the standard 8mm image, and about 3.5 times the

38 area of the super 8 image. We can therefore expect crisper images and also better sound quality since its track has a greater width and travels at a higher speed.

There are two distinct forms of the 16mm format: a double perforation, or double *perf,* and a single perf variety; 16mm was originally introduced in the double perf form—sprocket holes along both edges of the film. One of the perforation rows was eliminated to make room for the sound track. For decades this space was used exclusively for optical track, but magnetic sound tracks are now used here as well.

The narrow stripe in the lower figure (right side of the right frame) serves the same function as the balance stripe used in super 8. It helps to spool the film on the reel evenly. There is a second, rarely used 16mm magnetic (mag for short) sound format which uses double perf film, and has a mag stripe or coating along both rows of perforations. One of the stripes serves as a balance stripe, the other for sound information and is called the record stripe. This double perf format with mag stripe is compatible with projectors that will play the broader, 100 mil wide (a mil is 0.001 of an inch, therefore 100 mil is 0.100 inch), single perf track. The width of this subspecies is 30 mil, the same as 8mm or super 8, and it is principally used by filmmakers who want to add sound to double perf original footage.

There is no reason why silent prints cannot be released in single perf form. However, when projectionists see single perf film, they usually set the projector's speed control for sound instead of silent speed. If you've made a silent film that ought to run at sound speed, it could be released in single perf form to avoid confusion. Unless there is a good reason not to, filmmakers generally choose double perf film for their shooting stock, even when they are planning a sound film. This will be discussed in chapter 7, but for now, let's say that it simplifies certain editing procedures. On the other hand, single perf film should be used if the filmmaker plans to add mag stripe to his original footage.

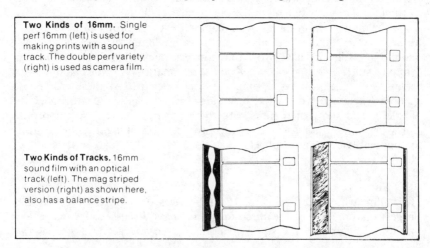

Two Kinds of 16mm. Single perf 16mm (left) is used for making prints with a sound track. The double perf variety (right) is used as camera film.

Two Kinds of Tracks. 16mm sound film with an optical track (left). The mag striped version (right) as shown here, also has a balance stripe.

Independent Filmmaking

Mag striped 16mm single perf raw stock is a standard item supplied by manufacturers for use in single system sound-on-film cameras, although it is also possible to have a lab stripe single perf film.

Film Availability

Sixteen mm film is supplied in many lengths in a wide variety of emulsions, on spools or on cores. Daylight loading spools of one or two hundred feet are commonly supplied, although the two hundred-foot spools are usually obtained only from professional outlets. Kodak, on special order, supplies many of its 16mm emulsions in metal magazines holding fifty feet of film. As far as I know, there are no general-purpose cameras currently made which accept these magazines. Film is also supplied on plastic cores in lengths of four and twelve hundred feet that must be loaded in camera magazines in total darkness.

Sixteen mm film is available in both negative and reversal emulsions for black and white. This is true for color as well, even though 16mm negative color is rarely used. Negative film is obviously designed for printmaking, but reversal film is often used and capable of producing high quality prints. The major suppliers of 16mm film are Eastman Kodak, Fuji and Agfa-Gevaert, and it is advisable to obtain your film directly from the manufacturers' own outlets because of their 20 percent or so discount below retail cost.

Following is a list of Kodak customer service centers in North America, from which professional motion picture film may be ordered.

Eastman Kodak Professional Film Outlets.

Dallas, TX 75234
2800 Forest Lane
Phone: (214) 241-1611

Oak Brook, IL 60521
1901 West 22nd Street
Phone: (312) 654-5300

Chamblee, GA 30341
5315 Peachtree Industrial Blvd.
Phone: (404) 455-0123

Hollywood, CA 90038
6677 Santa Monica Blvd.
Phone: (213) 464-6131

Rochester, NY 14650
1187 Ridge Road West
Phone: (716) 254-1300

Montreal, Quebec H3E 1A1:
2 Place du Commerce,
Ile des Soeurs
Phone: (514) 761-3487

Honolulu, Hawaii 96819
1122 Mapunapuna Street
Phone: (808) 833-1661

San Ramon, CA 94583
9100 Alcosta Blvd.
Phone: (415) 828-7000

Toronto, Ontario M6M 1V3:
3500 Eglinton Ave. West
Phone: (416) 766-8233

Dayton, NJ 08810
P.O. Box 1334
Route 130 at Georges Road
Phone: (201) 329-6600 &
(212) 879-1500, ext. 240

Washington, DC 20024
(Customer service
from Rochester)
Rochester, N.Y. 14650
1187 Ridge Road West
Phone: (716) 254-1300

West Vancouver, B.C. V7T 1A2:
100 S. Park Royal
Phone: (604) 926-7411

If you live in or near a large city, check the telephone book for an address of a regional office. Any size order will be filled, so don't be intimidated by what you consider a small order.

The Format

Laboratory Services

Because 16mm is primarily a commercial medium designed for the making of prints, extensive laboratory picture and sound services are available to handle this format. While the independent filmmaker who chooses to use 16mm has the advantage of these services, you must also be aware of their expense. Naturally you are free to ignore any or all of the supporting services, and can, for example, silently project your original footage with a tape recorded track in rough synchronization.

The main function of the laboratory is to process film, which can usually be done overnight or even the same day. Workers in 16mm often order a *workprint,* or a *cutting copy,* made from their original footage. This relatively inexpensive print, after it has been edited, will serve as a guide for cutting the camera film. Prints are usually contact printed, but on occasion the filmmaker may have need of optical prints (see chapter 9, under Optical Printers). Optical printers are used to make dissolves, special effects, frame line corrections, freeze-frame printing and so on. The optical printer is also ideal for the preparation of master printing material printed from original camera film. In the past, when it was felt by people who run laboratories that there was no demand for such services for the smaller formats, 8mm and super 8 filmmakers enjoyed few of these postshooting techniques. Present indications are that many laboratories are starting to offer very comprehensive services for super 8.

Laboratories also offer A and B printing, which can yield prints free from visible splice marks, and dissolves and titles without recourse to the optical printer (see chapter 6, under A and B Roll Editing). Extensive sound recording and rerecording services are available, including in-sync recording with a projected film, transfer of original tape recordings to magnetic film or optical track, etc. (see chapter 8, *Preparing the Sound Track*).

Equipment

Sixteen mm cameras are generally heavier and bulkier than their 8mm or super 8 counterparts. For example, a Leicina, a quality 8mm camera weighs in at about two pounds, and the 16mm Bolex H-16, another fine camera, weighs about eight pounds, with film and three lenses. Despite the fact that 16mm cameras are usually heavier and larger, 8mm and super 8 machines frequently have features often missing from the bigger format. It's a rare super 8 camera that doesn't have through-the-lens reflex viewing, automatic exposure control and electric drive; many offer power zoom as well. Once you've used cameras with these features, they cease to be luxuries. Part of the reason why the smaller format cameras are so advanced is that in a competitive market, features sell cameras. For another thing, most 16mm camera bodies have been on the market for a long time; new models are essentially only improved versions of older ones. The designer of the smaller format camera will often start from scratch, giving him a greater opportunity for innovation.

Sixteen millimeter cameras fall roughly into two categories: those offering up to one hundred-foot loads on 3¼ inch reels, and those offering longer magazine loads with capacities of two, four and twelve hun-

dred feet. Cameras with magazines, like the Arriflex and Eclair, are
driven with an electric motor. Many cameras accepting one hundred-foot
loads are spring-driven, although most can accommodate an accessory
electric motor, and recent one hundred-foot load cameras like the Canon
Scoopic or Beaulieu, have been designed around electric drive. A few
cameras of this capacity, like the Arriflex 16S, the Bolex H-5, and recent
Pathé and Beaulieu cameras, will also accept a magazine mounted above
the built-in film chambers. There is a wide camera price range with
spring-driven one hundred-foot load models at one end of the spectrum,
and electric-drive magazine cameras on the other. The filmmaker can
expect to pay between a few hundred to more than ten thousand dollars
for a camera outfit that includes accessories and lenses.

Sound projectors for 16mm are larger, heavier and costlier than
8mm or super 8 machines with recent models having greatly improved
optical sound, brightness and image quality. Most projectors in service
now, however, offer only optical sound reproduction for 16mm.

Editing equipment for the large format is more expensive and, in
general, of better quality. Most 8mm and super 8 editing equipment
comes in the form of an outfit containing winds, splicer and viewer. This
is the exception rather than the rule for 16mm equipment, and these
items have to be purchased separately.

Sound Track

Sound Track and Format

The positions, widths and running speeds of the sound tracks of the
various formats differ, and a filmmaker's working technique must suit
the individual demands of each. Although there will be a more complete
discussion of sound and its application to filmmaking in chapters 7 and
8, it will be introduced here because a filmmaker's choice of his
medium is influenced by the flexibility or limitations inherent in a format's sound facilities.

Running Speed

The speed originally chosen by Edison was 40 fps according to Thomas
Armat who helped to develop the motion picture projector. This meant
that forty times each second the film was advanced one frame and
held at rest in the camera and later in the projector. However, later
designers and engineers decided that too much film was used at this
speed; instead, a speed of 16 fps was found to be adequate. The introduction of sound brought about the general adoption of a running speed
of 24 fps facilitating better sound quality and less flickering of the projected image. These standards for 35mm theatrical films were also
applied to 16mm—silents at 16 fps and sound at 24 fps. Most 16mm projectors run at both speeds. Similarly, 16 fps was chosen as the running
speed for 8mm. The use of magnetic sound track for 8mm spread the use
of 24 fps for that format, but 8mm filmmakers have the option of using
either sound or silent speed for sound films since 8mm sound projectors
will record and play back sound at either speed.

In recent years the silent projection standard has been changed from 16 to 18 fps. Some filmmakers considered this a plot on the part of the film manufacturers to increase the use of film. The reason given by the companies for this change of standards was that as light sources in projectors were becoming brighter, after a certain screen brightness level is reached, there is increase in flicker. In order to suppress this flicker, it was maintained that a particular speed of 18 fps is necessary to get beyond the threshold of noticeable flicker. Although I do not doubt the word of those responsible for this research, I have never been able to see a difference between projection at 16 and 18 fps. Be that as it may, for some years now, 8mm and 16mm projectors have been set for 18 fps silent running speed, even though they may be marked 16 fps. Similarly, 8mm cameras are set to run at 18 fps for silent speed, while 18 fps has always been the standard for super 8 silent filming.

For European TV a sound speed of 25 fps has come into use because European television broadcasts 25 images per second. Footage shot specifically for the tube is done at 25 fps, while film for the theater screen at 24 fps must be boosted one fps for TV transmission.

Picture-Sound Separation

One other important standard that varies from format to format is based upon the different technical requirements for image projection and sound reproduction. The motion of the film through the projector's optical system must be intermittent. Although the film flows more or less evenly from feed to take-up reel, it must be held momentarily at rest as it reaches the projector's lens. Once it is held at rest, the projector's shutter opens, and the image is flashed on the screen. When the shutter moves to block the image from the screen, the film is advanced one more frame, held at rest again, and the process is repeated.

But just as magnetic tape must flow by the head of a tape recorder, or the grooves of a phonograph record pass by the stylus, the sound track must flow continuously by the sound reproduction device, or sound head. The continuous motion of the film past the sound head, and the intermittent motion of the film through the optical system are not compatible. Designers have solved the problem by allowing the film to form a loop and pass over rollers, between the optical and sound systems. The loop and rollers serve to smooth out the intermittent film motion converting it into a smooth, continuous motion needed for good sound reproduction. Therefore, the sound record for a particular image precedes that image by the distance necessary to form the loop. (The picture could also have preceded the sound—the choice is arbitrary.) The length of film between the image and sound has been standardized for the various formats and types of sound track.

Magnetic Sound

Film can in effect be converted into magnetic tape if it is striped with a layer of magnetic oxide. Magnetic oxide can be coated on raw film stock (unexposed film), or it can be coated after the film has been processed.

Although magnetic sound tracks are commonly used for 8mm or super 8 projection, the use of mag track for 16mm projection is not as common although it is used by the television industry. Magnetic sound is theoretically capable of better sound quality than optical sound.

Optical Sound

With few exceptions, magnetic tape is used for original recording and rerecording, or 'dubbing.' The use of optical sound is usually confined to release prints, and, at present, most of the optical sound work is in 16mm, although there are several 8mm and super 8 optical sound machines on the market.

Optical tracks are a photographic record of the variations in intensity that make up sound. The amplitude of the sound waves is translated into a record of varying density or area, which upon playback is turned into variations of electric current used to drive loud speakers. Because an optical sound track is a photographic record that uses the same film emulsion as the image part of the film, it is less expensive than magnetic tracks. Although 16mm magnetic tracks can be of high fidelity quality, it is rare that a good sound track, either optical or magnetic, displays its full potential because of room acoustics, projector noise and inadequate playback equipment.

Lip Sync

There are several 8mm and 16mm sound-on-film cameras used to record both a sound and picture record at the same time (in sync), usually, of people talking. The Fairchild 900 is an 8mm camera that records sound-on-film striped with mag oxide. There is only one sound-on-film super 8 camera as of this writing, the Wilcam which uses single super 8 stock. Auricon makes several 16mm camera models that record either optical or magnetic tracks on single perf stock. There are several other 16mm cameras that can produce sound-on-film with the addition of a

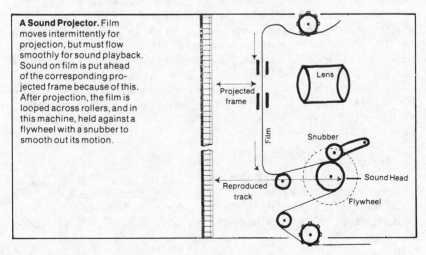

A Sound Projector. Film moves intermittently for projection, but must flow smoothly for sound playback. Sound on film is put ahead of the corresponding projected frame because of this. After projection, the film is looped across rollers, and in this machine, held against a flywheel with a snubber to smooth out its motion.

Projected frame

Lens

Film

Snubber

Reproduced track

Sound Head

Flywheel

The Format

magnetic head unit or module. Canon also manufactures a fairly compact magnetic sound-on-film camera. Such direct recording of sound-on-film with the camera is called *single system* sound, to distinguish it from the system in which a separate machine is used to record the sound track, called *double system* recording.

8mm Sound

Since magnetic track standard 8mm is capable of fairly good sound quality, there are many 8mm magnetic sound projectors on the market. A few machines made by Toei, Viewlex and one distributed by Petri Kine Camera Co. played back optical tracks. Optical sound standards for 8mm were never established. The image-sound separation for 8mm is fifty-six frames, which means that the magnetic sound recording precedes the picture by about eight inches. This makes editing of single system sound difficult, because there is a 2.3 second lag at 24 fps, and a 3.1 second lag at 18 fps between sound and image. If the filmmaker is cutting a single system film for sound track, he may lose important image. If he is cutting for picture image, he may be including 2 or 3 seconds of sound he doesn't want.

This is the usual procedure for preparation of an 8mm magnetic track: the filmmaker completes his editing of the film and sends it to a laboratory to have it magnetic sound striped or coated. The cost is several cents a foot for this service. There are also striping devices which allow the filmmaker to add his own magnetic track. Next he projects the striped film, and uses the recording facility of the projector to transfer sound from a variety of sources to the film: direct recording into a microphone, transfer of a tape or records, or mixing any of these or other elements.

Super 8 Sound

Most of the remarks made for 8mm sound apply to super 8. (Certainly the track can be prepared with the same general method.) There are a number of super 8 magnetic and optical sound projectors on the market. The image-sound separation for super 8 is 18 frames which means that there is a lag of only 2/3 second magnetic track between image and sound at 24 fps. The image-sound separation is 22 frames for optical track films. After shooting and sound recording with a super 8 single system, editing its film ought to be easier than the editing of 8mm single system films. Optical sound super 8 never really caught on, except for endless loop cartridge devices like those made by Technicolor.

16mm Sound

Magnetic recording, usually in the form of ¼ inch tape, at 7½ ips, is used for the original recording of most 16mm tracks. Many home tape machines have the quality to do the job, and these recorders have valuable features for the filmmaker. For example, the sound mixing facility of many multiple track tape machines allows the filmmaker to mix two or more sound tracks together with ease. In addition to recording wild or floating tracks — tracks unsynchronized at the time of shooting — these machines can be converted to record lip sync.

The next step usually is to bring the original recordings to a sound studio, often part of the film laboratory, and have this material transferred to 16mm mag film. This is single perf film, 16mm wide, coated entirely with iron oxide material. After the mag film is edited, it can be used for producing the magnetic or optical track of the print. All of the recording and rerecording needed is done with tape or 16mm magnetic film because of its ability to make copies without the quality losses inherent in optical sound dubbing. One of the major reasons why optical sound tracks of prints have improved in recent years is that original recording and dubbing is now done with magnetic tape or film.

The image sound separation for 16mm optical sound is twenty-six frames, and the separation for magnetic sound is twenty-eight frames. Editing 16mm single system involves the same difficulties as editing 8mm single system.

Which Format?

Quality

What do we mean by *quality*? There are many factors that contribute to the quality of a projected image. We have to consider the entire system used to get that image on the screen from film and camera to laboratory work and projection. Also, the conditions under which the film is projected influence its quality.

Obviously 16mm is capable of the highest 'quality' of the three formats. Its picture size is on the order of four times that of 8mm or super 8, and in a traditional sense, at least in terms of 'sharpness,' one would expect this increased quality to be the case. But as far as I am concerned, and I'm sure this is an opinion shared by an increasing number of filmmakers who consider such things, quality is entirely relative to purpose. For example, there are no good or bad film stocks. If a film is very grainy, then its use should exploit this quality. If smaller formats are not capable of the fine grain or the sharpness inherent in the 16mm image, why try to reproduce these things? Why not try to explore the qualities like motion and swirling grain, and the freedom of handling a small camera? Just as each kind of film can be considered to be another *color* on the filmmaker's palette, to paraphrase filmmaker Stan Brakhage, each format is capable of its own kind of quality.

The traditional concept of judging image quality in terms of fine grain, accurate color rendition (whatever that is), sharpness, gradation and so on, is hopelessly outmoded. A creative filmmaker must be aware of all of these factors which do contribute to the appearance of the final image. But the filmmaker is cheating himself if he fails to realize that the traditional concept of best or good quality, while it may be suitable

The Format

for commercial filmmakers, is of no value and may in fact restrict creative expression.

Costs

Film stock in 16mm costs about three to four times what the 8mm formats cost for the same screen time. But this is only the beginning of the story. An 8mm or super 8 filmmaker rarely has expenses beyond equipment and film stock, but the 16mm filmmaker, who uses more expensive equipment as well, usually is concerned with producing prints. This involves sound work, other laboratory services such as workprints, and the cost of the prints themselves. All in all, I estimate that it costs as much to put one minute of 16mm color sound film on the screen as it costs to put half an hour of color and sound 8mm or super 8 on the screen.

It's really impossible to compare the large format with the smaller formats in this manner, because 16mm as described here is a printmaking medium, and it might be more appropriate to compare the cost of 8mm sound color print from 8mm original with the cost of 16mm sound color print from 16mm original, even though such 8mm or super 8 prints are rarely made. Also, estimates will vary from filmmaker to filmmaker depending upon his way of working.

Distribution

If distribution is the filmmaker's goal, he must finally make prints of his films available. If 16mm distribution is considered, the filmmaker has the option of shooting in 8mm or super 8, and then blowing up these films to 16mm. If there is even the vague possibility that such distribution is in the offing, the filmmaker ought to shoot his film to be shown at 24 fps, especially if a sound track is contemplated. Although it is possible to show 8mm or super 8 sound films at the silent speed of 18 fps, such a procedure is uncommon enough in 16mm to make these sound films essentially undistributable.

The expense of blowing up 8mm or super 8 to 16mm varies greatly from lab to lab; the filmmaker will have to get his own estimates of such costs. There are filmmakers who prefer shooting in 8mm and planning subsequent 16mm enlargement. Depending upon the individual's working technique, some saving in total film cost is possible, but this will partly depend upon the ratio of discarded 8mm original footage to that finally used for the blowup. Filmmakers using this method can finish their films in 8mm, and then have a straight blowup made. Other filmmakers blow up their footage, and then manipulate it as if it were 16mm original. It has been my experience that a good 8mm to 16mm blowup can be better than an 8mm to 8mm print.

Most often, filmmakers seeking distribution shoot their films in 16mm. I think it highly probable that super 8 may replace 16mm as the distribution format. Super 8 prints of films shot in 16mm are comparatively inexpensive, and can have good quality. The challenge now is to make good super 8 prints of films shot in super 8.

The proliferation of three quarter and half inch video tape recorders makes tape distribution of films an interesting possibility.

Independent Filmmaking

My purpose has been to introduce some concepts of motion picture technology, and to help the filmmaker, or prospective filmmaker, choose the format best suited to his purposes. Hopefully, reading the rest of the book will continue to aid him in making that choice and even re-fine it. But let me point this out, if it hasn't as yet been made clear: choice of format is entirely relative to the filmmaker's purpose, distribution, expense and so on. I know several filmmakers who use more than one format, changing from one to another, even for the same film, as their whim or purpose changes.

The Future of the Formats

We'll start with the narrow gauges and work our way up. Since standard, or regular, 8mm is obsolete, we need not consider it further.

Super 8

Super 8 remains a provocatively interesting format for the independent filmmaker. There is lots of good super 8 equipment designed for the amateur or home movie maker. However, in recent years, super 8 has not fared terribly well in the marketplace, at least according to industry expectations of consumer activity. Every new ingredient to the super 8 cake has added first an up and then a down to sales, or so it seems. The original super 8 cartridge concept spurred lagging 8mm sales. A few years later the XL system, combining high speed film with fast lenses and a wider shutter opening—giving the ability to shoot in 10 footcandles or less—initially spurred sales. However, after a burst of momentary enthusiasm, sales curves subsided just as they had after the introduction of the cartridge itself. And the same story for the sound-on-film cartridge. After initial enthusiasm, sales curves dropped.

It may well be that super 8 sales were depressed by a seriously troubled economy and the threat of the introduction of video for home movies. Today as I stroll city streets, parks and tourist haunts, I see more and more video cameras and recorders used by people who a few years ago would have been making home movies on film.

The Original Two-Hundred-Foot Cartridge-accepting Camera. Not a terribly good camera, but it established a standard and paved the way for better cameras from Elmo, Chinon and Nizo. (Eastman Kodak)

The Format

Other factors may have contributed to super 8 sales becoming very soft; but whatever the causes, the important thing for the independent is the fact that there are still good super 8 products on the market. Most exciting for me is the two hundred-foot sound-striped cartridge, which gives ten minutes of good quality image and sound in a compact package that's easy to load. For my money, the most interesting camera accepting the cartridge is the Elmo 1200 SXL, a low-cost good performer whose main turn-off, running noise, can be helped with a barney.

Super 8 remains a viable means of production for many kinds of small-budget films, or films which cannot possibly be shot in 16mm. Try entering many of the nations of the world with 16mm gear and you will run into enough customs interference to make your head swim. But super 8 equipment, considered a home movie medium, won't even excite a second glance.

Super 8 transfers to video using the Rank flying spot scanner (discussed in chapter 11), for example, can be outstanding, and I defy the most knowledgeable technician to tell super 8 from 16mm, most of the time.

Super 8 has had difficulties establishing itself in the audio-visual marketplace. Here it is caught between the firmly entrenched 16mm infrastructure and the rise of three quarter and half inch video cassette equipment, not to mention the relatively recent addition of video disk formats. Nonetheless, it remains a viable means of expression for the independent, and those seeking further information on the subject are advised to read the author's *The Super 8 Book*, or *Lipton on Filmmaking*, both published by Simon and Schuster.

16mm Versus Video Tape

Sixteen millimeter has had an interesting history since the first edition of this book was published. Essentially, it has been all but totally eclipsed in the United States as a medium for television news-gathering by ENG (electronic news-gathering) equipment. The reasons for this are obvious: TV stations do not need to maintain processing labs to handle the news film chores when shot on tape. ENG can broadcast news as it happens from remote locations, and, most important, video engineers are into electronics—film is a technology sufficiently different to give them grief.

Nevertheless, 16mm documentaries for video continue to be shot, and 16mm (or 35mm, for that matter) remains the only truly universal means for moving image dissemination for video on an international scale. This is because film standards are the same the world over, whereas video standards are many, and conversions from one standard to another can be costly, leaving telltale artifacts in the transfer. (Video standards are discussed in detail in chapter 11.)

Sixteen millimeter production for sponsored films and for TV commercials remains high, but video is clearly making inroads in these arenas. Therefore, film and video are likely to coexist for years to come, and there may never be a final outcome to the much-written-about battle between film and video.

Independent Filmmaking

The Format

The Film

Film is made up of an image forming layer called the *emulsion,* coated on a transparent support material called the *base.* Photography is founded on the light sensitive properties of the emulsion which is, in part, made up of silver compounds called silver halides. Silver chloride, bromide and iodide are the photographically interesting *haloid compounds,* whose name derives from the fact that chlorine, bromine and iodine are members of the halogen group of elements.

Particles of silver halide are dispersed throughout a medium of more or less transparent gelatin. Although this combination of silver halide particles and gelatin is called the emulsion, strictly speaking, an emulsion is one liquid dispersed throughout another. Whole milk, for example, is an emulsion of liquid fat globules suspended in skim milk.

The emulsion of motion picture film is coated on a support, or base, which must be flexible, strong and transparent. It is bound to the base with a substance called the *substratum.* The base is usually cellulose triacetate, or, more commonly, cellulose acetate. In recent years manufacturers have begun to coat the emulsion on polyester plastics, commonly known under the trade name Estar (Eastman Kodak).

The particles of silver halide in the emulsions are activated in proportion to the amount and intensity of light striking them. After it is exposed to light, the film can be processed — immersed in a mild reducing solution, usually some organic compound and other ingredients called *developer.* Those particles that were struck by light are most susceptible to the chemical reaction induced by the developer; in a given time, some, but not all the halide, is reduced to metallic silver, which is black in color. If the film were left in the developer for an extended time, all the silver halide in the emulsion would be transformed into metallic silver.

After development metallic silver and silver halide dispersed in

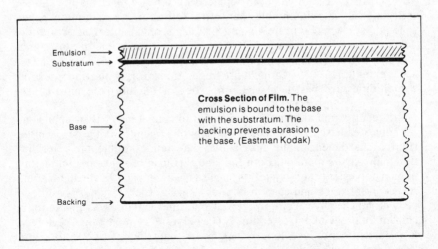

Emulsion ⟶
Substratum ⟶

Base ⟶

Cross Section of Film. The emulsion is bound to the base with the substratum. The backing prevents abrasion to the base. (Eastman Kodak)

Backing ⟶

The Film

gelatin is left. The undeveloped silver halide is removed at this point with a solution called *hypo*, or *fixer,* which does not react with the silver metal. This process is called *fixation.* If the undeveloped silver salts were not removed, the image would not have the necessary variations in density to form the image nor would it be stable. After fixation, areas of various densities of silver metal, and areas of clear gelatin remain. The densest portions of the film are where the greatest light intensity struck the emulsion; the least dense portions, those more transparent, are where moderate or small amounts of light struck the emulsion.

When an image is formed on the film through a lens, and the film is developed and fixed, we have what is called a *negative.* For example, a white shirt will appear black, and a black car, white. Printing this negative on another piece of film will result in a positive print of the original image. In other words, the tones of the print will match those of the original subject.

The other basic kind of film, reversal film, to be described in more detail in the following pages, produces images of normal — not negative — tones.

The Qualities of Film

All films — negative, reversal, color and black and white — have certain properties in common.

Film Base

The base, or support, for motion picture film must be flexible, transparent, and strong, even though its thickness is on the order of several thousandths of an inch. The material originally used, cellulose nitrate, met all these needs but was very flammable and sometimes explosive. Moreover, when stored for several years, it was subject to deterioration.

Nitrate base film has been replaced by *safety film,* usually cellulose triacetate, far less flammable than nitrate film, or even common paper. It is not subject to nitrate's aging problems or chemical deterioration. Today, nearly all motion picture film including camera film, intermediate printing master material and print film, consists of cellulose acetate material, even though fire regulations for projection in some communities are based on the properties of the obsolete nitrate base film.

Recently, manufacturers have begun to coat some of their emulsions on polyester bases stronger and thinner than acetate. Polyester is more transparent, dimensionally more stable and even less subject to deterioration than acetate material. Both Fuji and Eastman produce motion picture film on polyester base; Fuji for its single 8 cartridge, and Eastman for some release print stock and camera film, on special order. It is not possible to cement splice polyester; however, at one time DuPont was marketing a cement for use with polyester film. Since polyester is thinner than acetate, it is possible to produce longer lengths of film, and consequently more

Independent Filmmaking

shooting time, for standard size reels. For example, the reel which accepts 53
one hundred feet of 16mm acetate base material comes spooled with one
hundred twenty-five feet of polyester base material; the two-hundred-foot
reel with two hundred and fifty feet of polyester, and so on.

Because of its superior properties, polyester film is a likely candidate to replace not only camera film but print material as well. There are obvious advantages in print storage, shipping and distribution, as well as the increased running time per reel.

Halation

When a bright light source, such as a street lamp, is included in a photographic image, sometimes it appears to be surrounded by a halo of light. Bright sunlight passing through a window into a room can cause adjacent subjects to glow producing a similar effect.

This is called *halation,* caused by a scattering of reflected light by the film base. This halo-like image occurs when some of the incident light, as it passes through the emulsion and then the base, reflects back from the base to the emulsion. In order to suppress this halation, film manufacturers have added dye to the base to absorb the light that would have passed through the base in the first place, and also absorb any remaining light rays that might be reflected back to the emulsion. Although such a dyed base may appear to have a gray or blue hue, the tint is not usually noticeable when, for example, original reversal black and white film is projected.

For color film, another approach often used by manufacturers to suppress halation is to coat a carbon black layer on the base side of the film opposite the color emulsion. Called a *rem jet* layer by Eastman, this prevents halation by absorbing the light rays that passed through the base as well as protecting the base from abrasion. It is removed during processing. Halation is most evident in fast emulsions, but it's rarely troublesome in modern films even in difficult situations.

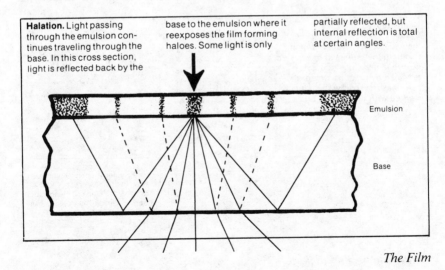

Halation. Light passing through the emulsion continues traveling through the base. In this cross section, light is reflected back by the base to the emulsion where it reexposes the film forming haloes. Some light is only partially reflected, but internal reflection is total at certain angles.

Emulsion

Base

The Film

54 **Film Speed**

The sensitivity or speed of an emulsion or film to light is given by a number, in the United States by what is called an ASA index, in Europe, sometimes by DIN numbers. The initials ASA come from the former name of the American Standards Association, which is now called the American National Standards Institute (ANSI). DIN derives from its German counterpart, Deutsche Industrie Norm.

The ASA numbers are an arithmetical system; that is, doubling the value of the index corresponds to doubling the film speed. For example, a film like Plus X reversal is 50 ASA, making it twice as sensitive to light as a film like Kodachrome II, with an index of 25.

DIN numbers are based on a logarithmic or exponential scale, and an increase of 3° DIN corresponds to a doubling of film speed. It is possible to convert one scale to the other. Most light meters have both ASA and DIN markings. Values in this book will follow the American standard.

Any testing laboratory following the standard procedure will arrive at the same ASA value for a specific film. These procedures have been agreed upon by the industry as far as still camera films are concerned. No agreements have been reached so far as motion picture film is concerned. For this reason motion picture film is usually referred to as having an E.I., or an exposure index rating as opposed to an ASA number. Strictly speaking, in the example above, I should have written that Plus X has a speed of 50 E.I., not 50 ASA. In point of fact it makes little difference whether you say ASA or E.I. People will know what you're talking about.

Although an arbitrary classification, film speed can be divided into usable categories: slow, medium, fast and very fast. By today's standards 10 to 50 E.I. would be considered slow, 50 to 200 medium, 200 to 400 fast and more than 400 very fast. A film speed of about 50 E.I. would serve for most outdoor conditions, ranging from bright sunlight to all but the

Comparative Film Speed Systems. The relations between the various types of film rating numbers that are used in exposure meter calculators, determined by practical comparison measurements with meters marked with the various types of scales. (Eastman Kodak)	ASA BSI	BSI (log)	OLDER* WESTON	DIN	SCHEINER	ASA BSI	BSI (log)	OLDER* WESTON	DIN	SCHEINER
	2.5	15°	2.0	5	16°	160	33	125	23	34
	3	16	2.5	6	17	200	34	160	24	35
	4	17	3	7	18	250	35	200	25	36
	5	18	4	8	19	320	36	250	26	37
	6	19	5	9	20	400	37	320	27	38
	8	20	6	10	21	500	38	400	28	39
	10	21	8	11	22	650	39	500	29	40
	12	22	10	12	23	800	40	650	30	41
	16	23	12	13	24	1,000	41	800	31	42
	20	24	16	14	25					
	25	25	20	15	26	*The numbers in this column are for the older Weston meters, such as Model Numbers 650, 715, 720, 735, 736, 819, and 850. Recent and current Weston meters are calibrated for ASA Exposure Indexes. These include Model Numbers 737, 852, and 853.				
	32	26	24	16	27					
	40	27	32	17	28					
	50	28	40	18	29					
	64	29	50	19	30					
	80	30	64	20	31					
	100	31	80	21	32					
	125	32	100	22	33					

deepest, darkest shade. An emulsion of 100 E.I. or more might be too fast for many situations outdoors, but it might be suitable for filming in the early morning, at twilight or in deep shade. The higher the E.I., the darker the environment it can record.

Studio lighting, which can be very bright (and hot), may not require film faster than that needed for outdoor filmmaking. Shooting in relatively dim interiors could require film with an index of 200 to 1000, or more.

Daylight and Tungsten Speed

Black and white film is usually provided with two speed numbers: a higher one for outdoor use and a slightly lower one for indoors. For example, Kodak Tri-X Reversal, 7278, has a daylight E.I. of 200, and a tungsten speed or E.I. of 160. Indoor illumination is usually provided by tungsten filamented electric lamps, hence the term tungsten speed.

The lower number is recommended for indoor work because tungsten illumination is relatively deficient in the blue-violet portion of the visible spectrum. Since photoelectric light meters (see chapter 5, under Exposure) may not respond to tungsten illumination as they do to sunlight, using such a meter indoors may result in a slight underexposure. However, the meter you use may be fully sensitive to the distribution of both indoor and outdoor light, and thus one index—the higher one—can serve for both environments. Only experience with your film and equipment will perfect your exposure technique. A film's published speed should serve only as a starting point for the filmmaker's efforts. Tests or trial and error will help determine the most comfortable working index.

Pushing Film

Many films can be pushed one stop amounting to an increase in effective film speed by a factor of two. In processing, the film is pushed by allow-

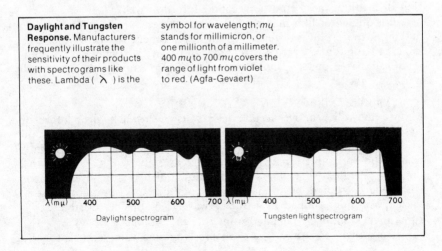

Daylight and Tungsten Response. Manufacturers frequently illustrate the sensitivity of their products with spectrograms like these. Lambda (λ) is the symbol for wavelength; $m\mu$ stands for millimicron, or one millionth of a millimeter. 400 $m\mu$ to 700 $m\mu$ covers the range of light from violet to red. (Agfa-Gevaert)

Daylight spectrogram

Tungsten light spectrogram

The Film

ing it to remain in the developer for a longer than usual period of time. For example, a 250 E.I. film pushed one stop reaches 500 E.I. If previously a proper exposure had been $f/1.0$, the new exposure would be $f/1.4$. (See chapter 4, under Lens Speed, for an explanation of f stops.)

This example illustrates the greatest use for pushing or forcing film: increasing the film's sensitivity to allow an exposure to be made under poorer lighting conditions. If you are using a lens with a maximum opening of $f/1.4$, and your exposure meter tells you that you need to expose at $f/1.0$, one solution is to push the film one stop. (Other possible solutions are to choose a faster film, increase the level of illumination, or undercrank — that is, shoot at a lower fps rate, thereby increasing the exposure time.)

Negative, reversal, black and white and color film may be pushed one, two or more stops. The laboratory doing the processing will acquaint you with their procedures and limitations on pushing. The lab will also be able to tell you what changes in quality can be anticipated with pushing, or, as it is often called, *forced development*.

The true measure of whether or not a film's speed has been increased through forced development is the quality of detail in dark or shadow areas. If detail is preserved in the dark portions of the subject, then pushing the film has actually increased its speed (and not merely increased its contrast or gamma).

Pushing film usually increases contrast and grain even though this will depend upon the film stock, the degree of forced development and the subject matter. Extended forced development of reversal, however, may result in a reduction in contrast, since the maximum density (D-max) may be diminished.

Many films can be forced one stop with slight changes in quality. Others can be forced two or more stops, with varying degrees of success, depending upon the quality the filmmaker wants, or is willing to accept. The usual practice is to force fast film to make it faster, although slow or medium speed emulsions can be forced as well.

Pushing color film may result in altering the overall color balance, making it more blue or green. Forced development is usually billed by the lab at about a 50 percent surcharge, and many labs may have a minimum rate based on, say, five hundred feet. Also usually, the entire roll must be forced.

Exposure Latitude

Many films will produce acceptable results even when given more or less than a 'perfect' exposure. For example, a negative film, black and white, of moderate speed, with an index of 80, may produce good prints when exposed from 20 to 160 E.I. In this case, one would say that this film will tolerate, or has an exposure latitude of two stops over and one stop under, a total exposure latitude of four stops. Assuming that at 80 the exposure determined by a meter was $f/5.6$, the permissible exposure range would have included stops $f/11$ to $f/4$.

This range, or latitude, in exposure is related to several factors in-

Independent Filmmaking

cluding the gradation of the film. Films with a long scale of tonal gradation, or films of low or moderate contrast, will have more exposure
latitude than higher contrast films.

Another contributing factor is the subject matter: if the subject is
contrasty — a dark-suited skier against a snowy sunlighted background —
the exposure latitude will be greatly reduced. If, on the other hand, the
subject has a limited contrast range — a room of subdued tones in fluorescent or indirect lighting — the exposure latitude will be effectively
increased.

Grain

Since the developed photographic emulsion is made up of suspended
particles of metallic silver in clear gelatin, as the projected motion picture image is enlarged, these become increasingly visible. Even a 16mm
image projected on a small screen (30 x 40 inches) must undergo an area
magnification of about 10,000 times.

The *graininess* (more properly, granularity) of a projected film depends not only on the original film's own inherent graininess, but is also
affected by the graininess of the stock on which it is printed. A grainy
original printed on a grainy stock will really show granularity.

The apparent graininess of a film is dependent on other factors
as well: the longer a film remains in the developer, the grainier it will
become because more silver halide particles convert into larger clumps of
silver grains as development time increases. Also, the temperature
changes from processing solution to solution, including the water rinse,
will emphasize the apparent graininess of the film. This effect is caused
by a minute buckling and swelling of the emulsion called *reticulation*.
Therefore if you do your own processing, this is one technique you can
employ to get very grainy images.

Perceiving Grain

Grain is most apparent in broad, solid toned areas, such as the sky, or a
wall. Detailed subject matter and different textures tend to conceal
grain. The grain of a photographic image may be likened to the dots in a
half-tone reproduction. The more per unit area, the less apparent they
are. The graininess of an image may vary within a single frame. For example, parts of the same image may appear to be grainier than others. A
sharper, pinpoint pattern of grain tends to be less obtrusive than large
blotchy clumps of grain. In color film grain is not made up of black silver
metal, but rather of the dyes that have replaced the silver.

There is a relationship between grain and film speed: slow films
tend to be less grainy than fast films. In recent years, however, the
granularity and overall quality of fast films has improved dramatically,
and many fast films are no grainier now than the fine grain slow emulsions of a decade ago. The 8mm, super 8-single 8 and 16mm filmmakers
all have benefited from this improvement in fast films. In the past there
has been some reluctance on the part of some major manufacturers to
offer faster films for the 8mm gauges, but this reticence is disappearing.

In motion picture work, we are dealing not with one photograph which can be studied at leisure, but with a constantly changing series of images, each with its own grain pattern. This helps reduce the apparent graininess of the projected image.

Contrast and Gradation

A high contrast emulsion is one which shows a great change in density with a small increase in exposure. For example, when light and dark gray subjects are photographed with a high contrast emulsion, they may appear black and white in the processed film.

A low contrast emulsion, on the other hand, compresses the tones of the original. The various densities of an image recorded on such an emulsion will not be very distinct. Low contrast films are described, often, as *flat*. High contrast films are characterized as *snappy*, or *contrasty*. In most cases, a successful original or print made for projection should have a scale of tones that appears to be normal, neither too snappy nor too flat.

Although the terms contrast and gradation are often used interchangeably, gradation refers specifically to the processed emulsion's tonal range. Films that record many tones faithful to the original have a good scale of gradation. The differences between the terms have become lost because emulsions with high contrast have a short scale of gradation, and emulsions with low contrast have a long scale of gradation. *Contrast*, then, refers to the change in density of the emulsion through a change of exposure. *Gradation* describes the entire range of tones that the emulsion is capable of recording.

Sharpness

The word sharpness, as applied to the photographic image, certainly has meaning, at least to the eye of the beholder; but trying to relate objective physical measurements to human perception is difficult.

In their *tech data* sheets, film manufacturers often refer to a film's *resolving power,* or its *modulation-transfer curve.* While the former is easier to understand, the latter actually conveys more information about the film's sharpness.

The *resolving power* of a film is determined by photographing a series of printed ruled lines, arranged in progressively closer sets. The distances between successive parallel lines are the same thickness as the lines. The test chart is photographed with a camera whose quality is known, the film is processed and the image is observed under magnification. The greatest number of lines per millimeter that the film is able to reproduce sharply is its resolving power. This test, then, determines how well the film can record fine image detail.

Unfortunately, resolving power tests frequently do not correlate well with the eye's subjective perception of sharpness. One difficulty is that contrast as well as resolving power plays a part in determining a film's apparent sharpness. In order to help overcome this difficulty, Eastman Kodak films have their resolving power rated for low and high contrast test charts. For example, the tech data sheet for Plus-X Reversal (a very sharp camera film) gives the following information: with a test-object contrast of 1.6:1 (very low contrast), the film has a resolving power of fifty lines per millimeter. With a test-object contrast of 1000:1, the resolving power of the film is given at one hundred and eighteen lines per millimeter. (A test-object contrast of 1000:1 means that the dark lines absorb one thousand times as much light as the white space around them, or conversely, the white space between the dark lines reflect one thousand times the intensity of light as the dark lines.)

Acutance

Acutance is a measure of sharpness that has a high correlation with an observer's subjective perception. Acutance has been described as a knife-edge measure of sharpness. In the resolution test, no account is taken of the fact that a ruled line of black on the test chart, when reproduced on film might appear, not as a strict change from light to dark, but rather as a diffused or gradual change from light to dark.

Acutance is a measure of the image that would be produced if a razor edge were laid on the photographic emulsion and the film exposed. A densitometer, a device very much like a photoelectric exposure meter, but used to determine the amount and intensity of light transmitted through the film, is moved across the developed film. An abrupt change in density between the exposed and unexposed areas is found in a film of high acutance, a gradual change in a film of low acutance. High acutance films appear sharp, low acutance films, less sharp. Instead of an abrupt change from dark to light, there might be a gradual, but very brief, change from light to dark. The gradual change in density comes from the fact that the photographic emulsion is made up of many grains of a certain depth of silver metal. In a thick emulsion — and fast films usually have thicker emulsions than slow films — light will scatter through the turbid combination of gelatin and silver halide. Such images may have less acutance than an image formed on thin, fine grained emulsion.

Modulation-Transfer (M-T) Curves

Modulation-transfer curves are now published by some motion picture film manufacturers in an effort to combine the concepts of resolving power and acutance. Very briefly, *modulation-transfer curves* are determined in the following manner: the film is exposed to a test pattern similar to the charts used to determine resolving power, with the exception that the lines are not solid bars separated by spaces of the same width. Instead, as we move across the pattern, the density of the lines varies like a sine curve. The information that would have corresponded to lines per millimeter is now given in terms of cycles per millimeter.

The film is exposed to targets with spatial frequencies from one to two hundred cycles per millimeter. For example, targets of spatial frequency of five, ten, twenty and so on, lines per millimeter will be exposed. For each exposure of each frequency, using a densitometer, a

The Film

modulation-transfer factor is calculated. The factor determined is given in terms of response percentages, which indicate how accurately the emulsion recorded each test chart. This information is plotted graphically, usually on what is called a log-log scale used to compress the size of the graph to record the information more readily.

Most films will produce a fairly straight curve until about ten or twenty cycles per millimeter. Although the response percentage of all films will fall off beyond this point (since it is more difficult to reproduce fine detail than coarse detail), the rate at which the curve falls off indicates a film's sharpness. Films that fall off slowly are sharper than films falling off more rapidly. I realize that many readers will find this information either totally incomprehensible, or if you have a background in such things, very sketchy. In practice the subject isn't that grim. To understand one M-T curve, it must be compared with other similar curves.

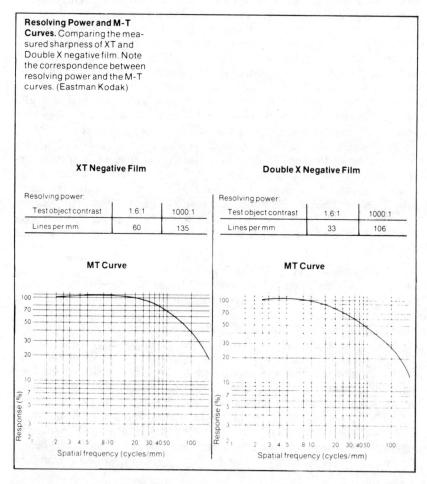

Resolving Power and M-T Curves. Comparing the measured sharpness of XT and Double X negative film. Note the correspondence between resolving power and the M-T curves. (Eastman Kodak)

XT Negative Film

Resolving power:

Test object contrast	1.6:1	1000:1
Lines per mm	60	135

MT Curve

Double X Negative Film

Resolving power:

Test object contrast	1.6:1	1000:1
Lines per mm	33	106

MT Curve

Independent Filmmaking

If your concern is printmaking, the sharpness of the projected film will naturally be influenced by both the camera film and the film used to make the print.

Lenses are also evaluated with M-T curves, but such curves are not often published by manufacturers.

Color Sensitivity

White light, or sunlight, is made up of the following colors in the following order: violet, blue, green, yellow, orange and red. On either end lie the invisible ultra-violet (beyond violet) and infrared (below red).

All photographic emulsions are sensitive to the violet and blue end of the spectrum. Films sensitive to only this portion of the visible spectrum are called *color blind*. Their use in motion picture work is limited to high contrast film, often used for titlemaking, and black and white printing stock. Dyes are added to the photographic emulsion in order to

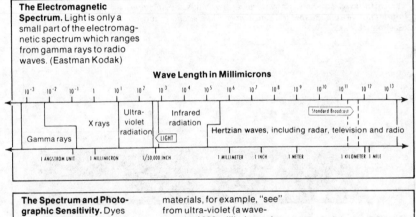

The Electromagnetic Spectrum. Light is only a small part of the electromagnetic spectrum which ranges from gamma rays to radio waves. (Eastman Kodak)

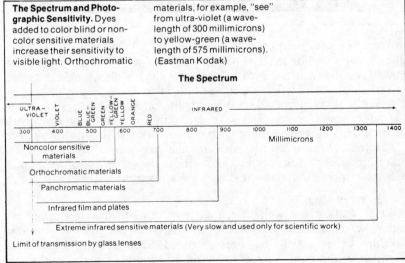

The Spectrum and Photographic Sensitivity. Dyes added to color blind or non-color sensitive materials increase their sensitivity to visible light. Orthochromatic materials, for example, "see" from ultra-violet (a wavelength of 300 millimicrons) to yellow-green (a wavelength of 575 millimicrons). (Eastman Kodak)

The Film

62

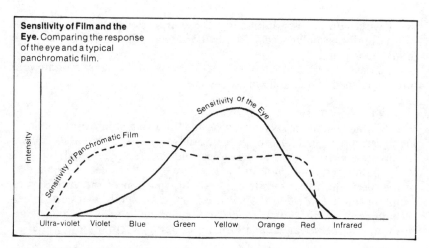

Sensitivity of Film and the Eye. Comparing the response of the eye and a typical panchromatic film.

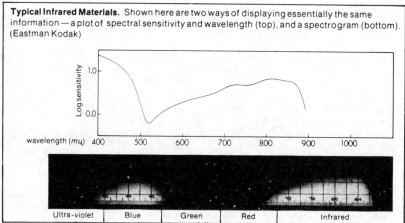

Typical Infrared Materials. Shown here are two ways of displaying essentially the same information—a plot of spectral sensitivity and wavelength (top), and a spectrogram (bottom). (Eastman Kodak)

increase the color response so that the image's colors will be reproduced in appropriate tones of black, white and gray. Films that have extended sensitivity through part of the spectrum, to the green, are known as orthochromatic (ortho), rarely used for filmmaking today.

Without exception, all black and white camera film is responsive to the full range of colors. This kind of emulsion is called panchromatic (pan). Panchromatic emulsions have good color sensitivity through to the red end of the spectrum. Although the color sensitivity of panchromatic film doesn't quite correspond to the color sensitivity of the human eye, the response in terms of tones of black is very similar.

Infrared Film

A kind of black and white film that may be of further interest to the filmmaker is infrared film whose sensitivity to the invisible infrared portion of the spectrum has been extended. Such film is available only as negative emulsion. In order to lop off, or suppress, the rest of the light

Independent Filmmaking

to which the infrared film is incidentally sensitized, deep red filters (Wratten 87, 88A, 89B) must also be used to achieve an exclusively infrared effect. (The more common Wratten 25 will give a good effect as well.)

Infrared film is difficult to expose, since the photoelectric exposure meters do not respond to infrared radiation. However, the manufacturer can supply exposure suggestions, and experience will help induce good results. Infrared film is useful for extreme haze penetration as well as the many weird effects it can produce. With the proper filter, it can turn the sky jet black, record foliage as white, and make all normal skin tones much lighter than they appear to the eye or on panchromatic emulsions.

Reciprocity

The law of reciprocity for photographic emulsions states that the product of the exposure time (in the following example the fps rate) and light intensity (f numbers) is a constant. That is, if the exposure time is doubled, say from 24 to 12 fps, and the f stop is halved from, say, $f/8$ to $f/11$, the density of the image of the processed film remains the same. Shooting at 24 fps (for most cameras 1/50 second: see chapter 3, under The Shutter), $f/8$ produces images of equal density as shooting at 12 fps (1/25 second) at $f/11$, and so on.

However, when the law of reciprocity breaks down — in the case of very long or very short exposures — the film will require additional exposure. This effect, called *reciprocity failure,* rarely concerns the filmmaker because the range of exposure times, say from one second to 1/500 second, which covers just about any fps setting, conforms to the law of reciprocity. Nevertheless, the filmmaker should be advised that either very long exposure of single frames (*time exposures,* as they are often called), or short exposures, produced with electronic flash, may necessitate an increase in exposure. Also, color film may require filters to restore the 'normal' color balance. If you are concerned with exposures of this kind, the film manufacturer will supply exposure correction and filtration information.

Characteristic Curve

The *characteristic curve* is also known as the H and D curve (after the men, Hurter and Driffield, who first plotted it) or the D log E curve. The last term derives from the fact that the curve is a plot of the density of a photographic negative as a function of the exposure that negative receives.

Although the details may vary, all photographic films have the same basic relationship between density and exposure, hence the name characteristic curve. The negative film shown is typical. For an increase in exposure (which is determined by both the length and the intensity of the exposure), there will be some corresponding increase in the density of the negative. A change in the logarithm of the exposure by 0.3 is equivalent to doubling the exposure.

The Film

64

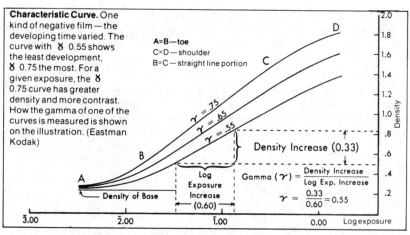

Characteristic Curve. One kind of negative film — the developing time varied. The curve with ᕐ 0.55 shows the least development, ᕐ 0.75 the most. For a given exposure, the ᕐ 0.75 curve has greater density and more contrast. How the gamma of one of the curves is measured is shown on the illustration. (Eastman Kodak)

A=B—toe
C=D—shoulder
B=C—straight line portion

Density Increase (0.33)

$$\text{Gamma}\ (\gamma) = \frac{\text{Density Increase}}{\text{Log Exp. Increase}}$$

$$\gamma = \frac{0.33}{0.60} = 0.55$$

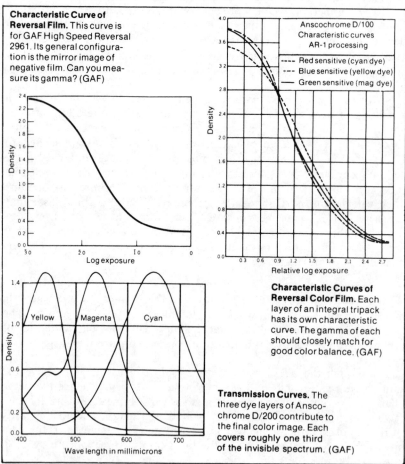

Characteristic Curve of Reversal Film. This curve is for GAF High Speed Reversal 2961. Its general configuration is the mirror image of negative film. Can you measure its gamma? (GAF)

Anscochrome D/100 Characteristic curves AR-1 processing
---- Red sensitive (cyan dye)
--- Blue sensitive (yellow dye)
— Green sensitive (mag dye)

Characteristic Curves of Reversal Color Film. Each layer of an integral tripack has its own characteristic curve. The gamma of each should closely match for good color balance. (GAF)

Transmission Curves. The three dye layers of Anscochrome D/200 contribute to the final color image. Each covers roughly one third of the invisible spectrum. (GAF)

Independent Filmmaking

Reversal curves are the mirror images of negative curves. Below point A, or for exposures less than point A, the film records no image. The portion of the curve from A to B is called the *toe,* from B to C the *straight-line portion,* and from C to D the *shoulder.* The highest point of the curve is a measure of the maximum density (D-max) the film is able to record.

In the toe portion, density increases rapidly with exposure. The straight-line portion shows a constant rate of increase of density with exposure, while for the shoulder portion, the rate of increase of density falls off.

The gamma (γ) is the slope (or derivative, or rate of change) of the straight line portion of the curve. It is a measure of contrast. The most important variable that affects contrast or gamma is the length of development (or temperature). The more the film is developed, the greater the gamma (contrast). This does not mean that all films can be developed to the same gamma. Some, depending upon the properties of the emulsion, are intrinsically able to be developed only to a certain gamma, or range of gammas. The contrast of photographic materials in use varies widely from about 0.5 to 10, from ordinary film to the very, very high contrast films used in graphic arts. Laboratories make frequent use of the characteristic curve to control film processing accurately. For more information about gamma, see page 355.

How Color Film Works

The effect of color film is very much like that produced by color printing used for color comic books. Except for the black outline of the drawings, the wide range of many colors for comics are reproduced by various combinations of three colors.

Color motion picture film, camera and print, negative and reversal, is composed of an arrangement of three layers of black and white emulsion, plus a yellow filter. These layers, one coated on another, each form a record of about one third of the visible spectrum. Each layer of reversal color film, appropriately dyed, helps to render the total image of the original subject.

The idea behind this color process is that the visible spectrum can be broken up into three portions, and an appropriate dye image used for each portion. If the dyes are well chosen, and the sensitive layers respond to the proper portions of the spectrum, a reasonable approximation of the colors of the original may be obtained. As we know, modern color film can produce very pleasing — in fact, beautiful — results.

The emulsion layers and a yellow filter are arranged in the following order: the top layer, sensitive for blue; then the yellow filter layer; a layer sensitive for green; finally the bottom layer, sensitive for red. The total thickness of the layers is on the order of twenty thousandths of a millimeter. The layers are coated on a base material, usually cellulose acetate. This three-layer arrangement is known as an *integral tripack.*

There are two types of reversal color film in use. The earliest introduced, Kodachrome, contains three layers of black and white emulsion without dyes incorporated into the film. Appropriate dyes are added to each emulsion layer during processing. However, the majority of color reversal film on the market, Agfachrome, Anscochrome, Ektachrome, etc, have what are called dye couplers integrated into the film itself. A specific dye replaces the metallic silver in each emulsion layer. During the processing procedure, the blue-sensitive layer is dyed yellow, the green, magenta and the red, cyan. Magenta might be described as a red lacking yellow; it looks like a deep pink. Cyan dye looks blue-green. The colors we call blue actually have a lot of red pigment in them. Cyan lacks any redness — it is a pure blue dye.

Let's trace what happens when we film one solid mass of color, red for example. The top layer and the middle layer receive no exposure. The red layer (bottom) is exposed and then made developable. Since we're dealing with a reversal process, after development the top two layers will be dense, or full of metallic silver. The bottom layer, the red one, will be clear. The metallic silver of the top two layers is replaced with yellow and magenta dye. When light travels through the processed film, it passes through the layer of yellow and magenta dye, producing the color that we call red.

Negative film consists of a similar three-layer arrangement. In order to correct for imperfections in the response of the dyes and color sensitivity of the layers, color masking layers, which appear orange or brown, are incorporated into the film. When printed on the appropriate stock, the negative produces the tones and colors of the original. The negative itself has an image made up of colors complementary to the colors of the subject. This may be somewhat difficult to see, because the masking layers give all the colors an overall orange tint.

The Qualities of Color Film

Color film has all the properties of black and white film — speed, grain, sharpness, gradation and contrast, exposure latitude. Practically everything said about these qualities in black and white negative and reversal applies to color negative and reversal; but color film has its own additional peculiarities.

Film Speed

Like black and white motion picture film, there are no industry standards for determining the film's speed, but each manufacturer provides an E.I. that is a useful starting point upon which to base exposures. Available emulsions range from the very slow (16 for standard 8mm outdoor Agfachrome), to the very fast (500 for 16mm Anscochrome D/500), and many color films can be pushed. A film like Ektachrome EF, for example, can be pushed as many as eight stops, although this is recommended for emergencies only. Indoor EF is rated at 125 E.I.

While it is true that the slowest color emulsions, like Agfachrome, Kodachrome II and Ektachrome Commercial, are the sharpest, finest grained color films available, it does not follow that the faster films,

Independent Filmmaking

like many of the Video News Film (VNF) Ektachrome emulsions, do not have good quality; high speed color films can have remarkably fine quality.

Grain

Since the silver metal in the emulsion is replaced by dye, we have an image composed of *grains of color*. A microscopic examination of color film reveals that it looks very much like color printing or a painting by a pointillist like Seurat. A color comic book, seen under a magnifying glass, is made up of a regular pattern of magenta, cyan and yellow dots; color film, seen under much greater magnification, is made up of randomly distributed masses of cyan, magenta and yellow *grains*.

Exposure Latitude

Color negative has more exposure latitude than color reversal but less than comparable black and white negative. Color reversal has practically no exposure latitude at all. However, it is usually better to underexpose,

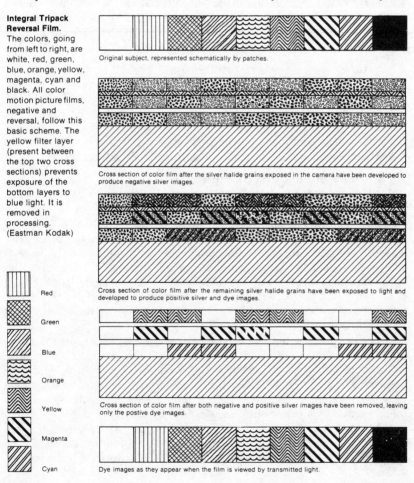

Integral Tripack Reversal Film. The colors, going from left to right, are white, red, green, blue, orange, yellow, magenta, cyan and black. All color motion picture films, negative and reversal, follow this basic scheme. The yellow filter layer (present between the top two cross sections) prevents exposure of the bottom layers to blue light. It is removed in processing. (Eastman Kodak)

Original subject, represented schematically by patches.

Cross section of color film after the silver halide grains exposed in the camera have been developed to produce negative silver images.

Cross section of color film after the remaining silver halide grains have been exposed to light and developed to produce positive silver and dye images.

Cross section of color film after both negative and positive silver images have been removed, leaving only the postive dye images.

Dye images as they appear when the film is viewed by transmitted light.

Red
Green
Blue
Orange
Yellow
Magenta
Cyan

to get a denser image, than to overexpose and get a thin image. If you've underexposed, at least there's something on the film, and it may be possible to save the shot when a print is made.

I might have made the case for color reversal film seem tighter than it actually is. Exposure latitude depends upon the particular emulsion. An emulsion like Commercial Ektachrome, with a very low contrast, has a useful range of about three stops, depending upon the subject matter. It may be possible to get good prints from such a film overexposing as much as one stop, and underexposing two stops. However, a contrasty subject decreases the effective latitude, a flat subject increases it.

Other color reversal emulsions, projection contrast materials, designed for good contrast with direct viewing, are more difficult to expose; but obviously, if these films were very difficult to expose, they couldn't be offered as they are on the amateur market. Once again, latitude greatly depends upon the subject matter. Some films tolerate underexposure better than others, and none that I know of can produce rich colors if overexposed more than one stop. The best way to find out what works is actually to expose some film and find out how it looks.

Saturation
This term refers to how rich the reproduced colors of a print or original reversal look. If the colors are deep and vibrant, they are richly saturated. If they are pale and ghostly, the colors are poorly saturated. This quality will vary from one brand of film to another. The saturation of the film depends both on the original colors and how the film is exposed. Underexposure of reversal encourages rich saturation of colors.

Color Balance and Color Temperature
Color film in order to communicate natural looking light and hues must be balanced or adjusted for the color temperature of the prevailing light. Color temperature is measured on the *absolute,* or Kelvin, scale where the low limit of temperature is minus 273 degrees centigrade. Since temperature is a measure of the molecular energy of motion, it is theoretically impossible for temperature to be less than -273°C, because all molecular motion ceases at this temperature. As an object is heated, it emits radiation, and depending on its temperature, much of this radiation is in the visible portion of the electromagnetic spectrum. That's what we call light.

The color of the light emitted by a substance as it is heated depends upon the substance itself and its temperature. Let us assume that there is a perfect radiator—a substance that radiates and absorbs light with absolute efficiency. Such a body would be *perfectly* black, and is referred to as a *black body*. Although there is no such perfect substance in the universe, many bodies or substances act very similarly.

The sun is one such body. It radiates energy as if it were a theoretically perfect black body heated to about six thousand degrees Kelvin (6000° K). For such large numerical values of absolute temperature, the scale might as well be in degrees centigrade. Light of this color temperature is called white light, or daylight.

When people want to find out the 'real' color of, for example, a fabric they are buying, they take it outdoors or to a window. Indoor light looks different from sunlight because electric lamps have a lower color temperature than the sun. In fact, depending upon their wattage, age and actual line voltage, household electric lamps have a color temperature of from 2800° K to 3000° K. This means that the heating of the tungsten filament by the electric current approximates the light intensity that would be given off by a black body heated 2800° K to 3000° K. Compared to sunlight, this illumination is deficient in blue. Remember what happens to a poker placed in a fire: first it glows dull red, then yellow and finally, at its hottest, blue-white. Tungsten illumination corresponds to the poker's glowing yellow or yellow-orange, the outdoor illumination compares to the poker's glowing blue-white.

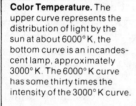

Color Temperature. The upper curve represents the distribution of light by the sun at about 6000° K, the bottom curve is an incandescent lamp, approximately 3000° K. The 6000° K curve has some thirty times the intensity of the 3000° K curve.

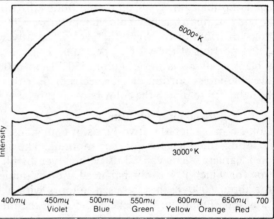

400mμ	450mμ	500mμ	550mμ	600mμ	650mμ	700
	Violet	Blue	Green	Yellow	Orange	Red

Sources of Illumination and Their Color Temperatures. This chart indicates that a fast color film for much available light shooting ought to be balanced for about 2900° K, instead of 3200° K.

Although present material is acceptable, experience indicates that 3200° K film with household illumination produces warm results. Ektachrome 160, super 8 film, has an emulsion more nearly suited to common indoor illumination than other products. (Eastman Kodak)

Source	Color Temperature (in K)
Sunlight (mean noon)	5400
Skylight	12000 to 18000
Photographic Daylight*	5500
Crater of carbon arc (ordinary hard-cored)	4000
White-flame carbon arc	5000
High-intensity carbon arc (sun arc)	5500
Clear zirconium foil-filled flash	4200
Clear aluminum foil-filled flash	3800
500-watt (photoflood) approx 34.0 lumens/watt	3400
500-watt (3200 K photographic) approx 27.0 lumens/watt	3200
200-watt (general service) approx 20.0 lumens/watt	2980
100-watt (general service) approx 17.5 lumens/watt	2900
75-watt (general service) approx 15.4 lumens/watt	2820
40-watt (general service) approx 11.8 lumens/watt	2650

Condition of daylight which best represents that encountered in typical photographic situations.

The Film

As a black body's temperature increases, not only does it give off more light, but more light in the more energetic frequencies, the blue-violet. Illumination with a comparatively low color temperature, such as an electric lamp at about 3000° K, is red or orange light; color film balanced for outdoors, lacking the automatic facility of the eye-brain to compensate for this change, will objectively report an overall orange tint to the subject. Color film for outdoor use must be balanced — have the sensitivity of its layers and dyes adjusted so that film exposed with the light of the sun will look natural. The eye automatically compensates for different color temperatures, so that indoor lighting provided by a tungsten filament electric light looks as natural to us as sunlight. Film used indoors must have the sensitivity of its layers and dyes adjusted for light of a lower color temperature.

To sum up: color temperature, a measure of the color of a source of illumination, is expressed by the Kelvin, or absolute, scale. A heated black body, which for photographic purposes can be the sun or an electric lamp filament, gives off a continuous distribution of colors of light. A body heated to a low color temperature, 3000° K, will emit a continuous distribution of light that is comparatively deficient in the blue-violet portion of the visible spectrum. The sun can be considered to be a black body radiating at about 5500° K to 6000° K, and so is richer in the blue-violet portion of the spectrum. For this reason, color film must be balanced to match the color temperature of the source of illumination.

Indoor and Outdoor Film

Color film is offered in two kinds of emulsions: one balanced for indoor shooting, the other for outdoor shooting. The use of an appropriate filter on a camera's lens can adjust either type of film for use with illumination for which it was not balanced. For example, outdoor film balanced for about 6000° K may be used indoors with a blue filter. Since indoor tungsten illumination is deficient in blue, the filter is needed to add blue to the exposure, or, if you like, hold back the red portion of the spectrum. Filters often used for this purpose are Wratten numbers 80A or 80B, but exact filter recommendations are provided by the film manufacturer. Because these filters are so dense, they may require an additional exposure of from one to three stops.

Usually indoor balanced film can be used outdoors with a filter like Wratten numbers 85 or 85B. Such filters are light orange and require less than a one-stop increase in exposure. Since greater film sensitivity is usually required with indoor illumination, it is preferable to use an indoor film filtered for outdoor use rather than the other way around.

With the proper tungsten illumination, indoor balanced film may be used without filtration. Outdoors, its effective film index will be somewhat lower, with appropriate filtration, but in all probability, acceptable. For example, Kodachrome II indoor film may be used unfiltered with 3200° K lamps at 40 E.I. With the outdoor conversion filter, Wratten 85, its E.I. is an acceptable 25. On the other hand, Kodachrome

II outdoor film has a speed of 25 balanced for sunlight. Used with photofloods indoors, it requires a Wratten 80B filter, resulting in 12 E.I., which is rather slow.

Most indoor color film (sometimes called Type B film) is balanced for illumination with a color temperature of 3200° K. Certain photoflood and halogen lamps operate at this color temperature. Other film (Type A) is balanced for 3400° K. Illumination for this film is also available.

Although ordinary tungsten lamps have a lower color temperature than 3400° K or 3200° K, Types A and B films will produce acceptable results with such sources. For more information about color film filtration, color temperature measurement with photoelectric devices and other related topics, see chapter 5.

Black and White Reproduced with Color Film
Color film ought to be able to reproduce black and white, as well as a full range of neutral grays. Most color films only come close to good reproduction of a 'gray scale.' Often, the white may be stained by some tone picked up from one of the layers. Usually this is totally unnoticeable. Grays, however, are something else. It's very difficult to photograph neutral grays with most color films and get neutral grays, even though some emulsions do better in this respect than others. The grays may have a slight magenta or cyan cast, for example. Usually this isn't of much concern unless you're into filming gray test charts.

Finally, the film should properly reproduce rich, deep blacks. Remember, with color film we are dealing with three dyed layers, not black metallic silver. In a reversal film, black is the product of three layers of dye holding back all, or very nearly all, of the incident light.

The maximum density of black that a reversal film is capable of producing is called its D-max. Color reversal films usually can't come close to a black opaque D-max. The film will often have a magenta toned D-max, or a green D-max. There's no reason why many subjects need a film with a deep black D-max. Often the D-max, though less than opaque, even semitransparent, will appear perfectly black because surrounding bright colors increase the black effect by comparison. If, however, you require rich blacks—a starry, black night sky, or the black that often surrounds a spotlighted performer—this property of color film will be very important to you.

A deep untinged D-max is important for shooting titles. If the background of the title is supposed to be black, you may be disappointed to discover that it photographs objectionably tinted.

One way to evaluate D-max is to run off a few feet of reversal in the camera with the lens cap on. Project the processed film, or examine it under a viewer, or hold it up to a clear light bulb. With practically any film, black and white or color, you'll see the filament of the light.

The Kinds of Camera Film

Black and White Negative
This kind of film is usually only available in 16mm, although it may be

possible to order double-8 or super 8 negative material. However, readily available 8mm or super 8-single 8 reversal black and white emulsions may be processed as negative.

A wide variety of negative films is available, from very slow, fine grained film meant for studio or bright outdoors, to very fast film for shooting in extremely dim light. In addition to the usual normal contrast panchromatic negative emulsions, infrared sensitive and high contrast copying film, blue sensitive, or color-blind stock, are also on the market. Some negative emulsions may be successfully processed as reversal film. Check with the manufacturer's tech data sheets or your lab to find out the possibilities. In general, negative processed as reversal roughly doubles in speed.

Black and White Reversal

Reversal film, unlike negative, produces normal tones and values. It is not necessary to make a print of reversal in order to see the positive image. Reversal film is processed so that it has a positive image, like that printed from a negative: it was originally introduced to save the amateur the additional cost of making a print. Today, use of reversal is the rule rather than the exception for 16mm, and certainly all 8mm and super 8-single 8 filmmaking.

Reversal film is available in all the formats: 8mm, super 8-single 8 and 16mm. There is almost as wide a range of reversal emulsions as there are negative—from medium speed to very fast material. High contrast and infrared emulsions are not available. All reversal camera films are panchromatic. Reversal film may be processed as negative. Check with your lab or the manufacturer to see if this is advisable for a particular film and to get an approximate recommendation for the film index. It has been said that reversal films are finer grained than negative material of comparable speed. However, prints from reversal have quality similar to that of positive prints from negative.

Black and White Reversal Processing. (Eastman Kodak)	Treatment	Processing Solution	Time of Treatment		
			68 F (20 C)	95 F (35 C)	110 F (43 C)
	1. First Development	D-94	2 min	40 sec	13 sec
	2. Rinse	Running Water	30 sec	20 sec	5 sec
	3. Bleach	R-9	50 sec	40 sec	10 sec
	4. Rinse	Running Water	30 sec	20 sec	5 sec
	5. Clear	CB-2	30 sec	20 sec	5 sec
	6. Rinse	Running Water	30 sec	20 sec	5 sec
	7. Reexposure	800 foot-candle-seconds			
	8. Redevelopment	D-95	30 sec	20 sec	5 sec
	9. Rinse	Running Water	30 sec	20 sec	5 sec
	10. Fix	F-10	50 sec	30 sec	5 sec
	11. Wash	Running Water	As required		
	12. Dry	As required (approximately 1 minute in a typical machine)			

Independent Filmmaking

Processing Reversal

Compared with negative processing, reversal processing is complicated. The reversal emulsion itself is very much like the negative emulsion; what makes a film into a reversal happens, essentially, during processing. Negative film processing involves the exposed film being run through a bath of developer, then a wash, or stop bath, and next the hypo, or fixer. After it has been washed in water again, the film is dried.

With reversal motion picture film, that part of the emulsion which would have been dissolved away by the hypo or fixer in the negative process, now forms the positive image.

The film is developed as in negative processing by converting silver halide struck by light into metallic silver. However, bleach is used to wash away the metallic silver negative image. Then the unexposed silver halide in the emulsion, which in the negative process would be washed away with the hypo, is made developable by reexposing the film to a controlled intensity of light. The film is redeveloped, turning the silver halide into silver metal. It is fixed to remove any remaining undeveloped silver halide and is washed and dried. I've left out several minor steps, such as the water washes, but the procedure is essentially as outlined.

Color Negative

This type of film is never used in the 8mm formats, although double 8 and double super 8 emulsions may be specially ordered. Negative color in the last few years has been greatly improved and is now frequently used for 16mm work. Negative color film, such as Eastman color, is regularly used by the theatrical motion picture industry in 35mm and 65mm (release-printed as 70mm) formats.

Processed color negatives have dyes which in the emulsion have replaced the metallic silver. These dyes are the complementary colors of the subject: red may appear as a shade of green, blue as orange, and so on. Color negative, when printed, produces film of normal colors.

Processing Machine. Unexposed film is spliced end-to-end and travels continuously through the machine, from one treatment to the next. (Consolidated Film Industries)

The Film

Color negative material has an overall orange cast. You might suspect that such a cast would produce a greenish tint in the print, but the orange tint, called a color mask, is added to the negative film to help correct colors and contrast, and make better prints. Prints made from camera original color negative, Eastman color film specifically, have translucent and open colors that have a light or airy look compared to the well saturated colors obtained from reversal prints of reversal camera original.

Color Reversal

Color reversal film, available for all formats, is processed so that it looks like the scene as it was shot, with colors approximating the original. It eliminates the immediate necessity to make a print. Prints from color reversal may be made on reversal print film. It is possible to process some color reversal emulsions as color negative. The resulting negatives lack the customary orange masking layers.

A wide range of color reversal films are manufactured by many companies. The great majority of color reversal films available in 16mm were designed to give good results when projected. That is, the projected color reversal film has good contrast and rich colors. It was not designed primarily for printmaking, although it is now possible to make very good prints from this kind of material, often called *projection contrast* film.

The second kind of 16mm color reversal is usually called commercial film, like Eastman's Ektachrome Commercial Film (7252). It is not recommended for projection because it is a very low contrast, chalky looking film, designed for making prints.

In the past it was very difficult to make quality prints from projection contrast reversal film, like Kodachrome II. The primary objection was a build-up of contrast in prints made from such film. In an effort to produce good quality prints from 16mm original reversal color film, a low contrast *commercial* film was used with release print stock compatible with this film.

While this system has been available for many years, research has nevertheless continued, and low contrast release print stock, for making prints from color reversal of normal contrast, has appeared. There are currently two systems for producing 16mm color reversal prints, one from low contrast original, the other from normal contrast original. Both systems can produce high quality prints. The low contrast original is slower than the normal contrast material, but, in general, it is quite sharp and has fine grain.

Film available through normal retail outlets in the 8mm formats is normal contrast color reversal, such as Agfachrome, Kodachrome II and various house brands. This should be of interest not only to the 16mm worker, but to the 8mm or super 8-single 8 worker who plans to make prints or blow up his film to 16mm. Optical 16mm prints made from 8mm originals ought to be made on the stock designed for printing normal or projection contrast reversal, like Eastman's 7389, Ektachrome R.

Independent Filmmaking

If your object is to project your original camera film, then your interest obviously is confined to how your camera film looks when projected. If you want to make prints of your films, then you will have to understand not only how the camera film portrays the subject, but how the print film works with your camera film. Given the variety of camera and print films, a vast range of effects is possible.

This is especially true with color material. Black and white emulsions of various manufacturers usually have similar characteristics. Color emulsions, however, have extremely marked individual characteristics.

Black and white film is so similar, in point of fact, that reversal or negative film of one manufacturer can be processed in solutions provided by other manufacturers for particular products. This is not true for color films. Although the principles of color filmmaking are similar, the specific process, dyes and chemical agents used are very different. The color sensitivity of each layer of an integral tripack, and the individual layer dyes, vary from film to film. The differences in dyes, especially, account for the various possible renderings of the same subjects with different color films. You'd be hampering your creative exploration of the medium by sticking to one kind of film or ignoring the possibilities of other materials.

What follows is not a complete catalogue of available motion picture films. Rather, it is a subjective appraisal of materials with which I have become familiar over a long period. Since manufacturers are constantly changing their products, and your impressions of a material's characteristics will not correspond to mine, I can only suggest that you not restrict your own experimentation. Remember too, printing one manufacturer's camera film on another's print film can produce unlikely and maybe even fascinating results. May I also suggest that deviations from professionally accepted practices will probably be more interesting and enlightening than filmmaking by the book.

8mm and Super 8-Single 8
Since many films available in 8mm are also available in super 8, these formats can be discussed together. There is also another reason for doing this: since image quality depends upon the area of the frame—the larger the frame the sharper the image, the finer the grain, for the same film, and so on—the roughly similar size frames of super 8 and 8mm make remarks applicable to one format relevant to the other.

Color
There are three super 8-single 8 filmstocks of traditional high quality—Kodachrome II, Fujichrome and Agfachrome. It is not altogether insignificant that they all end in the suffix -chrome. All color reversal films marketed in the United States end in that suffix. Negative color films end in the suffix -color, for example, Eastmancolor.

Fujichrome is only available in the single 8 format, in Fuji's own single 8 cartridge. It is available in two varieties, an indoor, or Type A, film, and an outdoor film balanced for sunlight. The indoor film has an E.I. of 50 (film speed after a product name will be given in parenthesis) and the outdoor film is 25 E.I. Like all Type A films, the indoor film may be used outdoors with a Type A or Wratten 85 filter. Fuji and 3M offer the only generally available film stocks coated on polyester base for the amateur.

Both Agfachrome and Kodachrome offer only Type A film in the super 8 cartridge. They both offer indoor and outdoor film in the 8mm format.

Agfachrome daylight (16), Kodachrome II daylight (25) and Fuji-chrome daylight (25) are about the same speed as the indoor Type A varieties of the film. Kodachrome and Agfachrome are both 40, and Fujichrome 50. Agfachrome's slightly slower outdoor film makes no difference for all practical purposes, and neither does Fujichrome's indoor 50, which is a tad faster than the competition.

Kodachrome and Fujichrome belong to that class of color films that lack color couplers. This is of concern only if you want to process your own film, in which case it is impossible to process film without couplers without elaborate machinery. Integral tripacks like Koda-chrome and Fujichrome must have each of their three layers reversed chemically or by exposure to light, and individually developed for color. Agfachrome has color couplers present in the emulsion layers, and so only one color development bath is necessary; even then few people take the trouble.

All three films are very sharp and fine grained. It would be difficult to say which was sharpest or finest grained. The differences between the three films lie in the areas of their contrast and subjective response to color. Fujichrome (which is not available in standard 8) is probably the most contrasty of the three, followed closely by Kodachrome and Agfa-chrome. For this reason it could conceivably look sharper than the other

Kodak Super 8 Cartridge Film. Ektachrome EF 7242 is listed here because it is still available. Unless you like a grainy look, stick with the far superior SM 7244.

	50 Foot Silent	50 Foot Sound	100 Foot Sound
Kodachrome 40	X	X	X
Ektachrome 160	X	X	
Ektachrome G	X		
Ektachrome EF 7242	X	X	X
Ektachrome SM 7244	X	X	X

Independent Filmmaking

two films under some circumstances. Fujichrome is the warmest film of the three, with more magenta in the yellows, giving them orange tones. All three produce good skin tones, greens and good blue skies. Kodachrome probably produces the best greens. It also has an openness that the other films don't quite match, a color expansiveness that makes it look 'pure.'

Both Agfachrome and Kodachrome are responsive to the moods of the day, and both can yield especially brilliant colors, but I'd choose Agfachrome for more mellow or sombre moods, say for late afternoons. Agfachrome has soul. It can give beautiful 'Dutch master' colors, that are often described as 'European' because of the decidedly magenta D-max. Fujichrome and Kodachrome appear to have neutral black maximum densities. All three films produce brilliant but different reds.

The films give better performance in the super 8-single 8 than in the 8mm format, essentially in long shots or shots with a lot of detail.

Eastman also offers Ektachromes just for the super 8 cartridge: Ektachrome 40, Ektachrome 160 and Ektachrome G Movie Film (consult the chart). Ektachrome 40 is exported from Rochester to various countries, but it is not available in the United States, and Ektachrome 160 is a tungsten balanced film with a fast E.I. of 160. Ektachrome G is a 'universal' type emulsion which reproduces good color for any type of lighting, without filtration. All of these Ektachromes use a special high speed developing process different from that of other Ektachromes.

Faster Ektachrome films can be specially ordered from Eastman Kodak for standard 8mm, and for double super 8. Fast Ektachrome indoor film is available in the super 8 cartridge as a standard item. One interesting item: on special order Eastman will also supply spools of 8 millimeter wide super 8 Ektachrome EF.

Probably the best fast Ektachrome is 7244, SM. It can be processed in the special SM processor, or in the same chemicals used for 16mm VNF.

There are a number of other outlets for both color and black and white 8mm stock in film speeds greater than those available through the usual channels. The principal sources for these fast stocks are Eso-S Pictures, 47th and Holly, Kansas City, Mo. 64112, and Superior Bulk Film Co., 442 North Wells Street, Chicago, Ill. 60610.

Black and White

People like color, and because of supply and demand this preference isn't any more expensive than black and white. Amateur use of black and white 8mm and super 8 reversal stock is practically nonexistent. In fact, black and white reversal is downright hard to get. For single 8 there are Fuji films, Fujipan R-50 and Fujipan R-200, with speeds of 50 and 200. These films are reported to be extraordinarily good.

You can get twenty-five-foot loads of standard double 8mm from Eastman. Both Plus-X (50) and Tri-X (200) reversal are available, but you may have to special order even though some of the larger camera stores sometimes stock them. They are good films in the 8mm formats. Super 8

Plus-X and Tri-X are also available, and you may be able to obtain the faster 4-X Reversal (400).

Many other interesting black and white 8mm and super 8 films are available from the sources listed above, namely Eso-S and Superior Bulk Film Company.

I should point out that all the black and white film speeds listed above are for daylight, and the tungsten speeds of these materials are almost always a quarter of a stop slower. For example, 200 daylight film is 160 under tungsten lights.

16mm

Before shooting a project, it's best to figure out what look the film ought to have, and then test a camera original film and take it through the intermediate print material (if any) and release print steps. Only in this way can you tell in advance whether the combination of films you have selected can do the job. I say 'combination of films' because, if you are going to make more than a few prints, you are going to use intermediate materials in order to preserve the life of your camera original film, and/or lower print costs.

When the first edition of this book was written practically all 16mm productions were shot on reversal materials. Not so today. Vastly improved films for the camera, intermediate master stages and release prints have been on the market for several years, and a great many 16mm workers use the negative-positive system.

In the following discussion of color films I will concentrate on the Eastman Kodak materials rather than on those of manufacturers such as Agfa-Gevaert, Fuji and 3-M. Agfa-Gevaert and Fuji provide negative and reversal camera films, and 3-M provides release print materials only. Today most materials from the various manufacturers are designed to be compatible with the Eastman processes, either VNF (Video News Film) for reversal, or the Eastman Color process for negative materials.

I strongly suggest that filmmakers seeking an alternative look check out the Agfa-Gevaert and Fuji camera films. Because the vast majority of people making films stick with the Eastman products, I haven't taken the trouble to write about the other materials. It is also possible to alter the look of a film shot with Eastman camera materials by having it printed on stock manufactured by other people. So testing is in order.

Color

Eastman offers several distinct families of films for 16mm workers. First, we will consider Kodachrome. You can buy it balanced for daylight (25) or tungsten (40 E.I. with photofloods, 20 with a Type A for daylight), and it is a fantastically great film in terms of all the traditional pictorial parameters: color, sharpness, granularity, gradation and so on. It is considered an amateur film, and you can buy it only through retail outlets and not directly from the manufacturer as you can their professional motion picture products. It was designed to be a projected film. The very film run through the camera runs through the projector. It can make good prints with the Eastman unit contrast reversal print materials, Ektachromes 7389 and 7899. I like the look but some people may not, so test it out. The results are very snappy and brilliant.

Kodachrome, because of its very dense black, or high D-max, is a good film for shooting titles, or for a B roll for titles that will be superimposed on a reversal A roll for white or colored writing superimposed over a background.

The next group of materials, ME-4 Ektachrome, I can hardly recommend, since they are really obsolete. I'll explain. Eastman offers three color reversal processes for 16mm professional work. I will repeat that the Kodachrome process is an amateur process, or so considered, and not part of the professional system. At any rate, here are the three professional 16mm processes: ECO (Ektachrome Commercial), the related ME-4 and VNF.

The ECO process was designed for one film: ECO. It's a low contrast film designed not to be projected, but rather used as a master material for making prints.

ME-4 is an older Ektachrome process, and three camera films—MS, EF daylight and EF tungsten—plus a print stock, 7389, are meant to be processed in it. The camera films have all been superseded in terms of pictorial quality by the new VNF family of emulsions. My research has uncovered the fact that most of the EF and MS Ektachrome is being purchased by misguided Uncle Sam, who can't change with the times, not only for vitally important social issues but for film as well. The ME-4 system is with us because the government of the United States is too dopey to switch to the clearly superior VNF family.

As a taxpayer and a filmmaker, I object.

It may well be that the only good reason for keeping ME-4 here is for print stock 7390, which has a gamma of about 1.5 and is designed for making good prints with ECO camera film.

We'll now consider the modern Ektachrome system, the VNF system. If I am not mistaken, there are more different films which can be processed with the VNF chemistry than has ever been the case for any motion picture system. This is certainly the case if we include films manufactured by entities other than Eastman. The VNF films have projection contrast; therefore, they need a low contrast print stock—the VNF processed Ektachrome 7399, which has unit contrast, or a gamma of 1.

The new VNF emulsions which are listed in the table, along with the other Eastman professional camera films, have finer grain, better exposure latitude, are sharper, have more pleasing color, lower contrast and in every way to my eye are pictorially superior to the EF films. We have VNF daylight 7239 (160 E.I.), VNF tungsten 7240 (125 E.I. for 3200 K°, 80 E.I. with 85B filter outdoors), VNF high speed tungsten 7250 (E.I.'s 400 and 250) and a VNF material, 7251, balanced for daylight (E.I. 400) but tweaked to give good color when filming with stadium illumination for sports.

VNF 7240 is such a good material that I wonder why the VNF family of emulsions is not extended to a film that might replace the slower ECO 7252.

The Film

7240 is the first pick of fast reversal films, and pushed one stop it hardly loses any quality. It is to be preferred to 7250, which is grainier and more contrasty. All the VNF films can be pushed a stop with hardly any noticeable change in image quality, and two stops with accompanying deterioration in granularity, color shifts and contrast buildup.

I'll repeat advice given earlier: Do tests with these films before shooting a project. Take the tests through the full print cycle to release print material as you think the film will be distributed. In other words, if you are contemplating making an internegative from which positive prints are to be made, have the lab do such a test.

The major change in filmmaking for 16mm independents and workers of all kinds is the introduction of new negative camera films and intermediate and release print materials from Kodak and other manufacturers such as Fuji and Agfa-Gevaert. I say again that I am giving practically all of my attention to Kodak materials because they really dominate the motion picture market. I suggest that filmmakers conduct their own tests to see for themselves the quality of competing materials from other manufacturers. Keep in mind that using one brand for camera stock and another for print stock can also be used as a creative control to change the look of the film.

Eastman color negative II film 7247 (100 tungsten without filtration, 64 outdoors with an 85) and Eastman color high speed negative film 7293 (250 E.I., and 160) have changed the way many filmmakers work. In particular, when 7247 was introduced it began a trend away from ECO reversal to negative film. The film is about as sharp and fine grained as ECO, but with four times the speed, and with better exposure latitude. The only thing against using it is that it takes very careful negative cutting techniques to avoid marring the emulsion. Scratches and dirt look like white blotches on positive prints. Although the theatrical film industry has always cut negative, the task is more demanding for 16mm, since the frame is about a quarter the size of 35mm. Therefore, I cannot recommend that most filmmakers actually cut the negative. Rather, I suggest you turn the task over to a lab or a specialist negative cutter.

Color negative film can make beautiful prints that sometimes have a more open and somehow transparent look than prints made from reversal. In most ways I think I prefer it, but the choice ought to depend upon your project and your way of working. I have seen 7247 and 7293, or rather the result of tests shot with their 35mm counterparts, and it was difficult for me to tell the two apart.

The addition of color negative to the range of 16mm materials is a positive step, but the addition of negative materials to super 8 would surely be a negative step, since scratches and other marks would almost certainly produce lousy-looking prints.

Other Color Films

There are other color films on the market you may like to try. Both Superior Bulk Film Co. and Eso-S distribute color film that may be of strange vintage. You can run any double 8mm film through your 16mm camera. The only problem here is making sure the lab doesn't slit the film. Put a note to that effect in with the film and hope for the best.

One of the most fruitful sources, if you're looking for new and different colors, and inexpensive stock to boot, is to use print or duplicating stock. Good films to try are Eastman 7387 and 7389.

These duplicating stocks were designed for the laboratory to be used to make prints from your camera film. They are balanced for tungsten illumination of about 2900° K. Actually the film's color balance may vary from emulsion number to emulsion number. Manufacturers make films in big batches and assign code numbers to each batch which has its own color balance. When preparing color film for camera use, the manufacturer must *zero-in* the film to very close tolerances for speed and color balance, but this isn't done to the same degree for print stock. Instead, individual labs must determine the proper exposure and color balance, through trial and error, by using different printing lights and filtering in their printing machines. Labs buy the film in great quantities and calibrate their equipment by using a sample of the emulsion number. Because duplication film, or print stock, was meant to be zeroed-in by the user, the price of print stock is much less than the price of camera film.

What this means is that you ought to try any print stock before you shoot a batch of it in your camera. Actually, if you aren't interested in results that are right on the nose, you don't have to go through the whole rigamarole every time you use some of this film. I've found that print stock can yield very good results with relatively simple filtration.

Black and White

When the first edition of this book appeared in 1972 there was considerable interest in black and white cinematography. This is no longer the case. Black and white filmmaking is a dying art, not only for the filmmaker, but for the lab as well. However, manufacturers like Kodak continue to supply very good black and white reversal and negative materials, as listed in the table of Kodak motion picture films.

Generally speaking, as film speed increases so does granularity and contrast, while sharpness decreases. As a general pattern, however, for Eastman black and white materials, subjective sharpness suffers very little with increased speed.

You can get good results whether you use reversal or negative material. Probably the best reason for using reversal is that it's easier to conform camera original to workprint. Easier for eye matching, and in the sense that dust and scratches take less of a toll on the final print, since reversal damage appears as black marks which are hard to notice, compared to negative damage which appears as very noticeable white marks.

I'm not quite certain of this, but it's my feeling that the Eastman black and white camera films are the only ones easily obtainable in the marketplace. Plus-X reversal film is probably the finest grained, sharpest camera film available for either color or black and white. While some sacrifice in pictorial quality has been made for the faster Tri-X and 4-X, these are beautiful films and deserve your consideration.

I've also had occasion to shoot negative material in 1965 for my film *We Shall March Again*. If you're careful, the negative-positive black and white system can look beautiful.

My impression is that most of the lab's work these days vis-à-vis black and white is for prints made from masters of films shot some time in the past. And my impression of filmmakers' use of black and white is that it is almost entirely confined to special sequences within color productions.

I shouldn't forget surveillance applications. Lots of black and white is shot in banks, of holdups.

Professional Motion Picture Films Available from Kodak. The chart omits Kodachrome (listed as an amateur film), and the newer fast VNF 7251 and Eastman color 7293 mentioned in the text. (Eastman Kodak)

Motion Picture Camera Films

Film Name	Film Code No.			Type	Exposure Index	
	35 mm	16 mm	super 8		Daylight	Tungsten (3200 K)
EASTMAN DOUBLE-X Negative Film	5222	7222	—	Black-and-White Negative	250	200
EASTMAN 4-X Negative Film	5224	7224	—	Black-and-White Negative	500	400
EASTMAN PLUS-X Negative Film	5231	7231	—	Black-and-White Negative	80	64
KODAK EKTACHROME Video News Film (Daylight)	5239	7239	—	Color Reversal	160	40 (With KODAK WRATTEN Gelatin Filter No. 80A)
EASTMAN EKTACHROME Video News Film (Tungsten)	5240	7240	—	Color Reversal	80 (With KODAK WRATTEN Gelatin Filter No. 85B)	125
KODAK EKTACHROME EF Film (Daylight)	5241	7241	—	Color Reversal	160	40 (With KODAK WRATTEN Gelatin Filter No. 80A)
KODAK EKTACHROME EF Film (Tungsten)	5242	7242	7242*	Color Reversal	80 (With KODAK WRATTEN Gelatin Filter No. 85B)	125
KODAK EKTACHROME SM Film (Type A)	—	—	7244*	Color Reversal	100 (With KODAK WRATTEN Gelatin Filter No. 85)	125‡ (With KODAK WRATTEN Gelatin Filter No. 82A)
EASTMAN Color Negative II Film	5247	7247	—	Color Negative	64 (With KODAK WRATTEN Gelatin Filter No. 85)	100
EASTMAN EKTACHROME Video News Film High Speed (Tungsten)	5250†	7250	—	Color Reversal	250 (With KODAK WRATTEN Gelatin Filter No. 85B)	400
EASTMAN EKTACHROME Commercial Film	7252	7252	—	Color Reversal	16 (With KODAK WRATTEN Gelatin Filter No. 85)	25
KODAK EKTACHROME MS Film	5256	7256	—	Color Reversal	64	16 (With KODAK WRATTEN Gelatin Filter No. 80A)
KODAK PLUS-X Reversal Film	—	7276	7276	Black-and-White Reversal	50	40
KODAK 4-X Reversal Film	—	7277	7277	Black-and-White Reversal	400	320
KODAK TRI-X Reversal Film	—	7278	7278	Black-and-White Reversal	200	160

*Super 8 200 ft (61 m) cartridge also available
†5250 (35 mm) available on special order in minimum order quantities
‡Exposure index is 160 with photoflood (3400 K) lamps, no filter required

This topic falls neatly into three areas. Storing film before and after exposure, and after processing.

Before Exposure

Film will change its properties with age. It can lose speed and contrast, pick up a higher background fog level; color film, in addition, can show shifts in overall color balance. The rate at which such deterioration takes place is related to the temperature at which it is stored, and to some extent, the relative humidity. If possible store your film in a refrigerator. Leave the film in its original tape-sealed cans or foil packages which provide good protection. Condensation of moisture can form on film placed in a refrigerator if the film is unprotected in this way.

According to Eastman, if their products are stored from 50° to 65°F, they'll be good for up to six months. A refrigerator usually operates at around 50°F or so, so there's no problem achieving the desired temperature. I've found that film stored this way will show no deterioration when used after two or even three years. Film stored in a freezer will probably remain in good shape for many years, or perhaps even decades.

Before using the film it must be allowed to warm up or moisture will condense on it and cause spotting or mottling. Eastman recommends, for a single 16mm roll, half an hour warm-up time if the difference in temperature between the refrigerator and the room is 25°F with a 70 percent relative humidity, and an hour at 90 percent. For a 100°F difference with 70 percent humidity, warming should take an hour, and at 90 percent an hour and a half. You can see that an additional 75°F of difference accounts for an increased warm-up time of only half an hour, so it's possible to safely estimate other inbetween times. The 8mm, super 8 and single 8 films will certainly warm up in the times given for 16mm. Do not remove the vapor seal tape, or take the film out of its foil package until after the warm-up time.

Filmmakers planning travel to Arctic or tropical regions should obtain all the needed information and advice of other experienced filmmakers. Cameras should be 'climatized' by the manufacturer or his representative. A good starting point to find out some of what you need to know would be the *American Cinematographer Manual*. Most of us won't come up against climates so cold that film will become brittle and snap, or so humid that mold will grow, but we do encounter automobile interiors that can reach 140°F, and cause as much deterioration of film in hours as years of storage at room temperature.

Exposed Film

Film should be processed as soon as possible after exposure. If this is not possible, store the exposed film like unexposed raw stock. Humid climates seem to present a great problem. If film is returned to its can and taped, you'll be sealing in the ambient air moisture which could possibly aid the growth of fungus or mold. I've read that you should and should not retape film cans under such conditions. A good solution might be to use a desiccant, like silica gel, with the film in a closed box, to dry it out. Then the film could be stored in a taped can, within the box containing silica gel.

After Processing

Black and white film properly fixed and washed, when stored at 40 to 50 percent relative humidity at 70° F — providing there are no harmful chemicals in the atmosphere — ought to last at least a century. If there are residual traces of hypo in the emulsion of processed film, it will deteriorate. There are established standards for the amount of permissible hypo or fixer for archival permanence. There are hypo-eliminating chemicals available, but as good a procedure would be a prolonged wash time in the lab.

Color emulsions are particularly susceptible to chemical deterioration. For this reason Eastman suggests storage of color master material at 0° F. Low temperatures slow down chemical reactions. However, at the present state of the art, nobody will guarantee that color film dyes will not deteriorate in time, no matter how well the film is stored. Accordingly, the usual procedure for very long term storage of color master material is to print separation negatives from the master, and store these. The color information in an intergral tripack film, like Ektachrome, can be stored in the form of three black and white separation negatives by printing on special panchromatic separation print stock through three successive color separation filters. Thus one roll of triple layered color film can be converted to a permanent record of three black and white rolls. These three rolls can be used to produce color prints or a new color master when required. Such a procedure, because of the costs involved, is certainly out of the question for most of us, but at least you now know such techniques are available.

For more information about film storage, consult Eastman Kodak's booklet, *Storage and Preservation of Motion Picture Film.*

Restoration of Damaged Film

Rejuvenation

If a film becomes damaged — its sprockets torn, emulsion scraped off, base scratched — sometimes it is possible to have the film *restored* or *rejuvenated.* Rejuvenation techniques may be applied to any film, in any format: to camera film, intermediate printing masters, or, for that matter, prints. How effective the rejuvenation process, naturally depends upon the extent of damage to the film and restoration techniques.

A particularly troublesome problem is *cinching,* or the yanking of the head or tail of a roll of film so that adjacent layers of emulsion and base rub against each other. Cinch marks look like a row of parallel lines, appearing periodically on the film. One possible cure for cinching is a rejuvenation process, another is liquid gate printing.

Rejuvenation is accomplished in essentially two stages: first, the film is cleaned, and then it is coated with a transparent liquid containing silicones to fill in scratches and abrasions. The silicone material has to have an index of refraction approximately equal to that of the film base. If the film is very badly wounded, this type of treatment may not provide much help. Damage such as torn sprocket holes can be repaired with polyester tape.

Film may also be coated with a wax or lacquer-type material used to shield the emulsion. Color film is often returned after automatic processing with such a protective coating. Three organizations that specialize in film restoration are Rapid Film Technique, Inc., 37-02 27th Street, Long Island City, N.Y. 11101, Comprehensive Filmtreat, 829 North Highland Avenue, Hollywood, Calif. 90038, and Filmlife, Inc., 141 Moonachie Rd., Moonachie, N.J. 07074.

Wet Printing

A technique that accomplishes much the same kind of restoration can be performed during printing, usually optical printing, which is used for making high quality printing masters; also, it is the only way that reduction or enlargement prints can be made from one format to another. The rejuvenation process is called *wet printing* or, sometimes, *liquid-gate printing* because the film, as it passes through the glass-enclosed printer gate, is immersed in a liquid bath. The liquid fills in the abrasions, and to some extent suppresses the grain pattern of the film. There is some controversy about the effectiveness of this procedure to suppress grain. It seems reasonable, though, to expect that the surface grain at least will be diminished.

Liquid-gate printing is useful not only for the restoration of damaged film, but also for maintaining the highest possible quality in undamaged film, especially in the preparation of printing masters and enlargements from the 8mm formats to 16mm or 16mm to 35mm.

The Camera

There is no ultimate, perfect camera. No one camera can do everything, even if a few designs try. A camera is something you, the filmmaker, have to like, have to feel comfortable with.

The choice of a camera is crucial because of the constraints each camera places on what you are able to film. But the filmmaker is far more important than the machine: many beautiful films have been shot with used, almost obsolete cameras. This chapter will try to present what you need to know about what happens inside the camera, and what can be done with the controls on the camera body; this will give you a more concrete idea about the camera you would like to use.

While it isn't precisely true that if you've worked one camera, you can work them all — for there are striking individual differences — it is true that they all operate through the same principles. This chapter is organized to serve as a general guide to camera operation, not as a particular manufacturer's instruction book.

How It Works, A Basic Rundown

A motion picture camera is a device for exposing, in sequence, a series of still photographs. Raw stock, or unexposed film, is stored in a light-tight chamber. In some cases it is wound on a daylight loading roll; in others, on a plastic core which can be loaded into a special magazine only in total darkness. If the film is stored in a super 8 or single 8 cartridge, then the cartridge itself protects the film from light. The portion of the cartridge, or magazine, or camera body in which the raw stock is stored is called the *feed chamber*.

From the feed chamber the film is brought to the camera's image-forming or optical system. Nearly all cameras — super 8 and single 8 machines and the vast majority of 8mm cameras — use a *shuttle*, or *claw*, to advance the film. The shuttle is shaped like a hooked finger. It engages the film, depending upon format standards and design peculiarities, a few frames above or below the frame to be exposed. The shuttle enters the perforation and moves downward, so that the film will be moved down the height of one frame — the distance between perforations for the formats discussed in this book. Then the shuttle helps hold the film at rest while it is being exposed.

In addition to the shuttles which are employed in nearly all cameras, 16mm cameras, and a few double 8 or double super 8 cameras, have *sprocket wheels*. Sprocket wheels have teeth which engage the film's perforations to advance the film. The area where the film is exposed is called the *gate*. The term 'gate' refers to the *pressure plate* as well as associated contraptions that hold the film firmly against the *aperture plate*. The aperture plate and spring-loaded pressure plate are usually of well machined metal, at least in the better cameras, although plastic has been used in some good designs. The super 8 cartridge and some 16mm magazines include the pressure plate in their design, and not in the camera. The hole in the aperture plate, corresponding to the dimensions of the frame, allows light from the lens to pass through, exposing

88 the film. In addition to the pressure plate, which holds the film flat against the aperture plate, the film is also secured with spring-loaded *side guides* to prevent the film from side wobbling, or weaving. They are located above and below the aperture and hug the sides of the film. The pressure plate, usually running the length of several frames, pushes against the film. Provision is made for the complete removal, or swinging away, of the pressure plate, so that it and the aperture region—in other words, the gate—may be cleaned. After a few hundred feet of film, fragments of the film, base or emulsion dust build up and are even caught in the aperture opening where they may appear on the exposed and processed film as 'nasty' shadows.

Most cameras employ the shuttle both to transport the film and to hold it at rest at the moment of exposure. Several of the more expensive 16mm cameras use a *registration pin* to hold the film while it is being exposed. The pin usually enters a perforation just before the moment of exposure, holds the frame steady and leaves the perforation immediately after the exposure.

Although cameras with registration pins invariably expose steady images, it is not true that machines lacking this refinement cannot. Similarly, you might suspect that 8mm, super 8 and single 8 cameras without even sprocket wheels would have indifferent steadiness. In well designed cameras, a shuttle can transport the film and does a good job of registering the film as well. Perhaps the smaller mass of film to be advanced and the lower linear rate of advance account for the ease of good registration of some 8mm machines. This discussion of the innards of the camera has omitted any mention of the camera shutter, and how it works, because this will be covered in detail.

When the film leaves the gate after it has been exposed, it is driven by another sprocket wheel to the take-up chamber. (Most 8mm machines do not have this take-up sprocket wheel.) From here the film goes to a take-up spool, or in the case of a magazine or cartridge, to a plastic core.

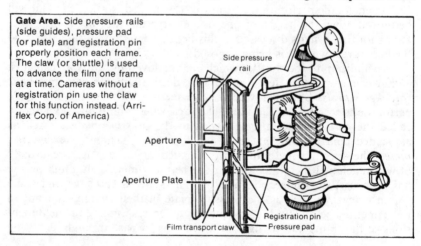

Gate Area. Side pressure rails (side guides), pressure pad (or plate) and registration pin properly position each frame. The claw (or shuttle) is used to advance the film one frame at a time. Cameras without a registration pin use the claw for this function instead. (Arriflex Corp. of America)

Side pressure rail

Aperture

Aperture Plate

Film transport claw

Registration pin

Pressure pad

Independent Filmmaking

A spool has side walls which prevent the film from being light-struck; the walls also allow for loading in subdued light. Cameras which accept a spool have a take-up spindle that fits through a hole in the spool. In the super 8 and single 8 cartridges, a similar device, a *dog,* drives the take-up chamber. The rate at which the take-up roll rotates must vary because as the film is taken up, the larger its diameter the greater the yank on the film. The take-up spindle, or dog, has a slipping clutch device to compensate for the increasing radius of the roll.

The Shutter

Reviewing how each frame is exposed reinforces the concept that in effect a movie camera is a still camera making a series of exposures in rapid succession. A hook-shaped shuttle engages the film's perforations to bring one unexposed frame into position behind the aperture. The film is held against the aperture plate during the exposure by a spring-loaded pressure plate so that the film will be at the theoretical distance (the film plane) for which the lens is adjusted. (See chapter 4, under Back Focus.) At the same time, the pressure plate must be sufficiently flexibly sprung not to impede with the film's motion as successive frames are being brought into position.

Once the film is held perfectly stationary, the exposure is made. While the frame to be exposed has been moving into position, the *shutter,* a rotating metal disk, placed between the lens and the aperture, has been preventing light from making an exposure. An exposure can be made only when the shutter admits light. The opening is a segment on the order of 180 degrees, actually just half of a disk, whirling in synchronization with the shuttle or the film's motion.

The film's exposure is determined by two things: the amount of light passing through the lens, or the f stop, and the amount of light passing through the shutter. Since it takes a finite amount of time for each frame to be brought into exposure position, the exposure can never be as long as 1/24 second at sound running speed, for example. The shutter's being half a disk indicates that the film spends about equal time in transport and exposure. This is verified by the fact that exposures at this speed are about 1/50 second. As a rule of thumb, the exposure, given as a fraction of a second, is roughly equal to one half the reciprocal of fps rate. (At 24 fps, $1/24 \times 1/2 = 1/48$ second, and so on.)

In some cameras there is a variable shutter which can be controlled, making it possible to reduce the opening of the shutter and even, on many such cameras, to close the shutter completely. In the case of a shutter with a 180 degree opening, for example, if we reduce the opening by half its maximum to 90 degrees, the exposure is now one stop less, or one half what it was. If the film in the camera is fast, and the lens has been closed down to its minimum aperture, the exposure can be further reduced with the variable shutter.

By controlling the exposure, the variable shutter can, in effect, control depth of field (see chapter 4, under Depth of Field). If you wish to decrease

The Camera

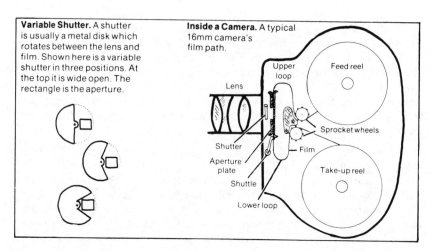

Variable Shutter. A shutter is usually a metal disk which rotates between the lens and film. Shown here is a variable shutter in three positions. At the top it is wide open. The rectangle is the aperture.

Inside a Camera. A typical 16mm camera's film path.

the depth of field of a shot, close down the variable shutter. In order to maintain the same exposure, the diaphragm must be opened, reducing depth of field. This, for example, helps to isolate foreground subjects from the background.

Sharpness

If you have any experience with still photography, you know that a shutter speed of 1/50 second won't arrest, or freeze, action. Movie images, on the other hand, tend to look smooth because the brain fuses all the blurry individual frames together into a smooth appearing whole. In fact, when individual frames are too sharp, there is the danger that the motion will appear jittery. That's why puppet models, like those used in *King Kong*, appear to have muscular or neurological disorders. The puppets aren't moving; only their position is changed for each exposure. Since the puppet is actually perfectly still for each frame's exposure, each frame is so very sharp that we get the jittery effect. This effect can be duplicated by freezing the action in every frame by closing the variable shutter so exposures of 1/250 or 1/500 second are made.

Fades and Dissolves

If during a shot the variable shutter is gradually and completely closed, the shot will fade out, or go to black. If at the start of a shot the closed shutter is gradually opened, the result is a fade-in. Perfectly combining a fade-out over a fade-in creates what is called a *dissolve*. This is a descriptive name for an effect in which one shot seems to blend (or dissolve) into another. At one time it was customary to call this effect by its full-blown name, lap-dissolve.

In order to achieve reasonably good in-the-camera dissolves, the camera should be equipped with more than a variable shutter: it needs a frame counter and provision for backwinding the film. You must know which frame began the dissolve, so that you can tell how much film to rewind on the feed reel. The fade-out is made, noting the frame counter

Independent Filmmaking

position. Next, by leaving the variable shutter closed, or capping the lens, the film is wound back to the start of the dissolve. As the shot begins, the shutter is opened for the fade-in part of the dissolve.

Fades and dissolves are typically twelve to ninety frames in length. Since it is usually difficult to make a smooth dissolve in the camera, the technique requires practice. Paillard offers the Rexofader, which automatically operates the variable shutter of their 16mm Bolex cameras, and some super 8 cameras can make dissolves automatically.

If possible, it's usually best to avoid in-the-camera dissolves. Even if the shot going into the dissolve may be perfect, you have no guarantee that the shot coming out of the dissolve, the fade-in, will be what you want. If the second shot isn't quite right, both shots now welded together by the dissolve, can be ruined. Filmmakers working in 8mm or single 8, or double super 8, may have no choice but to try in-the-camera dissolves, although labs are now offering this service for super 8. Filmmakers working in 16mm can combine any two shots with a dissolve after shooting, with the appropriate laboratory printing procedure.

Viewing and Focusing Systems

In the past not enough attention was paid to the motion picture camera's viewing and focusing systems. As nearly as possible, these show the filmmaker what the shot or scene will look like. Cameras were designed with superb mechanisms and totally inadequate viewing systems. And yet what can be more important than a good viewfinder?

Direct Optical Finder

The simplest kind of finder in use is the optical finder. The filmmaker sights his subject through an eyepiece, a device resembling a telescope. Hopefully, the field of view covered by the finder coincides with the lens.

There are two kinds of optical finders in use to accommodate lenses of different focal lengths. One uses interchangeable objectives (a fancy word for lens), corresponding to specific focal lengths of taking lenses. The Kodak K-100 mounts its finder lenses on the same turret as the taking lenses. They move into place as the lens is positioned. The Bell & Howell 70-DR has a similar arrangement (discussed later this chapter).

The second type of optical finder is an all-in-one arrangement, to cover a wide variety of focal lengths by 'tuning-in' with a twist of a knob. The finder either restricts, or masks, the field of view or optically changes the magnification of the image, in other words, by zooming.

The Bolex Octameter, one of these kinds of devices, uses both masks and variable magnification to achieve a range of sixteen to one hundred and fifty millimeter coverage in the 16mm model. An attached supplementary lens can slide over the front of the device to increase the field of view of the sixteen millimeter focal length to that of a ten millimeter focal length lens. The finder clips to the side of a Bolex body but may be used independently as a *director's finder*.

The Camera

Vision through an optical finder should be crisp, contrasty and bright. In addition the finder ought to have provision for what is known as *parallax compensation.*

Parallax Compensation

Since the finder objective and the taking objective must be an inch or two apart, their field of view coincides for subjects only at relatively great distances from the camera. If the filmmaker unquestioningly relied on such a finder for shooting close subjects, say under eight or ten feet, he would cut off parts of the subject. For this reason, optical finders often incorporate some kind of device for correcting this discrepancy between the views of the taking lens and finder, called *parallax compensation.* From the dictionary: Parallax is 'the apparent change in the position of an object resulting from the change in the direction or position from which it is viewed.'

When working at close distances, one solution to the problem is to place lines within the finder corresponding to the field. The other solution is more accurate but can consume valuable seconds before shooting can begin. By changing the angle of the finder, it is possible to get it to cover more or less the same field as the taking lens. A manually operated control, set to correspond to the taking lens' focusing distance, is used.

No matter how well constructed to compensate for parallax error, an optical finder cannot display the exact image the film is receiving, that is, the image that eventually will be projected on the screen. Despite the fact that the finder and taking lens may be covering the same outline of a scene, the juxtaposition of foreground and background subject will vary because of the different position of each optical system. Moreover, the angle of view of a lens actually changes as it is focused, and no optical finder for a movie camera has been made to compensate for this effect.

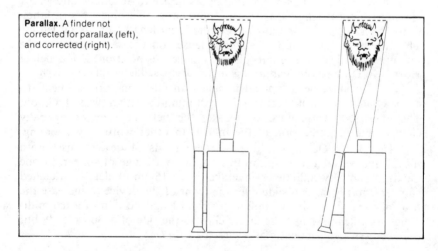

Parallax. A finder not corrected for parallax (left), and corrected (right).

Independent Filmmaking

The kind of composition that works in film would often be considered noncomposition in still photography terms. It is dynamic composition, and following the flow of action is as important as perceiving the relationships of the elements of the picture.

Therefore, you must have a feeling that what you are seeing through the viewfinder will closely resemble what is finally projected on the screen. Also, a viewfinder should be fun to use, not torture. Optical viewfinders, no matter how good they may be, simply cannot achieve the proper psychological conditions. There is always some doubt about the 'authenticity' of the image viewed. For this reason, reflex finders are now widely used. The image is obtained through the actual taking lens, but it is a projected image, similar to the one on the theater screen, and, in fact, the image projected on the film itself.

Advantages

For one thing, the reflex systems allow for parallax-free viewing of the scene. While an optical finder must necessarily be a certain distance from the taking lens, a reflex system uses the light gathered by the taking lens for forming the viewfinder's image. No parallax correction is necessary with the reflex finder. This is the reflex finder's chief advantage, especially for close working distances. For subjects near the lens, the optical type finder is useless. The reflex system will automatically display the angle of view or field of the lens being used — no matter what focal length. For this reason, reflex finders are especially useful with zoom lenses. Also, since the reflex finder sees through the taking lens, the filmmaker will be aware of colored filters in place, or other accessory devices such as an intruding lens cap.

One great advantage that the reflex system has, and many would rank it as great an advantage as any already discussed, is its focusing capability. Focusing is accomplished with a ground glass, or a similarly grained focusing screen in most 16mm models. A ground glass screen usually allows the filmmaker to gauge depth of field (discussed more fully in chapter 4, *The Lens*). Reflex viewing on a ground glass, or similarly surfaced viewing screen, allows the filmmaker to see the limits of acceptable focus of objects in the field of view.

To sum up: The reflex finder can show exactly what the film *sees*. It is particularly useful for zoom lenses, and indispensable for close-up filming. If filters and other optical accessories such as prisms, distortion mirrors and so on, are used, their effects can be seen immediately and used to better advantage.

Disadvantages

The major disadvantage of the reflex system is that it may be somewhat dimmer than the direct viewing optical system. In low level lighting situations, viewing through a reflex system, even with the lens wide open, may not allow you to see what's going on, and focusing becomes hard. There are two things the filmmaker can do: first, choose the

The Camera

shortest focal length lens possible, so that focusing becomes less critical. Short focal length lenses, or wide angle lenses, have more depth of field at a given stop for the same subject distance than longer lenses. Next, use the rubber eyecup attached to the finder eyepiece to exclude extraneous light. If you wear glasses, and it's possible to adjust the finder focus for your eye, do so to keep the eye and finder in contact and isolated from interfering light.

Although it's possible to describe reflex systems in a number of ways, I've chosen to classify them into these three categories: the moving mirror system, the beam splitter within the lens and the beam splitter or similar optical device behind the lens.

Moving Mirror Reflex Systems

The mirror is located directly behind the lens, between it and the film. When the film is exposed, the shutter opens exposing the film. At this moment, the mirror is out of the way. Once the shutter closes, and blocks the light from reaching the film, the film is advanced and the mirror moves into position.

The mirror may have, for example, a rotating motion, the system used in the Arriflex camera, or as in the case of the Beaulieu cameras, it may reciprocate. In either case, light reflected from the mirror follows a path through the viewfinder's optical system, usually consisting of lenses, prisms and a ground glass screen. The viewfinder image should appear contrasty, crisp and right way 'round—proper left to right orientation, that is. Because of the mirror's motion, the image in the finder will flicker.

Beam Splitter in the Lens

A beam splitter is a block of glass, made up of two cemented prism segments. At the surface where the segments meet, a thin metallic coating reflects part of the light to the finder system, leaving most of it to expose the film. The usual arrangement for this system is to locate the beam splitter within the elements of the lens, before the diaphragm.

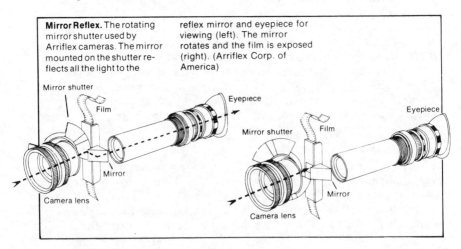

Mirror Reflex. The rotating mirror shutter used by Arriflex cameras. The mirror mounted on the shutter reflects all the light to the reflex mirror and eyepiece for viewing (left). The mirror rotates and the film is exposed (right). (Arriflex Corp. of America)

Mirror shutter

Film

Eyepiece

Mirror

Camera lens

Mirror shutter

Film

Eyepiece

Mirror

Camera lens

Independent Filmmaking

A good beam-splitter system will take only a quarter or a third of the light available for the total exposure. Inefficient designs actually rob as much as one full stop, or more. As shown, since the beam splitter is before the diaphragm, the finder will always maintain the same brightness level and not flicker.

Used in most super 8 and late model 8mm cameras offering built-in zoom lenses, such a system, because of the placement of the beam splitter, precludes lens interchangeability. The design also suggests the use of a built-in automatic diaphragm system. Because the light for the finder is taken before the lens diaphragm, depth of field may not be viewed.

Several manufacturers, such as SOM Berthiot and Angenieux, offer models of their zoom lenses with built-in beam-splitter reflex finders. These lenses are meant to be used with 16mm camera bodies lacking a reflex finder. Some have been manufactured for use with 8mm cameras.

Behind-the-Lens Beam Splitter

It is also possible to place the beam splitter behind the diaphragm, as was done, for example, in the Leicina 8mm interchangeable lens component camera. The Bolex H-8 and H-16 offer a beam splitter behind the lens, while the Pathé super 8 and 16mm models offer reflex viewing through a *pellicule* (sometimes called pellicle) placed behind the lens. A pellicule is a very thin sheet of glass, coated with a partially reflecting surface. It functions just like the beam splitter, diverting some of the light to the finder, while allowing most of it to pass through to expose the film.

Pros and Cons

Each system and its variants has its own advantages and disadvantages. In the case of cameras offering built-in zoom lenses and beam-splitter reflex systems, the plus factors are compactness and a maintained brilliance of image; such a system will also easily accommodate an automatic behind-the-lens (BTL) diaphragm system. The negative

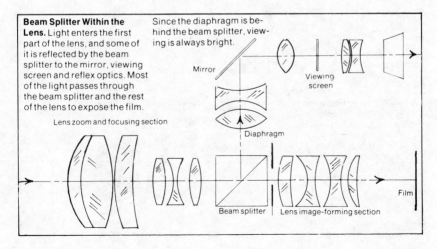

Beam Splitter Within the Lens. Light enters the first part of the lens, and some of it is reflected by the beam splitter to the mirror, viewing screen and reflex optics. Most of the light passes through the beam splitter and the rest of the lens to expose the film.

Since the diaphragm is behind the beam splitter, viewing is always bright.

Mirror

Viewing screen

Lens zoom and focusing section

Diaphragm

Beam splitter

Lens image-forming section

Film

The Camera

features start with the lack of lens interchangeability. This may or may not be of importance to the filmmaker depending upon the use to which the camera will be put. If the range and speed of the zoom lens is acceptable, then there will be no problem.

Since the light is taken before the diaphragm, it is also not possible to view depth of field in this finder. But this system assures maximum focusing accuracy since the finder system 'sees' through the lens wide open, and consequently, depth of field is at a minimum. But for this 'advantage,' the filmmaker must sacrifice the ability to observe the range of sharp focus. How an image looks out of focus can be as important as how it looks in focus.

Reflex systems whose light is taken from behind the lens diaphragm, be they moving mirror, beam splitter or pellicule, allow the filmmaker to view depth of field. Unlike the beam-splitter or pellicule systems, which have a continuous image, the viewfinder image of the

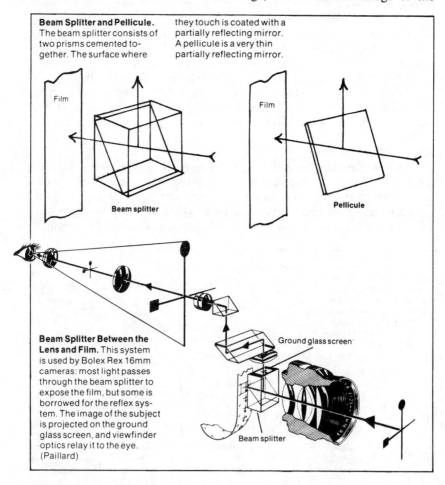

Beam Splitter and Pellicule. The beam splitter consists of two prisms cemented together. The surface where they touch is coated with a partially reflecting mirror. A pellicule is a very thin partially reflecting mirror.

Film

Film

Beam splitter

Pellicule

Beam Splitter Between the Lens and Film. This system is used by Bolex Rex 16mm cameras: most light passes through the beam splitter to expose the film, but some is borrowed for the reflex system. The image of the subject is projected on the ground glass screen, and viewfinder optics relay it to the eye. (Paillard)

Ground glass screen

Beam splitter

mirror system flickers. Although some filmmakers may find this flickering annoying, most have no trouble working with such a finder. This system does have the distinct advantage of allowing all of the light passing through the lens to expose the film.

The beam-splitter camera takes part of the light for the finder, reducing the effective exposure. This factor must be accounted for in computing exposure for such cameras and can be if an automatic light meter is part of the system.

It has been claimed that finder systems incorporating the moving mirror are brighter than other behind-the-lens systems, beam splitter or pellicule. Just as the mirror allows all of the light passing through the lens to expose the film, it also uses all the light for the finder. The behind-the-lens beam-splitter system taking only part of the light for the finder, it is argued, must be dimmer.

When the intermittent nature of the light coming through the finder of the moving mirror system cameras is considered, its intensity should prove to be on the order of the light viewed through the beam-splitter finder. However, before shooting, with the mirror in place, the image is decidedly brighter. And cameras using the moving mirror system do seem to have brighter finders.

One other factor that influences the apparent brightness of the finder image is the kind of *viewing screen* incorporated in the finder.

Viewfinder Screens

There are, in general, two kinds of viewfinder screens: ground glass, or grained, and brilliant. Ground glass screens are most frequently featured as part of the finder system in cameras which take their light from behind the lens. The advantage of such a finder screen is that focus can be viewed over its entire surface, and depth of field observed. The ground glass finder, or etched finder, or one of the new extremely bright *divided grain* finder screens, as found in the Beaulieu cameras, has great psychological advantages for the filmmaker. Better than any other finder screen, it simulates the quality of the image as it will be when projected.

The other kind of finder screen, the brilliant screen, is usually a part of a system deriving its light from in front of the diaphragm. The important advantage of the ground glass finder, viewing depth of field, is absent in this scheme. Therefore designers are free to choose a clear nonfocusing, or brilliant finder screen. Often such a screen will contain a focusing device — usually the ground glass circle or a split image range finder — incorporated within a circle in the center of the screen. The use of the ground glass focusing circle is self-evident; the split image device calls for the alignment of broken halves of vertical or sharp-edged elements in the subject.

Viewfinder Eyepiece Adjustment

In order to focus as accurately as possible, the viewfinder eyepiece must be focus corrected for the filmmaker's eye. Some eyepieces adjust from plus or minus two to three diopters, which should cover most vision from farsighted, through normal, to nearsighted. Diopters are a measure of lens *power* used by opticians. A nearsighted person will have a prescription with a negative diopter sign (like -3.00 diopters), a farsighted person, positive. It is also possible to have a correction lens mounted, or dropped in place, before the rear element of the finder system. Such lenses can be supplied by the camera manufacturer or by an optician, but they can also be cut out of an old pair of spectacles.

If you want to wear glasses when using the finder, leave them on when adjusting the finder. In most cases, then, it is not possible to see the entire field at one glance. This makes it necessary for many filmmakers, like myself, who are rather nearsighted, to keep popping their glasses on and off, when they want to see the world with or without the camera. If you ever lose your glasses, you could walk around with your camera to try to find them. Contact lenses may turn out to be the best solution for the nearsighted filmmaker.

How does one properly adjust the finder eyepiece? If your camera has a ground glass or a similar focusing screen, and interchangeable lenses, remove the lens and point the camera at a bright light source— the sky or an electric light at least several feet away. Turn the finder adjustment until the grains or texture of the finder are as sharp as they can be. The finder is now focused for your eye.

If the camera does not have interchangeable lenses, or a ground glass screen, in which case it invariably will be fitted with a zoom lens, turn to maximum focal length, adjust to the maximum lens opening, and focus the lens at infinity. Now sight a distant object that's easy to focus on, like a tree, and focus the finder eyepiece until the image is as sharp as possible. This procedure can work with either type of finder screen— brilliant or grained.

The instruction book that comes with the camera should be able to explain about focusing the finder. If the finder is not properly focused,

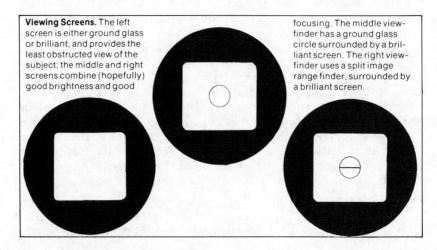

Viewing Screens. The left screen is either ground glass or brilliant, and provides the least obstructed view of the subject; the middle and right screens combine (hopefully) good brightness and good focusing. The middle viewfinder has a ground glass circle surrounded by a brilliant screen. The right viewfinder uses a split image range finder, surrounded by a brilliant screen.

Independent Filmmaking

it is impossible or, at the very least, very difficult to focus the lens
accurately. Once the finder has been individually adjusted, some cameras offer a locking device; others, unfortunately, do not.

Drive Mechanisms

Three kinds of 'motive' power are used to drive movie cameras: human,
spring and electric.

Human Power

Most of us know that the first motion picture cameras were driven by
the cameraman who actually turned a crank or lever. Today many
cameras may still be powered by hand, even though the manufacturer's
instructions may specifically advise against it. The Bolex H camera
models have such a cautionary note, for example, but the Bell & Howell
DR-70 offers a large cranking lever, presumably because its mechanism
is suitable for hand-cranking. Since many cameras are not specifically
designed for hand-cranking, uneven cranking would cause variation in
the rate of film speed through the camera which would produce variations in exposure. Any spring-powered camera which accepts an electric
motor as an accessory may be hand-cranked with an appropriate cranking key. But let me point out that there may be instances in which an
uneven rate of frames per second exposed is just what the filmmaker
wants.

Spring Drive

The recent trend in design of super 8 equipment has been away from
spring-powered drive. In fact, I know of only one new spring-powered
super 8 camera, and it was offered in Europe by Bell & Howell. Even
when 8mm cameras were still being manufactured, there was a gradual
change from spring power to electric drive. There are still many spring-
driven 16mm cameras, virtually all of which offer an electric motor as an
accessory drive.

Obviously the main disadvantage of spring drive is that when the
camera mechanism runs down the spring needs to be rewound, or re-
tensioned. The spring mechanism, much like a clockwork mechanism, is
found in 16mm cameras like the Bolex with a sixteen-foot run, or 27 seconds at 24 fps; the Bell & Howell DR-70, twenty-two feet, or 37 seconds,
and the Kodak K-100, with an impressive forty-foot run, or one minute
and 7 seconds. Kodak achieves this lengthy run with what it calls a 'prestressed spring drive.'

Standard 8mm cameras had spring motors which ran from seven to
fifteen feet, or 23 to 50 seconds at 24 fps. The same running length
naturally gave more time to the silent speeds of 16 or 18 fps. Agfa offered
an astounding double 8mm camera which when fully wound could run
through the entire twenty-five-foot length of standard 8mm film.

Electric Motors

Professional 35mm cameras progressed directly from hand-cranked

The Camera

models to machines powered by electric motors. For many years, however, amateur cameras were powered with spring-driven mechanisms, and only in their last years of production were there electric-powered 8mm cameras. Many 16mm models were, and still are, spring-powered, even though the trend is toward electric drive. Many of the better electric-drive cameras offer rechargeable cells (usually nickel cadmium [nicad] cells). And it is even possible to replace disposable cells, used in the less expensive 8mm or super 8 cameras, with rechargeable cells.

It is generally true that electric-drive 8mm and super 8 cameras have a smaller choice of running speeds than spring-driven cameras. Many super 8 cameras with electric drive have settings for only 18 fps and a slow motion speed, usually from 24 to 36 fps. Many offer only one running speed, nominally 18 fps. A great many spring-driven standard 8 cameras have speed ranges that are fairly broad, from 8 to 32 fps for example, in the case of the Carena and Camex.

The Beaulieu 4008 ZM super 8 camera has a wide range of continuously variable speeds from 2 to 70 fps with its electric motor and solid state controlled circuitry. Electric- and spring-driven 16mm cameras generally have an acceptable range of speeds.

Clearly, the introduction of compact electric motors, solid state circuitry for controlling and varying the motor's rate and compact, long lasting rechargeable power supplies have made the spring motor all but obsolete.

Having said that, I ought to say that many good spring-driven 8mm cameras are available, and many 16mm cameras such as the Bolex, Pathé and Bell & Howell DR-70 will probably be manufactured for years to come and deserve the filmmaker's consideration.

Varying Film Speeds

Fast and Slow Motion

The standard running speeds for silent and sound films are, respectively, 18 and 24 frames per second. The assumption is that both camera and projector run at the same speed. If, however, the camera is *undercranked,* so that less than the standard numbers of frames per second are exposed, the projected motion will appear to be very rapid, or accelerated. The term comes from the days when hand cranking cameramen reduced the rate of rotation of the crank to achieve comedy effects or, sometimes, when running out of film at the end of a day of shooting.

Then we have *overcranking,* or slow motion filming, in which more than the standard number of frames per second is exposed. For example, if the intention is to show a film at 24 fps, and we shoot at 48 fps, it will take twice as long for the filmed action to transpire on the screen as it did during filming.

At one end of the spectrum of filming speeds, is time-lapse photography, in which exposures are not measured in frames per second, but rather, frames per minute, hours or even days. This effect is familiarily used to show the unfolding or blooming of a flower or the transition from dawn to dusk in only a few minutes. An auxiliary timing device, called an *intervalometer* is often used in this connection. The Nizo S80 and S56 super 8 cameras have built-in intervalometers.

For intervals of seconds, transistorized circuitry can be used, but for intervals of several minutes or hours, an electric motor can be employed. In either case, the intervalometer usually produces a current which actuates a solenoid which in turn depresses the single frame control of the camera. If the camera has a *remote control* device, the connection from the intervalometer may be made directly to this input. Electronic flash can be used in conjunction with time-lapse work. Some cameras have a connection for triggering electronic flash, and others can be so modified. It is also possible to construct a relatively inexpensive intervalometer. However, the zealous filmmaker can take the place of this device by timing intervals with a watch or by *feel*, and making the exposures himself, using a cable release for the tripod-mounted camera.

There are ways of achieving marked undercranked effects without going to the trouble of either using an intervalometer or becoming a human intervalometer. Many subjects just aren't that demanding. For example, swirling cloud effects can be achieved with filming rates of only one half to one quarter normal fps, say 12 to 8 fps. The Beaulieu super 8 and 16mm electric-drive cameras operate at a frame rate as low as 2 fps.

Moderate undercranking can be used to give impetus to a fight or a chase sequence, and more drastic undercranking, say 12 fps, gives decidedly silly effects. Undercranking below 20 fps, assuming the sound running speed, for projection, is easily detected. This figure is probably not sufficiently conservative, and usually most undercranking looks phoney.

There are cameras, usually used for scientific and engineering purposes, that take hundreds or thousands of frames per second. The top speed of most standard production cameras is generally 48 to 64 fps, although the Pathé 16mm and double super 8 cameras offer a top speed of 80 fps.

The uses of slow motion are fairly obvious. Almost any kind of action can be made to appear more fluid and graceful, while it is possible to study the motion. Slow motion is also used to make filming of models more believable. By adjusting the rate of a model car's crash, a fall from a cliff can appear less obviously faked. The Bell & Howell 70-SR filming at 128 fps is available for rental as are other high speed cameras which will film at thousands of fps.

Exposure

Changing the fps rate in the middle of a shot will alter the exposure since exposure is directly proportional to the filming speed. For example, shooting at 12 fps lets in twice as much light as filming at 24 fps, and filming at 48 fps lets in half as much light as filming at 24 fps. For this reason varying the filming speed, in addition to altering the f stop, can also be used as a form of exposure control. Undercranking is

The Camera

useful for increasing the exposure in low light levels even though the subject will appear to move more swiftly than normal; but this may not be objectionable, depending on the subject and the filmmaker's purpose.

On the other hand, if you want exposure to remain constant, the diaphragm, or variable shutter, can be moved in synchronization with the fps control. This requires unusual dexterity and if you don't have a third hand, an assistant can help work the necessary control. There are several cameras with automatic exposure control which adjust the exposure as the fps rate is changed. These allow the filmmaker to experiment with continuously varying rates of filmed action.

Getting Up to Speed

It is difficult for a camera to get up to the set speed the first few frames exposed, especially with high fps settings. If the first few frames are not up to speed, they will appear overexposed. This may be a blessing in disguise, because it allows easy finding of where shots begin and end. In addition, since frames are always needed, and consequently lost, when making a cement splice, there should be a few frames for this purpose.

Most cameras for the 8mm formats and many 16mm cameras get up to speed quickly for sound speed settings and below, probably to satisfy the demand of amateurs who hate to see a frame wasted. Even these cameras, however, have a hard time getting up to speed instantly for slow motion shooting.

Light Meter Systems

For many years light meters have been built into motion picture camera bodies. Most often, in the case of 8mm and super 8-single 8 equipment, they are coupled with the lens diaphragm for automatic exposure control. A few built-in meters arrive at the proper exposure when the filmmaker manually operates the lens diaphragm. In this case he can observe an indicator, or align a pointer usually placed in the viewfinder.

The photoelectric cell may be placed within a small optical system that limits its field of view to correspond with that of the lens. A photoelectric light meter is a device which uses a sensitive cell to measure the intensity of light. Such a cell will either generate or modulate an electric current in proportion to the intensity of the light which it 'sees.' If it is found above or below the lens it is called an *adjacent* meter. On the other hand, the light-sensitive cell may monitor light coming directly through the lens. A usual method is to take a reading of part of the light from the reflex finder for this purpose. In the case of a meter system that automatically controls the diaphragm of the lens by seeing light through it, the stimulus-response situation is directly analogous to the human eye and its iris.

Selenium, Cadmium Sulfide and Silicone Blue Cells

Selenium metal photocells were once extensively used for camera light meter systems, and some cameras were even built with selenium meters;

the light striking such a selenium cell penetrates an electric current.

A great impetus for automatic or built-in meter design has been the cadmium sulfide (CdS) cell. The greater sensitivity of cadmium sulfide cells, compared with the selenium cell, allows them to be used in a way selenium cells cannot be used, namely in behind-the-lens (BTL) systems. CdS cells have generally replaced selenium cells for built-in camera applications. Their resistance, or ability to pass an electric current, varies with the intensity of light that strikes them. The more light striking the cell, the less its resistance. Since the cell itself doesn't generate current, but rather modulates or controls current, they are often powered with small disk-shaped mercury power cells.

As of this time only Fuji single 8 cameras use silicone blue cells, but there's no doubt in my mind that new designs and advanced models will be equipped with these devices. Silicone blue cells must be used in circuitry in conjunction with field effect transistors. They offer several advantages over the popular CdS cells: under low light levels they rapidly respond to changes of light intensity. CdS cells can give inaccurate readings of low light levels after exposure to bright light. Silicone cells are not subject to this light fatigue. And lastly, the spectral response of these new cells more nearly matches the response of film. By 'seeing' more like film, silicone cells should give more accurate results.

Manual Override

Most creative filmmakers will want to override the automatic meter. Some cameras make this possible, and some have a limited provision for this. They may allow for over- or underexposures of plus or minus a stop or so. However, such limited control leaves much to be desired. Automatic diaphragm control may be fine for most situations, but the ability to set the stop manually is mandatory for the fullest creative control. A camera without automatic lens setting is more desirable than one which completely prevents the filmmaker from making decisions about exposure.

It is possible to change the f stop on many cameras by adjusting the film index setting, but this is a slipshod method. Filmmakers using most super 8 and single 8 cameras don't even have this option, since the film speed is keyed by the cartridge. Many cameras don't reveal what f stop is being used, and one must be content with warning devices in the viewfinder, like lights or flags, indicating over- or underexposure.

BTL Automatic Exposure

Behind-the-lens (BTL) automatic systems are usually found in cameras with built-in zoom lenses. Many 8mm cameras were produced with automatic BTL, and most super 8 and single 8 machines feature this system. In a typical BTL automatic exposure system, light passes through the zoom section of the lens system. Part of it is reflected by a beam splitter to the viewfinder system. The rest of the light passes on through the diaphragm blades to the prime- or image-forming section of the zoom lens. In the illustrated layout, light is reflected by a reciprocating mirror mounted on or before the shutter to the CdS photocell. Between the mirror and the photocell lies the film speed mask which sets the light level for the proper exposure. The mask has different neutral gray sections on it, corresponding to different film indexes. It is usually a piece of photographic film with sections of differing densities. There can be some variation in the system as pictured here. For example, light for the meter system could be obtained from another beam splitter placed within the viewfinder system.

As mentioned, the CdS photocell, usually powered by one or two mercury cells, varies its resistance according to the intensity of light reaching it. As the light level increases, resistance of the CdS cell drops, and the current through the photocell increases. This controls the power to operate the iris diaphragm blades which may actually be the vanes of a galvanometer, or the diaphragm may be operated by a small motor.

The electric circuit is designed to seek a specific current or light level. If the diaphragm blades close down too much, less light reaches the photocell, and since current to the diaphragm is accordingly diminished, the blades open. If they open too much, more light reaches the CdS cell, and the diaphragm closes down.

Such a system is called a *closed-loop servomechanism*. The circuit notes the difference between the light level falling on the photocell and its established standard or reference level. The entire system is regulated by the constraining film speed mask. The BTL meter seeks a certain intensity of light. If the intensity is not correct, the diaphragm blades adjust the opening. Since the diaphragm is part of the lens, the closed-loop servo BTL meter system is used almost exclusively on cameras with built-in lenses—invariably zoom lenses. Such cameras offer reflex viewing as well.

Adjacent and BTL Meters
The BTL meter has decided advantages over the adjacent type meter.

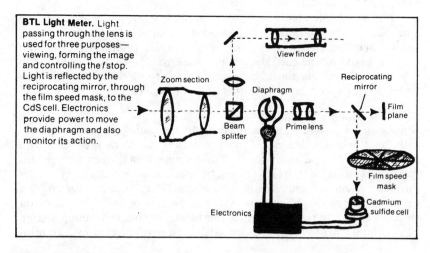

BTL Light Meter. Light passing through the lens is used for three purposes—viewing, forming the image and controlling the *f* stop. Light is reflected by the reciprocating mirror, through the film speed mask, to the CdS cell. Electronics provide power to move the diaphragm and also monitor its action.

Zoom section · Diaphragm · View finder · Reciprocating mirror · Beam splitter · Prime lens · Film plane · Film speed mask · Cadmium sulfide cell · Electronics

Independent Filmmaking

However, it should be made clear that well constructed systems of either design give effective results; it is preferable to have a first-rate adjacent type meter, than a BTL meter which falls short of the mark.

The major advantage of a well designed BTL meter is that it sees the same field of view that the lens sees, no matter what the focal length. (With a zoom lens, if it is possible to hold the setting, this kind of meter can work as an effective *spot meter*. The spot meter is discussed in chapter 5, *Shooting*.)

Just as either type of meter would change the *f* stop when panning from light to shady regions, the BTL meter will change the *f* stop when zooming from light to dark regions. A simple example: a girl standing under a tree, in the shade. We start with an overall view, a long shot if you like, of the tree, the background, mountains, hills, whatever, and then zoom in on the girl's face. The diaphragm would then automatically open up to properly expose the girl's shaded face. Such a transition must be totally unobtrusive.

The BTL meter has the additional advantage of automatically compensating for lens filters. In cameras with interchangeable lenses, like the Pathé 16, double super 8 or Beaulieu cameras, the use of extension tubes with manual BTL systems, which would normally call for some kind of calculation, becomes an automatic matter. Such cameras are ideal for many difficult exposure situations; for example, filming through a microscope.

BTL Manual Systems

In the manual BTL system, the filmmaker makes the *f* stop setting while looking through the viewfinder and observing an indicator, usually a pointer. Once the pointer is perfectly vertical, for example, the filmmaker knows that the camera 'thinks' it has the correct exposure.

Just as in the fully automatic system, this system is adjusted to seek a specific light level that depends upon settings made on the camera

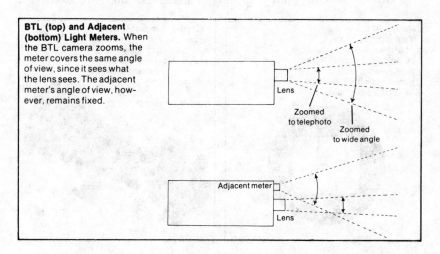

BTL (top) and Adjacent (bottom) Light Meters. When the BTL camera zooms, the meter covers the same angle of view, since it sees what the lens sees. The adjacent meter's angle of view, however, remains fixed.

Lens

Zoomed to telephoto

Zoomed to wide angle

Adjacent meter

Lens

The Camera

body for film speed and fps. But once the system is given these parameters, it lacks the means to set the stop itself. The filmmaker has to open or close the diaphragm, until the pointer tells him the proper level has been reached.

The final exposure, however, is determined by the filmmaker's experience and judgment. He may decide that the light distribution across the frame calls for no alteration of the setting obtained, or he may wish to open or close the diaphragm if the region of principal interest would, in his judgment, suffer from such an exposure.

Calibrating the Meter

Most built-in camera meters, BTL or adjacent, offer no opportunity for calibration of their meter systems. This is not serious if they offer manually set film indexes. If a reversal film of 50 E.I., for example, is found to be underexposed when the meter scale is set for 50, you can always try rating the film at some lower index, 32 or 25, or whatever works. By doing this, you are in effect calibrating your meter empirically, probably the best way to do the job. Usually a meter that is off-scale by a stop for a 50 E.I., will be off-scale by the same factor for a film of any speed. In other words, the meter could be set to 25 for the 50 E.I. and 200 for a 400 E.I.

Super 8 and single 8 machines, however, with few exceptions have their built-in meters set or keyed by the cartridge. If these cameras make no provision for calibrating the meter, and the meter is inaccurate, the camera must be returned to the factory or repair station.

Inertia and Hunting

Inertia of the system describes how rapidly the automatic meter makes a change corresponding to the light level in its field of view. If the diaphragm tends to move slowly, the system has a high inertia; quickly, a low inertia.

One of the most annoying things a meter can do, is to *over-react*

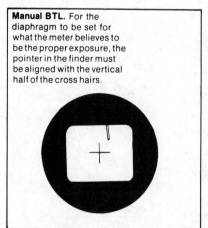

Manual BTL. For the diaphragm to be set for what the meter believes to be the proper exposure, the pointer in the finder must be aligned with the vertical half of the cross hairs.

BTL Interchangeable Lens. Angenieux zoom lenses, with automatic light meter, may be used with many 16mm cameras. The model shown here is the 12 to 120 millimeter f2.2. (Angenieux Corp. of America)

Independent Filmmaking

through an excessively low inertia. BTL meters, perhaps because they see such a restricted field of view, are often subject to this defect. An automatic meter system which is not properly damped, can oscillate until it finds the proper exposure. Such *hunting* will produce rapid fluctuations of exposure.

Some meters react to the extent that a man with a white shirt walking into the scene will cause the lens to stop down. This usually doesn't look too good on the screen. Of course, such a meter is ideal for some circumstances, such as panning from the shade to a bright sunny region. A more sluggish meter might work very well with the man and the white shirt, but it might close down too slowly when panning from shade to sun. The effect on the screen, in this case, is visible as overexposure of the sunny region until the correct exposure is belatedly reached.

Creative Camera Controls

Lenses and the Turret

Although the chapter on lenses will deal with the subject fully, a few words ought to be said here about the relationship between the lens and camera body. Many 8mm and super 8 cameras offer built-in zoom lenses that are not interchangeable. This means that the filmmaker is 'stuck' with one 'all-purpose' lens. However, the picture isn't really bleak, because many of these lenses, such as those made by Angenieux, Canon, Schneider or others, are as good as the best available fixed focal length lenses.

The 16mm filmmaker usually can change his lens by simply screwing it in or out of the camera turret. Sixteen millimeter cameras frequently offer a three-lens turret on which a selection of lenses may be mounted. By rotating the turret, each lens can rapidly be brought into position. The only constraining feature is that the longest focal length lens must not obstruct the field of view of the widest angle lens. That is, because of its length and width, it must not intrude into the image. The divergent turret of the Arriflex allows for a wider selection of focal lengths by angling each lens.

Lenses most often found on a 16mm turret camera—10, 25, and 75 millimeter focal lengths—have speeds ranging from $f/0.95$ to $f/2.8$ or less. Many other focal lengths are available, the most frequent being 5.7, 12.5, 15, 50, 150 millimeters and so on. Actually the list is incomplete, because such a wide variety of focal lengths and speeds are now included.

It is possible to mount a zoom lens on such a turret, in which case it is likely to be the only lens mounted. As their quality improves, zoom lenses are taking the place of fixed focal length lenses for most purposes. The turret used with zoom lenses, or very long lenses, will frequently need some sort of additional bracing—because of the long hefty lens' effective lever arm—to prevent warping. The torque produced by a sharp tap at the front of the lens is likely to bend the turret out of shape.

The Camera

Power Zoom

Many 8mm cameras offered, and many super 8 machines presently offer, motorized or power zoom. Pushing one button will zoom the lens to telephoto, another button will control zooming to wide angle. The advantage of the power zoom is in its producing smooth zooms. Often there are two rates at which the lens may be zoomed, moderate and fast, or on some cameras, slow and moderate. It is difficult to specify what is a slow, fast or moderate zoom. This will depend upon the zoom ratio of the lens, the filmmaker's taste and the subject being filmed. For this reason, it is important that some convenient form of manual override be provided for cameras incorporating power zoom. You should be able to select any zooming rate, continuous or even, that's appropriate for your purpose.

Accessory power zoom motors are available for 16mm zoom lenses. These motors, controls and power supplies can cost as much or more than many fine super 8 machines. What was once considered a frivolous luxury is now regarded as a necessity by professionals, as was the case with automatic light meter systems.

Release or Drive Button

The release button, or shutter release button, is used to turn on the camera transport system. The button should be well placed and comfortable to use without too much pressure required to depress it. Some release buttons incorporate a locking device which prevents making inadvertent exposures once it is set. Others have a locking device which allows the film to keep on running, without your having to constantly depress the button.

The Tachometer

Some electric-drive 16mm cameras, like the Beaulieu and Arriflex, have a device called a *tachometer* which is used to calibrate film speed accurately. This can be especially crucial if you are trying to shoot double system lip-sync sound. In this case, it is best to come as close as possible to 24 fps (25 fps European TV).

The tachometer uses a swinging indicator or pointer which must align with an appropriate marking to ensure the desired fps setting—8, 16, 24-25, 48 and/or 64 fps. By playing with the fps control the filmmaker can, in short order, achieve the desired speed.

The tachometer becomes necessary when power supplies with different voltages run the electric motor at different speeds for the same fps setting. A good time to set the tachometer for the desired speed is while the head leader is being taken up into the camera. For greatest accuracy, film should be in the camera when you use the tachometer.

Single Frame Control

Many cameras provide a socket which accepts a cable release, to activate the single frame mechanism. The object of this device is to allow a single frame to be exposed at a time, for use, for example, in animation. Since the single frame exposure will usually vary with the fps setting, consult the manufacturer's instructions for exact exposure times. Some single frame devices also allow for *time exposures;* that is, the shutter will remain open as long as the release is depressed.

Frame Counter

The frame counter is a useful device for animation, or the coordination of double or multiple exposures. It works by counting each frame exposed. For example, Ed Emshwiller's *Lifelines* (CCM, FMC) was done entirely in the camera, a Bolex, through the use of the frame counter to coordinate the painted animation with shots of the dancer. The frame counter is also a useful device for measuring short lengths of film for in-the-camera dissolves and fades.

Electric-Drive Camera Controls. The controls and indicators of the Beaulieu R 16: *a*, film speed setting for through-the-lens meter; *b*, remote control input; *c*, mode control (off, battery check, forward, reverse); *d*, finder focus ring; *e*, footage counter; *f*, fps range selector; *g*, frame counter; *h*, tachometer; *i*, electric power input; *j*, cover for sync pulse generator shaft; *k*, single frame cable release socket; *l*, hand grip; *m*, ni-cad power cell (it's part of the grip); *n*, main release or drive button, with cable release socket; *o*, turret locking device; *p*, fps selector; *q*, magazine (when used) fits here. (Photograph by Cinema Beaulieu)

The Camera

Footage Counter

There are two kinds of footage counters in use: one is geared directly to the transport mechanism, and as such can be accurate to the frame. The other uses a feeler arm resting on either the film spooled on the feed or take-up reels. As the radius of the film increases or decreases, the counter reads how much film has been used, or is left. Either kind of counter could start at zero and proceed to twenty-five or one hundred or whatever the maximum load may be, or start at maximum and go to empty, or zero. Both kinds of counters usually make some sort of provision for head leader.

The geared counter is more desirable since it is not influenced by variations in the thickness of different kinds of film: color film, or mag striped film, for example, can be thicker than a black and white film. If

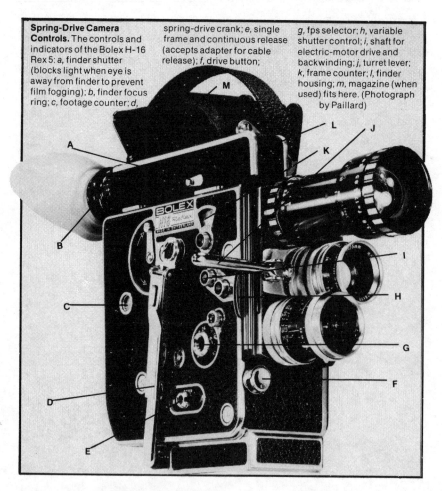

Spring-Drive Camera Controls. The controls and indicators of the Bolex H-16 Rex 5: a, finder shutter (blocks light when eye is away from finder to prevent film fogging); b, finder focus ring; c, footage counter; d, spring-drive crank; e, single frame and continuous release (accepts adapter for cable release); f, drive button; g, fps selector; h, variable shutter control; i, shaft for electric-motor drive and backwinding; j, turret lever; k, frame counter; l, finder housing; m, magazine (when used) fits here. (Photograph by Paillard)

Independent Filmmaking

a feeler type is used, it is better for it to work in conjunction with the take-up reel so that it can detect whether the film is actually being taken up.

A feeler-operated footage counter is ideal for polyester base film. Even though the exact footage cannot be registered, the end of the roll will be indicated. For example, a two hundred and fifty-foot spool of polyester base film is offered on the standard two hundred-foot spool, which is 4 7/8 inches in diameter. Once two hundred and fifty feet of film have passed through the camera, the indicator will read empty because the feeler counter is radius dependent, and not influenced by the actual length of footage which went through the camera.

Backwinding

Some cameras have provision for winding film back on the feed reel or into the feed chamber; some allow for unlimited backwinding, some for only a few feet. Backwinding is useful for double exposing film — used for adding titles or making a dissolve or for multiple image filming. Only a few cameras allow limited backwinding in the super 8 cartridge.

To prevent film exposure during backwinding, use a lens cap to cover the lens, or if the camera has one, close down the variable shutter. Once you've backwound as far as is necessary, proceed to shoot.

Some electric motor cameras offer power-driven reverse. These cameras can be used for backwinding, or they can be used to film action backwards. The 16mm filmmaker seeking to shoot action backwards has the additional option of being able to turn his camera upside down. If this footage is reversed end to end in editing, it would then appear to have been shot *backwards*. The double 8 or double super 8 or single 8 filmmaker can also get this result if his camera operates in reverse. Filming upside down with these formats will result in backwards action, only if upon projection the emulsion position of such footage is reversed with respect to normally shot footage.

Electric Power Supplies

Most super 8 and 8mm electric-drive cameras are powered by several 1.5 volt manganese alkaline penlight size batteries. From three to six batteries are commonly used in series. Once these power cells have been exhausted, replace them with new cells; sometimes it is possible to re-energize the cells. Avoid photoflash or other kinds of penlight batteries, which will have a relatively short life if used to drive a camera motor. Typically the maximum number of fifty-foot super 8 cartridges run on a set of batteries will vary between ten and thirty, or five hundred to fifteen hundred feet of film. Such batteries usually have a decent shelf life of many months which can be greatly extended if kept refrigerated. (They must warm to room temperature before use.)

Power cells for these 8mm cameras are usually stored within the camera body or the camera's pistol grip. Sixteen millimeter cameras

The Camera

are often powered by nickel cadmium rechargeable cells which probably give a lifetime of use. The Canon Scoopic 16mm camera contains its ni-cad battery within its body. Others such as the Arriflex or Bolex, using the accessory motor, are powered with various kinds of batteries, lead acid or ni-cad 'dry cells,' that are worn over the shoulder, on the belt or around the waist. The Beaulieu 16mm camera offers a pistol grip that accepts a ni-cad power cell. It may take between ten and fifteen hours to charge such cells, using a special charger unit powered by house current. Newer charging devices can do the job in less than an hour. Some cameras, using either the appropriate motor or a suitable transformer-rectifier, will operate directly from house current. (Units for car battery charging are available too.)

Battery Check

Electric-drive cameras often incorporate some means for checking the battery's charge. Without such a check, the filmmaker has simply no way of telling whether or not his power supply is up to par. A battery check usually involves pressing a button, and observing whether a meter's indicator deflects into the charged or uncharged zone.

Cameras often use a separate mercury cell for powering the light meter. Some argument can be made for omitting any battery check for these meter-powering cells; they are extremely long lived, and when they finally fail, they lose power very rapidly.

It would be more convenient not to have to use a separately powered light meter in an electric-drive camera. This may involve additional circuitry, but some recent cameras have the ability to use one set of power cells for both meter and drive. The Zeiss Ikon Moviflex super 8 cameras, for example, use a bridge circuit for their BTL system and draw power for meter and motor from one source.

Matte Box

Although used in conjunction with the lens, I consider the matte box to be a camera accessory since it is directly attached to the camera body. The matte box, sometimes called a *compendium,* sits in front of the camera body, held in place before the lenses by a rail or rails. The matte box itself is made of a bellows, the kind found in folding or view cameras. By adjusting the extension of this bellows, the matte box serves as a lens shade for many focal lengths. The rear of the matte box can hold gelatin filters or mattes of various shapes. Two of those most familiar are the keyhole and binocular mattes.

The matte box has often been used for the ever-popular split screen effect where one character acts with himself. This is accomplished by filming the shot with half the frame masked, backwinding and shooting the shot again with the matte properly repositioned. Although the matte box may be a useful tool for tripod shooting, it can be an impediment for hand-held work.

A brilliant use of the matte box, for combining images, can be found in Bruce Baillie's *Castro Street* (CCC, FMC). By using images in various portions of the screen, each shot through its own matte, or the film-maker's black-gloved hand, Baillie created an impressionistic vision of freight trains and their industrial environment.

Filter Slot

The filter slot is a device built into the camera body, behind the lens and before the aperture, to hold gelatin filters mounted in a metal frame. Some cameras, like the Bolex H-16, come equipped with a filter slot. Others may be converted to accept gelatin filters this way. When the filter holder of the Bolex, for example, is left out of the filter slot, the

Mattes and Matte Box.
Mattes, like these corny ones for binocular and keyhole effects, are cut out of black card stock and mounted in the matte box. Supported on rails, attaching to the front of the camera, the matte box bellows can serve to hold mattes for special effects, as a variable lens hood and as a filter holder. (Photograph by Paillard)

The Camera

114   film will be fogged. Even when no gelatin is used, the empty holder has
to be left in place.

The filter slot is extremely useful for cameras with turret-mounted
fixed focal length lenses, or zoom lenses. Once a gelatin is in the slot,
any lens in shooting position will be influenced by that filter. Instead
of mounting several glass or gelatin filters in front of each lens, as
usual, filter slots make life easier by replacing, say three operations,
with one.

The filter slot is a good feature to have even if you're using a zoom
lens. Filters for zoom lenses are often rather expensive because of their
large size. At least this is true of glass filters for many 16mm zoom
lenses. It is possible to carry dozens of very inexpensive framed gelatin
filters in the same space that would be taken up with just a few glass
filters.

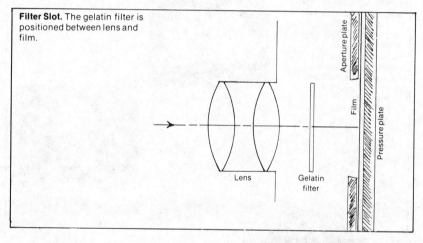

Filter Slot. The gelatin filter is positioned between lens and film.

Magazine Only. The Arriflex BL was designed to be used with a magazine; it has no internal film capacity. (Birns & Sawyer)

Independent Filmmaking

Magazines

There are two kinds of cameras that accept magazines. Those, like the Eclair or Arriflex 16M or Elmo Tri-Filmatic, cannot operate without a magazine in position, and those, like late models of the Bolex H-16 Rex, Pathé or Beaulieu accept an auxiliary magazine.

Once film is loaded in the magazine of the former camera types, the magazine can be affixed to the camera body, and the film is threaded through it. (In the case of the Eclair, no threading is necessary.) The magazine contains the feed and take-up chambers, and the camera body performs the distinct function of exposing the film. It has no chambers for feed or take up of film.

The Beaulieu, Bolex or Arri 16S, have feed and take-up chambers for one hundred-foot spools of 16mm film. A larger capacity auxiliary magazine may be fixed to these cameras. The Arri and the Bolex will accept four hundred-foot magazines, which may use core-wound four hundred-foot loads, or two hundred-foot spool-wound daylight loads. The Beaulieu accepts two hundred- and four hundred-foot capacity magazines.

With the exception of the Elmo camera listed above, all the cameras mentioned are 16mm models. Pathé offers a double super 8 model of its machine which will accept a four hundred-foot load of double super 8 film (eight hundred feet slit). The Elmo Tri-Filmatic, distributed in the United States by Honeywell, accepts magazines for 8mm, super 8 and single 8 cartridges, and one hundred-foot spools (two hundred feet slit) of double super 8. The (no longer manufactured) Fairchild 900, double 8mm sound on film camera, accepts a two hundred-foot magazine, or fifty feet internally without the magazine.

Magazines need some method for taking up film within them. Some offer an electric *torque motor* coupled to the take-up spindle; others use a drive belt run by the camera motor.

Magazine or Internal Loads. The Bolex H-16 Rex 5 has the capacity to hold one hundred feet of film without a magazine, or four hundred feet with a magazine. Shown here with accessory electric motor. (Paillard)

The Camera

Cable Release

The cable release socket is usually found in the center of the release button but sometimes it will be on some other portion of the camera body. To this threaded socket a cable release, a foot or two or longer in length, may be attached. When the button, or plunger, on the cable release is depressed, it drives a metal wire, encased in a sheathe, into the cable release socket causing the camera to start. Relaxation of pressure on the cable release button will stop the camera. Some cable releases lock, allowing continuous filming until the release is unlocked. Other kinds of releases are operated by pushing or even stepping on a rubber bulb. This is very useful for animation, because it frees both hands. The cable release is invariably used when the camera is tripod mounted to achieve maximum steadiness and the elimination of any camera shake during shooting.

Pistol Grip

One of the most useful accessories for a camera, if it doesn't already come equipped with it, is the pistol grip. The pistol grip often makes hand-holding the camera easier than holding the camera by its body. There are exceptions. You may find it easier to hold some cameras by their bodies than with a grip, for example, the Bell & Howell DR-70 16mm camera, the Arriflex 16S or the Leicina 8mm cameras.

Pistol grips usually attach to the tripod socket or sometimes couple to the shutter or drive button. Cameras with built-in pistol grips usually house the spring-drive mechanism, or the power cells for operating the motor, making them awkward when tripod mounted.

It is important for the grip to comfortably fit your fingers. It is more important for the grip-camera combination to form a balanced whole. A heavy, poorly balanced pistol grip-camera (and lens) combination can become a torture machine after a few minutes of shooting.

Tripod Socket

The camera should have a threaded hole bored into its base so that it may be attached to a tripod. There are two standard size tripod sockets, 3/8 and 3/16 inch. For use with a 3/16 inch tripod, an inexpensive double threaded adapter sleeve can be inserted into a camera's 3/8 inch tripod socket. Some cameras have both sizes of tripod sockets, but most cameras simply have the smaller diameter thread.

Camera Design

The 16mm filmmaker has every reason to envy the 8mm, super 8 or single 8 filmmaker, at least as far as camera selection is concerned. The super 8 filmmaker has a great variety of reasonable, well designed cameras — Canon, Bolex and Nizo, for example — from which to choose. Cameras like these offer built-in zoom lenses, automatic exposure control, extremely bright viewfinders, well placed controls and many feature power zoom.

Independent Filmmaking

Zoom lenses available in super 8 have such a wide range and high
speed, that the filmmaker might not miss lens interchangeability.
There are fast $f/1.8$ zoom lenses like the Angenieux 8 to 64 millimeter
zoom, or the Schneider 7 to 56 millimeters. Canon offered one camera,
model 1218, with a 12-to-1 zoom ratio. Its speed is $f/1.8$, and it zooms
from 7.5 to 90 millimeters. Many of the zoom lenses found on super 8
cameras are in the range of $f/1.4$ to $f/1.8$, and have good quality at all
f stops and focal lengths.

It's rare that you'll find a zoom lens for a 16mm camera faster than
$f/2$. The Canon Scoopic lens, $f/1.6$, with a range of 13 to 76 millimeters
comes to mind. Another Canon lens, for 16mm, zooms from 15 to 120
millimeters and has a speed of $f/1.3$.

High speed and extensive zoom range aren't the only virtues of
super 8 cameras. They're easier to hold than most 16mm cameras because they are smaller and lighter. I've heard it said, by some filmmakers, that they like a camera with a certain amount of weight. There
is something to be said for this point of view. If the mass of a camera is
well distributed so that it balances properly, its weight will act to help
hold it steady. If it's hefty, they contend, it's easier to hold. But as far
as I'm concerned, a feather is easier to carry than a sack of potatoes, and
filmmakers who crave heavy cameras, deserve heavy cameras.

Left-handed Cameras

I believe that one of the worst design failures of most 16mm cameras is
that the controls are on the wrong side of the body, that is, the left side
as seen from the front.

If you're left-handed, the controls are well placed, but most people
are right-handed, and holding the cameras with the right hand makes
reaching the controls difficult. In order to turn the camera body toward
him, the filmmaker must turn his hand, so that the knuckles are toward
the face. Compare holding an imaginary camera in your right hand this
way. Now turn the wrist so that the palm is away from you, with fingers
toward your face. It's much easier to reach the controls when held palm
facing the face. One hundred-foot load 16mm cameras, like the Pathé,
Bolex, Canon, Beaulieu and Bell & Howell, have their controls designed
to be used by a lefty. Not only that, many of these cameras are also most
conveniently designed for the left eye at the finder; most people are
right-eyed.

How did these 16mm cameras come to be designed to accommodate left-handed, left-eyed people when the vast majority of people
are right-eyed and right-handed? Super 8 cameras, on the other hand,
are, in general, designed for the majority of right-handed, right-eyed
filmmakers.

Position of Indicators

While I believe that most of us would be better served with the camera
controls on the right side of the camera body, as one faces the front of the
camera, the indicators should be placed on the back panel under the

118 viewfinder. A quick glance away from the finder could then show the filmmaker the f stop, battery charge, film consumed or remaining and whatever else might be necessary.

A better approach might be to place this information within the viewfinder, away from the actual area of the image. Some cameras already offer exposure information with numbers, but within the image area obscuring the most important information of all.

Testing the Camera

Finder Accuracy

The reflex viewfinder ought to be tested for focusing and field accuracy. It may surprise you to learn that a reflex finder's field might not coincide with the image projected by the lens on the film plane, but this is sometimes the case. If the optics of the finder system are improperly positioned, the finder may see slightly to the right or left, up or down.

On a sheet of paper, draw a series of ruled rectangles, in the proportion 3 x 4, one inside another. To identify each rectangle they can be numbered or colored. Viewing of film shot of such a test target will easily reveal if the finder image is properly centered. Also bear in mind that the finder is often masked to correspond to the projector's aperture which is somewhat less than the full frame.

Working the Controls

Run through all the controls to make sure they work. It's possible to learn a lot about the camera before exposing any film. (Don't operate a camera above 24 fps if it isn't loaded.) Next, expose a roll of film, trying to use every control the camera offers, repeatedly. Make sure the footage counter works, the film keeps its loops, the viewfinder is bright and easily focused and so on.

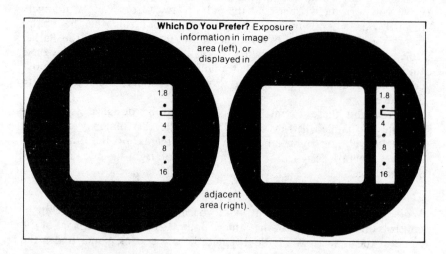

Which Do You Prefer? Exposure information in image area (left), or displayed in adjacent area (right).

Independent Filmmaking

The most basic mechanical test to determine a camera's quality is the steadiness test. The results of this test can be used as a yardstick of the general mechanical soundness of the camera. If the camera fails the steadiness test, something is wrong with it.

Run a roll of film through the camera, exposing a black cross drawn on a white piece of paper or cardboard. Actually, you can use black tape on a wall or a door. Any convenient distance from the target to the camera will do. The camera should be mounted on a firm tripod. After the film has been exposed, remove it from the camera or backwind it, and run it through a second time after having moved the cross or the camera slightly. The purpose of this test is to double expose the *crosses,* so that they will be on top of each other, or rather, very nearly together. If you're working in 8mm or double super 8, the film would have to be run through the camera three times to make the proper double exposure, or backwound and then reexposed.

Let us suppose you tried to make this test with only one exposure of the cross. Upon projection, the cross would be subject to the unsteadiness of the projector, and it will be difficult to isolate the source of unsteadiness. By double exposing the cross, we can observe the relative unsteadiness of cross compared to cross, eliminating the contribution of the projector. Look closely at the twin crosses from as close to the screen as you care to go, and see if the crosses are moving with respect to each other.

One way to perform such a test would be to use a microscope and measure the unsteadiness, giving figures in terms of percentage of frame height. Such a procedure is out of the question for most film-makers, so I'm going to try to give you some way to judge the results. Side to side movement, or weave, is more tolerable to the eye than up

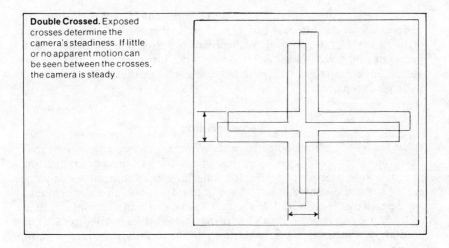

Double Crossed. Exposed crosses determine the camera's steadiness. If little or no apparent motion can be seen between the crosses, the camera is steady.

and down, or vertical unsteadiness. It has been my experience, that projecting the image on a 30 x 40 inch screen, a fairly standard size, and getting about a foot or two from the screen, will tell all that needs to be told. Well running cameras will display little or no motion between the crosses under these conditions, at least as far as the naked eye is concerned.

The steadiness test assumes that the film's perforations are accurately cut, and this is usually the case. Although the registration error may cancel out some of the time, the virtue of this test is that part of the time the film is being exposed, we must see double the error, or the worst possible error. The proper evaluation of this test heavily depends upon the judgment of an observer, and does require some experience.

Unfortunately, the steadiness of super 8 in the cartridge cannot be evaluated by this method. (Single 8 and double super 8 can be evaluated since they can be backwound.) If the filmmaker is sure he has a perfectly steady projector, he can observe a single exposure of a cross and learn about the super 8 camera's steadiness. In general, super 8 cameras are very steady.

The test should be conducted at a variety of fps settings. Such a test will also reveal any frame line drift. It sometimes happens that cameras will register the frame at slightly different positions relative to the film's sprocket holes at different fps settings. Each section of such a test should be exposed and reexposed at the same fps setting, if the test is to have any meaning. If you are using more than one camera, or a camera with shifting frame line position, intercutting such footage can prove troublesome since during projection, shifting frame lines may annoyingly appear on the screen. Visual examination of exposures made with only one pass through the camera can make clear a poorly registered frame line. By running the film through the camera twice, in different directions, misregistered frame lines will overlap. The steadiness test is also a good frame line test.

Certainly most of the interesting independent, experimental or underground films have been made on cameras that were not put through any of these tests. If such procedures are contrary to your temperament, or if you have better things to do, don't try the tests. Use the camera, and if anything seems to be wrong with it, that's the time to test it, or get it repaired.

Camera Guide

What follows is a brief guide to motion picture cameras. It is personal, based upon my own experience, that of my friends and colleagues, and in some cases, extensive testing. It would have been difficult for any one person to have operated, and to have gotten to know, all the machines I am describing. However, I have used many of them. The information about those cameras I have not personally used, I have tried to acquire accurately. Naturally enough, those that I have used may receive more attention. This may not be fair to the camera, but it will be to film-makers.

121

Ridiculously Low Prices.
Taken from the back pages of a circa 1982 photography magazine, these prices for super 8 cameras are laughably low.

MOVIE CAMERAS & PROJECTORS	
Canon 310 XL	129.95
Canon 514 XL	184.95
Canon 514XL-S	264.95
Canon 514 XL-S AF	394.95
Canon 1014 XL-S	584.95
Elmo 412-XL	144.95
Elmo 614 XL	174.95
Elmo 230S XL	159.95
Elmo 240S XL	224.95
Elmo 260-S-XL	269.95
Elmo 1012 SXL	399.95
Elmo 2400 AF	299.95
Elmo 2600 AF	384.95
Sankyo EM 40XL	164.95
Sankyo EM 60XL	193.95
Sankyo XL 320S	189.95
Sankyo XL 420S	264.95
Sankyo XL 620S	349.95
Chinon 30 RXL	288.95
Chinon 30 AFXL	274.95
Chinon 60 AFXL	309.95
Chinon 60 RXL	284.95
Chinon 405 MXL	304.95
Chinon 60 SMXL	327.95
Chinon 12 SMR	444.95
Chinon 200 8XL	574.95
Minolta XL 401	173.95
Minolta XL 601	199.95
Minolta XL 42S	208.95
Minolta XL 64S	245.95
Minolta XL 84S	295.95

In prior printings of this book there has been discussion of standard or regular 8mm camera equipment. I am dropping these words of advice aimed at the 8mm camera user, since 8mm is obsolete and cannot be considered a viable means of filmic expression.

Super 8-Single 8

Since this book was first written, I wrote a book on the subject of super 8 filmmaking, *The Super 8 Book* (Simon and Schuster). The interested reader might look to this work as a source of information. Accordingly, I have abbreviated my comments herein.

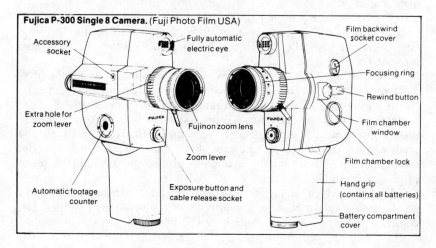

Fujica P-300 Single 8 Camera. (Fuji Photo Film USA)

Accessory socket

Fully automatic electric eye

Film backwind socket cover

Focusing ring

Rewind button

Extra hole for zoom lever

Fujinon zoom lens

Film chamber window

Zoom lever

Film chamber lock

Automatic footage counter

Exposure button and cable release socket

Hand grip (contains all batteries)

Battery compartment cover

The Camera

Beaulieu 4008 ZM Super 8 Camera. (Cinema Beaulieu)

I call to the reader's attention the listing of new super 8 cameras and their prices from a circa 1982 advertisement in a major photography magazine. The advertiser is an East Coast discount house and the prices given are typical. There probably isn't a camera on this list that isn't worth giving a try, and they are at such good prices!

Super 8 cameras fall into several categories. There are simple box-type cameras for shooting silent or sound-on-film. There are box-type XL cameras with $f/1.2$ lenses, with or without sound capability. There are more complex cameras, which we might call production cameras, which run at not only the 18 fps to be found on the box cameras, but also at 24 fps, slow motion speeds, perhaps 56 fps, and intervalometer speeds down to a few fps. Of course such cameras all have through-the-lens metering, reflex viewing, zoom lenses and diopter adjustments for the viewfinder to suit different people's eyes. A few super 8 cameras offer sophisticated automatic focusing.

The XL feature is often found on production cameras—as are remote control operation and sync pulse output, often combined with electronic flash-triggering capability which can be coupled with the intervalometer function for time-lapse work.

Then we have the sound-on-film cameras which can accept the fifty- and two-hundred-foot sound-striped cartridges. The best of these cameras, like the Elmo 1012 SXL, give first-rate voice recording. Some of these cameras, like the Elmo, combine XL and sound-on-film, and some combine production camera features. There are cameras that can do sound and picture fades and dissolves, and most have their systems, meter, zoom motor, camera and capstan drive, and electronics all powered by a set of pistol-grip household AA cells.

Such riches! And many of these really are fine machines that will give good results. We attribute the low prices to a combination of factors: The cameras are mass produced, there is competition among several manufac-

Independent Filmmaking

turers and, quite simply put, the bottom fell out of the super 8 market. It's a buyer's market.

It's such a buyer's market that manufacturers have been going out of business. I'm not talking about some fly-by-night outfit, but a major like Eumig. Or, almost as bad, take the case of a fine camera line like Nizo, which has not had an American distributor for many years.

While the bottom may have fallen out of the amateur market, the situation is O.K. for the independent seeking to pick up bargains in brand new classy equipment like the beautiful Elmo 1012 SXL, selling for an astonishing $399.95. When first introduced, its list price was over $1000, and when I bought one for $700 I thought I was getting a deal!

16mm

16mm movie cameras can be as simple as the Bell & Howell–designed spring-driven 70-DR, or as complex and sophisticated, and as costly I might add, as an Arriflex 16SR. Figuring what a camera can cost, and if it can do the job for you, may not be easy. Practically all the cameras listed here are obtainable on a rental basis from individuals or from companies who specialize in professional motion picture equipment. There is a flourishing market for used 16mm gear. While I would not recommend used super 8 equipment, a used 16mm purchase can make good sense, if it's the right camera at the right price.

Remember that additions to the basic camera body can in some cases, depending on the camera design, include costly zoom lenses, matte boxes, special purpose motors, special viewfinders, magazines and who knows what else. These add-ons, hardly luxuries since it can be quite impossible to do the job without them, can multiply the cost of the camera far beyond the basic price.

Aaton 7

The Aaton 7 is exceedingly advanced, and expensive. Like its direct competition, the Arri SR and the Eclair ACL II, a basic outfit without lens is in the 20 to 25K range. The camera was designed specifically for hand-held verité work. It runs very quiet and, if they are telling the truth, gets quieter with age, like a wise man. The camera accepts four hundred-foot magazines, which snap on and off the camera head very quickly. A built-in exposure meter looks at the film emulsion surface, so you have, in effect, reflex metering without losing any exposure light to a beam splitter system. A video tap is also available.

The camera can print Aaton Clear Time Recording Code on the film itself, which, unlike other time code systems, can be read by a human being as well as a computer sensor. If quarter inch tape is similarly time coded and clock regulated, the syncing up of dailies can be greatly facilitated, providing you have a suitably modified editing table which can read the encoded transferred mag film and workprint. Time code systems for filmmaking, in general, have not caught on in the United States.

The Camera

It's a really interesting and highly individualistic design. It has a wonderful viewfinder system, and the Aaton feels good to hold on the shoulder. Because the design is so bold, some people love it and some hate it.

Arriflex

The Arriflex S and GS are identical except that the GS has a built-in sync pulse system and an electric blooper (clap stick). The camera was designed to be hand-held, and it has provision for one hundred-foot loads, but will accept external or accessory two hundred- and four hundred-foot magazines. It uses registration pins for reputedly rock steady registration. Arriflex cameras have an outstanding reputation for registration and superiority of construction.

One word comes to mind when describing the view through the Arri finder, which is of the reflex type and uses a rotating mirror: beautiful. Lenses provided for the Arri—I am familiar with those by Schneider—are not only optically superb, but their lens mounts leave little to be desired. Following focus with the Arri is extraordinarily easy. The camera lenses were designed to be used in conjunction with the Arri matte box. Check out the Zeiss high speed prime lenses, which are superb. The designs were commissioned by Arri and introduced in the late seventies.

The variable speed camera motor will drive film from 5 to 50 fps. The motor is interchangeable, and special motors for sync sound and animation are available. If you purchase the single frame animation motor, you will also need to have the external shutter to prevent unwanted exposures.

The Arriflex M is somewhat like the 16S, but it cannot be used without a magazine. Three magazines are available: two hundred, four hundred and a coaxial twelve hundred feet. The camera is best used on a tripod, but I have seen many staggering cameramen using it hand-held, even with the aid of a shoulder harness and belt pod. These devices tend to make the upper portion of the body rigid, decreasing the fluidity of camera motion.

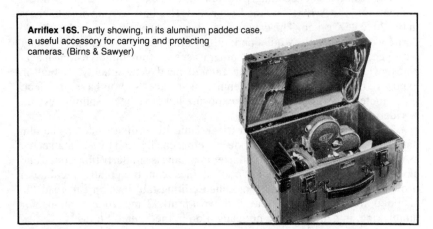

Arriflex 16S. Partly showing, in its aluminum padded case, a useful accessory for carrying and protecting cameras. (Birns & Sawyer)

The Arriflex BL, similar to the M model, was specially designed for lip-sync sound recording. It is self-blimped and, as such, very quiet. Special blimped zoom lenses are necessary to maintain the required low noise level. The camera will shoot single or double system sound. A special module, easily installed, will convert the camera to single system sound-on-film recording on magnetic-striped film. Although people use the camera hand-held, it's a klutz used this way, and better left on a tripod.

The Arriflex 16SR would be my first choice amongst Arri models, if I had the bucks to buy it. It will do everything all the other Arri models will do, and it's really easier to use and more fun, too. Naturally it's very expensive. It is a flat-based camera, unlike the Aaton or Eclair ACL, which are designed to fit around the shoulder. It accepts four hundred-foot coaxial quick-loading magazines, and it has all the features you'd expect in a no-compromise production verité camera, including the usual crystal controlled motor and internal exposure system. The viewfinder image is beautiful.

Arriflex has introduced a high speed model, which runs a little louder. The basic 16SR can be used without a barney for sync sound filmmaking.

Auricon

There are several models of Auricon single system sound cameras. They record optical sound-on-film, but with simple modification they can record magnetic sound-on-film as well. Models are the Cine-Voice II (one hundred-foot spool loads), the Pro-600 (six hundred-foot capacity), the Super-1200 (twelve hundred-foot capacity) and the Pro-600 "Special" (four hundred-foot capacity), all of which run quiet. These cameras are primarily of interest to people who do television interviewing, although any film-

Auricon Cine Voice II.
Filmagnetic recording
unit in place.
(Bach Auricon)

The Camera

maker interested in single system sound-on-film may find the cameras useful. General Camera, F&B Ceco, Birns & Sawyer and many other people by the late sixties had created a subindustry to improve upon and convert these cameras to reflex viewing. Gone, gone are the days, now that we have ENG.

Beaulieu

There are variations of the Beaulieu R16 lightweight, electric-drive, one hundred-foot spool camera that accepts an accessory two hundred-foot magazine. All versions have a through-the-lens light meter, adjusted by operating the diaphragm until the pointer in the finder is vertical. One version, the R16B, couples with fully automatic zoom lenses, like the Angenieux $f/2.2$ 12 to 120 millimeter lens with *Reglomatic* servo zoom motor. Some models of the nonautomatic model may be converted to the fully automatic camera. The fully automatic exposure camera allows the f stop to be set manually. The system is identical to that used by the Beaulieu 4008ZM super 8 camera. Another model, the R16B(PZ), offers variable speed power zoom lenses.

Present models of the camera use a single power supply for both light meter and motor, and, in addition, for the magazine torque motor, which has electric contacts automatically made as it is seated atop the camera. The light meter is accurate and, as mentioned, the meter pointer is visible in the finder. The finder is of the moving mirror type, and it is very bright and easy to use. Focusing is difficult with shorter focal length lenses.

The camera has solid state electronically governed speeds from 2 to 64 fps, and a built-in tachometer to set the speeds accurately. The tachometer has a second scale which is used for accurate setting of the sound speeds of either 24 or 25 fps. A single frame shaft accepts a compact sync pulse generator for double system lip sync recording.

The Beaulieu is a very steady camera at all forward speeds. The camera has electric drive for reverse, which is essentially useful for backwinding film, but not for exposing backward action. I advise against using it for this purpose, because it exhibits marked frame line shift and is grossly unsteady when run backward. Bearing this in mind, the electric rewind is useful for backwinding film for in-the-camera effects or multiple exposures. For backward action turn the camera upside down, as you would using any 16mm camera.

Versions of the camera with the turret accept three C mount lenses. A heavy-duty plate, which accepts but one lens, is used in place of the turret for zoom lens operation. I cannot advise the use of the turret model with hefty lenses, like many zoom models. The turret is supported only at the center and may not be able to handle much of a load.

The camera has a battery check for its rechargeable ni-cad cells. There are two versions of ni-cads used with the Beaulieu. One will drive about seven hundred feet, and the other about sixteen hundred feet, at 24 fps. These cells, cylindrical in shape, become an integral part of the grip and camera combination when screwed in place. The manufacturer's estimated capability of the power cells is quite conservative.

The Beaulieu is one of the easiest-to-hold 16mm cameras on the market, even with the magazine in place. This is in part attributable to its extremely well-designed *pistol-anatomical* grip, and certainly to its light weight. The camera also features electric remote control and single frame control for animation. It is a reasonably sturdy, well-designed, versatile, beautifully finished and easy-to-use machine.

Bell & Howell

The 70-DR is a robust, spring-driven camera with a variable fps rate of from 8 to 64. One wind will tension a run of twenty-two feet of film through the camera, or a running time of thirty-seven seconds at 24 fps, which is quite adequate. The camera accepts one hundred-foot spool loads. The turret accepts three lenses, and the viewfinder objectives are mounted on a side turret, geared to the taking lens turret. Rotation of the larger turret brings into place the finder objective that "sees" the appropriate field of view. (Older models do not have the geared finder and lens turrets.) The image through the finder is a trifle small, but crisp and bright. There is a control for manual parallax compensation.

This camera is easily held with the wrist through the strap, with the fingers grasping the finder barrel. There is a small window for reflex focusing, which can be used only when the camera is not running. This device is a nice try, but not very easy to use. It's dim, and you see only the center of the field. Many accessories are available, such as finder lenses and external motors.

The machine is easy to use, highly dependable and capable of making superb films. Its most severe limitation is that it lacks a true reflex finder system. However, there's not much point in criticizing an apple because it doesn't taste like a pear. . . . You can probably find a zoom lens with a built-in finder to use with the 70-DR body.

Bolex

There are several models of the Bolex from which to choose. They break down this way: those with reflex viewing, and those that accept only one lens; and those that accept the four hundred-foot accessory magazine, and those that do not. As I understand the Bolex catalog, those without reflex finders lack the turret and are meant essentially to be the line's economy cameras, or to be used in conjunction with one of the many zoom lenses with built-in reflex focusing and viewing that the company supplies.

In the past, Bolex turret models with optical finders were available. All Bolex cameras accept the Octameter optical finder that clips to the cover side of the camera. The basic body accepts one hundred-foot spool loads.

Having gotten that out of the way, let me say that I don't know if there would have been an independent filmmaking movement without this

128

70-DR. (Bell & Howell)

Bolex H-16 Rex 5. (Paillard)

K-100. (Eastman Kodak)

Independent Filmmaking

camera. There is no other machine at such a comparatively low price with so many features and so much quality.

Models H-16 Rex 4 and 5 (the 5 has the capability to accept the four hundred-foot magazine) have reflex viewing and focusing through a behind-the-lens beam splitter. Fixed focal length lenses from 10 to 50 millimeters, and zoom lenses, are specially adjusted for the 4 and 5 bodies because of the beam splitter. These lenses are marked *Rx*.

The camera has practically everything a camera could have, with the notable exception of a through-the-lens meter. It has a filter slot, fully closing variable shutter, film rewind, single frame release, automatic threading, frame counter and speeds from 12 to 64 fps. It is spring driven, and one wind will run sixteen and a half feet of film (or twenty-eight seconds at 24 fps) through the camera. I consider this short run to be inadequate: although it is long enough for most scenes, it forces too-frequent winding and that race-against-sudden-death feeling when shooting.

The camera accepts two kinds of electric-drive motors, one for filming at variable fps and another constant speed motor for filming at 24 fps. The latter, the MST motor, has a sync pulse generator which may be used for lip sync shooting with tape recorders like the Nagra or Uher 1000.

The camera's registration is very good, or what is usually described as rock steady. The reflex finder is adequate, but dim under low light conditions. Most of the time it is very easy to focus with and to observe depth of field.

Like most machines that have developed over the years with design modifications, the Bolex shows signs of growing pains. The controls are rather crowded, but easy to use. The reflex finder system was added to the basic design, but done so well that there's no point in arguing with it. Perhaps the oddest feature of the Bolex is its turret, which accepts three C mount lenses. It is shaped like half a circle or a split pie plate. When used in any but the central position, the turret extends over the control side of the camera. This would make cranking the spring lever difficult, if the lever wasn't able to telescope inward to avoid the turret. With the Bolex, one design modification has led to another; but designers have solved these problems adequately, even if with a Rube Goldberg flair, and by using the same basic camera for many years they have kept the cost of the machine down to a low price.

The Bolex has a variety of accessories, including lenses of many focal lengths, the four hundred-foot magazine, a matte box, a bellows close-focusing device with built-in 75 millimeter Yvar lens, copying stand, light meter and most important, for hand-held shooting, a pistol grip. The grip and camera lens combination balances very well, although the outfit is hefty for my taste. The camera is beautifully finished and workmanship is of a high order.

Two of the best things about the Bolex are the Yvar and faster Switar lenses that Paillard provides for the camera. Not only are they optically superb, their mounts, or barrels, are beautifully designed.

Continuing the evolution of the camera, Paillard designers have added

130

Bolex 16 Pro. (Paillard)

Eclair NPR. (Eclair)

some additional models to the line. The EBM is a battery-powered Bolex
with a built-in electric motor. More properly it might be placed in the next
higher priced category, but it shares much in common with the spring-
driven Bolex. Gone is the spring drive, but the body retains the old features.
There's a selection of speeds from 10 to 50 fps, and the camera will run at 24
or 25 fps while generating a sync pulse signal. Bolex has developed their
own extra large bayonet lens mount, especially designed for use with hefty

Independent Filmmaking

zoom lenses. Both electric- and spring-drive bodies can offer this mount
which may be adapted to accept standard C mount lenses.

While the older Bolex models accept external or add-on electric
motors, a new series of Bolex camera, using the basic Bolex box, has
appeared in the last decade. The model designations are SBM, EBM and
EL. The cameras have a new type of very large breach locking bayonet
mount, quartz crystal controlled motors, internal metering, and they
accept four hundred-foot magazines. To get the lowdown on exactly what's
what with which model, see your dealer.

The Bolex 16 Pro, according to the designer, was conceived for the
coverage of news events, with either single or double system sync sound. It
has a number of interesting design points, such as a moving mirror reflex
finder and a specially designed electric motor which is the heart of the
camera. The camera accepts four hundred-foot magazines, and it was
meant to be shoulder supported. Essentially designed for zoom lens use, it
will accept a variety of interchangeable lenses. Zoom lenses with automatic
diaphragm and focusing devices are available. The hand grips have controls
which can operate motors for the zoom, focus and exposure control. The
BTL meter may be set for speeds from 12 to 1600 E.I., and filming speeds
may be varied from 12 to 50 fps.

This weird and awkward camera never caught on, and production was
halted shortly after it was introduced.

Canon

Although the Canon Scoopic is a marked design departure for 16mm
equipment, it is old hat for 8mm or super 8. It is an electric-drive, one
hundred-foot roll-loading, automatic-threading camera with a built-on
anatomical grip.

What's really different about this camera for 16mm is that it has a built-
in zoom lens with a reflex viewing and focusing system that takes its light
before the diaphragm. Also, its ni-cad power cell is placed within the
camera body. The zoom lens has focal lengths of 13 to 76 millimeters, and is
extraordinarily fast, $f/1.6$. With such a noninterchangeable system you
might suspect that the designers would have chosen to employ a BTL
automatic meter system. They haven't. Instead they've used an adjacent
CdS meter cell that sits above and slightly to one side of the zoom objective.

The camera has provision for setting film speeds to 320, and an
inexpensive modification allows for doubling that maximum index. Film
running speed settings are: 16, 24, 32 and 48 fps. The zoom lens stops down
to $f/22$ and focuses to five feet. The camera is well finished, and workmanship seems to be of a high order.

The lens is extremely good. The only flaw I was able to detect was the
slightest amount of pin-cushion distortion (consult chapter 4, under Distortion) at the extreme telephoto position. Focusing was not easy in dim light
levels. I found the inability to focus closer than five feet annoying even

Canon Scoopic. (Canon, USA)

Beaulieu R 16. (Cinema Beaulieu)

GSMO Shown with Four Hundred-Foot Magazine. (Cinema Products)

Independent Filmmaking

though with the telephoto position at five feet it is possible to cover an area of about 6 by 8 inches. When zoomed to the wide angle position of 13 millimeters, depth of field is great enough when focused at five feet, at many f stops, to get fairly close. Supplementary close-up lenses are also available.

The automatic threading is well engineered, and the film registration is very good. Unfortunately, the camera lacks a single frame release for animation, and with this omission the lack of a frame counter is consistent. It is possible to have an electric blooper and sync pulse generator added to the camera.

The camera was obviously designed for hand-held newsreel-type shooting (Scoopic must derive from *scoop*), and the designers have tried to work everything toward that end. By eliminating some features they may have reduced the cost of the camera, but they have also reduced its versatility and usefulness.

It's curious that the requirements of the amateur and the newsreel filmmaker should so closely coincide, as in fact they do. What makes working the Scoopic so easy for the newsreel filmmaker—the automatic light meter, automatic loading and the built-in zoom lens—also makes it easy for the home movie maker to use.

There's a variation of the Scoopic, the Sound Scoopic 200. It was meant to be used for single or double system sound, and it can hold a two hundred-foot daylight loading reel. The camera operator wears, over the shoulder, a separate amplifier-power supply, which plugs into the camera. Although based on the Scoopic design, having the same general configuration and similar lens, the automatic exposure system works through the lens (instead of an adjacent-type metering system), and the reflex viewing system uses a moving mirror (instead of a beam splitter).

Cinema Products

Hooray for Cinema Products. This is an innovative Los Angeles–based company that has proved that high quality movie cameras can still be made in the United States. The cameras are fully competitive in terms of quality and price.

The CP-16 was probably the most widely used 16mm TV news camera. It shoots picture with sound on mag-striped film. My guess is that quite a few of these are available used, at good prices. Check them out.

The GSMO is a jewel of a camera, definitely vying for that part of the market inhabited by the Eclair ACL, the Aaton 7 and the Arri SR. A worthy contender, since it is significantly less expensive than the alternatives. It is relatively lightweight, a little louder than the competition, and it takes a number of the CP-16 accessories but not the CP-16 magazine, which is a displacement Mitchell-style device. Instead the GSMO accepts its own four hundred-foot quick-loading coaxial magazines similar to those offered by the competition.

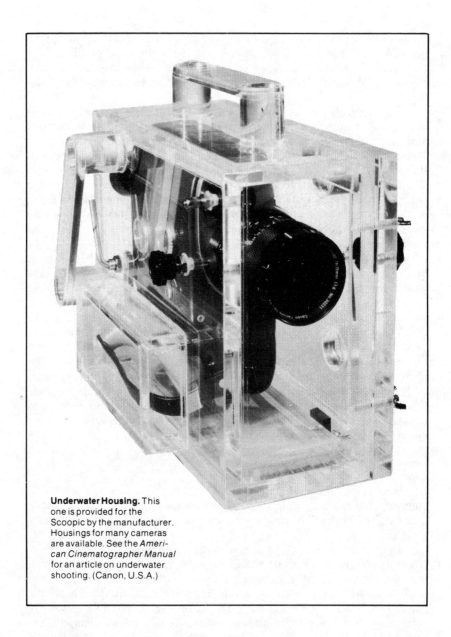

Underwater Housing. This one is provided for the Scoopic by the manufacturer. Housings for many cameras are available. See the *American Cinematographer Manual* for an article on underwater shooting. (Canon, U.S.A.)

Eclair NPR and ACL

The NPR was the first *unblimped* low-noise reflex camera designed for lip sync single or double system shooting. It attacks the problem at its source: its mechanism is quiet. In the past years it has become an increasingly familiar sight at news events, or wherever documentary

Independent Filmmaking

filmmakers tend to gather. The camera rests on the shoulder, and may be easily held for long periods of time, I am told by some people who have used it. I find it awkward to handle and painful to hold for any length of time. It has many features and many accessories. Although the camera has a good reputation, the smaller and lighter model ACL is a more advanced design.

In fact, the ACL II is so much lighter weight, easier to use, more pleasant to hand-hold and in just about every conceivable way a more pleasant machine, that unless you know something I don't, there's no reason to consider the NPR. A beautiful camera, a good viewfinder, an interesting design—and it runs quiet and accepts both two hundred- and four hundred-foot coaxial magazines.

Kodak

The K-100 is spring driven at speeds from 16 to 64 fps. One wind of the *prestressed* spring will run forty feet of film, or one minute seven seconds running time at 24 fps—the longest-running spring-wound motor of any camera. It will accept accessory electric-drive motors, and it takes one hundred-foot spool loads.

The camera has a three-lens turret that uses C mount lenses and mounts finder lenses as well. Rotation of the turret will position both taking and finder objectives. The direct optical finder of the K-100 is the best I have ever used: large, bright, crisp, and has lines surrounding the picture area so that subject matter adjacent to the frame, or about to move into the frame, can be observed. It uses an etched line as a guide for parallax compensation when focusing close. Although this is a fudge, it does work well and has the advantage of eliminating the extra step required to manually set other kinds of parallax compensation devices.

Like other optical finder cameras, its usefulness will be greatly extended if it is used with a zoom lens offering a built-in reflex viewing system. This is a good, sturdy camera that is backed up by an extensive service organization. The only drawback, of the particular camera that I used, was that the frame line position shifted slightly with different fps settings.

I should mention one other drawback. The camera I used had termites in it and in its case. So check your K-100 for insect infestation.

Pathé

Pathé cameras have very complete features. The last Pathé (the previous model) I used was quite different, so it is not really possible to draw upon that experience for this description; but that camera was awful. It had terrible registration, and it was awkward to hold by hand.

The PR/BTL uses one hundred-foot spools and accepts a four hundred-foot accessory magazine. The finder system is of the reflex type, and it uses a pellicule to divert a portion of the light to the finder system. Like the

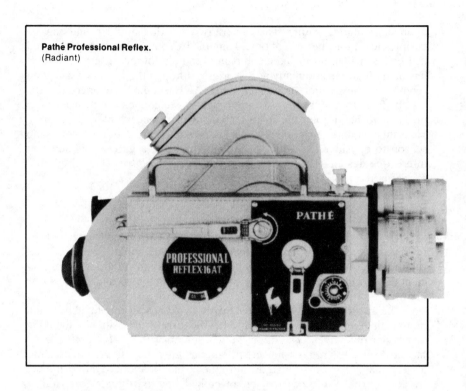

Pathé Professional Reflex.
(Radiant)

Bolex, this results in a flickerless finder image. A through-the-lens exposure meter measures light passing through the lens, and the proper *f* stop is selected by aligning a needle to a cut-out located in the finder as the diaphragm is moved. Threading is automatic.

The camera has a three-lens turret that accepts C mount lenses. It has a variable shutter, and spring motor with speeds ranging from 8 to 80 fps, with a twenty-two-foot run. An accessory electric-drive motor is available. The camera allows for backwinding. A pistol grip, matte box and other accessories are available. The double super 8 version of this camera is known as the DS8/BTL. Electric-drive versions of these cameras are available.

Repairs and Service

Camera repair and service is a grim problem, an opinion based on sad experiences with my cameras (and projectors, and especially tape recorders). Conversations with other filmmakers on the subject of repairs are usually an exchange of horror stories. Although distributors and manufacturers of equipment have the most at stake, and some of them do a good job, many of the really fine repairmen work for themselves in their own shops.

Unless made under the original guarantee, even the smallest repair can cost $50, and you must be prepared to spend at least that much every year

Independent Filmmaking

to adequately service your camera—which really isn't that much to keep a good machine running. After a few years of use it's not at all unusual to discover that you've spent many hundreds of dollars servicing your camera. What is unusual is getting the machine repaired in under a month, and getting the job done right.

The Lens

Basic Optics

One of the constructs (or models) that scientists use to explain the nature of light, is that light is propagated in the form of a wave, traveling in a straight line from the source of origin. For our purposes this statement is essentially correct for light traveling through a medium like space or air. But when light travels from one medium to another, from air to glass or to water, its rate of propagation through that medium changes. Light travels through air or space at about 186,000 miles a second; it loses about one third of that velocity through glass.

The fact that light is a wave phenomenon and that it travels at different speeds through different media accounts for the fact that light is bent as it moves from one medium to another.

When light travels from air to glass, it is bent towards the normal. The normal is a line drawn perpendicular to the surface at the point where the light enters or leaves. Light is always bent toward the normal when it enters a denser medium. This process of light bending is called *refraction*. Each transparent medium can be assigned a number, determined experimentally, which serves to indicate how much that medium will bend light. This number is called the *index of refraction*. The index of refraction of air, with respect to a vacuum, is 1.0003, so that its value may be taken as unity, for most purposes. Water has an index of refraction of 1.334, diamond 2.419 and crown glass, sometimes used for lenses, has an index of 1.517.

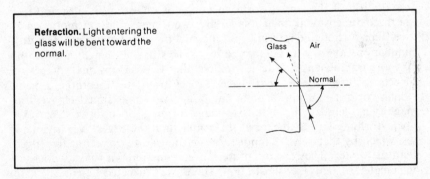

Refraction. Light entering the glass will be bent toward the normal.

Newton and the Prism

Newton's famous experiment with a prism showed that sunlight, or what we call white light, after passing through the prism, is made up of a combination of colors, or a spectrum of light. This phenomenon has important implications for lens design. It actually demonstrates that each color of light is refracted a different amount.

A simple lens can be thought to be two prisms placed end to end. In this case, and in the case of simple lenses made with spherical surfaces, white light cannot be focused at one point. The changes in refrac-

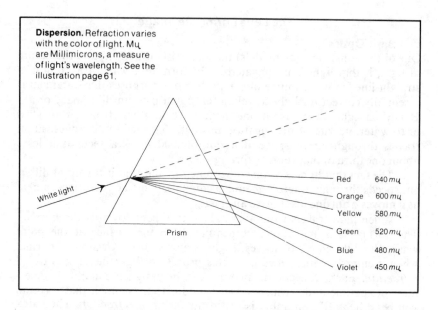

Dispersion. Refraction varies with the color of light. Mμ are Millimicrons, a measure of light's wavelength. See the illustration page 61.

White light

Prism

Red	640 mμ
Orange	600 mμ
Yellow	580 mμ
Green	520 mμ
Blue	480 mμ
Violet	450 mμ

tion of light for different color — or wavelength — which is actually a decrease in the index of refraction as we go towards the red end of the spectrum is called *dispersion.*

The Simple Lens

It is the job of the lens to form an image of objects. While the objects are three dimensional, their images are two dimensional on motion picture film. Although depth in a motion picture may be suggested in any number of ways, the image formed by the lens has but height and width. A photographic lens is a device for creating two dimensional images of objects in three dimensional space. A lens translates the three dimensional world it *sees* into a point for point two dimensional effigy. The magnifying lens is the simplest image-forming or positive lens. An image-forming lens is thicker at the center than the edges. Negative lenses, which by themselves cannot form an image, are thicker at the edges than the center. They are often used in conjunction with positive lenses in complex systems (see illustration, The Basic Corrected Lens).

Focal Length

The focal length of a lens is a fundamental quantity that determines the size of the image. The focal length of a simple positive lens, like a magnifying glass, is easily determined. It is the distance from the center of the lens, along the lens axis (the line running through the center of the lens) to the point at which a sharply focused image is formed by an object at a great distance. For example, if the distance from a magnifying lens to its focused image of the sun is three inches, the lens has a focal length of three inches.

Independent Filmmaking

Because most lenses used in filmmaking are made up of many pieces of glass (called *elements*), the center of the complex lens isn't as immediately obvious as the center of a simple lens. Usually the *optical center* is located roughly midway between the front and rear elements; its *principal point* can be thought of as equivalent to the geometric center of the simple lens. *Focal length* is defined in terms of the distance from the principal point to the image point.

Image Magnification

The longer the focal length of a lens, the larger the projected image size. The image size, or the length of one dimension of the image, is

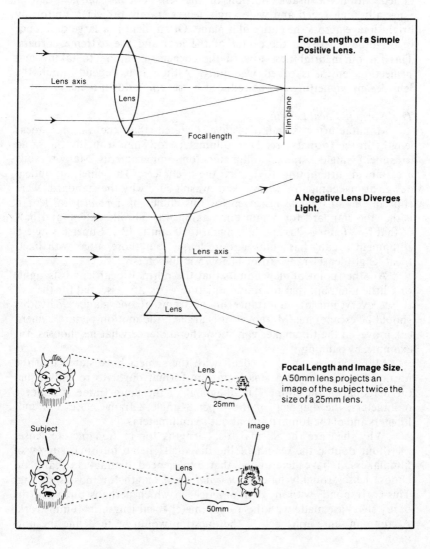

Focal Length of a Simple Positive Lens.

A Negative Lens Diverges Light.

Focal Length and Image Size. A 50mm lens projects an image of the subject twice the size of a 25mm lens.

The Lens

proportional to the focal length. For example, suppose an image of a house on the frame of a 16mm camera is one millimeter high, when filmed with a ten millimeter lens. If the camera isn't moved, and we substitute a hundred millimeter lens, the image size will now be ten times the height, or ten millimeters. The most basic use of lenses of different focal lengths, then, is to vary the size, or magnification, of the image.

Coverage

A lens forms a circular image; the shape of the exposed motion picture frame is very nearly square. The frame's dimensions are contained within the usable portion of the lens' circular image. Lenses, especially high speed and wide angle lenses, rarely project a uniformly bright image across the entire film plane. Often there is a large difference in brightness between the center of the lens and the extreme corners. This fall-off in brightness toward the corners, common to taking and projecting lenses, is called *vignetting*. Although it depends upon the lens design, vignetting can be reduced by stopping down the aperture.

The 'Normal' Focal Length

Manufacturing standards have dictated that the *normal* focal lengths in the formats are: 12.5 millimeters for 8mm, roughly the same for super 8-single 8, and 25 millimeters for 16mm cameras. Many reasons are offered, attempting to justify these choices. The chief of optical design at one company, when asked, wasn't sure why the standards were chosen. One of the reasons given for this choice of *normal* focal length is that the standard for 35mm filmmaking was 50 millimeters, and half of that for 16mm is 25, and half again for 8mm is 12.5. Super 8-single 8 equipment usually has built-in zoom lenses, but those fitted with fixed focal length lenses range from 11 to 15 millimeters.

Another point of view admits that the normal focal length is tight, or a little long, but that for motion picture work it is essential for the eye to see everything of importance in the frame at one glance. Why this should be escapes me. Moreover, it is argued, the motion picture camera can move, so the filmmaker can show the audience what he chooses, for example, by panning.

Many writers who have dealt with the subject have stated that the normal focal length of a lens for a film format ought to roughly equal the diagonal of the frame. The diagonal of the 8mm frame is about 6 millimeters, the diagonal of the super 8-single 8 frame close to 7 millimeters and of the 16mm frame about 13 millimeters.

Why then are the normal focal lengths for motion picture lenses all about double the length of the diagonal? In an informal survey of filmmakers, I have determined that experienced filmmakers really do choose lenses roughly half the *normal* focal length for most shooting. This corresponds with my own practice, in which perhaps three fourths of my shots are made with the 10 millimeter focal length in 16mm work. A common sense approach to the question would be to define the nor-

Angle of View and Focal Length. To find the horizontal angle of view, pick the focal length that interests you, and read the value from the curve for the appropriate format. For example, a 20 millimeter lens has a horizontal angle of view of 15° for the super 8 format. To obtain the vertical angle of view, multiply the horizontal by 0.75. For our example this would be about 11°. The angles of view are based on the projector aperture which is slightly smaller than the camera aperture.

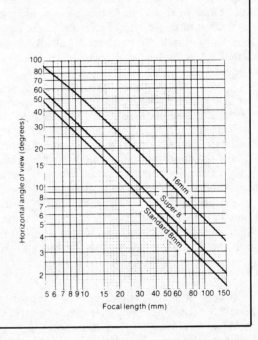

mal lens in terms of your own work. If you generally work with a 10 millimeter lens in 16mm, that's your normal lens.

Unfortunately, manufacturers do not manufacture many lens designs of focal lengths less than the diagonal of the frame. There are several lenses in the 5 to 6 millimeter category, for 16mm work, for example, but these cost as much as many a good camera body. Zoom lenses in all formats rarely zoom to decently wide angle focal lengths.

One motion picture lens design problem is that the back focus (distance from the rear element to the film plane) must be rather long, to clear the turret and viewfinder prism or mirror. It is difficult to design high speed lenses in short focal lengths if the rear element isn't fairly close to the film. But in recent years film speed has greatly increased, and filmmakers may be willing to sacrifice some speed for the sake of a reasonably priced wide angle lens. Certainly the designs exist. They have been employed for several years now in 35mm single lens reflex cameras for lenses with focal lengths approximately half, or less than half the 35mm still frame's diagonal.

Wide and Long Lenses

Once we've established what we mean by a 'normal' lens, we can go on and talk about wide and long focal length lenses. A wide angle lens,

The Lens

or a wide field lens, or a lens of short focal length, covers a greater angle of view than the normal lens. For example, a 12.5 millimeter lens for 16mm work will have twice the vertical and horizontal angle of view of a 25 millimeter lens. From the same camera distance, a subject will be recorded half the height it would have with a lens of twice the focal length. A wide lens will cover more of the subject, or put more of it on the frame.

These terms, wide *angle,* wide field, short focal length, have more or less precise slightly *differing* definitions; but in general usage the terms are interchangeable. Similarly, the terms long lens, long focal length lens and telephoto lens are used pretty much interchangeably. It will be explained that there are technical differences between a long lens and a telephoto lens, but the important thing about such lenses is that they have a focal length greater than the standard lens, and so magnify the subject. The linear dimensions of the image will be magnified in direct proportion to the focal length. Shooting a subject with a 50 millimeter lens at ten feet results in the same size image on the film as shooting with a 25 millimeter lens at five feet. A long focal length lens will show only a portion of the subject shown by a normal lens.

Sharpness

It is very difficult to describe what appears to be a sharp image in objectively measurable physical quantities. (If you recall, we had the same problem evaluating the quality for film.) The most recent attempt to evaluate definition in photographic systems has been the introduction of the modulation-transfer curves (see chapter 2, *The Film*). I'm not sure that this approach makes the subject more meaningful to the filmmaker, even if it may satisfy lens designers, engineers and technicians.

Prior to the introduction of modulation-transfer functions, lenses were tested by exposing high resolution film to a target of ruled lines. Presumably, defining the sharpness of the lens is closely related to the number of lines that the lens can record on a given area of film. Such a test is called a *resolution test,* determining the *resolving power* of the lens. In order to give sharp images for large screen projection, the 16mm lens should be able to resolve about one hundred lines per millimeter.

As it turns out, it's possible for a lens to have high tested resolution, and still produce pictures that may not look sharp. A lens produces sharp pictures if it has sufficient resolving power *and* can form a suitably contrasty image. But the sharpness of the image, as it is finally projected on the screen, is a function of many factors besides the quality of the taking lens. So, we must also consider the taking conditions, such as the use of filters, camera shake, film registration, quality of the film stock, processing of the film and procedures involved for making release prints. The quality of the projector used (its brightness is especially crucial) and even the surface of the screen are also factors that contribute to the apparent sharpness of the image.

Lens Speed

The term *speed* is often used to express the light-gathering facility, or light-gathering power, of a lens. A fast lens makes available a lot of light for exposures. A slow lens makes relatively little light available.

To help make the proper exposure, lenses are marked with *f* numbers or stops. The same *f* numbers, on any two lenses of any manufacturer, design or focal length, theoretically have the same speed. The *f* stop is the ratio between the focal length and the diameter of the lens. A lens that has a focal length of 25 millimeters, and an effective maximum diameter of 12.5 millimeters, has a maximum stop of *f*/2. Just as the determination of the focal length is less than straightforward for a complex lens system, it is also difficult to judge the effective diameter simply by looking at it.

The pupil of the eye increases or decreases in diameter with varying lighting conditions; similarly, it is possible to vary the size of the effective diameter of the lens. Most lenses accomplish this with an iris diaphragm made up of moveable segments; these form circular openings of different diameters depending upon what value the filmmaker chooses for the *f* stop. Varying the diameter, or aperture, changes the *f* stop.

The *f* stop is usually selected by moving a ring on the lens mount. Lenses are usually calibrated so that each successive turning of the ring admits either one half or twice as much light. Since there is no standardization of direction in which the aperture or diaphragm ring ought to be turned, this will vary with the manufacturer. But a line of lenses will conform to the same standard. Nearly all lenses made for many years have these markings in the following sequence:

1, 1.4, 2, 2.8, 4, 5.6, 8, 11, 16, 22, 32, 45, 64

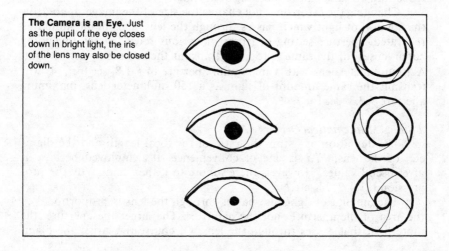

The Camera is an Eye. Just as the pupil of the eye closes down in bright light, the iris of the lens may also be closed down.

The Lens

The lens may not have all these markings, especially those at either end of the scale. The maximum openings of many lenses for motion picture use are comparatively high, especially for short and intermediate focal lengths, say from 10 to 50 millimeters for 16mm work. Openings are on the order of $f/0.95$ to $f/2$.

Moving from numerically low values for f to high values decreases the light transmitted by the lens. Half the exposure of $f/2$ is $f/2.8$, $f/4$ is a quarter the exposure and $f/5.6$ is an eighth the exposure of $f/2$. Moving from the high to low values of f is an increase in the amount of light passing through the lens. For example, $f/5.6$ is twice the exposure of $f/8$, and so on. It's also possible to set a lens for intermediate values of f that aren't marked. If the lens is set at $f/2$ and we want to cut the exposure in third, we could set the diaphragm for a value between $f/2.8$ and $f/4$, or to about $f/3.5$.

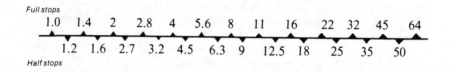

Full stops

| 1.0 | 1.4 | 2 | 2.8 | 4 | 5.6 | 8 | 11 | 16 | 22 | 32 | 45 | 64 |

| 1.2 | 1.6 | 2.7 | 3.2 | 4.5 | 6.3 | 9 | 12.5 | 18 | 25 | 35 | 50 |

Half stops

Remember, the larger the f number, the less light the lens transmits. Many people find this strange at first, because they associate a high number with a lot of light. But the definition of f stop, the ratio of focal length to aperture, indicates that the value of f must increase as the diameter decreases.

The most obvious effect of changing the f stop is the change in the light level reaching the frame. The filmmaker may alter the exposure by changing the f stop to suit lighting conditions, or he can also change the fps setting, variable shutter opening or use filters.

Changing the f stop does not change the size of the image. It controls the amount of light which passes through the lens. This point should be reiterated: aperture setting of lenses of various focal lengths (including zoom lenses) of the same f stop will transmit the same amount of light. A 10 millimeter lens with a maximum aperture of $f/1.8$, set for $f/4$, will transmit the same amount of light as a 150 millimeter lens, maximum aperture $f/3.3$, set for $f/4$.

f Stop's Mathematical Origin

The definition of f stop, the ratio of the focal length and the diameter of the lens, F/d, is one of convenience. It's employed because it gives useful values. However, there's more to it than that. Why the progression 1, 1.4, 2, 2.8, etc.?

The amount of light that passes through the lens is proportional to the area of the aperture, not the diameter. The larger the aperture, the more light that passes through the lens. Of course the larger the diameter of the aperture the greater the area. Now area is a function of diameter. The formula for the area of a circle is πr^2. We're interested in the diameter, which is twice the radius, so we'll use the formula in this form: $\pi (\frac{d}{2})^2$, or for our purposes, more simply: $\frac{\pi}{4}d^2$.

Let's suppose we double d, the diameter. In such a case we'd have four times, not double, the area since d is squared, or multiplied by itself, or four times the light will pass through the lens. What number could we use instead of 2 to increase the diameter of the circle by a factor of 2? The answer is the square root of two, or $\sqrt{2}$, for $(\sqrt{2})^2$ is 2. $\sqrt{2}$ is approximately equal to 1.4. Now our progression becomes more meaningful. By multiplying or dividing each f number by $\sqrt{2}$ we obtain the next f number.

T Stops

The definition of f stop needs the following qualification: light losses caused by reflection from air to glass surfaces in the lens must be accounted for. In complex lenses, this can amount to a stop, or more. Lenses used for professional motion picture work are often calibrated with T (for transmission) stops. The T stop is actually the *effective f* stop, since it takes into consideration these light losses in the lens system. For example, if a lens that *loses* half the light passing through it were set for, say, $f/8$, it would have a value of $T/11$.

Antireflection coatings for most lens systems have reduced the need for T stops, by making the difference between these and f stops negligible. The introduction of zoom lenses, with many air to glass surfaces, makes the T stop system more interesting.

Minimum Aperture Setting

Lens designers have had a difficult time designing good quality lenses with very large or very small apertures. The theoretical upper limit to lens speed is $f/0.5$. There is a theoretical limit to the other end of the f stop scale as well. For very small diaphragm openings, diffraction sets in.

Diffraction

Ordinarily, light rays can be said to travel in straight lines. When light passes from one transparent medium to another, with a different index of refraction, it travels in straight lines, even if it may make abrupt changes in direction. Light will no longer travel in straight lines when it passes through an opening whose dimensions are comparable to the wave length of light itself. Rather it will spread out from such an opening. This phenomenon is called *diffraction*. In fact, diffraction may not cause most of the problems with small diaphragm openings. They are essentially mechanical. It's very hard to manufacture iris diaphragms which can be calibrated for small openings accurately. In practice, movie lenses stop down to from $f/16$ to $f/32$, depending upon focal length, with the smallest openings usually reserved for lenses with long focal lengths.

The Lens

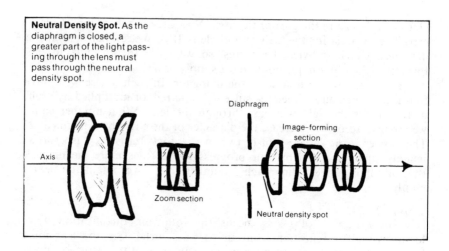

Neutral Density Spot. As the diaphragm is closed, a greater part of the light passing through the lens must pass through the neutral density spot.

Axis

Zoom section

Diaphragm

Image-forming section

Neutral density spot

Neutral Density Spot

The introduction of high speed quality film stock makes the use of small diaphragm openings increasingly attractive. Kodak first introduced an 8mm camera that pointed to a solution to this problem, and Bell & Howell and Zeiss, in their original super 8 cameras, developed the idea.

By coating a semitransparent metallic spot on the lens surface (like that used for a beam splitter or pellicule coating) immediately behind the iris diaphragm, some light can be transmitted. The spot has a small diameter when compared to the maximum aperture of the lens. For large lens openings, an insignificant amount of light is influenced by this *neutral density spot*. As the iris diaphragm gets smaller, the spot holds back more of the light. Past a certain point, such a lens needs to be calibrated so that the f stops actually read on a scale would be effective f stops, or in fact, T stops. If the camera uses a closed-loop servo type through-the-lens automatic diaphragm, the system is self-calibrating, since the BTL metering system sees the light that actually passes through the lens. It doesn't know the difference between real and effective f stops.

Depth of field will not increase beyond a certain point, since it is determined by the actual f stop, and not the T stop. Some of the Bell & Howell cameras stop down to $T/64$ which actually corresponds to an f stop of about $f/11$. More manufacturers should think about adopting this device because of the importance of controlling the amount of light which passes through the lens at either end of the f stop scale.

Aberration

Aberrations play a part in any lens; in fact, every lens must have aberration. If a lens were perfect, it would project an image of three dimen-

Independent Filmmaking

sional space that would be a point for point two dimensional representation of whatever it was 'seeing.' Departures from this perfect image are
called *lens aberration.*

The success of a lens design can be measured only in terms of purpose. The present stage of the technology comes very close to allowing
aberrations to be controlled or suppressed. It is not that new and fundamental laws of optics have been discovered, but rather that high speed
computers, new optical glasses, knowing designers and better manufacturing techniques have refined lenses used in filmmaking to an amazing
degree. Modern photographic lenses can be, practically speaking, free
of aberration. One value this discussion of aberration can have, is not
only to help you spot lens flaws, but also to appreciate the beautiful and
unusual effects that result from less than perfectly *corrected* lenses.

Color fringing, bowed horizontal and vertical lines, weird patterns,
hazy images, can all be achieved through lenses rich with aberration.
Such lenses can be purchased used, or existing lenses can be modified,
by removal of an element, for example; one of the best sources of aber-
ration-inducing images is the dime-store magnifying glass (glass or
plastic). Mounted at the end of extension tubes, or a cardboard roll of a
suitable length, such a simple lens can produce unexpectedly desirable
effects.

Chromatic Aberration

Newton believed that it was impossible to correct *dispersion*—color
fringing— or *chromatic aberration,* as it is called when applied to lens
design. He thought a refracting telescope (one with lenses) could not be
corrected to suppress the halo or rainbow of color surrounding an image
point, in his case a star.

Newton was wrong. It soon was possible to correct such telescopes
or lenses. It was the most important discovery in lens design—that led,
in the early nineteenth century, to the use of more than one lens in an
image-forming system. A concave, or negative, lens which would
'spread' the light, rather than bring it to focus at a point, was added to
an image-forming lens, producing a simple lens system. The negative
lens (thinner at the middle than at the edges), was made of highly dispersive flint glass. In conjunction with the positive, or image-forming,
lens of crown glass (a lower dispersive material), a lens system was
organized that had less chromatic aberration than any lens that preceded it.

When several lenses are used in an image-forming system, each is
called an *element.* This simple two-element lens design was the precursor of all subsequent lenses, which often use seven or more elements for
correction of aberration.

Spherical Aberration

In the case of chromatic aberration, the simple lens, with spherical
surfaces, was unable to bring light of many colors to focus at one point.

Spherical aberration is the inability of the lens to focus rays of light of the same color to a point. As we move off the axis, or away from the center of the lens, the light is bent more than at the center. While chromatic aberration would show itself by fringes of color, spherical aberration results in fuzzy images. Luckily the cure for spherical aberration is the same as that for chromatic aberration, namely the use of appropriately designed negative lenses used with the image-forming lens.

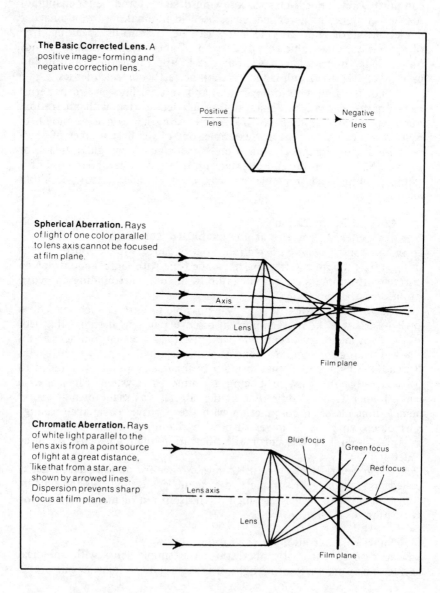

The Basic Corrected Lens. A positive image-forming and negative correction lens.

Positive lens

Negative lens

Spherical Aberration. Rays of light of one color parallel to lens axis cannot be focused at film plane.

Axis

Lens

Film plane

Chromatic Aberration. Rays of white light parallel to the lens axis from a point source of light at a great distance, like that from a star, are shown by arrowed lines. Dispersion prevents sharp focus at film plane.

Blue focus

Green focus

Red focus

Lens axis

Lens

Film plane

Independent Filmmaking

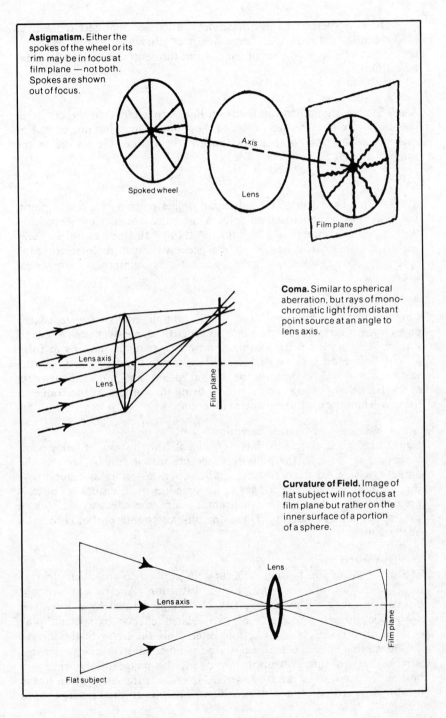

Astigmatism. Either the spokes of the wheel or its rim may be in focus at film plane — not both. Spokes are shown out of focus.

Axis

Spoked wheel

Lens

Film plane

Coma. Similar to spherical aberration, but rays of monochromatic light from distant point source at an angle to lens axis.

Lens axis

Lens

Film plane

Curvature of Field. Image of flat subject will not focus at film plane but rather on the inner surface of a portion of a sphere.

Lens

Lens axis

Film plane

Flat subject

The Lens

The two aberrations that have been discussed manifest themselves at the center of the image. There are five other aberrations which, if present, can be seen off axis or away from the central portion of the exposed film.

Astigmatism
A lens with astigmatism can focus on lines either radial to the center of the lens, or on lines perpendicular to these radial lines, but not both. For example, when photographing a spoked wheel either the spokes or the rim, not both, can be in sharp focus.

Coma
The failure of the lens to reproduce an object point as a circular point, but rather as a comet-shaped splotch, is called coma. Coma produces blurring in the corners of the frame. Although this aberration is easily corrected in many lens designs, it is especially difficult to correct in high speed or wide angle lenses. Coma is the off-axis counterpart of spherical aberration.

Curvature of Field
This would be no problem, if the photographic emulsion were coated on a concave surface. A simple lens will focus sharply over such a curved surface. The motion picture camera, however, requires the lens to form a sharp image on a plane surface. A lens which is uncorrected for curvature of field will be sharp in the central region, but blur at the corners of the frame. Adjusting such a lens to bring the corners of the frame to focus will blur the central portion of the frame.

Transverse Chromatic Aberration
Sometimes this is also called lateral chromatic aberration, or color magnification error. Like the preceding aberrations, it can be seen at the corners or sides of the frame. This aberration is visible as color fringing. With color film, the fringes or color edges will, naturally, be colored; with black and white panchromatic film, the effect would still be present as a kind of blurring. This is the off-axis counterpart of chromatic aberration.

Distortion
The word distortion is often inaccurately applied to the other aberrations, and confused with perspective distortion. Aberrations are not distortions. They are always part of the image formed by a lens. The aberration *distortion* consists of two related effects: barrel and pincushion distortion. These distortions affect only the shape of the image.

Assuming that the lens axis is perpendicular to a chart of ruled straight lines, if this aberration is present, the image of the lines will bow either outward or inward. *Barrel distortion* is the name given to the bowing outward effect, and *pin-cushion distortion* to the bowing inward

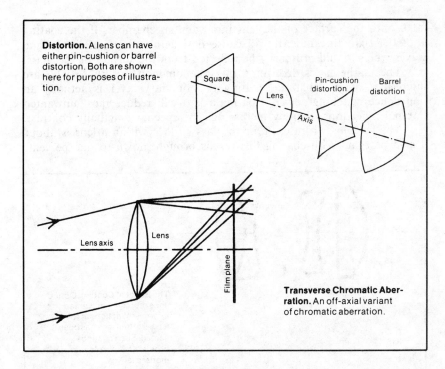

Distortion. A lens can have either pin-cushion or barrel distortion. Both are shown here for purposes of illustration.

Square

Lens

Axis

Pin-cushion distortion

Barrel distortion

Lens axis

Lens

Film plane

Transverse Chromatic Aberration. An off-axial variant of chromatic aberration.

effect. Some small amount of this distortion is tolerable, but the effect can become annoying when shooting a subject with straight lines, like a building.

Aberration and *f* Stop

No simple statement can be made about the relationship between aberration and aperture setting. However, the aberrations which vary with *f* stop improve with stopping down the lens. Spherical aberration and coma will decrease as the size of the aperture decreases, or if you like, as the numerical value of the *f* stop increases. Astigmatism will improve as well, and curvature of field will become relatively unimportant as the lens is stopped down, because its effect will be masked by increased depth of focus.

Antireflection Coatings

The light which is internally reflected by a lens, and consequently not available for image-forming, does eventually reach the film. Rather than helping to form the image, it produces an overall exposure which tends to reduce the contrast of the image. For most purposes, this background *noise,* or fog, is undesirable.

For many years, manufacturers have been *coating* their lenses so that the glass to air surfaces have a *surface film* of extremely thin material, such as calcium or magnesium fluoride. This material is evapo-

The Lens

rated onto the surface of the lens in a vacuum chamber. If the coating is of the right thickness, it will cause destructive interference of light waves which would ordinarily be reflected from the surface of the glass.

The mathematics describing this phenomenon, for those who are interested, suggest that the coating or boundary layer is actually an impedence matching device. Coating a lens will reduce most unwanted internal reflections, thereby increasing lens speed, or actually contrast.

The light loss from each air to glass surface within a lens is about 4 or 5 percent. With coating this loss is brought down to one percent.

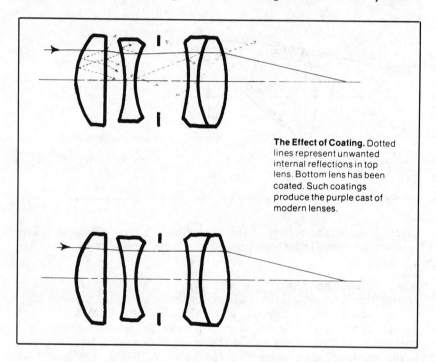

The Effect of Coating. Dotted lines represent unwanted internal reflections in top lens. Bottom lens has been coated. Such coatings produce the purple cast of modern lenses.

Optics with many air to glass surfaces, like high speed lenses, or wide angle retrofocus designs or zoom lenses, profit greatly from this coating. Without coating these lenses can lose a full stop. With coating most lenses lose an unnoticeable quarter of a stop or less. However, some complex designs, especially zoom lenses, can still lose from half to a full stop even with coating.

In addition to light losses within the lens, spurious reflections can produce overall fogging or flair. When shooting into a bright light, like the sun, with the subject backlit, there will be a terrific amount of flair in addition to spotty internal reflections. Coating helps to suppress these effects. But complex designs with many air to glass surfaces, like zoom lenses, may still have a great deal of flair.

Independent Filmmaking

In order to improve both the light transmission and reduce the flair of complex lenses, some manufacturers are now offering multiple coatings. Three (or more) carefully controlled layers instead of one are deposited on the air to glass surface. These *high efficiency* coatings can drastically reduce flair and reduce light losses to better than ½ percent for each air to glass surface.

Complex Lenses

It is simpler to design well corrected sharp slow speed lenses, in any focal length, than well corrected (relatively aberration-free) sharp high speed lenses. As the speed of a lens increases, it is usually necessary to increase the number of elements in the construction. Perfectly good three-element movie lenses for the *normal* focal lengths in speeds from

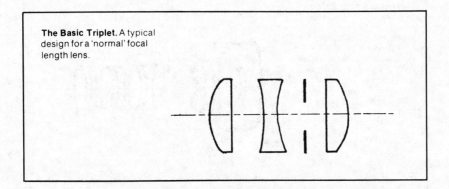

The Basic Triplet. A typical design for a 'normal' focal length lens.

$f/1.9$ to $f/3.5$ have been produced. Many of these lenses appear to be sharper or crisper than their high speed counterparts, because they produce images of higher contrast. They are also cheaper to manufacture.

In order to correct aberration and maintain sharp images, high speed lenses usually have to use at least double the number of elements. Although good modern high speed lenses are well corrected wide opened, that is they are free of aberration and are sharp, most lenses are at their best closed down two stops or so, less than the maximum aperture. For example, a good $f/1.4$ 25 millimeter lens might become a really fine performer stopped down three stops to $f/4$. This is a usual pattern for lens performance. Some filmmakers will want to know when their lenses are at their optimum stop. You can find this out for yourself by simply shooting a subject at various stops. Typically the above lens might remain at its best from $f/4$ to $f/11$, with quality beginning to fall off slightly at $f/16$, because of diffraction effects.

It is possible to correct chromatic and spherical aberration by using two or more lenses to make an image-forming system. By choosing the proper combination of many *elements,* or individual lenses, it is possible

The Lens

to correct nearly all aberration. Optical designers have the choice of varying the radius of the lens surfaces, which is usually the section of a sphere, or of using glasses of different dispersion and indexes of refraction. In recent years, they have chosen glass containing rare-earth ingredients, such as lanthanum, and most recently crystalline fluorite—artificially grown crystals. Designers can also use nonspherical shapes, such as ellipses, parabolas or higher degree curves, for greater correction. While many kinds of glasses for elements have been used for a hundred years, difficulty in manufacturing lenses with nonspherical surfaces has severely restricted their use.

The elements of many designs are often cemented together, in groups of two or three, and a complex lens may be made up of several

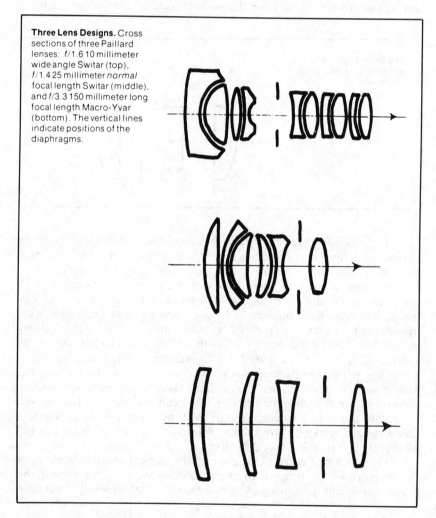

Three Lens Designs. Cross sections of three Paillard lenses: *f*/1.6 10 millimeter wide angle Switar (top), *f*/1.4 25 millimeter *normal* focal length Switar (middle), and *f*/3.3 150 millimeter long focal length Macro-Yvar (bottom). The vertical lines indicate positions of the diaphragms.

such groups. It is not at all unusual to find photographic objectives with six or seven separate lenses, or pieces of glass, in two or three groups.

Plastic objectives are not in general use, although there are several cameras of American manufacture that use plastic elements in their reflex viewfinder systems, and for the taking lenses in less expensive cameras. In these capacities, plastic works very well.

Lens Mount

The elements of any lens are mounted in a metal shell, called a mount or barrel, accurately positioned with respect to one another and to the film plane. The lens usually can vary its focus from very distant scenes, marked with the infinity sign ∞, to close subjects. Distance markings, calibrated in feet, meters or both, are adjacent to the rotating focusing collar or mount.

Some extremely short focal length lenses, or lenses used for very simple cameras, do not warrant the additional cost of a focusing mount, because it is felt by their designers that depth of field is sufficient at all *f* stops. A supplementary lens has to be used with such lenses for close-ups.

The majority of lenses, however, do focus by one of two methods. Focusing is accomplished by rotating the focusing collar of the lens. In some cases the entire lens can be moved—within a shell in the mount— various distances from the film plane, corresponding to subject distance. The best mounts of this kind are called *helical* mounts in which the front of the lens does not rotate as it is focused, and accessories such as a polarizing filter or a squared lens hood maintain their proper orientation. In addition, the *f* stop and focusing scales remain in a fixed position on the mount. In the second focusing method, the entire lens may rotate in a simple *screw* mount, bringing the lens closer or farther away from the film plane.

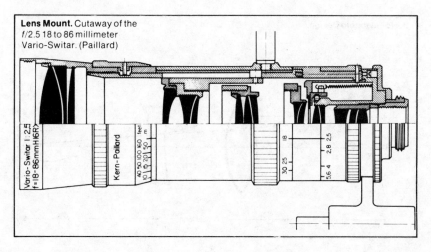

Lens Mount. Cutaway of the f/2.5 18 to 86 millimeter Vario-Switar. (Paillard)

The shorter the focal length, the closer the lens usually focuses in its mount. Wide angle lenses may focus to within a foot or less, whereas normal focal length lenses can focus to a foot or two; long focal length lenses can be focused to several feet—as a rule.

Zoom lenses, and a few fixed focal length lenses, focus by moving a front component—group or element—while the rest of the lens remains fixed. The front focusing section is usually rotated in a simple screw mount. As a rule, zoom lenses do not focus as close as their fixed focal length counterparts.

The term lens mount can have another meaning: in order to make lenses interchangeable from camera body to body, standardization of the method of mounting lenses has been adopted by most manufacturers. Although such standardization is neither complete nor compulsory, it has been fairly thorough.

For 16mm and super 8 cameras, the standard mount—a screw mount —is called the 'C' mount, and most 16mm cameras conform to this standard. Several bayonet mount series of lenses have also been offered. These lenses are simply put into place and firmly locked by a short rotation. Some Kodak cameras have accepted an 'S' type mount, and Arriflex cameras accept an 'A' bayonet mount. The standard screw mount of 8mm cameras is the 'D' screw mount.

Adapter Mounts

Many lenses for 35mm cameras may be used with movie cameras. Since the super 8 and 16mm standard mount thread is the C mount, it is necessary to obtain an adapter from whatever mount the lens was designed for, to the C mount. Such adapters are supplied by Cinema Beaulieu, Burke & James, and others. Adapters are available for Leica thread to C, Leica bayonet to C, Nikon to C, Pentax to C and so on. Quality 35mm lenses work very well for filmmaking. As it turns out, their focal lengths are generally rather long for our movie formats.

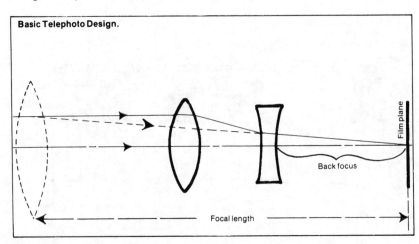

Basic Telephoto Design.

Film plane

Back focus

Focal length

Independent Filmmaking

Telephoto Lens

Lenses several times greater in focal length than the *normal* lens are generally called *telephoto* lenses. Technically this may be a mistake. There is a specific definition for a telephoto lens, based on its particular optical design, and not every lens of long focal length qualifies.

The true telephoto design has one specific advantage: it is shorter, that is physically more compact than a long lens of the same focal length. By using a negative rear element, spaced some distance away from the positive image-forming element, the telephoto design pushes the *optical center* of the lens forward, so that it will be in front of the positive image-forming element. This enables the telephoto lens to be mounted in a barrel shorter in length than its focal length would usually require.

Back Focus and the Retrofocus Lens

Back focus is defined as the distance from the rear glass surface of the lens to the film plane, when the lens is focused at infinity. Since the lens at infinity is closest to the film plane, the back focus specifies the nearest the rear element of the lens will come to the film.

Back focus is an important parameter in motion picture cameras, because the lens must not interfere with either the turret or the reflex viewfinder system. Because of the difficulty in designing wide angle lenses with a back focus long enough to satisfy these requirements, designers have come up with what is called the inverted or reversed telephoto, or *retrofocus* design.

Looking through a pair of binoculars the wrong way gives a wide angle view. This is an example of the inverted telephoto effect. In principle, such wide angle lenses are actually telephoto lenses turned wrong way 'round. In practice, however, retrofocus designs are more sophisticated than this.

Catadioptric Lens

Earlier, Newton's belief in the impossibility of correcting a refracting

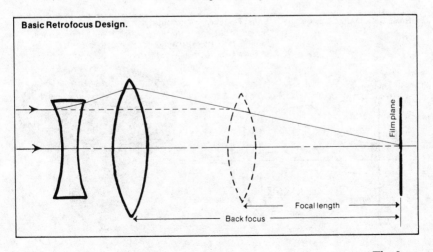

Basic Retrofocus Design.

The Lens

telescope was mentioned. It was this erroneous belief that lead to his discovery of the reflector telescope. Today this design is used for extremely long focal length lenses because it is appreciably more compact, both shorter and lighter in weight than conventional telephoto or long focal length designs. Such reflector telescope objectives, in their presently improved form, are known as *catadioptric* lenses. Although a few are provided specifically for 16mm, most work with 35mm single lens reflex still cameras, but may be adapted for the 16mm C mount movie camera.

In a catadioptric lens, after light passes through a correction plate or lens, it is reflected by a concave mirror to another mirror, mounted near or on the front correction lens. From the second mirror, the light passes through a hole in the concave mirror and through additional correction elements, to form the image.

These lenses are about the same speed as comparable long focal length lenses, say from $f/5.6$ to $f/11$, and range in focal lengths of from about 500 to 2000 millimeters. The lens may be focused, but it cannot be stopped down. The catadioptric lens does not have an iris diaphragm. In order to reduce the exposure, the filmmaker could use a different fps rate, a filter in a filter slot or the variable shutter. The lens itself usually comes equipped with several filters, mounted internally, which may be rotated into position.

Fisheye and Very Wide Lenses

The *fisheye* lens gets its name from the fact that it resembles the eye of a fish. Its very large front section precedes its image-forming section. A similar effect could be duplicated with an ordinary lens by shooting into a lawn reflector, or a mirror coated hemisphere. Fisheye lenses can be made to cover an amazingly great angular field.

The $f/1.9$, 1.9 millimeter Kinoptic (distributed by Karl Heitz) covers most of the 16mm frame, but produces an image with rounded edges. It actually sees behind itself. Its angular coverage is 197 degrees.

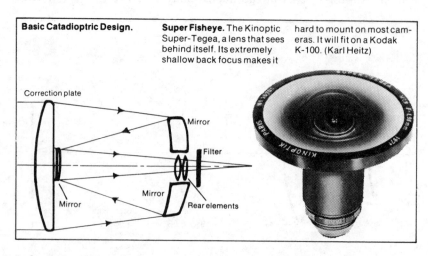

Basic Catadioptric Design.

Super Fisheye. The Kinoptic Super-Tegea, a lens that sees behind itself. Its extremely shallow back focus makes it hard to mount on most cameras. It will fit on a Kodak K-100. (Karl Heitz)

Correction plate

Mirror

Filter

Mirror

Mirror

Rear elements

Independent Filmmaking

There are a few very wide lenses for 16mm work. Two, a 5.9mm by Angenieux, and a 5.7mm by Kinoptik come to mind. They have a horizontal angle of view of about 90 degrees. Century Precision Optics also offers some interesting wide and fisheye lenses.

For the most part, there just aren't any very wide angle lenses for the super 8-single 8 format.

Zoom Lens

The zoom lens has been perfected only in recent years, in part because of legal battles concerning proprietary rights. Also, the use of computers for calculation has facilitated zoom lens design, as well as the design of fixed focal length lenses.

A *zoom lens* is capable of continuously varying the magnification of its image. From a fixed camera position, this enables the filmmaker to *zoom* in close to an important portion of the image, or to zoom away

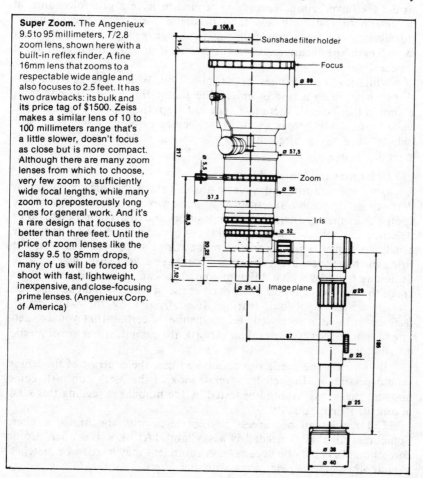

Super Zoom. The Angenieux 9.5 to 95 millimeters, *T*/2.8 zoom lens, shown here with a built-in reflex finder. A fine 16mm lens that zooms to a respectable wide angle and also focuses to 2.5 feet. It has two drawbacks: its bulk and its price tag of $1500. Zeiss makes a similar lens of 10 to 100 millimeters range that's a little slower, doesn't focus as close but is more compact. Although there are many zoom lenses from which to choose, very few zoom to sufficiently wide focal lengths, while many zoom to preposterously long ones for general work. And it's a rare design that focuses to better than three feet. Until the price of zoom lenses like the classy 9.5 to 95mm drops, many of us will be forced to shoot with fast, lightweight, inexpensive, and close-focusing prime lenses. (Angenieux Corp. of America)

The Lens

and show more area. At one time zoom lenses were used only when the zoom effect was an absolute necessity. Fixed focal length lenses, because of their superior quality and speed, were used wherever possible, and replaced the zoom lens when variable magnification was not needed.

Today there are many zoom lenses on the market with quality comparable to the best fixed focal length lenses. Typical zoom lenses for 8mm or super 8 equipment are in the 6 to 50 millimeter range. Double these focal lengths for the 16mm zoom lenses.

Most important, for design purposes and cost of the lens, is the zoom ratio, and the minimum rather than maximum focal length. Changing the short focal length a few millimeters more heavily influences the zoom ratio than changing the high end the same amount. If a lens zooms from a focal length of 8 to 64 millimeters, it has a zoom ratio of 8:1. If we change the specifications of the short focal length by just one millimeter to 7 to 64 millimeters, the ratio is now about 9:1. Probably, to attract the buyer, zoom lenses have tended to have a generous range in the telephoto end, with less than dramatic wide angle focal lengths. However, it has been more difficult to design zoom lenses with short focal length specifications, even though such designs are beginning to appear.

While the lens changes its magnification, which is usually accomplished by turning a ring or collar, the f stop should remain constant, as should the focus. If there is a shift in f stop, the exposure will change while zooming. If there is a shift in the focused distance, it will be impossible to keep the subject sharp while zooming. Most modern designs maintain focus and f stop.

Color Bias and Matched Lenses

A lens will not transmit all wavelengths of light with equal impartiality. Portions of the visible spectrum may be somewhat filtered. Depending upon the elements used, their composition and the color of the anti-reflection coating, each lens will have its own *color bias*. Such lenses are usually spoken of as being warm — emphasizing the red — or cold — emphasizing the blue; there are lenses which can have a yellowish tinge as well. Switching to a lens with a different color bias can be noticed if the shots are of the same subject, photographed at the same time and cut together. Usually lenses supplied in various focal lengths by the same manufacturer will match very well. To be absolutely certain that you are getting a matched set of lenses, you can ask the manufacturer or domestic distributor.

If you are concerned, also be advised that the contrast of the lenses should be similar. In fact, the overall look of the lens—contrast, color bias and sharpness—should be tested by the filmmaker seeking this kind of control of image quality.

Color bias can be successfully corrected with the use of a filter. Sometimes all that is needed is a skylight (1A) or a UV filter. Color correction filters may be necessary. A zoom lens may have to be matched to your other lenses, or vice versa, with such filters.

Independent Filmmaking

When a filmmaker focuses his lens on a subject at a certain distance, there will be a range of acceptably sharp focus in front of and behind this particular subject. Just how much is in focus, or what may be the extent of acceptable focus, becomes the definition of *depth of field*.

Depth of field, or the amount of depth of field, measured in space in front of the camera, is a measure of the extent of acceptably sharp focus. There are many rules pertaining to depth of field, and they will be presented here essentially as rules, with little substantiation in a formal sense; some appeal to intuition should be made to make the subject more comprehensible.

Necessary for the formal treatment of the subject is a definition of the term *circle of confusion*. For every point in space we have a corresponding projection of such a point on the film plane. The lens is, practically speaking, incapable of rendering the point in space as a perfect point on the film plane. In fact, this point will actually become a small circle. It is this circle that is given the terrible name, circle of confusion. The circle of *least confusion* is obtained when the lens is precisely focused for a subject a particular distance from the camera. By arbitrarily setting up a standard for the tolerable size of this circle of confusion for anything less than perfect focus, or the circle of least confusion, tables can be calculated which will give us the range of acceptable focus, or depth of field.

The size of the circle of confusion that we can accept is dependent on how we view the projected film. The closer the spectator is to the screen, the smaller the acceptable circle of confusion, and conversely, the farther away from the screen, the larger the acceptable circle of confusion. Experience bears this out. The greater the distance from any object, be it a projected motion picture image, a still photograph or a woman's face, the less flaws we see, the more perfect it appears.

Therefore, the choice of an acceptable maximum diameter for the circle of confusion is based upon the projected film as it is viewed by some hypothetical viewer, a certain distance from a screen of a certain size. The choice that has been made for the circle of confusion for 16mm is 0.001 inch, and for 8mm 0.0005 inch. The circle of confusion for super 8-single 8 would be very nearly that of 8mm, actually 0.00065 inch.

We've made two assumptions in this discussion, namely that we are dealing with essentially aberrationless lenses, and that the size of the grain of the film is much smaller than the circle of confusion. For most well made modern lenses the first assumption is valid, but with some 8mm or super 8-single 8 films, the grain size may approach the size of the circle of confusion, and therefore may set a limit on the actual depth of field.

For the time being, we are going to assume that we are discussing the depth of field of a particular format. Toward the end of this section, a comparison will be made of the depth of field relationships among the formats.

The Lens

Standard 8 Depth of Field Tables. (Eastman Kodak)

6.5mm Lens

Distance Focused On (in feet)		f/2.7		f/4		f/5.6		f/8		f/11		f/16	
		ft.	in.	ft.	in.	ft.	in.	ft.	in.	ft.	in.	ft.	in.
∞ (INF)	NEAR	4	⅜	2	8⅝	1	11⅜	1	4¼	0	11⅞	0	8⅛
	FAR	∞		∞		∞		∞		∞		∞	
25	NEAR	3	5¾	2	5½	1	9⅝	1	3½	0	11⅜	0	7⅞
	FAR	∞		∞		∞		∞		∞		∞	
15	NEAR	3	2¼	2	3⅝	1	8⅝	1	3	0	11⅛	0	7¾
	FAR	∞		∞		∞		∞		∞		∞	
10	NEAR	2	10½	2	1¾	1	7½	1	2⅜	0	10¾	0	7⅝
	FAR	∞		∞		∞		∞		∞		∞	
6	NEAR	2	5	1	10½	1	5⅝	1	1⅜	0	10⅛	0	7¼
	FAR	∞		∞		∞		∞		∞		∞	
4	NEAR	2	⅛	1	7½	1	3¾	1	¼	0	9½	0	7
	FAR	253	6⅝	∞		∞		∞		∞		∞	

9mm Lens

Distance Focused On (in feet)		f/2.7		f/4		f/5.6		f/8		f/11		f/16	
		ft.	in.	ft.	in.	ft.	in.	ft.	in.	ft.	in.	ft.	in.
∞ (INF)	NEAR	7	8⅞	5	2⅝	3	8¾	2	7⅜	1	10¾	1	3⅝
	FAR	∞		∞		∞		∞		∞		∞	
25	NEAR	5	11	4	3⅞	3	3	2	4⅜	1	9⅛	1	2⅞
	FAR	∞		∞		∞		∞		∞		∞	
15	NEAR	5	1⅜	3	10½	2	11⅞	2	2¾	1	8¼	1	2⅜
	FAR	∞		∞		∞		∞		∞		∞	
10	NEAR	4	4⅜	3	5¼	2	8⅝	2	⅞	1	7⅛	1	1⅞
	FAR	∞		∞		∞		∞		∞		∞	
6	NEAR	3	4⅝	2	9½	2	3⅝	1	9⅞	1	5⅜	1	⅞
	FAR	26	1½	∞		∞		∞		∞		∞	
4	NEAR	2	7⅝	2	3¼	1	11¼	1	7	1	3½	0	11⅞
	FAR	8	2⅜	16	7⅛	∞		∞		∞		∞	

13mm Lens

Distance Focused On (in feet)		f/2.7		f/4		f/5.6		f/8		f/11		f/16	
		ft.	in.	ft.	in.	ft.	in.	ft.	in.	ft.	in.	ft.	in.
∞ (INF)	NEAR	16	1⅝	10	10¾	7	9⅜	5	5¾	3	11½	2	8⅝
	FAR	∞		∞		∞		∞		∞		∞	
25	NEAR	9	9⅞	7	7¼	5	11⅜	4	5¾	3	5⅛	2	5½
	FAR	∞		∞		∞		∞		∞		∞	
15	NEAR	7	9½	6	3⅞	5	1⅝	4	0	3	1⅝	2	3¾
	FAR	∞		∞		∞		∞		∞		∞	
10	NEAR	6	2¼	5	2¾	4	4⅝	3	6⅜	2	10⅛	2	1¾
	FAR	26	¼	114	⅛	∞		∞		∞		∞	
6	NEAR	4	4½	3	10½	3	4¾	2	10⅜	2	4¾	1	9¼
	FAR	9	6	13	2¼	25	5¼	∞		∞		∞	
4	NEAR	3	2½	2	11⅛	2	7¾	2	3¾	2	0	1	7½
	FAR	5	3½	6	3¼	8	1⅜	14	6⅝	∞		∞	

Standard 8 Depth of Field Tables (continued).

30mm Lens

Distance Focused On (in feet)		f/2.7		f/4		f/5.6		f/8		f/11		f/16	
		ft.	in.	ft.	in.	ft.	in.	ft.	in.	ft.	in.	ft.	in.
∞ (INF)	NEAR	85	4½	57	9⅜	41	4⅛	28	11⅝	21	1	14	6
	FAR	∞		∞		∞		∞		∞		∞	
50	NEAR	31	7¾	26	10¾	22	8⅜	18	4¾	14	10½	11	3¼
	FAR	118	10⅞	∞		∞		∞		∞		∞	
25	NEAR	19	4⅝	17	6	15	7½	13	5½	11	5⅝	9	2½
	FAR	35	2	43	8¾	62	5½	174	7¼	∞		∞	
15	NEAR	12	9⅜	11	11¼	11	⅜	9	10⅞	8	9½	7	4¾
	FAR	18	1⅝	20	2	23	4¾	30	9⅜	50	10⅛	∞	
10	NEAR	8	11½	8	6½	8	⅞	7	5⅛	6	9⅝	5	11¼
	FAR	11	3½	12	⅝	13	1½	15	2	18	9¾	31	4⅝
6	NEAR	5	7⅜	5	5¼	5	3	4	11¾	4	8¼	4	3⅛
	FAR	6	5¼	6	8⅛	6	11⅞	7	3¼	8	3⅞	10	1⅛
4	NEAR	3	9⅞	3	8⅞	3	7⅞	3	6¼	3	4½	3	1¾
	FAR	4	2¼	4	3⅜	4	4⅞	4	7⅜	4	10¾	5	5½

Super 8 Depth of Field Tables.
(Eastman Kodak)

9mm Lens

Distance Focused On (in feet)		f/2.7		f/4		f/5.6		f/8		f/11		f/16	
		ft.	in.	ft.	in.	ft.	in.	ft.	in.	ft.	in.	ft.	in.
∞ (INF)	NEAR	5	11⅜	4	¼	2	10⅜	2	⅛	1	5½	1	0
	FAR	∞		∞		∞		∞		∞		∞	
25	NEAR	4	9¾	3	5⅝	2	6⅞	1	10¼	1	4½	0	11½
	FAR	∞		∞		∞		∞		∞		∞	
15	NEAR	4	3¼	3	2⅛	2	4⅞	1	9¼	1	4	0	11¼
	FAR	∞		∞		∞		∞		∞		∞	
10	NEAR	3	8⅞	2	10½	2	2¾	1	8⅛	1	3¼	0	10⅞
	FAR	∞		∞		∞		∞		∞		∞	
6	NEAR	2	11⅞	2	4⅞	1	11⅜	1	6⅛	1	2⅛	0	10⅜
	FAR	∞		∞		∞		∞		∞		∞	
4	NEAR	2	4¾	2	⅛	1	8⅛	1	4⅛	1	⅞	0	9⅝
	FAR	11	11⅝	∞		∞		∞		∞		∞	

13mm Lens

Distance Focused On (in feet)		f/2.8		f/4		f/5.6		f/8		f/11		f/16	
		ft.	in.	ft.	in.	ft.	in.	ft.	in.	ft.	in.	ft.	in.
∞ (INF)	NEAR	12	5	8	4⅝	5	11⅞	4	2¼	3	⅝	2	1⅛
	FAR	∞		∞		∞		∞		∞		∞	
25	NEAR	8	3¾	6	3½	4	10	3	7⅛	2	8⅝	1	11¼
	FAR	∞		∞		∞		∞		∞		∞	
15	NEAR	6	9⅝	5	4⅝	4	3½	3	3⅜	2	6½	1	10⅛
	FAR	∞		∞		∞		∞		∞		∞	
10	NEAR	5	6⅚	4	6⅞	3	9	2	11½	2	4⅛	1	8⅞
	FAR	50	1½	∞		∞		∞		∞		∞	
6	NEAR	4	⅝	3	6	3	0	2	5¾	2	⅜	1	6¾
	FAR	11	6⅛	20	7⅞	∞		∞		∞		∞	
4	NEAR	3	⅜	2	8½	2	4⅞	2	⅝	1	8⅞	1	4⅝
	FAR	5	10⅜	7	6¾	11	9⅛	69	9½	∞		∞	

Continued on next page

Super 8 Depth of Field Tables (continued).

28mm Lens

Distance Focused On (in feet)		f/2.7		f/4		f/5.6		f/8		f/11		f/16	
		ft.	in.	ft.	in.	ft.	in.	ft.	in.	ft.	in.	ft.	in.
∞ (INF)	NEAR	57	4⅜	38	9½	27	8⅞	19	5⅛	14	1⅝	9	8⅝
	FAR	∞		∞		∞		∞		∞		∞	
25	NEAR	17	5½	15	2⅞	13	2¼	10	11⅝	9	⅝	7	¼
	FAR	43	11¾	69	4⅛	∞		∞		∞		∞	
15	NEAR	11	11	10	10⅛	9	9⅛	8	5⅞	7	3⅝	5	11
	FAR	20	2⅝	24	3½	32	3¾	63	11⅝	∞		∞	
10	NEAR	8	6⅜	7	11⅝	7	4⅜	6	7½	5	10½	4	11⅜
	FAR	12	⅞	13	4⅞	15	6⅜	20	4¼	33	3⅜	∞	
6	NEAR	5	5¼	5	2½	4	11⅜	4	7⅛	4	2¾	3	8¾
	FAR	6	8⅛	7	¾	7	7⅜	8	7¼	10	3½	15	3
4	NEAR	3	8⅞	3	7½	3	6	3	3⅞	3	1½	2	10¼
	FAR	4	3⅜	4	5¼	4	7¾	5	0	5	6¼	6	8⅛

36mm Lens

Distance Focused On (in feet)		f/2.7		f/4		f/5.6		f/8		f/11		f/16	
		ft.	in.	ft.	in.	ft.	in.	ft.	in.	ft.	in.	ft.	in.
∞ (INF)	NEAR	94	5¾	63	11⅝	45	9¼	32	1	23	4¼	16	¾
	FAR	∞		∞		∞		∞		∞		∞	
25	NEAR	19	9⅞	18	⅜	16	2⅝	14	1⅛	12	1⅜	9	9¾
	FAR	33	9⅞	40	8⅞	54	5⅝	110	1	∞		∞	
15	NEAR	12	11⅝	12	2⅛	11	3⅞	10	3	9	2	7	9½
	FAR	17	9¼	19	6	22	2	27	10⅝	41	2	198	9⅞
10	NEAR	9	⅝	8	8	8	2¾	7	7¾	7	⅜	6	2¼
	FAR	11	1¾	11	9¾	12	8¾	14	5⅛	17	3⅝	25	10¾
6	NEAR	5	7¾	5	5⅞	5	3¾	5	⅞	4	9½	4	4⅝
	FAR	6	4⅝	6	7⅛	6	10½	7	4	8	⅛	9	5⅜
4	NEAR	3	10	3	9¼	3	8¼	3	6¾	3	5⅛	3	2⅝
	FAR	4	2	4	3	4	4⅜	4	6½	4	9½	5	3¼

45mm Lens

Distance Focused On (in feet)		f/2.7		f/4		f/5.6		f/8		f/11		f/16	
		ft.	in.	ft.	in.	ft.	in.	ft.	in.	ft.	in.	ft.	in.
∞ (INF)	NEAR	146	10⅛	99	7⅛	71	4⅛	50	½	36	5⅜	25	1
	FAR	∞		∞		∞		∞		∞		∞	
25	NEAR	21	5	20	½	18	6⅞	16	8¾	14	10⅝	12	6⅞
	FAR	30	0	33	2⅜	38	2½	49	4⅞	77	11½	∞	
15	NEAR	13	7⅝	13	¾	12	5⅛	11	6⅞	10	8	9	5⅛
	FAR	16	7⅞	17	7⅛	18	10⅞	21	3⅜	25	3	36	7½
10	NEAR	9	4½	9	1¼	8	9½	8	4¼	7	10½	7	2⅛
	FAR	10	8⅜	11	1	11	7	12	5⅛	13	8⅛	16	5¼
6	NEAR	5	9¼	5	8	5	6½	5	4⅜	5	2	4	10⅜
	FAR	6	2⅞	6	4⅜	6	6⅜	6	9⅜	7	1⅝	7	9¾
4	NEAR	3	10¾	3	10⅛	3	9½	3	8½	3	7⅜	3	5½
	FAR	4	1¼	4	1⅞	4	2⅝	4	3⅞	4	5⅝	4	8⅝

For a lens of a given focal length, stopping down the lens will increase the depth of field. The smaller the opening of the iris diaphragm, the greater the range of focus. For example, assuming the circle of confusion given above, a 25 millimeter lens for 16mm filmmaking, focused at ten feet at *f*/2, will have a depth of field of from eight to fourteen feet. Stopped down to *f*/5.6, the depth of field becomes six to thirty-two feet, and at *f*/22, three feet to infinity.

How does the filmmaker know the depth of field at a given distance with a particular focal length? For one thing, and this is probably the most cumbersome method, he can consult a depth of field table. Such tables are sometimes provided in the lens or camera manufacturers instruction booklets, or appear in a book like the *American Cinematographer Manual.* These tables are calculated to the nearest inch, or fraction of a meter, and give the impression that depth of field is a very precise quantity. However, depth of field falls off gradually, at least as perceived by an observer. Tables calculated on the basis of a circle of confusion standard do not take this into account. The near and far limits of depth of field are not abrupt.

The next method for determining depth of field is very convenient but is limited to lenses of fixed focal length. An indicator is engraved

Depth of Field Scale. Typical engraved on-the-lens mount depth of field scale. This lens focused at 9 feet has a depth of field of, for example, from 6 to 40 feet at f/11.

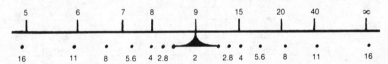

on the lens mount, and the depth of field may be read off this scale once the lens is focused. There are several types of scales in use, but all follow the same general principle. If the filmmaker relies on these scales, or on the depth of field table, he can ensure that near and far objects will be in focus by using the next *f* stop of numerically greater value in order to determine the range of focus. By choosing to regard the depth of field of the next smallest stop (using a table or inscribed scale), a safety factor can be added to critical shots. For ordinary purposes, however, the normally determined values work nicely.

All the remarks that can be made about depth of field for fixed focal length lenses can be made about zoom lenses. At a particular focal length, *f* stop and focusing distance, the depth of field will be that of a corresponding fixed focal length lens.

Zoom lenses invariably lack a depth of field scale. The filmmaker must then rely either on a depth of field table, choosing the focal length that most nearly corresponds to his working focal length, or he may use the method that can be employed with any lens and camera with reflex finder and ground glass, or overall focusing screen.

The Lens

16mm Depth of Field Tables.
(Eastman Kodak)

15mm Lens

Distance Focused On (in feet)		f/2.8		f/4		f/5.6		f/8		f/11		f/16		f/22	
		ft.	in.	ft.	in.	ft.	in.	ft.	in.	ft.	in.	ft.	in.	ft.	in.
∞ (INF)	NEAR	11	7	8	2	5	10	4	1	3	0	2	1	1	6
	FAR	∞		∞		∞		∞		∞		∞		∞	
12	NEAR	5	11	4	10	3	11	3	1	2	5	1	10	1	4
	FAR	∞		∞		∞		∞		∞		∞		∞	
6	NEAR	4	0	3	6	3	0	2	6	2	0	1	7	1	3
	FAR	12	2	21	0	∞		∞		∞		∞		∞	
4	NEAR	3	¼	2	8½	2	5	2	¾	1	9	1	5	1	2
	FAR	6	0	7	8	12	2	104	6	∞		∞		∞	
2	NEAR	1	8¾	1	7⅝	1	6¼	1	4½	1	3	1	¾	0	10⅞
	FAR	2	4½	2	7⅛	2	11⅜	3	8½	5	6	29	11	∞	

25mm Lens

Distance Focused On (in feet)		f/2.8		f/4		f/5.6		f/8		f/11		f/16		f/22	
		ft.	in.	ft.	in.	ft.	in.	ft.	in.	ft.	in.	ft.	in.	ft.	in.
∞ (INF)	NEAR	30	0	21	0	15	0	10	6	7	9	5	4	4	0
	FAR	∞		∞		∞		∞		∞		∞		∞	
30	NEAR	15	0	12	0	10	0	7	10	6	2	4	6	3	6
	FAR	∞		∞		∞		∞		∞		∞		∞	
15	NEAR	10	0	9	0	7	6	6	3	5	2	4	0	3	2
	FAR	29	0	50	0	∞		∞		∞		∞		∞	
10	NEAR	7	6	6	10	6	0	5	2	4	5	3	6	2	10
	FAR	14	10	18	9	29	0	155	0	∞		∞		∞	
6	NEAR	5	0	4	8	4	4	3	10	3	5	2	10	2	5
	FAR	7	5	8	3	9	9	13	6	25	0	∞		∞	
4	NEAR	3	7	3	5	3	2¼	2	11	2	8	2	4	2	0
	FAR	4	7	4	10	5	4¼	6	3	8	0	15	0	∞	
2	NEAR	1	10¾	1	10¼	1	9½	1	8⅝	1	7½	1	6	1	4½
	FAR	2	1½	2	2	2	3	2	5	2	7	3	0	3	9½

50mm Lens

Distance Focused On (in feet)		f/2.8		f/4		f/5.6		f/8		f/11		f/16		f/22	
		ft.	in.	ft.	in.	ft.	in.	ft.	in.	ft.	in.	ft.	in.	ft.	in.
∞ (INF)	NEAR	120	0	80	0	60	0	40	0	30	0	20	0	15	0
	FAR	∞		∞		∞		∞		∞		∞		∞	
50	NEAR	35	0	30	0	25	0	20	0	18	0	14	0	12	0
	FAR	80	0	100	0	300	0	∞		∞		∞		∞	
25	NEAR	21	0	20	0	18	0	16	0	14	0	12	0	10	0
	FAR	32	0	35	0	40	0	60	0	150	0	∞		∞	
15	NEAR	13	3	13	0	12	0	11	0	10	0	9	0	8	0
	FAR	17	0	18	0	20	0	25	0	30	0	40	0	∞	
10	NEAR	9	0	8	9	8	6	8	0	7	6	7	0	6	0
	FAR	10	8	11	0	12	0	13	0	15	0	20	0	30	0
6	NEAR	5	8	5	7	5	6	5	4	5	0	4	8	4	4
	FAR	6	4	6	6	6	9	7	2	7	6	8	6	10	0
4	NEAR	3	10½	3	9½	3	9	3	8	3	7	3	5	3	3
	FAR	4	1½	4	2	4	3	4	4	4	5	4	11	5	6

63mm Lens

Distance Focused On (in feet)		f/2.8		f/4		f/5.6		f/8		f/11		f/16		f/22	
		ft.	in.	ft.	in.	ft.	in.	ft.	in.	ft.	in.	ft.	in.	ft.	in.
∞ (INF)	NEAR	200	0	140	0	90	0	65	0	48	0	33	0	25	0
	FAR	∞		∞		∞		∞		∞		∞		∞	
50	NEAR	40	0	35	0	33	0	30	0	25	0	20	0	16	0
	FAR	68	0	80	0	100	0	200	0	∞		∞		∞	
25	NEAR	22	0	21	0	20	0	18	0	16	0	14	0	12	0
	FAR	28	0	30	0	33	0	40	0	60	0	100	0	∞	
15	NEAR	14	0	13	6	13	0	12	0	11	0	10	0	9	0
	FAR	16	0	17	0	18	0	19	0	21	0	25	0	40	0
10	NEAR	9	6	9	3	9	0	8	6	8	0	7	6	7	0
	FAR	10	6	10	9	11	0	12	0	12	6	13	0	15	0
6	NEAR	5	10	5	9	5	8	5	6	5	3	5	0	4	9
	FAR	6	2	6	3	6	5	6	7	6	9	7	0	7	6
4	NEAR	3	11	3	10½	3	10	3	9½	3	8½	3	7½	3	6
	FAR	4	1	4	1½	4	2	4	3	4	4	4	6	4	8

102mm Lens

Distance Focused On (in feet)		f/2.7		f/4		f/5.6		f/8		f/11		f/16		f/22	
		ft.	in.	ft.	in.	ft.	in.	ft.	in.	ft.	in.	ft.	in.	ft.	in.
∞ (INF)	NEAR	500	0	300	0	200	0	170	0	120	0	85	0	60	0
	FAR	∞		∞		∞		∞		∞		∞		∞	
100	NEAR	85	0	80	0	70	0	65	0	55	0	46	0	40	0
	FAR	125	0	140	0	170	0	250	0	600	0	∞		∞	
50	NEAR	46	0	44	0	42	0	38	0	35	0	31	0	27	0
	FAR	55	0	60	0	65	0	70	0	85	0	125	0	300	0
30	NEAR	28	0	27	6	27	0	25	6	24	0	22	0	20	0
	FAR	32	0	33	0	34	0	36	5	40	0	50	0	60	0
20	NEAR	19	3	18	11	18	6	17	11	17	0	16	3	15	0
	FAR	20	10	21	3	21	9	22	7	23	9	26	0	30	0
15	NEAR	14	7	14	4	14	2	13	10	13	5	12	9	12	0
	FAR	15	5	15	8	16	0	16	5	17	0	18	0	20	0
8	NEAR	7	11	7	10	7	9	7	8	7	6	7	4	7	2
	FAR	8	1½	8	2	8	3	8	4½	8	6	8	9	9	0
6	NEAR	5	11¼	5	11	5	10½	5	10	5	9	5	8	5	6
	FAR	6	¾	6	1	6	1½	6	2	6	3½	6	5	6	7

152mm Lens

Distance Focused On (in feet)		f/4		f/5.6		f/8		f/11		f/16		f/22	
		ft.	in.	ft.	in.	ft.	in.	ft.	in.	ft.	in.	ft.	in.
∞ (INF)	NEAR	800	0	540	0	375	0	275	0	190	0	140	0
	FAR	∞		∞		∞		∞		∞		∞	
200	NEAR	160	0	140	0	130	0	120	0	100	0	80	0
	FAR	270	0	300	0	425	0	700	0	∞		∞	
100	NEAR	90	0	85	0	80	0	74	0	65	0	60	0
	FAR	110	0	120	0	140	0	160	0	200	0	360	0
60	NEAR	56	0	54	0	52	0	50	0	46	0	40	0
	FAR	65	0	67	0	70	0	75	0	90	0	100	0
40	NEAR	38	0	37	4	36	0	35	0	33	0	30	0
	FAR	42	0	43	0	44	0	46	6	50	0	55	0
20	NEAR	19	6½	19	4	19	0	18	9	18	3	18	0
	FAR	20	6	20	8	21	0	21	6	22	0	23	0
12	NEAR	11	10½	11	9	11	8	11	7	11	4	11	2
	FAR	12	1½	12	3	12	4	12	6	12	8	13	0
8	NEAR	7	11¼	7	11	7	10½	7	10	7	9	7	8
	FAR	8	¾	8	1	8	1½	8	2¼	8	3¼	8	4½

The Lens

Such a screen allows the filmmaker to judge the depth of field directly. He can actually view the depth of field, or an approximation of it through such a finder. There are several drawbacks to the practice, in theory at least. For one thing, the grain of the finder can interfere with the filmmaker's judgment, particularly for fine detail. Since detail in more distant objects is smaller than detail in close objects, it is possible to underestimate their depth of field because of the grained screen. Actually this usually turns out to be a good thing because depth of field tables and scales—since these are computed on a strictly mathematical basis—tend to be generous in their distant values. In fact, they do not take into consideration that detail in distant objects tends to get lost much more easily than detail in close objects. The real problem with judging depth of field through the reflex finder is that the relative magnification and brightness of the image can influence your judgment.

Take the case of the size of the finder image. What guarantee does the filmmaker have that the audience will see an image of relatively equal size projected on the screen? If they don't, then the gauging of depth of field through the finder is very arbitrary indeed. Practically speaking, though, things seem to average out, and gauging depth of field through a good reflex finder is an effective method.

Depth and Distance

For a particular f stop and focal length, the closer the filmmaker focuses his lens, the less the depth of field. For example, according to the depth of field tables, a 25 millimeter lens for 16mm filmmaking, assuming an f stop of $f/5.6$, focused at two feet has a depth of field of from one foot 9 inches to 2 feet 4 inches, or if you like, depth of field sufficient for filming something flat, like a card or a painting. Certainly the depth of field is very shallow here, only about half a foot. The same f stop and focal length, now focused at ten feet yield a depth of field of six to thirty-two feet. Depth of field tends to rapidly diminish as the lens is focused close.

Switar Scale. Switar lenses have an unusual type of depth of field scale. Dots *light up* as f stop is changed. Lens is focused at about 30 feet, with f stop at about $f/3.5$. Depth of field is approximately 25 to 45 feet. Paillard at one time made a full range of prime Switars. The lenses are optically awe-inspiring, and a good buy for the money. Concentration on their zoom lenses has made them neglect interesting lenses like the $f/1.4$ 50mm Switar. Check out their 10mm $f/1.6$ Switar in "C" or "Rex" mount.

For usual working distances, most of the depth of field lies behind the focused distance—approximately two thirds behind, only one third in front of, the focused distance. If you shoot a portrait of a man and focus on his ears, his nose may go out of focus; but if you focus on his eyes, the entire head will usually be in focus.

Hyperfocal Distance

When the lens is set at the hyperfocal distance, for a particular f stop and focal length and circle of confusion, the far end of depth of field will be in focus at infinity. Somehow, that seemingly simple statement takes a lot of thought to work its way into one's head. Put it this way: when focused at some distance, there will be a near and far limit of acceptable focus. When the lens is focused at the distance at which the far limit of acceptable focus is infinity, that distance is called the *hyperfocal* distance. The easiest way to set a lens for the hyperfocal distance is to set the infinity mark of the focusing scale opposite the f stop mark engraved on the depth of field scale.

The lens set for the hyperfocal distance will maximize depth of field, and on sunny days with high numerical f stops, frees the filmmaker from focusing for all but the very closest distances. The hyperfocal distances may be obtained from a depth of field table, if you like; if you have a zoom lens, it may be the only way. Users of zoom lenses who don't want to drag around depth of field tables covering the range of their zoom lens focal lengths, might do well to tape a chart of hyperfocal distances for f stops and focal lengths to the camera body.

Depth and Image Size

So far we have considered only the case of a lens of a particular focal length, but what happens to depth of field when we switch to a lens of a new focal length, or zoom to another focal length? This question touches on the richest source of confusion concerning depth of field. It is usual for filmmakers to say that they are going to choose a lens of short focal length in order to increase depth of field. It's true that lenses of short focal length will increase depth of field, but only if the filmmaker is willing to accept the accompanying reduction in subject image size.

The perverse fact of the matter is that all lenses, no matter what focal length, have the same depth of field for the same image size, with the same f stop (for the same format). This means that if the filmmaker wishes to film a subject so that it is the same image size with a long lens as for a short lens, he will have to get closer to the subject. Now remember, the image formed by the lens in this example is the same size—it remains constant. As the filmmaker approaches the subject to increase the image size in the viewfinder, or on the film, if you like (or to maintain the same magnification, if you prefer this terminology), depth of field will be correspondingly altered so that the depth of the short lens and long lens will become the same.

The Lens

More About Depth and Distance

If the camera is kept at a fixed distance from a subject, with a fixed f stop, and various focal length lenses are used, shorter lenses will have more depth of field than long lenses. Unlike the previous case, the size of the image projected on the frame will naturally change as the focal length of the lens changes. The longer the lens, the larger the image of the subject, and the less the depth of field. Conversely, for the same focus setting, from the same position, using a wide angle lens will decrease the image size but increase the depth of field. The assumption has been that the lenses of varying focal lengths used have all been set at the same f stop.

Depth of Field and the Formats

For the same image recorded on the smaller 8mm and super 8-single 8 formats, as on 16mm film, the smaller format images will have more depth of field, provided we have the same subject distance and f stop. If we are shooting a scene in 8mm with say a 12.5 millimeter lens, and we are shooting the same scene in 16mm with a 25 millimeter lens, from the same distance to the subject, with the same focusing setting, we will record images that closely cover the same angle of view. When projected on the same size screen, viewed from the same distance, the 8mm scene, shot with the same f stop as the 16mm scene, will have more depth of field.

Depth of Field—A Look Back

We can make these statements about depth of field that may help the filmmaker untangle the subject: depth of field increases as a lens is stopped down. Depth of field increases as we choose a short focal length lens, but only if we are willing to accept a shot which reduces the size of the subject—naturally including more of the subject. If the filmmaker attempts to restore the subject size by decreasing the camera-subject distance, all advantages of using the shorter focal length lens, at least

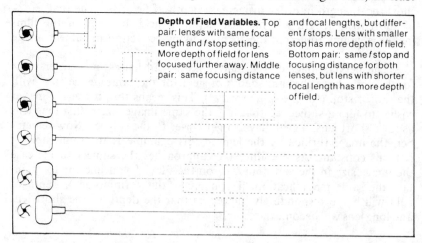

Depth of Field Variables. Top pair: lenses with same focal length and f stop setting. More depth of field for lens focused further away. Middle pair: same focusing distance and focal lengths, but different f stops. Lens with smaller stop has more depth of field. Bottom pair: same f stop and focusing distance for both lenses, but lens with shorter focal length has more depth of field.

as far as depth of field is concerned, must necessarily be lost.

The closer the subject to the camera, the less the depth of field. Depth of field decreases sharply as subject-camera distance decreases. When focusing at a particular subject distance, about two thirds of the zone of acceptable focus lies behind the subject when projected on the same size screen; the smaller formats have more depth of field, with the same f stop, subject distance and lenses of comparable angle of view, than the 16mm format.

I feel that the subject of depth of field could use even a few more words: consider the following variables—f stop, focal length and subject distance. Assuming that we are talking about one particular format, keeping subject distance and focal length fixed, increased depth of field results from a decreased f stop (increased numerical value—a smaller opening). Keeping the focal length and f stop fixed, an increased subject distance increases depth of field. Now, finally, let us suppose that we keep the subject distance fixed. In this case, increased focal length causes decreased depth of field, and the converse is true.

In actual practice, when a filmmaker wants more depth of field, he usually goes to a shorter focal length.

Depth of Focus

This term is often confused with depth of field. *Depth of focus* is measured at the film plane, not at the subject, and sets the tolerable limits of lens-film plane distance. Like depth of field, depth of focus increases with the numerical value of the f stop. Unlike depth of field, depth of focus increases as focal length increases, and increases as subject distance decreases. Depth of focus is measured equally in front of and behind the film plane. The filmmaker ought not to confuse these terms. Depth of field is his concern, depth of *focus* is essentially the concern of the manufacturer.

Focusing the Zoom Lens

The subject of focusing the zoom lens is given here because it is closely related to depth of field. To understand the conditions necessary for accurate focusing of such a lens, it is necessary to apply some of what was discussed about depth of field.

A zoom lens is focused by rotating the front of the lens mount. This changes the distance between the lens' front component, or elements, and the zoom and image-forming section of the lens. In other words, zoom lenses focus by front element focusing. They cannot be focused by racking the lens forward, as is the case with fixed focal length lenses. Zoom lenses must maintain a constant back focus in order to properly form an image. For this reason extension tubes or bellows—devices for close focusing—may not be used with the zoom lens.

In his introduction Stan Brakhage makes the point that he has used extension tubes in conjunction with a zoom lens for close focusing. Brakhage is right. However, when used this way, you cannot zoom and maintain a focused image.

The Lens

Zoom lenses should be focused wide open—that is, at maximum aperture and focal length. By focusing at the widest aperture and longest focal length, depth of field will be minimized to make focusing as accurate as possible. If focusing is done at a wide or moderate focal length, zooming to a longer focal length can throw the subject completely out of focus.

Since depth of field is greater at shorter focal lengths, focusing is less precise, and an error in focusing is likely to be masked. This depth of field cushion disappears as the lens zooms toward long focal lengths.

Users of 8mm and super 8 equipment usually focus at the widest opening, since light for their viewing systems is taken before the iris diaphragm. For these filmmakers, all that is needed to ensure good focus is to zoom to longest focal length.

Although it is a good idea to focus at the lens' maximum focal length for the most accuracy, especially if there is the possibility of zooming to a longer focal length from a shorter focal length, there may be some disadvantage to a too strict application of this method. If you are planning to use your lens fairly close to the subject, you might assume that the subject is out of focus, when actually, for the short focal lengths, it would not be. Part of the problem here is that, generally speaking, zoom lenses focus to three to five feet. If you want to use the shortest focal length, both the focusing scale and the method of zooming to a long focal length would make you believe it was impossible to get close to the subject. However, this is probably not the case. Let us take the case of a 16mm zoom lens which focuses to four feet, and has a short focal length of 12.5 millimeters. Assuming that we are shooting at $f/5.6$, we'll have a range of focus of two feet two inches to thirty-six and a half feet, when focused at four feet. Obviously in this case, which has fairly typical conditions, we are able to safely approach the subject as close as about two feet. A filmmaker who likes to get close with such a zoom lens, used at the shortest focal length, might draft a close focusing limit table at various f stops and tape it to the camera body.

Perspective

The term *perspective* refers to the relative juxtaposition of foreground and background objects in the filmed scene. The rules of perspective developed by Renaissance painting correspond to the results obtained with photography. Each point in the scene being shot is represented by an image point on the exposed film. The main concern of the filmmaker is not so much with vanishing points and placement of horizontal or vertical lines in the composition, but rather with the size of the image, and the relative size of foreground and background objects.

The filmmaker is able to decide not only what portion of the world will appear within the frame's rectangle, but under given conditions, he may control the relationship of the sizes of objects in the scene.

Image Size

With a camera of a given format and a fixed distance, the size of the object formed by the lens on the film plane varies with the focal length of the lens. The shorter the lens, the smaller the subject will be reproduced and, naturally, more of the scene will be included in the shot. Increase the focal length of the lens, and the image increases in size, restricting the field of view of the scene.

The most important use of varying focal length, whether with fixed focal lengths or zoom lenses is to control the image size of the main subject. If it is difficult for the filmmaker to approach a subject, a lens of long focal length is usually chosen. If the filmmaker wishes to present as much of the scene as possible, without increasing the camera-subject distance, he must choose a lens of relatively short focal length.

With the conditions of a given format and fixed camera position, the perspective of all the shots taken, no matter what focal length lens,

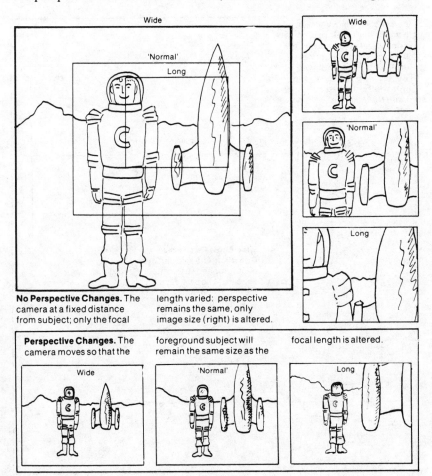

No Perspective Changes. The camera at a fixed distance from subject; only the focal length varied: perspective remains the same, only image size (right) is altered.

Perspective Changes. The camera moves so that the foreground subject will remain the same size as the focal length is altered.

The Lens

will be the same. The situation is exactly like *cropping* a still photograph. If a cropped portion of the frame were to be enlarged, the relative size and juxtaposition of foreground and background objects would be the same. However, in movie work we are not concerned with enlarging portions of the frame. The final image is chosen at the time of filming.

Control of Relative Sizes

As I have said, the most important function of lenses of different focal lengths is to control the image size of the subject. Naturally, the size of the subject may be controlled by changing the distance between camera and subject. In this case, the relationship between foreground and background will be altered. In the example shown, the camera is moved so that the size of the astronaut is always the same, no matter what lens is chosen. The astronaut is standing still, and the rocket is always the same distance from him.

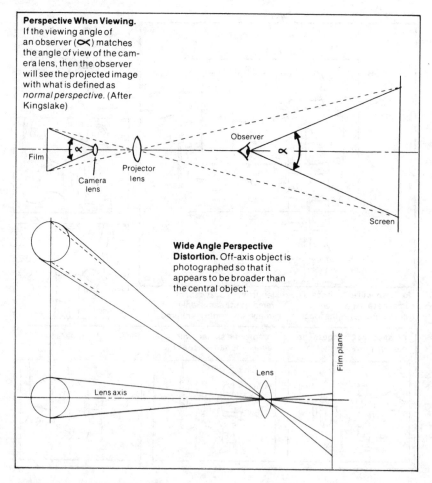

Perspective When Viewing. If the viewing angle of an observer (α) matches the angle of view of the camera lens, then the observer will see the projected image with what is defined as *normal perspective*. (After Kingslake)

Film · Camera lens · Projector lens · Observer · Screen

Wide Angle Perspective Distortion. Off-axis object is photographed so that it appears to be broader than the central object.

Lens axis · Lens · Film plane

Independent Filmmaking

When the short focal length lens is chosen, and the camera is brought close to the astronaut, the size of the rocket seems to diminish. The height of the astronaut is fixed, that is one of the conditions, but the rocket seems to have either receded or diminished in height. Whether it's a small rocket, or one far away from the astronaut, must be learned from other clues in the film. For example, if there is intervening haze, the rocket may seem to be in the distance. This particular distance gauging phenomenon is called *aerial perspective*.

In the case of the use of the long lens, the size of the rocket is emphasized, while our condition prevails—the image size of the astronaut remains constant. The camera is moved back to maintain the astronaut's size.

For these reasons, it is often said that long lenses *flatten* perspective, while short lenses tend to exaggerate perspective, or depth, if you like.

Some Remarks About Normal Perspective
A line of argument concerning *normal* perspective often given in books dealing with photographic perspective concludes that there is one right and proper distance from which to view a film taken with a lens of a particular focal length and projected on a screen of a certain size.

There's little you can do about where the viewer will sit when he watches your film. Perhaps the filmmaker ought to design his perspective effects for those conservatives who tend to sit in the middle of the theater. As for those who prefer the side sections of the theater or screening room, would consideration have to be given to whether or not they are sitting left or right of center?

However, nobody would argue that the audience should get up and change seats each time a shot appears on the screen taken with a different lens. Those who prefer to sit very close to the screen are going to get one point of view—*normal* perspective for close viewers is achieved when filming with a wide lens. Those who prefer to sit a long distance from the screen will see *normal* perspective in long focal length shots.

It really doesn't matter what the *normal* perspective is anyway. We don't usually peer out at the world as if everything were happening beyond our grasp through a black rectangle. It is the power of the filmmaker's art that he can make the viewer forget the existence of this rectangle. The filmmaker must be aware of the effects he is producing and how they will appear on the screen.

Perspective Distortion
Any *perspective distortion* caused by very long lenses would be noticed most in the filming of an object coming toward the camera. For example, if a character is shown running toward the camera, his size will scarcely change—he seems to be making no headway. This constancy of size is explained by the fact that the distance covered by the runner is only a small percentage of the distance of the camera from the runner, when a shot is made with a very long lens.

An interesting wide angle *distortion* is most easily understood by looking at the illustration. Objects at the side of the image tend to appear to be wider than they are, and certainly wider than they would photograph in the center of the field. The effect is particularly noticeable in faces caught at the extreme edges of the frame.

A Note on Portraits

The rules of perspective also apply to the human face. For this reason, longer than *normal* lenses are often preferred because they tend to flatten the features, especially the nose. In other cultures, Semitic for example, it is entirely possible that some filmmakers, unaware of Western standards, might prefer to use shorter lenses emphasizing the size of the subject's nose.

Close-ups

There are some lenses, called *macro lenses,* which allow continuous focusing from infinity to within several inches of the subject. Actually, the most important factor for many close-up purposes isn't how near you can get to the subject, but rather the size of the rectangle you can cover. For example, for a 16mm camera, a 25 millimeter lens, which focuses to 18 inches will allow coverage of a 4½ x 6 inch rectangle. Unless there are instructions to the contrary, the minimum distance, in this case 18 inches, is measured from the film plane (a few lenses measure distance from the front of the lens mount). There are two ways that most lenses can be made to cover less than their usual minimum rectangle. The first method, close-up lenses, will work for any lens, and is, perhaps, the simplest to use.

Close-up Lenses

Close-up lenses in different diameters are available to fit in front of the lens. They should be placed as close to the front element of the lens as the mount will allow. There are two ways to fit these to the lens, or two styles of securing them in place: they may be screwed into the front thread of the lens mount, which is usually used for attaching the lens shade; or they may be dropped into an adapter-retaining ring set, which in turn is screwed in place.

These lenses require no increase in exposure. They are available with antireflection coated surfaces. They are rated in *diopter* power, as are eyeglasses. A diopter is the reciprocal focal length of the lens in meters. For example, a lens with +2 diopter power is actually half a meter in focal length. Lenses are ordinarily supplied in strengths of 1, 2, 3, 4 and 5 diopters, although higher diopter powers are available, and sometimes lenses of ½, 1½ and so on are offered. It's possible to use two of these lenses at once, in which case the strongest ought to be closest to the taking lens. The usual advice when using these attachments is to use the lens stopped down to about $f/8$ in order to secure maximum correction.

Close-up lenses have positive diopter values which means that they are converging lenses. When placed in front of the taking lens, they

effectively shorten the focal length. Because of the shortened focal
length, the lens may now be racked out far enough to form sharp images
at the film plane. In a pinch, a magnifying glass, or spectacles for correcting farsightedness, can replace a close-up lens. Use of the close-up
lens is the preferred method for extending the close-focusing range of
the zoom lens.

Bellows and Extension Tubes

When a lens focuses close, it is moved away from the film plane. Some,
notably zoom lenses, focus by moving their front elements, or section,
away from the film plane. In the case of all lenses except zoom lenses,
it's possible to extend the close-focusing range by moving the lens farther away from the film plane. (Naturally, this method cannot be used
for cameras with built-in lenses.)

Extension tubes are often used to extend the close-focusing range.
They are, simply, hollow cylinders threaded at either end to screw into
the camera body as a lens would. The lens is, in turn, screwed into the
other end of the tube. A number of extension tubes may be used in any
combination in order to achieve the desired image size. Extension tubes
are usually sold in sets. Bolex for example, makes a very useful set of
C mount type thread extension tubes of 5, 10, 20 and 40 millimeters,
allowing the filmmaker to combine extensions of from 5 to 75 millimeters, in steps of 5 millimeters.

As the lens moves away from the film plane, the light available for
exposure decreases as the inverse square of the distance from the principal point or optical center of the lens, to the film plane. A new exposure must be calculated. Here's how to do it: add the focal length to the
length of the extension tube(s), and divide this sum by the focal length.
The length of the tube is usually marked, in millimeters, on the tube
itself. Naturally, all lengths must be in the same units. The number which
results from this simple computation is the f number multiplying factor.
Multiply the f number by the factor to get the new effective f number.

For example, suppose we are using a 25 millimeter lens, with a set
of extension tubes adding up to another 25 millimeters. The length of
the focal length plus the length of the added distance, or the length of
the extension tube is 25 plus 25 millimeters. This sum must be divided
by the focal length, 25 millimeters. The resulting factor is 2. If the lens
is set for $f/4$, exposure should be calculated on the basis of an effective
exposure of $f/8$. Written as a formula we have:

$$\text{effective } f \text{ number} = \frac{\text{(focal length)} + \text{(length of extension)}}{\text{focal length}} \times \text{marked } f \text{ number}$$

In this particular example, when the length of the extension equals
the focal length, the image size will equal the object size. This is called a
1:1 reproduction, or image magnification.

Here's another example to help you compute the proper exposure
when using extension tubes. Suppose you're using a 75 millimeter lens,
with an extension tube of 40 millimeters length. Your light meter tells

The Lens

you that you need an exposure of $f/11$. We know that setting the lens to $f/11$ will result in an underexposure, so the lens will actually have to be set for some f stop numerically less than $f/11$.

Plugging the numbers into our equation we get:

$$f/11 = \frac{(75mm + 40mm)}{} \times \text{marked } f \text{ number}$$

or
$$f/11 = 1.5 \times \overset{(70mm)}{\text{marked } f} \text{ number}$$

$$\frac{f/11}{1.5} = \text{marked } f \text{ number}$$

$$f/8 = \text{marked } f \text{ number}$$

I've gone to this trouble because I think it's valuable to know how to do this calculation, and like me, you may have been away from algebra for quite some time. Remember, if you use a light meter to find out what f number is required, the f number that must be set on the lens with extension tubes has to be numerically less than the f number without the tubes.

Since you're going to lose perhaps a stop or more using these tubes, high speed film, like Tri-X or one of the fast Anscochromes for example, are very helpful for maintaining adequate depth of field. They will allow you to use a numerically large f stop, and still have the proper effective f stop.

The same kind of calculation can be carried out for bellows close-focusing devices. The device allows for continuous close-focusing, since the bellows may be moved to any point along its length of travel. Few bellows devices are available specifically for 8mm or 16mm work. Bolex supplies a unit with built-in $f/2.8$, 75 millimeter Yvar lens which may be used with its H reflex cameras. The many bellows units designed for 35mm still camera work may possibly be employed with a suitable adapter.

More About Getting Close

One trick in filming the motion of models used by Stanley Kubrick in *2001: A Space Odyssey,* was to use extreme undercranking to increase his exposure to the point where he could use very small apertures. Each frame for the model shots was exposed for seconds, not fractions of a second. Movement of the models had to be scaled down so that motion would appear natural when the film was projected at the normal 24 fps rate. This is a marked departure from the traditional method when models are shot overcranked in order to make their motion appear more natural on the screen. This costs the filmmaker depth of field, which is precisely what's needed to make model work convincing.

It is often best to use a lens two or three times the *normal* focal length in order to get enough working distance between the front surface of the lens and the subject. For example, 50 or 75 millimeter lenses used with 16mm are convenient focal lengths. For 8mm or super 8, half these focal lengths should provide good working distances.

Filmmakers are sometimes put off by this bit of information, thinking that they should use short focal length lenses to maximize depth of field for close-ups. If you remember the discussion of depth of field, you will see that this cannot be the case. For the same magnification, or projected image size of the object on the film, depth of field is the same for a lens of any focal length. All that can be changed with the focal length, if the subject remains a constant image size, is the relative size of the background.

Variable Power Close-up Lenses

Close-up lenses of variable diopter power, sort of a zoom-a-power arrangement have recently been introduced. The one offered by Spiratone is called the *Proxivar,* and Tiffen Optical Company offers a unit, called the *HCE Vari-Close-Up Lens,* with a range of from +1 to +10 diopters. Like fixed diopter lenses, they attach to the lens like filters and require no increase in exposure.

Split-Diopter Lenses

These lenses, very much like bifocal eyeglasses, allow the filmmaker to focus on two separate distances at once. Part of the lens has a curvature, hence a diopter power, and the other part of the lens is flat glass. It takes careful composition to mask the edge of the split field. Split field lenses are available from Spiratone, Tiffen and Century Precision Optics.

Lens Accompaniers

Focal Length Convertors

A lens of normal focal length can be altered for longer or shorter focal length. Convertors, or auxiliary lenses, attached to the front of the lens will change its focal length. For the wide angle convertor, the new focal length is the product of the old focal length and a factor usually of about

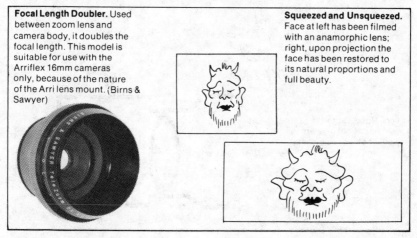

Focal Length Doubler. Used between zoom lens and camera body, it doubles the focal length. This model is suitable for use with the Arriflex 16mm cameras only, because of the nature of the Arri lens mount. (Birns & Sawyer)

Squeezed and Unsqueezed. Face at left has been filmed with an anamorphic lens; right, upon projection the face has been restored to its natural proportions and full beauty.

The Lens

0.75; the telephoto conversion results in a new focal length on the order of 1.5 times the former focal length. Such devices, known as *afocal convertors,* are available for both fixed focal length and zoom lenses. They are used for projector lenses, as well as for cameras.

The original focusing scale of the lens will be totally altered when the attachment is in place. Sometimes such attachments do not use the lens' focusing mount. Rather, the lens is set to infinity, and the convertor is focused itself, with its own scale, by rotation in its mount.

Monocular attachments for more drastic increases of focal length are also available. Healthy focal lengths can result from the use of such attachments, but they produce a very low effective *f* stop. If such attachments are well designed and manufactured, they can give very good results.

There is another type of convertor, used between the camera body and the lens, to increase the lenses' focal length anywhere from two to four times. They may be used with zoom or fixed focal length lenses. To get the highest quality image, it's usually best to stop down quite a bit when using any of these devices.

Anamorphic Attachments

An *anamorphic convertor,* when placed on the camera, results in a lens combination that has a short horizontal and a long vertical focal length. Anamorphic lenses or attachments were made popular by the introduction of CinemaScope, by 20th Century Fox in the early fifties. *Scope* films, are shot in the wide aspect ratio of 2.35:1.

When projected with the same sort of lens system that was used to take the picture, the proportions of the image are restored to normal. If projected without the proper anamorphic lens, the subjects appear squashed together. For 35mm and 70mm commercial films, Panavision and others supply fully integrated anamorphic lens designs. Formerly, the professionals did what the amateur or independent must do today;

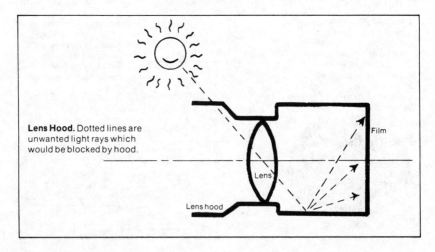

Lens Hood. Dotted lines are unwanted light rays which would be blocked by hood.

Film

Lens

Lens hood

Independent Filmmaking

if scope motion pictures were desired, they used a convertor.

The convertor is attached to the front of the lens. Convertors achieve their effect through two means: in the first case, they use cylindrical lens elements. Such a lens, since its surface is the section of a curved cylinder rather than a sphere, will refract light rays in one plane only, producing the desired squeeze effect. The other type of convertor uses prisms and a cylindrically curved front surface mirror. The mirror squeezes the light. It works very much like a fun-house mirror.

For 8mm or 16mm, the same convertor is often used for both taking and projection lenses. These lens attachments are usually designed to give best results on the camera. Their projection quality is rarely better than mediocre.

Typical compression factors are 1.5X and 2X. This factor is used to multiply the horizontal dimension. For example, the 4:3 aspect ratio with the 1.5X anamorphic convertor will produce a new aspect ratio that is 6:3, or 2:1. Usually, these attachments will not cover less than the *normal* focal length for that format, that is 12.5 millimeters for 8mm, and 25 millimeters for 16mm. Each format needs an attachment designed for its size. Since the important design factor is the diameter of the attachment compared to the diameter of the lens with which it will be used, a 16mm unit will usually work with 8mm and super 8 lenses, but not the other way 'round.

Lens Designations
How can you tell the vital information of a lens by the markings on the lens mount? Let's take the case of a lens of 50 millimeter focal length, with an opening of $f/1.8$. Here are some of the designations that manufacturers may use. They are found engraved somewhere, often on the front of the lens mount:

        F:1.8   50mm
        1:1.8/50mm
        1:1.8 f = 50mm
        1:1.8   F.50

The focal length range of a zoom lens, with a range of from say, 10 to 50 millimeters might be expressed as follows:

        F.10-50mm
        f=10   50mm
        f=10 to 50mm

The Lens Hood
The *lens hood,* sometimes called the sunshade, is the most useful lens accessory. Its secondary purpose is to protect the lens from harm, by protruding beyond the end of the lens mount. Its primary function, however, is to increase the contrast of the image and reduce spurious images produced by bright light sources.

If we consider that the lens forms a circular image larger than the

184 rectangle of the frame being exposed, we realize that the light beyond the rectangle does not contribute to the image. Rather, it is reflected within the camera, in the space between the film plane and the lens; it adds an overall exposure to the film. In other words, it does not produce a specific image, but rather, raises the overall level of illumination within the camera, which tends to reduce the contrast, or *fog* the image. Depending upon the subject matter, the lighting and the *f* stop used, this may be a major or unnoticeable effect.

Most lens hoods are conical in shape. The best shape is a rectangle conforming to the aspect ratio of the frame. It is important that the hood does not cut off any part of the image. If you have a reflex finder, you may observe if this is the case. A conical type lens hood may be masked to the rectangular shape, by taping black photographic masking tape over its outer lip. Once again, the reflex finder is useful for determining whether or not a portion of the image is cut off.

Lens hoods for zoom lenses must be shaped so that they will conform to the coverage of the widest angle or shortest focal length. As such, they are probably not very effective for most of the lens' zoom range. The matte box, which may be used in conjunction with many camera bodies, can perform the function of the lens hood with better results.

Lens Testing

I am in favor of completely subjective lens testing. Shoot the kind of pictures you usually shoot, or intend to shoot, at a variety of *f* stops, under many lighting conditions. Shoot subjects close to the camera, and far from the camera. Project the film. Are the pictures sharp enough from corner to corner to suit you? Remember that your projector may be less than perfect. Projection lenses often suffer from curvature of field. You can improve the overall sharpness of the projection lens by making a black cardboard stop, and taping that over the lens. The hole ought to be about half or three quarters the radius of the lens' cross section.

Lens Cleaning

Rarely clean a lens. A little dust won't hurt, but a fingerprint, a grease smudge, acid or salt water, for example, may permanently *etch* the glass. Clean, if you must, with lens cleaning tissue made especially for camera lenses, and not for eyeglasses. Eyeglass tissue is bad for your lens: it will scratch the antireflection coating.

Try blowing on the lens surface to remove the dust before you clean the lens with fluid, or if you just want to get rid of dust. Unfortunately you may wind up spitting on your lens, which means you'll have to use fluid anyway. A blower or a small syringe works well. Don't use a brush. Brushes get greasy and spread it around. Try breathing on the lens with a wide-open mouth. The condensed breath, essentially distilled water, helps the tissue pick up grease and dirt deposited on the lens.

To clean a very dirty or grease smeared lens, put a drop of lens cleaning fluid on a bunched-up tissue, and gently use this tissue to wet

the lens. A drop of fluid directly on the lens surface can creep under the   185
edge of the lens, and work the cement loose. Use another tissue, bunched
up nicely, and gently — do not apply pressure — to swab the lens dry.

Some filmmakers like to use a haze or ultra-violet filter to protect
the lens from damage and the need for cleaning. This filter does not
change exposure and can be used at all times. Spiratone offers coated
optical glass lens caps to take care of this need.

If you use interchangeable lenses, it's wise to occasionally clean the
flange — that portion of the lens mount that sits directly against the
camera turret and determines the lens-to-film plane distance. Any build-
up of dirt on the flange, or the portion of the turret that comes in contact
with the flange, can alter the distance, producing soft images, particularly for short focal length lenses with their limited depth of focus. A
good way to clean the lens mount, its flange and the entire camera body
is with cotton swabs and discarded cotton editing gloves very sparingly
dampened in denatured alcohol to prevent damage to cemented parts.

Operating a Lens

After all of these words, it might be nice to make some sort of a summa-
tion about working a lens. First focus the lens. If you have a reflex finder,
open the lens up to its widest f stop (lowest numerical setting); this will
minimize depth of field and make the image through the finder as
bright as possible. Both of these factors will help you focus the lens
better. Now when the lens is focused, set the proper f stop. You may
have determined this with a hand-held light meter or with a through-
the-lens meter, or the camera may have a built-in automatic light meter,
in which case the lens will have set itself.

If your camera has a reflex system that takes its light before the
diaphragm, you do not have to open the lens up in order to reduce depth
of field to a minimum or to gain the maximum light transmission for
focusing. However, if your camera has a zoom lens—built-in or interchangeable—zoom to the longest focal length before you focus. This will
minimize depth of field and help you to focus accurately.

If you have a camera with reflex viewing, you can observe the depth
of field at a particular f stop, for the focal length employed, provided
the reflex system takes its light after the diaphragm. Depth of field
may be given on the lens mount of fixed focal length lenses, but is not
inscribed on zoom lens mounts. For cameras with a built-in zoom lens
which invariably employs a reflex viewing system that precludes visual
evaluation of depth of field, you can consult depth of field tables to get
an idea of the range of sharp focus. Knowing the exact depth of field of
a particular shot is often totally unimportant.

Now you can shoot. While shooting, it is possible to follow focus,
that is focus the lens as the distance between the subject and camera
changes. It is also possible to zoom to another focal length while shooting, and possibly to change the f stop (the camera may perform this function automatically).

The Lens

Shooting

There are two prime reasons for working the camera: the joy of doing and the anticipation of how what you've done will look on the screen.

The camera may be moved in many ways; or, of course, it may be held still. What camera motion produces on the screen can be broken down into two broad categories: rejuxtaposition of objects within a shot or a change in perspective, and camera movement which will cause no such rejuxtaposition, for example between foreground and background. Moving the camera is like animation, since it imparts motion to that which is static.

The camera's actual movements, and not simply pivoting about some point in the camera body, causes perspective changes in the shot. These perspective changes take place when the camera moves toward or away, rotates about or simply moves by or alongside the subject. If the camera is held in the filmmaker's hand as he walks, perspective changes are going to take place. If the camera is shooting through the side window of a moving car, perspective changes are going to take place—foreground objects will pass by more quickly than the background.

However, if the camera is rotated through an axis drawn through it, in any direction, from side to side, or up and down, no perspective changes take place. Moving the camera in such a way either on a tripod or held in the hand, is called *panning,* short for panoraming. The effect of a pan is what you'd expect to get if you filmed a movement across the surface of a photograph. The camera's transition through space is very small, so the image will not show a rejuxtaposition of subjects.

Without moving the camera from its fixed position, you can make the subject larger or smaller by using a zoom lens. Here there will be no change of perspective, because there is no rejuxtaposition of foreground and background. Once again we can use the comparison of filming a still photograph.

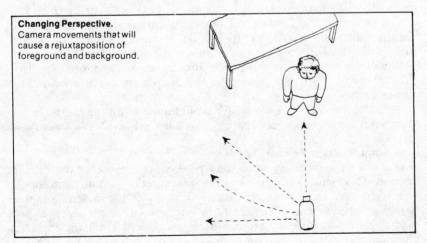

Changing Perspective.
Camera movements that will cause a rejuxtaposition of foreground and background.

Shooting

In practice, a shot will often combine changes in perspective with motion producing no changes in perspective. For example, moving a camera through space while panning or zooming.

Spatial and Temporal Parallax

We perceive three dimensional images because our eyes are about two inches or so apart. The brain combines what these two receptors see, and for relatively close distances, say within a hundred yards, we perceive depth. Because the eyes are some distance apart, *spatial parallax* produces depth perception. At one instant in time then, the eye-brain receives two slightly different images and combines them into a single three dimensional image. The eye-brain interprets other clues about distance and depth. Intervening haze, color, relative size—all play a part in the judging of distance or gauging of depth. But spatial parallax is the same principle which is applied to certain camera focusing devices, and for that matter, by astronomers to measure the distances to the nearer stars.

At this point in the history of film, most movies are two dimensional, and clues about the depth of the scene must come from some source other than spatial parallax. Temporal parallax can serve as an effective substitute for spatial parallax. *Temporal parallax* comes about not in one instant of time, as is the case for spatial parallax, but rather over a length of time. In the interval, the eye-brain is given the information it needs for gauging the depth of a scene. This information can be imparted by, for example, the camera's moving through space so that foreground and background are rejuxtaposed. This is the perceived motion of a camera shooting through the side window of a moving car: trees and rocks in the foreground move by quickly, but hills and more distant objects move by much more slowly. The sky, clouds, will hardly seem to move at all. Such a shot, if well executed, can be as satisfying for the purposes of perceiving depth as a motionless, fully three dimensional view of the scene as perceived with two eyes. Panning or zooming cannot supply the information needed for temporal parallax gauging of depth.

It is within the filmmaker's power to emphasize or deemphasize the three dimensional aspect of his subject. Filmmakers like Max Ophuls and Ed Emshwiller, for example, in many of their films, use the device of the moving camera to mold their subjects three dimensionally. The filmmaker may 'flatten' his subject, if this is his purpose, by choosing to pan or zoom.

At the very least, the filmmaker should understand the means at his disposal to control apparent depth.

Smoothness and Focal Length

The shorter the focal length of the lens used, the smoother the camera motion. This includes any kind of hand-held camera motion, from simply moving the arms and torso, to walking around with the camera. Suppose you want the camera movement to be very smooth. Every weave, bob and jiggle made while shooting will be reproduced when the image is projected on the screen. But the longer the focal length of the lens, the greater the image magnification, the greater the appearance of the jiggle. If you shake a camera, and on film this shake is recorded as a one millimeter high displacement of the image, a lens of half the focal length will only record a height of half a millimeter.

It's usually quite easy to produce smooth motion on the screen hand-holding a camera with a lens half the *normal* focal length, say 5 to 7 millimeters for 8mm and super 8, or 10 millimeters for 16mm. Short focal lengths also help to take the place of a tripod you're trying to hold steady, with no intended motion. With practice, it's very nearly possible to reproduce the steadiness of a dolly or tripod mounted camera. Accomplishing this is really no great feat. To help hold a motionless shot steady, you can lean against anything available, a wall for example, but really, this isn't necessary.

Why use a tripod, if it doesn't matter? The traditional advice for filmmaking is to use a tripod whenever possible. My practice is to avoid using a tripod whenever possible.

The Steadicam. Expensive and cumbersome, it is the last word in smooth hand-held cinematography, and has been used to good effect on many features. (Cinema Products)

Selecting the Lens and Focal Length

One consideration that the filmmaker must take into account when choosing a specific lens, or focal length, can be stated in the form of a question: what will be the size of the image, or how much of the scene or subject will I be including in the frame? Another consideration is the necessary distance between the camera and the subject. For distant subjects which are physically impossible or dangerous to approach, a long focal length may be required. If it is impossible or difficult to move the camera away from a scene or the subject, and you must include more of it on the frame, a short focal length is required. Of course, you may wish to control the perspective of the shot, and for a discussion of this, please see chapter 4, *The Lens*.

Here are some other reasons for selecting a lens or focal length: a wide angle lens will allow you to hand-hold shots appreciably more steadily than a long focal length lens. In addition, for a given distance, wide angle lenses have more depth of field, often making following focus unnecessary. You may choose a longer focal length so that the camera will be farther away from the subject for sync-sound recording. The farther the camera is from the microphone, the easier it is to avoid picking up the mechanism's noise. Or you might choose a long focal length to reduce depth of field for selective focus to isolate the subject from the background.

You may choose a lens because it is particularly fast. The fastest lenses usually are available in the *normal* 25 millimeter focal length for 16mm. In low light level situations, such a lens may make otherwise impossible exposures possible. There are several $f/0.95$ 25 millimeter lenses in C mounts for use with 16mm or super 8 cameras that will accept interchangeable lenses. There is a very fast C mount Kinoptic lens (distributed by Karl Heitz) with a speed of $f/0.7$ in the 60 millimeter focal length.

The filmmaker may choose to use the zoom lens, not only because of its possible variable magnification or zoom effects, but also because it allows choice among a great number of intermediate focal lengths. Now that there is little quality differential between a good zoom lens and a good fixed focal length lens, many zoom lenses may be used where formerly fixed focal length lenses were used exclusively. However, prime, or fixed focal length lenses can still be quite a bit faster than zoom lenses, and generally they have the advantages of being more compact and able to focus much closer.

Hand-holding the Camera

So far, I haven't mentioned the most obvious, and I suppose for that reason the most important purpose for moving the camera: to show something new, or to follow a subject as it moves. Traditionally, the single criterion used to judge successful camera movement was smoothness. The more mechanical, or pneumatic, the camera's motion, the more it was applauded. It is difficult to convince people brought up on this con-

cept of quality that it is an arbitrary esthetic, and not an absolute or a
fact of life.

Times have changed, and it is now more often the smooth camera, not the jerky one, that calls attention to itself, because of its inhuman artificiality. Many contemporary filmmakers, even relatively traditional directors like Truffaut and Godard, have demonstrated that a little camera shake never hurt anything, especially the audience. People who've made home movies have been acquainted with this technique, and have certainly found it to be useful. Perhaps, because of its association with the home movie or newsreel, it is the shaking camera that speaks *truth*. And why shouldn't the filmmaker use techniques that are easy? Shouldn't the act of making a film be a joy itself? In the realm of the independent film, we run a spectrum of styles of hand-held cameras, from Stan Brakhage, and his wild and free camera which imitates the motion of the eyeball, to Ed Emshwiller, who is able to use all of the grace of a dancer to caress his subject with flowing camera movement.

Moving the Camera
There are a number of ways that a man holding a camera can get it from place to place. The simplest way is to walk with the camera. If smoothness is your goal, choose the shortest possible focal length lens compatible with the situation, and walk with the camera; develop a kind of gliding shuffle. Practice moving this way without jerking or sudden movement; save money by practicing without film in the camera; you can even practice without a camera. When you know how to hold a camera smoothly, you can then proceed to hold it any way you like. Having perfectly smooth camera motions is, after all, no virtue, unless your purpose is to have smooth motion.

Sometimes it's easier to retreat, or walk backwards with the camera, when you want forward motion on the screen. If you're shooting in 16mm, hold the camera upside down and move backwards; the projected image, when properly oriented, will appear to have been shot normally. The technique can also make forward motion appear backwards when the film is projected.

The body and the camera can be turned into a disciplined choreographic unit. Camera motion can be achieved by moving from the waist, by bending and twisting the body. Such motions can be combined with walking as well. These maneuvers can be accomplished without the help of any assistants also. It may take practice to get a shot just right, and this may mean several takes of the same shot to accomplish your end; by the controlled use of the body, you can eliminate the need for tripods, dollies, cranes and other mechanical devices that would complicate your work and do restrict your freedom.

The Pan
The simplest kind of body-camera motion is the pan. Like other elementary body-camera motions, it can also be accomplished with a mechanical device, in this case the most basic camera aid, the tripod.

A *horizontal pan* can be accomplished by twisting from the waist, rotating the head, neck and arms, knees and ankles in a coordinated movement. The shorter the pan, or the less of an arc the camera swings through, the less anatomy need be brought to play.

A *vertical pan,* sometimes called a *tilt,* can be accomplished as easily. A tilt uses the upper part of the body, essentially waist, head, neck and arms. It can be incorporated with the horizontal pan, so that you can pan the camera in any direction, or you can smoothly transfer one kind of pan into another. Any camera motion, pan or camera-body movement can be combined with any other.

When panning across a static scene, such as a distant landscape, the usual tendency is to pan too fast for detail to be visible. Such panning looks like a blur on the screen. Now this may be what you want, but if it isn't, you'll have to keep your pan slow—be the camera hand-held or on a tripod. You can try slowing down your motion as you pan, or you can try choosing a higher fps rate, in effect shooting the pan in slow motion. There's a lot to be gained by this last method if smoothness and clarity are your goal. However, if there is action in the shot that must be identified realistically, such as a man walking, the effect could be spoiled by the apparent slow motion of the pan.

I've seen published tables that, correlating focal length with panning arc, inform the filmmaker how much time such a shot should take. I think such tables are silly; the best guide to smooth panning is experience. If you are not certain of the results, repeat the pan several times, at different rates.

When panning a moving subject, simply follow the subject by keeping it in the finder. Don't worry about your rate of panning. The eye of the viewer concentrates on the subject and not on details in the background. It is possible to follow a subject's action, unaided by a tripod, with a very long lens, and get very good results.

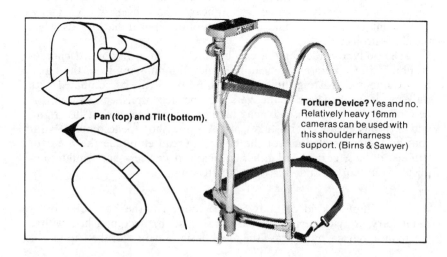

Pan (top) and Tilt (bottom).

Torture Device? Yes and no. Relatively heavy 16mm cameras can be used with this shoulder harness support. (Birns & Sawyer)

Independent Filmmaking

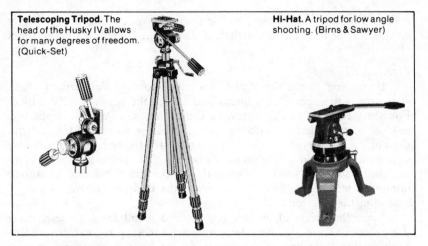

Telescoping Tripod. The head of the Husky IV allows for many degrees of freedom. (Quick-Set)

Hi-Hat. A tripod for low angle shooting. (Birns & Sawyer)

On a Tripod

A tripod is used for filming from a fixed point of view. The camera is held perfectly steady when mounted on a tripod. This is useful for shooting titles, single frame animation and so on; the camera can also be pivoted on the moveable head of the tripod. (On some tripods the head is a separate unit which may be interchanged.) This head is called a *pan head,* and it is usually adjustable for panning, tilting and swinging from side to side.

To properly position the tripod, it may be necessary to control its side-to-side and up and down motion. It is important that the controls allow the proper framing of the shot, as well as permitting the camera to be rotated (panned) in any number of ways. A simple ball joint head is not suitable for most motion picture work.

Tripods are made out of wood or metal. Their legs usually collapse from full extension, making them portable. The legs of the tripod may be fitted with rubber-tipped stops, or spikes, for securing into the ground. It is difficult to find an adequate tripod for less than, say sixty dollars. In this price category, there are several serviceable units, such as the Husky IV. These tripods, usually made out of a light aluminum alloy, are equipped with telescoping rubber-tipped legs and an elevator section which, for additional height or fine positioning, may be raised or lowered with a crank control. The separate pan head rests on top of the elevator section.

It is possible to pay several hundred dollars for the pan head alone. The expensive pan heads, such as the Miller, are so designed that they force the filmmaker to make a smooth pan. They offer a resistance to the intended motion of direction and smooth out motion by forcing a fluid from one chamber to another. Other pan heads use different precision gear designs, or nylon fittings so tightly enmeshed that rapid or jerky motion of the camera is impossible. Whether or not an expensive tripod and pan head is worth the money will have to be determined by the film-

Shooting

194   maker. For many purposes, the less expensive tripods are perfectly serviceable, flexible machines that, if well treated, will give many years of service.

Fixed on a Tripod

If you wish to use the tripod as a fixed shooting platform, all that's necessary is to mount the camera and adjust the height of the tripod. For heavy cameras do this in reverse order; that is, adjust the tripod legs as close as possible to the desired position before mounting the camera. Do not use the elevator section of the tripod for long lenses in a breeze or a wind. The wind acting on the camera body could cause the elevator section to sway or jitter. In general, for the most steadiness, use the minimum elevator extension, achieving the desired camera height by extending the legs alone.

Since the object of using a tripod is to maintain steadiness, make it a practice to use a cable release to start and stop the camera mechanism so that your fingers and hands do not have to touch the camera body. This will avoid any sudden jar at the beginning or end of a shot or, in fact, during a shot.

Panning with a Pan Head

Comparatively little skill is required for a smooth pan with any of the more expensive pan heads. If the filmmaker is using the less expensive tripod fitted with its own pan head, practice will produce a smooth pan. The proper technique will develop perfectly good pans.

The best procedure is to lock the head securely for all degrees of freedom, except the desired pan direction, or directions. If, for example, you are trying for a horizontal pan, tighten all the controls that permit freedom of motion in any other direction. Loosen the control for the horizontal pan so that the camera swings freely without drag. Some filmmakers leave a small degree of tension or tightness, believing that this will guarantee a smoother pan. This is not usually the case, since such pan heads may have rough spots that will prevent smooth rotation. If the head is adjusted to swing freely in the desired direction, with practice you can ensure a steady pan.

Tactile Control

There may be occasions, in very tight corners or for close-ups, when it is best to hold the camera like a flashlight, without your eye at the finder. This may seem outrageous, but it is possible to achieve beautiful and dynamic effects with this essentially *tactile* technique. Guesswork is required since you can't be perfectly sure of what's in the finder. The use of a wide angle lens helps in this problem, and at the same time, smooths out the movement.

Suppose you wanted to shoot a tree limb, traveling from one end to the other. With this technique you could combine arm and body motion to train the lens of the camera along the length of the limb. Slow motion can help smooth apparent movement and control the duration of such a shot. It may

require several takes, however, until you're satisfied that you've gotten
what you want.

The Dolly

The word *dolly* can have two meanings: it can describe a kind of camera movement, or it can be the name for the instrument producing that motion. A dolly shot is one in which the camera moves, usually on some device equipped with wheels. The wheeled device is called a dolly. There are many kinds and prices of commercially available dollies, from rather large units, to what are described as portable units.

The dolly is usually propelled by an assistant. The camerman rides along with the camera on the dolly. It usually requires a flat surface on which to move, or its motion will be less than steady. When shooting *on location* (whenever a commercial filmmaker is not working in a studio), commercial filmmakers frequently lay tracks, like railroad tracks, for the dolly to ride on smoothly.

A dolly may move toward the subject or back away from the subject; moving in is called dollying in, and out, dollying out. If the dolly is following the action, the camera pointing roughly perpendicular to the direction of travel, it's still dollying, but the shot is usually called a *traveling shot,* or sometimes a *trucking shot.*

The camera's movement on the dolly may make many demands on the filmmaker. For example, if the distance between camera and subject changes, it may be necessary to refocus or *follow-focus* the lens. Sometimes smooth and continuous refocusing of the lens requires an assistant's cooperation. As the camera moves, it may go from a region requiring one exposure to one requiring a different exposure. This, of course, can happen during a pan as well. For that matter, there's nothing to prevent the filmmaker from panning or zooming while dollying. In any event, such exposure control may require an assistant to reset the *f* stop; if the camera is equipped with automatic exposure control, it

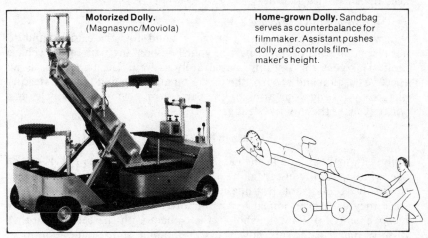

Motorized Dolly.
(Magnasync/Moviola)

Home-grown Dolly. Sandbag serves as counterbalance for filmmaker. Assistant pushes dolly and controls film-maker's height.

Shooting

maintains the proper exposure. Or, in this case, it can be easier to use the variable shutter to control changes in exposure.

Improvised Dollies

The most basic improvisation, or substitution for the dolly, has already been discussed—the human body. Without the use of the dolly—and all of its inconvenience—it is possible to achieve wonderfully effective traveling shots, free of the financial and mechanical restrictions of the dolly. However, when a dolly is needed and isn't available, all kinds of devices can be improvised to replace it. In every case, the camera is hand-held, and the filmmaker rides with the 'dolly.' Here are some improvised dollies: a wheelchair (can work superbly), a table with roller wheels, a rug on a polished or very smooth surface, a child's wagon (usually painted red), a shopping cart, and although this is not the end of the list, a car, which is especially smooth with the engine turned off, as it rolls or is being pushed.

Homemade Dollies and Cranes

A dolly can be made without too much trouble. One simple design is a four-wheeled platform on which a tripod is mounted. An interesting design for a dolly has been suggested by filmmaker Hillary Harris. It combines both the dolly, and what is know as a *crane*. You can see that it is based on the design of a child's see-saw or teeter-totter. In this design for a crane-dolly, the filmmaker lies prone on one end of a board and hand-holds the camera. His weight is counterbalanced with a sand bag. The pivot, or fulcrum, of this dolly-lever, is built on a wheeled platform. It requires an assistant to control the motion of the dolly and the crane functions of the device.

Professionally available cranes are very expensive, and massive. They are used to elevate the camera platform. The cliché Hollywood ending, in which the camera backs off higher and higher, is usually accomplished with a crane.

Shooting from a Moving Vehicle

When shooting from a car, boat or plane, hand-hold the camera, and do not rest your arms or upper part of your body on any part of the vehicle itself. This goes for any improvised dolly as well. The body acts as an effective cushion and absorbs the jars. You are not going to get a steadier picture by resting your arms or the camera on a vibrating vehicle; this will only make the shot less steady.

Effects in the Camera

If you can make a fade in the camera, and the camera has provision for backwinding film, you can make a dissolve. The serious limitation here is that the second shot, if it doesn't come out right will spoil both shots since they have been joined by the dissolve. Moreover, it may be very inconvenient to follow the shot in the camera with the second shot. A dissolve made in the lab, however, can combine shots made months or

Independent Filmmaking

years apart, at locations hundreds or thousands of miles away from each other. Be that as it may, here are some other ways to make fades (and possibly dissolves) in the camera.

One simple method might be to stop the lens down. Some lenses stop down totally, and admit no light, but most don't. Let's suppose that you're shooting an outdoor shot with medium speed film, and your exposure is $f/8$. Now stopping down the lens all the way, to say $f/16$, will not leave a completely dark image since some image, or at least some density, will probably be recorded three or more stops past the point of good exposure. If the lens were opened to $f/2$, then stopping it down to $f/16$ would create a complete fade. A neutral density filter, or any other filter with enough of a factor, can be used to change the $f/8$ aperture to $f/2$; the fade-in can be made by starting from the mimimum numerical f stop.

Another method for making a fade would be to pass a graduated strip—opaque at one end and transparent at the other—past the lens. You can make such a strip with sheet film, for example, if you do still photography, and have some sort of a darkroom setup. Eastman supplies such strips on special order.

One last method for making fades: polarizing material. Fuji, for example, makes a fade-out fade-in polarizer that fits in front of the lens. The device actually consists of two polarizing sheets of plastic or glass. As the axes of polarization are aligned, the maximum amount of light passes through the filter combination. When the axes of polarization are crossed, or at right angles, no light will reach the film. Gradual rotation of one of the pieces of polarizing material will produce a fade. Since polarizing sheet material is available from scientific supply houses, you can make your own fading device but this material may not be of first rate photographic or optical quality.

Polarizing filters are often known by the proprietary name Polaroid, which is the trade mark of the Polaroid Corporation. Many other companies also manufacture similar material.

Animation

It's hard to start classifying types of animation, but not nearly as difficult as to explain what it is. At the risk of explaining the obvious, animation in film is creating motion, or imparting motion to that which is inanimate. Movies are made of a string of frames, and if the object or objects to be animated are slightly moved in each exposed frame, then, upon projection, the objects will appear to move.

The objects can be dolls, or cutouts or *cells* (transparent celluloid sheets used by animation studios), or in fact, anything at all. If each frame has some new motion in it, then the animation tends to be smoother. In order to save himself effort, the animator often exposes not one, but often two or three frames of the same setup before going on to the next one. This may be acceptable for many subjects. Films made for television often use the two or three frame technique.

Shooting

Collage Animation

Stan VanDerBeek used clusters of two or three frame animation in his collage films, like *Science Friction* (FMC). The collage technique consists of cutting out a subject and animating it against or around a background. Plate or heavy glass can be used to hold the subject flat. The set-up for this kind of animation usually requires the camera looking down on the subject matter. Special animation rigs are available, usually at some expense. They provide many controls for zoom and pan effects. Less expensive tilting devices can serve as well as commercial animation rigs. Most independents build their own animation stands. The complexity and flexibility of such a stand is limited only by what the animator wishes to do, and his expertise as a carpenter and engineer.

A very simple animation setup is a tripod mounted camera aimed downward at the subject. Many tripods have reversable heads which makes animation work easier. The head or elevator section may be removed and can be inserted upside down. Sometimes, the geometry of such a setup makes the work of animation easier.

Cell Animation

Collage animation differs drastically from cell animation. *Cell animation* is a technique that is essentially geared to mass production procedures, allowing for assembly line techniques in the preparation of backgrounds, and especially foreground subjects. Most commercial animation, Disney films and so on, are produced through this method.

A background is drawn on paper, and characters are drawn on celluloid sheets which are placed over the paper background. The transparent celluloid sheets are inked and colored, drawn by different people in different parts of the studio. Every step is planned in advance. Usually, or in fact, invariably, all action is determined by the already recorded track. The camera operator follows instructions during the actual shooting. Each successive cell is held in position for each shot by a system of peg registration pins. Holes are cut along the top of the cell, and are aligned over the background with pegs on the animation board.

By separating the foreground and background this way, a great deal of labor is saved. If each frame had to be photographed from a complete drawing, the effort involved would be enormous. Even as efficient as it is, cell animation involves great effort, which is why many independents have attempted other forms of animation.

Other Techniques

Actually, there are so many ways to animate that I won't begin to cover the subject. But animation isn't any more difficult than other kinds of filmmaking. If you doubt these words, look at the films made by the children of Yvonne Anderson's Ball Workshop. *The Yellow Ball Catch,* and *Menagerie,* are to my mind, the two best animated films made in years. They were made under Yvonne's direction, by children aged 3 to 14. They have used clay animations, moving them a little for each new exposure, and they have used animated drawings with articulated or hinged joints against painted backgrounds.

The films of Carmen D'Avino, in which objects, like pianos or rooms, become progressively painted ought to be seen, as should Ed Emshwiller's *Lifelines* (FMC, CCC) for an example of the superb work that can be done with in-the-camera combinations of live figures and drawings. Another kind of animated film is illustrated by VanDerBeek's *Mankinda* (FMC) in which the painted film grows before your eyes. Actually, it might more properly be called a drawn film, or an inked film. The dazzling films of Harry Smith (FMC) illustrate yet another technique of animation, that is, drawing right on the film. Stan Brakhage (FMC, CCC) has combined drawing or painting on film with live action, simply by painting over the shots of live action. His *Art of Vision* and Smith's *Early Abstractions* should be seen and studied by anyone interested in animation, or film, for that matter.

The general technique for photographing animation is very much like copy work. A camera that will be used for animation ought to have a single frame release; a frame counter is also most helpful. Reflex viewing is not a must, but it is useful. Zoom lenses are usually shunned by professional animators because the center of field tends to shift as the focal length is changed. While this would not be obtrusive for most filmmaking, such sidewise or up and down swings of the image might be objectionable in very precise animation. Many of the latest designs of zoom lenses do not suffer from this defect to any distracting extent.

Exposure

Much of what can be said about exposure is related to the characteristics of film, and so has been broached in chapter 2, *The Film*. What will be presented here is within the context of this chapter: that is, factors controlling exposure at the time of shooting. Given a certain lighting setup, whether in or out of doors, the filmmaker's principal means of control is the variation of the f stop. Commercial films are often shot just the other way 'round. That is, the director of cinematography, as he is usually known, will light a shot for *his* favorite f stop, say $f/4$ or $f/5.6$.

At any rate, given an already existing lighting setup, the filmmaker can control the film's exposure by altering the opening of the lens diaphragm. If the camera is equipped with a variable shutter, this too becomes a means of exposure control. As the shutter is 'closed-down,' or the variable sector decreased, the exposure is correspondingly decreased.

The filmmaker may also choose to control exposure by changing the fps rate. Increasing the fps rate will decrease the exposure, and vice versa. Any change in the fps rate, either over- or undercranking, can respectively show up on the screen as slow or fast motion.

Finally, the filmmaker can control the exposure with filters. Neutral density filters are designed expressly for exposure control, and they will neither alter the relative tones of a black and white shot nor the colors of a color shot. With these filters, it is possible to 'stop down' the lens ten or more effective stops. Other filters can also be used, such as a polarizing filter (with a factor of about 2.5) for either black and white or color. For black and white filmmaking, colored filters will also control exposure.

With the exception of opening the f stop and undercranking, all of these methods decrease exposure. Under certain lighting conditions, the filmmaker has the option of using a faster film if it is impossible to get a decent exposure with slower stock. In addition he can have the film pushed. Most film stock—but there are exceptions—can be pushed at least one stop or, in some cases, two or more. Forced development, or pushing film one stop, is equivalent to doubling its exposure index; pushing it two stops, quadrupling the index, and so on. If the film is 'too fast' for the situation, it is possible to employ any of the enumerated methods for decreasing the exposure. Of course, it is also possible to use a slower film.

Determining the Exposure

The exposure can be accurately determined with the use of a device, named appropriately enough, an *exposure meter*. Some cameras have built-in exposure metering systems with varying degrees of automaticity. Whether or not the camera has such a meter, you can determine the exposure with the use of a separate device. There are two techniques, and two kinds of 'unattached' or in-the-hand meters. One type measures light reflected by the subject, and it is called a *reflected light meter*. This is the kind of meter built into camera exposure systems. The second meter measures *incident light*—light which falls on the subject—and not light reflected by the subject.

An exposure chart for various lighting conditions is sometimes supplied with film, and with a lot of experience and luck, it can get a fair percentage of good exposures. But the exposure meter takes nearly all of the guesswork out of exposure determination. However, the use of such a meter is not cut and dried, and improper technique, even with such a device, will result in disappointingly inaccurate exposures.

In the chapter devoted to film, film speed and latitude were discussed: film speed describes a film's relative sensitivity to light. Film speed can be determined objectively, and the value called the exposure index is given as a number. Once the E.I. is determined for a particular film, set the meter for that index. The index of film speed supplied by the manufacturer is generally accurate, but it is meant to be used as a starting point, because modifications—the calibration of the meter, the method of use, the effective f stop (or T stop) of the lens, the shutter speed of the camera or light lost by the reflex viewing system—have to be taken into consideration.

The manufacturer may recommend an index of 50 for his product, let us say a reversal black and white film. The filmmaker could make a

series of exposures with neighboring indexes of 32, 40, 50, 64 and 80.
The index yielding the best exposure should naturally be adopted. Film-makers whose work demands especially critical exposures can buy a large quantity of film stock—all of the same manufacturer's code for that emulsion batch—and run a test on one of the rolls, and use the results as a guide for future exposures on all subsequent rolls.

Even with all of the care in the world, however, errors in exposure can occur. Whether or not such errors can be corrected by the laboratory in printing will depend upon the degree of the error, and the subject matter of the shot.

Using the Reflected Light Meter

Reflected light meters measure light reflected by the subject to the light sensitive or *photoelectric* cell. There are two kinds of light cells in use—the selenium and cadmium sulfide cells. The selenium cell generates a current proportional to the light falling on it; the CdS cell modulates a current, provided by a battery or power cell, according to how much light falls upon it.

Meters—either separate or built into a camera—using either kind of cell can have good accuracy. The CdS cell is more sensitive: it can take readings under dimmer light conditions. Although it has this distinct advantage, it uses batteries which must be replaced periodically—every year or so—while the selenium cell meter will work indefinitely.

Usually, the reflected light meter is held at some reasonable distance from the subject. For landscapes, it would be pointed at the landscape, say at a forty-five degree angle to the ground, to exclude registering the sky's illumination. Including the bright sky would make the meter see the overall scene as brighter than it is. This could result in under-exposure. In the case of an exposure determination of a person's face, the meter could be brought to within a foot or inches of the face; care must be taken not to cast a shadow which would make the meter see less than the full measure of light striking the face.

One method of using a reflected light meter: take a reading for the

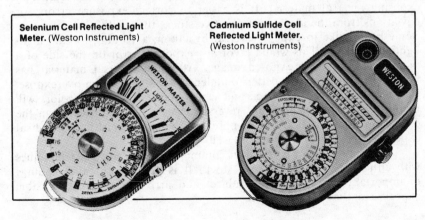

Selenium Cell Reflected Light Meter. (Weston Instruments)

Cadmium Sulfide Cell Reflected Light Meter. (Weston Instruments)

Shooting

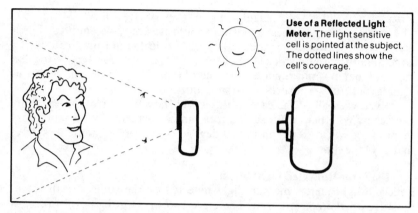

Use of a Reflected Light Meter. The light sensitive cell is pointed at the subject. The dotted lines show the cell's coverage.

most important portion of the scene, and base the exposure on that. As is often the case, the most important subject is usually someone's face. The meter can be brought close to the face, and the reading taken from this position. Such an exposure, if the face is evenly lit, will properly reproduce face detail. However, if other portions of the scene are appreciably darker or lighter, they may not be properly exposed. At this point it might be well to adjust or weight or bias the exposure according to the rest of the subject that will be recorded in the field of view of the lens.

The usual recommendation for negative film is to base the exposure on the shadow areas. If shadow detail is caught, the negative material usually has enough latitude to reproduce the rest of the tones of the subject. Best negative material results are produced by the minimum possible exposure capturing the full range of tones of the scene. If the film is given the minimum exposure, it will have the least possible grain. If there is any question about an exposure, overexpose negative stock. It is easier for a lab to make a decent print from a dense, or overexposed shot, than a thin, underexposed one.

Exposing negative material is somewhat less critical, however, than exposing reversal material. It is easier to correct exposure errors, or deviations from the ideal, with negative stock, than with reversal stock. Some people like to expose reversal by taking a reading for the highlights of the shot. This would favor any exposure error on the side of a more dense, or underexposed image. Although reversal material has very limited latitude, it is better to underexpose slightly than overexpose. This is true for color or black and white stock. At least the colors will be saturated, when using color reversal, even if important detail in the darker portions of the scene is obscured. Thin, or very light, reversal exposures are very difficult to print well.

At any rate, there is much in common in reflected light techniques with either negative or reversal stock. It is possible to take readings of important portions of the subject and arrive at the best possible exposure for the whole situation.

Independent Filmmaking

Using Spot Meters

Spot meters are a very special kind of reflected light meter. They make a reading for a small field of view, perhaps a few degrees, by sighting the subject through a finder. Reflected light meters usually take in a rather broad field of view, generally on the order of fifty or sixty degrees. Because the spot meter takes in such a narrow field of view, it is useful for measuring a small subject area from a relatively great distance. A spot meter is ideal, for example, for determining the exposure of events taking place on a stage, within a spotlight. Ordinary reflected light or incident meters would not be useful under such conditions unless they were brought within reach of the subject. If the camera is equipped with a through-the-lens metering system, it may be capable of making spot readings if it has a zoom lens.

In addition to this specialized use, the spot meter can also function as a highly accurate general purpose meter. By aiming the meter at various parts of the scene, and noting the various readings, a composite for a good reading may be obtained.

Suppose the sun is about forty-five degrees above the horizon, and someone is standing with his back to it. We're facing the subject and we're going to take a shot of him. Even though the sun is low in the sky, it's still a very bright day. We're using Kodachrome II, daylight or indoor corrected, with an 85 filter: our E.I. is 25; we're shooting at 24 fps, and our camera has a shutter speed of 1/50 second.

A meter reading of our subject's face indicates that $f/8$ would be a good exposure. Looking at other portions of the scene before us we get these readings: green grass in the field about $f/16$, a clump of rocks $f/11$, the subject's clothes $f/5.6$, yellow hay $f/22$ and sky $f/32$.

A close-up of the subject's face would call for an exposure of $f/8$. If we want to include more of the field, say in a head and shoulders shot, we'd stay with $f/8$, or if we wanted more saturation of background color we might stop down to $f/9$ or $f/10$. For a shot of the full figure of the man and the field, $f/11$ might be a reasonable compromise. If we wanted to silhouette the man against the field and the sky, at least $f/22$ would be called for.

Spot Meter. Spotron Pentaview Zoom reads a variable but narrow angle of view. (EPOI)

However, there is no *right* exposure. We have to relate exposure to purpose. And this example is fairly typical of situations the filmmaker is likely to meet.

Using the Incident Meter

Although some reflective meters are convertible to incident reading, and vice versa, each type of meter invariably works best for the job it was designed to do. The incident meter is used at the subject, and its light sensitive cell is aimed at the camera. The cell of the incident meter is covered with a hemisphere of some translucent material. The light passing through the hemisphere is metered by the sensitive cell within. In this way the meter takes an integrated look at all of the light falling on the subject. Once the reading is determined, the filmmaker can judiciously determine the final exposure according to the density, or densities, of the subject.

Generally speaking, the incident meter will give accurate readings for Caucasian faces if held with the hemisphere pointing directly at the camera from the position of the subject. If we're using the meter outdoors, and uniform lighting conditions prevail, the meter can be used at the camera position. If this method were strictly applied to the shooting of black people, we'd have to underexpose their faces, often half or a full stop more than what the meter indicates may be required.

The incident meter is preferred by professionals who often claim that it gives more accurate readings than the reflective meter. The incident meter is attractive to people who are working under conditions of controlled studio lighting, although it can give good results outdoors as well. It is particularly well suited for measuring the lighting contrast ratio.

Contrast Ratio

The *key light* on a set is the main light used to illuminate the subject's face. The *fill light* consists of the subsidiary lighting used to model the

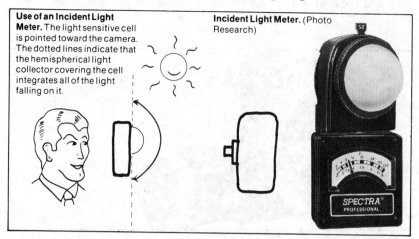

Use of an Incident Light Meter. The light sensitive cell is pointed toward the camera. The dotted lines indicate that the hemispherical light collector covering the cell integrates all of the light falling on it.

Incident Light Meter. (Photo Research)

Independent Filmmaking

face. The *contrast ratio* is the ratio of the brightness of the combined key and fill lights to the fill light alone. It is a measure of the ratio of the brightest area of light falling on the subject to the area of fill light. The lighting ratio may be determined with the incident meter by replacing the hemispherical integrating light shell with a flat white translucent disk. With the disk facing toward the lights — away from the face — we can measure the key plus fill and then the fill along. (See the illustration later in this chapter for a typical key and fill setup.)

Incident meters can give readings either in f stops or foot-candles. Foot-candles are a measure of the amount of light falling on the subject. If the meter says the light falling on the brightest portion of the subject's face is 250 foot-candles (or $f/8$), and the fill light is 125 foot-candles (or $f/5.6$), we have a lighting ratio of 2:1.

Usually, studio lighting technicians try to hold the lighting ratio for color film to no more than 3:1, because color film has less latitude than black and white film. If I were to try to apply the motion picture film manufacturer's strict advice about the use of his product, and use a ratio of 3:1, I could rarely film anything. Practically the only time you have to worry about light contrast ratios is if you've shot a scene and have to reshoot it later. In such a case, if you know the lighting ratio, it's a relatively simple matter to relight the shot to match already filmed footage.

Using the Polaroid Land Camera

A light meter is best suited for exposure determination. Sometimes, though, a Polaroid camera can be of assistance as an exposure measuring device. Not only can the exposure be gauged, but the tonal relationships among portions of the image can be seen. This method requires the more expensive Polaroid Land cameras without fully automatic exposure control, or a Polaroid back on a sheet film camera.

Suppose we are exposing film with an index of 50, and we are using the Polaroid black and white material with an index of 400. Using a neutral density filter with a factor of 10, an ND10, will yield a film-filter combination with a working index of 40, or very close to the motion picture film we are using with a 50 E.I. Suppose the motion picture camera's shutter operates at 1/50 second exposure. By setting the Polaroid camera for 1/50 second, we can readily determine which aperture to use for the motion picture camera by making exposure with the Polaroid camera, because its f stop setting now corresponds with our motion picture camera's lens stop. Black and white Polaroid material gives more consistent results than their color material.

Some experimentation may be necessary before you find the proper conversion factor between the Polaroid exposure and the motion picture camera exposure.

Flashing

This technique is used to increase the speed and reduce the contrast of black and white and color film. Some people like it and some people think it doesn't work very well. Flashing falls into two categories: preexposure fogging, or hypersensitizing, and postexposure fogging, or latensification. Some labs will perform this controlled exposure to film. Or, you can do it yourself by shooting a Kodak Neutral Gray Card, out of focus, to eliminate the card's texture. The color temperature of the illumination should be matched to the film. You'll have to find the proper flashing exposure by testing.

Just how much the film speed is increased is a matter best determined by experimentation. I've heard that you can gain one stop. Flashing produces a reduction in contrast and color saturation that must be determined by experimentation and observation as well. Flashed images often look gossamer with sparkling highlights.

Filters

There are so many possible uses for filters, that no general statement can be made about them except that they control, or change, the exposed image. There are several kinds of filter material and ways to mount them.

Gelatin Filters

Least expensive, and best suited for many purposes, are dyed gelatin filters, lacquered to resist abrasion. Since they are inexpensive but easily damaged, discard and replace them if there is any question about their quality. They can be dusted off, but it is difficult to remove fingerprints or grease from them even with careful wiping.

Gelatin filters are placed in front of the lens in the rear portion of a matte box, or between adapter and retaining rings mounted on the lens. They are usually held between the lens shade and the lens. First, they must be cut to the appropriate size and then dropped into place. To help hold them in the matte box and keep them flat and firm, border them with black photographic masking tape, or frames are available in which they may be mounted.

Some cameras, like the Bolex H models, are equipped with a filter slot. The gelatin filters are inserted in metal frames; a frame is placed in a slot behind the lens and in front of the film. Some cameras can be converted to accept this kind of filter slot. One advantage of using gelatins in a filter slot or matte box arrangement is that the filter remains in position even when the lens is changed.

Gelatins, like other filters, will change color, or fade, in time. Since this deterioration is related to exposure to light, storing them in the dark will retard fading.

Glass Filters

Colored material may be sandwiched between two pieces of flat glass to form one variety of glass filter. The other kind of glass filter uses colored glass. It's often difficult to tell what kind you're buying, but it doesn't really matter. Glass filters with an antireflection coating may also be purchased.

Glass filters are held in front of the lens. One type of glass filter

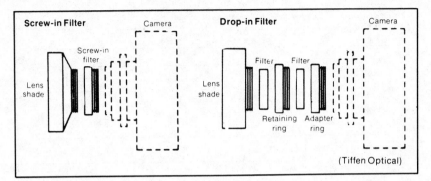

| Screw-in Filter | | Camera | Drop-in Filter | | | | | Camera |

(Tiffen Optical)

comes fitted with a screw-in thread that matches the thread of the front section of the lens mount. If this screw-in type filter doesn't have a threaded front end to attach a sunshade to, its usefulness is limited. There are other kinds of filters with their own mounting devices, ranging from bayonet to push-on type arrangements.

There are several standard *series,* or sizes of filters, from series V to series IX; the larger the Roman numeral, the greater the diameter of the filter. The most useful glass filters are either rimless or simply mounted in a metal rim. It is possible simply to drop the filter of the appropriate diameter into place in the front of some lens mounts. The lens shade could then be used to secure the filter in place. In some cases, an *adapter ring* may have to be used, screwed into the front of the lens (or pushed into place over the outside of the front of the lens), so that standard series lenses may be employed. In this case, the filter may be held in place with the proper lens hood. If a retaining ring is used to secure the filter in place, another filter may be added to the retaining ring which may be held in place by another retaining ring, or a lens hood. Combinations of glass filters, gelatin filters and close-up lenses may be held in place with such retaining rings.

Filters for Black and White

The major use for filters in black and white filmmaking is to control the tonal relationship of subjects. Sometimes the filmmaker might want to emphasize aspects of the scene by darkening or lightening parts of the image. On some occasions, it might be accurate to say that the use of such filters makes the tones of the scene reproduce more naturally. Although there must be dozens, if not hundreds, of filters available, most effects can be created with a handful of filters. These are colored yellow, red, blue and green, and are available in many densities for each color.

The guiding principle in the use of a colored filter with black and white film (negative or reversal) is that the filter will render similar colors as lighter tones, and complementary colors as darker tones. For example, a green filter will lighten green foliage, but darken red lipstick. A yellow or orange or red filter will darken the blue sky; if the blue sky is deepened then clouds will stand out.

Shooting

Filter Factors for Black and White Materials. (Eastman Kodak)

WRATTEN Filter Number	Color of Filter	Non-Color-Sensitized		Orthochromatic		Pan-Chromatic	
		Sunl't	Tung	Sunl't	Tung	Sunl't	Tung
3	Light Yellow	4	3	2	1.5	1.5	
4	Yellow	8	5	2	1.5	1.5	1.5
6	K1—Light Yellow	4	3	2	1.5	1.5	1.5
8	K2— Yellow	12	10	2	2	2	1.5
9	K3— Deep Yellow	20	16	2.5	2	2	1.5
11	X1—Yellowish-Green					4	3
12	Yellow			3	2.5	2	1.5
13	X2—Dark Yellowish-Green					5	4
15	G—Deep Yellow					3	2
23A	Light Red			3	3	6	3
50	Very Dark Blue					20	40
25	A—Red					8	6
58	Green			6	5	8	8
47B	Blue			5	8	6	12
29	F—Deep Red					25	12
61	Green					12	12
47B	Blue			6	8	8	16
Pola-Screen	Gray	For darkened sky effects, use a factor of 2.5 in addition to the exposure increase required for side lighting; or increase the exposure four times as compared to the exposure for the same subject with front lighting and without a Pola Screen.					

Filter Factors

Since filters hold back part of the light which might have reached the film, they usually require an increase in exposure. This is determined by a number provided for the particular combination of filter and film, called the *filter factor*. A filter factor is not a constant, but varies according to the subject and the desired effect. That's another way of saying that a change in the exposure using a filter will affect the relative tones of the subject as they will be recorded.

The assumption is that we have been considering panchromatic films—motion picture film is invariably panchromatic. This means that the film will be able to reproduce properly all the colors of visible light as tones of black and white. Since different emulsions emphasize or deemphasize various portions of the visible spectrum, individual filter factors will vary according to the kind of black and white panchromatic film used. Manufacturers publish filter factors and technical data sheets containing such information. If such a sheet does not come packaged with the film, it is available from the manufacturer.

A film-filter combination with a factor of 2 means that the lens must be opened one stop. If you prefer, divide the E.I. by the filter factor, and use your exposure meter accordingly. For example, a film with a 50 E.I., and a medium yellow filter with a factor of 2, could be considered to have a 25 E.I. If the factor were 3, we'd have to open the lens a stop and one half, or if you prefer, divide the E.I. by the factor to get the effective index.

Filters of similar color used in combination have a factor that is the result of the product of these two numbers. For example, using a 2 factor and a 3 factor filter would result in a factor of 6. However, this is to be taken only as a guide for exposure determination: only experimentation can determine the proper exposure. Filters with complementary colors, like the combination of a blue and a red filter, won't follow this rule. There, the factor will be much greater than the product of the two factors.

Black and white filters can be used for color film as well, and the effect they will produce can be easily judged by looking through the reflex finder of a camera mounted with such a filter, or by simply holding the filter to the eye. The filter factors given for their use with black and white film are a good starting point for determining the exposure with color film. A list of common filters, and their effect on black and white film follows. Since these filters, in at least gelatin form, are available in many outlets from Kodak, the Wratten designation is given in parentheses. Other manufacturers use other designations.

YELLOW (K2) is the most popular filter for use with black and white film. Since panchromatic film tends to be overly sensitive to the blue-violet end of the visible spectrum, a yellow filter suppresses transmission of the blue-violet. This will help reproduce the colors of the subject more accurately in tones of black and white. Aside from this consideration, which is primarily of theoretical interest, the filter deepens the blue sky, leaving other colors in the scene essentially unaffected. The filter factor is 2.

DEEP YELLOW (G) filter produces even greater darkening of the sky than the medium yellow, K2. It is claimed that use of this filter helps pene-

Filters and Their Effects. (Eastman Kodak)

Subject	Effect Desired	Suggested Kodak Filter
Clouds against Blue Sky	Natural	K2
	Darkened	G
	Spectacular	A
Blue Sky as Background for Other Subjects	Almost Black	29 (F)
	Night Effect	A plus Pola-Screen, A or 29 (F) with infrared material
Marine Scenes when Sky Is Blue	Natural	K2
	Water Dark	G
	Natural	None or K2
Sunsets	Increased Brilliance	G or A
	Addition of Haze for Atmospheric Effects	47 (C5)
	Very SLIGHT Addition of Haze	No Filter
	Natural	K2
Distant Landscapes	Haze Reduction	G
	Greater Haze Reduction	A or 29 (F)
	Haze Elimination	A or 29 (F) with infrared material
Nearby Foliage	Natural	K2 or X1
	Light	58 (B), or G with orthochromatic
Outdoor Portraits against Sky	Natural	K2 or X1
Red, "Bronze," Orange, and Similar Colors	Lighter to Show Detail	A
Dark Blue, Purple, and "Foliage" Plants	Lighter to Show Detail	None or 47 (C5)
	Lighter to Show Detail	58 (B), or G with orthochromatic material
Architectural Stone, Wood, Fabrics, Sand, Snow, etc, when Sunlit and under Blue Sky	Natural	K2
	Enhanced Texture Rendering	G or A

Shooting

trate haze, so that detail in distant views will be recorded more clearly. For this reason it is often recommended for long or telephoto lenses. My own experience with this filter leads me to offer this advice: do not expect too much of its alleged ability to penetrate haze. The K2 is preferable for close-ups of faces which include a sky background, because the G tends to change the values of lips and skin. The G has a filter factor of 3.

RED (A) filter has a high factor, about 8. It will produce very dark and dramatic skies. It can be used in conjunction with underexposure in attempting to simulate nighttime effects during the day. Greens, such as foliage, will be darkly rendered.

GREEN (X1). The use of this filter will result both in a darkening of the sky, and a lightening of the tones of green foliage. Leaves, foliage and green plants gain an astonishing degree of detail. It has a filter factor of 4.

Other Black and White Filters

It ought to be stressed that there are many other filters that can be used by the filmmaker for control or correction of the black and white image. For example, B is a deeper counterpart of X1; it has a factor of 8, and its effects follow in the same direction, but more strikingly. Similarly, there are a wide variety of yellow, red and orange filters.

In addition to these filters, there is one special kind of filter recommended only for infrared photography. Infrared movie film, as negative stock, is available. In order to filter out all but the infrared rays, it is necessary to use a very deep red filter, like an 87, which cuts off most of the visible light. A red filter like the A may be used successfully with infrared film.

Color Film Filters

Filters for color film fall into two general, but not distinct, categories. The first category contains *conversion filters,* and the second, *light balancing* or *color compensating filters.* The application of the factors of these filters is identical to the practice used with black and white film.

Information about conversion filters is supplied by the manufacturer, and so may differ from manufacturer to manufacturer and film

Controlling Tonality of the Sky for Black and White Films. (Eastman Kodak)		
Material	WRATTEN Filter	Monochromatic Rendering of a Clear Blue Sky
Non-Color Sensitized	None	Lighter than correct
Orthochromatic	None	Lighter than correct
Panchromatic	None	Lighter than correct
Orthochromatic	K2 (No. 8)	Practically correct
Panchromatic	K2 (No. 8)	Practically correct
Panchromatic	G (No. 15)	Darker than correct
Panchromatic	A (No. 25)	Very dark
Panchromatic	F (No. 29)	Almost black
Infrared-Sensitive	A (No. 25)	Black

Light Balancing and Conversion Filters. To use this chart: if you're using film balanced for 3200° K and you plan to use it with a source close to 3200° K, you'll need a light balancing filter. For example, with a 2900° K source an 82B filter is recommended. Conversion filters produce greater control. For example, a film balanced for 5500° K that will be used indoors (3200° K), needs an 80A (3200° K to 5500° K). (Eastman Kodak)

	Filter Color	WRATTEN Number	Exposure Increase in Stops*	To obtain 3200 K from:	To obtain 3400 K from:
Light Balancing Filters	Bluish	82C + 82C	1 1/3	2490 K	2610 K
		82C + 82B	1 1/3	2570 K	2700 K
		82C + 82A	1	2650 K	2780 K
		82C + 82	1	2720 K	2870 K
		82C	2/3	2800 K	2950 K
		82B	2/3	2900 K	3060 K
		82A	1/3	3000 K	3180 K
		82	1/3	3100 K	3290 K
		No Filter Necessary		3200 K	3400 K
	Yellowish	81	1/3	3300 K	3510 K
		81A	1/3	3400 K	3630 K
		81B	1/3	3500 K	3740 K
		81C	1/3	3600 K	3850 K
		81D	2/3	3700 K	3970 K
		81EF	2/3	3850 K	4140 K
Conversion Filters	Blue	80A	2	3200 to 5500	
		80A	2	3400 to 5500	
		80B	1 2/3	3400 to 5500	
		80C	1	3800 to 5500	
		80D	1/3	4200 to 3200	
	Orange	85C	1/3	5500 to 3800	
		85	2/3	5500 to 3400	
		85B	2/3	5500 to 3200	

Color Compensating Filters. (Eastman Kodak)

Peak Density	Yellow (Absorbs Blue)	Exposure Increase in Stops*	Magenta (Absorbs Green)	Exposure Increase in Stops*	Cyan (Absorbs Red)	Cyan-2 (Absorbs Red)	Exposure Increase in Stops*
.025	CC025Y	—	CC025M	—	CC025C	CC025C-2	—
.05	CC05Y	—	CC05M	1/3	CC05C	CC05C-2	1/3
.10	CC10Y	1/3	CC10M	1/3	CC10C	CC10C-2	1/3
.20	CC20Y	1/3	CC20M	1/3	CC20C	CC10C-2	1/3
.30	CC30Y	1/3	CC30M	2/3	CC30C	CC30C-2	2/3
.40	CC40Y	1/3	CC40M	2/3	CC40C	CC40C-2	2/3
.50	CC50Y	2/3	CC50M	2/3	CC50C	CC50C-2	1

Peak Density	Red (Absorbs Blue and Green)	Exposure Increase in Stops*	Green (Absorbs Blue and Red)	Exposure Increase in Stops*	Blue (Absorbs Red and Green)	Exposure Increase in Stops*
.025	CC025R	—	—	—	—	—
.05	CC05R	1/3	CC05G	1/3	CC05B	1/3
.10	CC10R	1/3	CC10G	1/3	CC10B	1/3
.20	CC20R	1/3	CC20G	1/3	CC20B	2/3
.30	CC30R	2/3	CC30G	2/3	CC30B	2/3
.40	CC40R	2/3	CC40G	2/3	CC40B	1
.50	CC50R	1	CC50G	1	CC50B	1 1/3

*These values are approximate. For critical work, they should be checked by practical test, especially if more than one filter is used.

to film. Here is some general information and a few guiding principles of filter application.

Color film is *balanced* for use in outdoor or indoor applications. The assumption here is that outdoors the light comes from the sun and the sky, and reflected from surrounding objects. Outdoor film, exposed under most outdoor conditions and without a filter, will reproduce

Shooting

colors, for lack of a better word, naturally. Outdoor film is balanced for 5500° K to 6000° K.

Indoor film is balanced fo. tungsten illumination or, more precisely, indoor film is balanced for a lighting source with a color temperature of 3200° K or 3400° K. There are many incandescent and quartz-type lamps that have a color temperature of 3200° K; others with a color temperature of 3400° K are also common.

In order to use tungsten balanced film outdoors, it is necessary to use an orange colored filter, the most frequently used is Wratten designation 85. Please check with the manufacturer's tech data sheets for exact recommendations.

It is common practice to use indoor film with filtration outdoors, but not vice versa. The deep blue filters required to convert outdoor film to tungsten balance have high filter factors which discourage this practice for all but emergencies. For example, Ektachrome EF Tungsten film can be used without filtration with 3200° K illumination sources with a 125 E.I. For use outdoors, with an 85 filter the index is 80. Ektachrome EF Daylight balanced film may be used outdoors without a filter with an index of 160, but in order to use it with 3200° K illumination, it must be filtered with a blue 80A filter giving a 40 E.I.

The orange filters for tungsten to daylight conversion have a factor of about 1.5, while the blue daylight to tungsten filters have a factor of about 2 or 4. Because of illumination problems, filmmakers need higher speed film shooting indoors than outdoors. For most purposes, an outdoor film converted to indoor use would present a handicap. Color film for the professional motion picture industry is usually supplied only in the tungsten balanced form. For outdoor use, it is filtered with an 85. Nearly all theatrical films are shot this way. Kodak's introduction of super 8 has been accompanied by their packaging of only one type of Kodachrome in their cartridges: indoor balanced Kodachrome II. This is an effort to make amateurs accept the professional practice of a *universal* film type.

Color Compensating and Light Balancing Filters

Color compensating or light balancing filters are supplied in many

Color Temperature Meter.
The model shown here, a Rebikoff, "sees" through two colored filters, red and blue, like most color temperature meters.

DM Exposure Factors.
(Tiffen Optical)

R SERIES	F STOP	B SERIES	F STOP
R 1 1/2	1/4	B 1 1/2	1
R 3	1/2	B 3	1 1/4
R 6	3/4	B 6	2
R 3 + *R6* = R 9	1	B 3 + B 6 = B 9	2 1/2
R 12	1 1/4	B 12	2 3/4
R 12 + R 3 = R 15	1 1/2	B 12 + B 3 = B 15	1/2
R 12 + R 6 = R 18	1 3/4	B 12 + B 6 = B 18	3/4

DM Film Types and Light Sources. (Tiffen Optical)	Bluish daylight, open shade, overcast DM 14	Average Sunlight 9 a.m. to 3 p.m. DM 18	Late afternoon sunlight, reddish DM 20	Photofloods 3400° K DM 29	3200° K Studio-Type Floods DM 31
Daylight Type DM 18	R3	NONE	B1 1/2	B9 & B1 1/2	B12
Type A and 3400K Tungsten DM 29	R12 & R3	R6, R3 and R1 1/2	R6 & R3	NONE	B1 1/2
Type B and 3200K Tungsten DM 31	R12, R3 and R1 1/2	R12	R3, R6 and R1 1/2	R1 1/2	NONE

colors and densities by several manufacturers such as Kodak, Tiffen and Harrison & Harrison. They may be used in conjunction with a color temperature meter, like the Gossen, Rebikoff or Spectra. The meter is used to determine the color temperature of the lighting, and then, depending upon the film's balance, a filter is chosen to adjust the film to the color temperature of the prevailing light.

Meters like this may be useful indoors, for example, because tungsten lamps tend to change color temperature with age or changes in the line voltage. They are useful outdoors as well, for example, early in the morning or towards sunset when light becomes much warmer, or redder. If it is the filmmaker's desire to maintain the illusion that the shot was taken midday, the use of a color temperature meter will determine the filter for this need.

Color compensating and light balancing filters may also be used to distort creatively the balance of the color. Instead of attempting to reproduce color as perfectly as the state of the art permits, these filters can be used for 'dramatic' effect. Overall tones can be added to the shot. Kodak color compensating filters, for example, come in six colors and six densities: yellow, magenta, cyan, red, green and blue; they call for exposure increases of a fraction of a stop to slightly over a stop. They may be used in combinations as well.

Decamired Filters

One system of color correction is the decamired system. Very briefly, here's how it works: color temperature values may be expressed in the *decamired scale*. Decamired values are obtained for a particular color temperature value in Kelvin by dividing 100,000 by the color temperature. For example, let us find the decamired value of daylight put at 5500° K.

$$\frac{100,000}{5500} = 18 \text{ decamired (or DM)}$$

Other useful similarly determined decamired values are 29 for 3400° K and 31 for 3200° K. The decamired system uses two sets of filters of varying densities of blue and red for *cooling* and *warming*. Each filter is assigned a number according to its density. Common red filters are R3, R6 and R12. Since they may be used in combination, for example R3 and R6 used together produce the effect of an R9, a few filters can produce a variety of densities. Blue filters are often supplied in the same densities, namely B3, B6 and B12.

In order to find out what filter to use with a particular combination of illumination and film type, make the following calculation: the de-camired value of the film minus the decamired value of the illumination equals the value of the correction filter. If the result of this calculation yields positive numbers, one chooses red filters; negative numbers, blue filters. Don't try to figure it out; it's like a game and those are the rules.

Here's a sample calculation. Suppose we want to use film balanced for 5500°K (18 DM) with 3200°K (31 DM) illumination. Applying the rule, we then have:

$$\begin{array}{r} 18 \text{ (the value of the film)} \\ -31 \text{ (the value of the illumination)} \\ \hline -13 \end{array}$$

The result -13 indicates that we need a blue filter of a value about B12. Some color temperature meters read directly in decamired values making any computation unnecessary.

Other Color Filters

Two popular filters for use with color film are the skylight (1A) and ultra-violet filters. The skylight and the UV have similar functions, and neither requires any exposure increase. The blue layer of the triple sandwich of layers making up color film emulsion is sensitive to radiation invisible to the eye—ultra-violet light. Ultra-violet light which is less able to penetrate haze present in distance scenes will be recorded as blue mist. The UV or 1A filter attenuates the ultra-violet light reaching the film, lessening the haze effect. At least it eliminates the bluish cast.

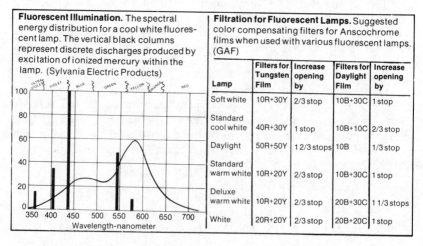

Fluorescent Illumination. The spectral energy distribution for a cool white fluorescent lamp. The vertical black columns represent discrete discharges produced by excitation of ionized mercury within the lamp. (Sylvania Electric Products)

Filtration for Fluorescent Lamps. Suggested color compensating filters for Anscochrome films when used with various fluorescent lamps. (GAF)

Lamp	Filters for Tungsten Film	Increase opening by	Filters for Daylight Film	Increase opening by
Soft white	10R+30Y	2/3 stop	10B+30C	1 stop
Standard cool white	40R+30Y	1 stop	10B+10C	2/3 stop
Daylight	50R+50Y	1 2/3 stops	10B	1/3 stop
Standard warm white	10R+20Y	2/3 stop	10B+30C	1 stop
Deluxe warm white	10R+20Y	2/3 stop	20B+30C	1 1/3 stops
White	20R+20Y	2/3 stop	20B+20C	1 stop

Independent Filmmaking

The UV and 1A filters are recommended for telephoto lenses because of this ability to diminish the effects of haze. The skylight filter is slightly pink, and UV filters are slightly yellow. The skylight is often useful for *warming up* shots made in the shade, without direct sunlight. In this case, much of the illumination comes from the sky, making the overall color balance of the shot tend toward the cold side.

These filters can be used in conjunction with black and white film as well. Some filmmakers like to leave the front mounted glass versions of these filters in place all the time because they offer protection for the lens.

Fluorescent Light

One particularly difficult color problem is shooting under fluorescent illumination. Fluorescent illumination cannot be measured on the Kelvin scale since fluorescent tubes emit light in selected portions of the spectrum, and color temperature has no real meaning applied to such a source.

Several manufacturers make filters especially for balancing color film to fluorescent illumination. Also, the manufacturer of the film you plan to use publishes filtration information for use with fluorescent lamps. Not only is the particular color sensitivity of the film a factor in determining filtration, but there are many kinds of fluorescent lamps on the market, making a difficult problem of correction even worse. However, try not using any filters with fluorescent illumination. You may like the results. Everything usually looks very blue or green.

Some people like to add enough supplementary tungsten illumination, say from halogen lamps, in order to produce a more pleasing color balance.

Black and White and Color Filters

Neutral Density Filters

I'd like to reiterate that any of the color filters available for black and white film can be used with color film for overall color changes. *Neutral density (ND) filters* which reduce the amount of light reaching the film may also be used with either color or black and white film. They are gray filters and favor no portion of the spectrum more than any other. For this reason, while reducing the transmitted light, they will neither alter the tonal balance of black and white reproduction of colors, nor shift the color balance of colors reproduced by color film.

Neutral density filters are one way of diminishing depth of field, if this is the filmmaker's goal. Or, these filters can be used with cameras that may have been loaded with film that's too fast for the situation. One way to get an acceptable *f* stop so that, for example, very fast film may be used outdoors, is to use a neutral density filter. Filters for color conversion to daylight used with high speed tungsten balanced film may be manufactured together with a neutral density filter to achieve a reasonable aperture. Eastman offers 85N3 and 85N6 combination filters.

Shooting

Like the neutral density filter, the *polarizing filter* may be used with either black and white or color film without altering relative colors or tones. The filter comes mounted in a rotating collar, and its effect is clearly visible through a reflex finder. Lacking such a finder, the filter can be held up to the eye to observe the effect. Polarizing filters have two major uses: to darken the sky and to reduce or eliminate reflection from some substances. Because reflections are suppressed, color saturation of some subjects may be increased. In addition, some haze penetration may be achieved.

A digression about polarization: light can be thought of as a wave, very much like that produced by shaking a rope tied at one end. The motion of the wave or the up and down action of the rope, can be thought of as being confined to a plane. Like the wave in the rope, waves of light travel in planes. Usually, light reflected from an object, or produced by a source, orients waves in planes at all angles with respect to each other. Such light is unpolarized. Polarized light is light whose waves are oriented in the same plane. When light is reflected by some substances at certain angles, some or all of it can be polarized. Very often reflections from glass or water, for example, can either be kept down or totally eliminated, because these reflections are made up of polarized light.

A polarizing filter allows full transmission of light waves oriented in one plane only. In other words, it polarizes the light it transmits. Light attempting to pass through the filter at any other angle will be attenuated or totally extinguished. If the light striking the filter is polarized, and the axis of the filter is oriented at 90 degrees to the plane of that light, none of it will pass through the filter. It's similar to a stick trying to pass through a slot set at right angles to its length.

In practice, the filter is mounted in front of the lens, and its effect can be seen through the reflex finder. By rotating the filter, its axis of polarization is rotated. If the plane of polarization of reflected light is at

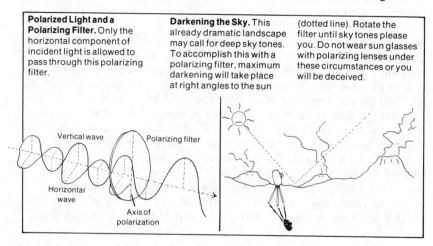

Polarized Light and a Polarizing Filter. Only the horizontal component of incident light is allowed to pass through this polarizing filter.

Darkening the Sky. This already dramatic landscape may call for deep sky tones. To accomplish this with a polarizing filter, maximum darkening will take place at right angles to the sun (dotted line). Rotate the filter until sky tones please you. Do not wear sun glasses with polarizing lenses under these circumstances or you will be deceived.

Vertical wave   Polarizing filter

Horizontal wave

Axis of polarization

right angles to the axis of polarization of the lens, the reflection can be suppressed or eliminated. The filter is very successful for seeing the bottoms of lakes or pools of water, by cancelling out surface reflections. It can be used to suppress reflections from oil paintings, glossy photographs or many other objects that have undesirable reflections. A successful polarizing filter can be overdone. For example, it is possible to suppress reflections from a car's windshield to the extent that it looks like there just isn't any glass.

Light as it passes through a medium like air can be polarized by what is called *scattering*. As a matter of fact, this is exactly what happens to light in the blue sky. Some of it is polarized. If a polarizing filter is used to shoot the sky, it is often possible to deepen the color of the sky. With the sun, camera and sky forming a right angle, the camera at the vertex, the maximum polarization of the blue sky takes place, and consequently the maximum darkening of the sky can be achieved without darkening the tones or colors in the rest of the shot. Depending upon the orientation of the filter, it is possible to obtain moderate to almost black or purple skies.

Unfortunately, as the angle between sun, camera and sky is changed, the polarization of the skylight decreases. Care must be used when panning with such a filter in place. Toward the sun, or 180 degrees away from it, there is no effect. At intermediate positions, there is the possibility of darkening.

A polarizing filter has a factor of about 2.5. It can be used in place of a neutral density filter. Polarizing filters, like other filters, tend to lose their moxie with time and exposure to light.

Special Purpose Filters
For lack of a better name I've grouped the following as special purpose filters. The best way to understand these filters is by using a camera with a reflex finder. The effect of the filter will vary with the distance it is placed from the front of the lens, the *f* stop used and the focal length of the lens.

The first filter we'll consider is the *graduated filter*. One form of this filter is half clear, and half neutral density, although it is possible to have part clear and part yellow or some other color. It is the deep half of the filter that is used to darken a portion of the scene. The simplest application of a graduated filter is to produce a dramatic sky effect without influencing tones in the lower portion of the shot.

Diffusion filters are available for softening the quality of the picture. They are useful for close-ups of Hollywood stars, if you have any around who have to mask or conceal their blemishes. The filters also add a soft or ghost-like effect to the scene. Filters are available with extremely varying diffusion effects. *Fog filters,* somewhat similar to diffusion filters, will add a foggy effect to the shot.

All of these glass filters are available from Harrison & Harrison, 6363 Santa Monica Blvd., Hollywood, California. They also provide a

Shooting

complete line of regular filters and will make filters to order for special purposes.

Another good source of filters—UV's, K2's, 85's and so on, and some weird filters as well—is Spiratone, 369 Seventh Avenue, New York, N.Y. They supply a filter called the *Crostar,* which will give 'star-like patterns from highlights and light sources.' Actually, with the diffusion, fog and Crostar filters we've sort of crossed over the boundary from filters into lens-like devices, since these 'filters' achieve their effects through the refraction of light. Spiratone also supplies a multiple image 'filter' that can produce rotating patterns of from three to five concentric or rotating images.

If you're interested in this sort of thing, several manufacturers (Spiratone, Tiffen Optical and Harrison & Harrison) make similar devices to be used in conjunction with your lens. You can also get odd effects by using plastic bits and pieces from the dime store or local glass suppliers.

Lighting

The emphasis here will be on lighting hardware and technique, rather than advice on specific setups or placement of lighting units. Commercial practice and independent, or if you like, *experimental,* lighting techniques have had, until recent years, little in common. Most often, independent filmmakers take the light as it is. This practice is called available light shooting and reproduces natural looking, or realistic effects.

Professionals generally shun this approach, and can give you many reasons why they are right and any other way wrong. Essentially, the issue is really a matter of esthetics. If you are interested in lighting a bottle of cola, so that it glimmers and glistens, or if your concern is to light a starlet's face so that she looks fantastically like a piece of stone, you will go to very nearly insane lengths to control the lighting. If you have virtually unlimited resources and a large crew, then you don't have to question established lighting procedures.

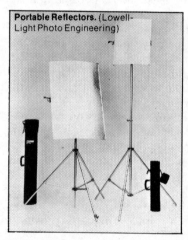

Portable Reflectors. (Lowell-Light Photo Engineering)

Use of a Reflector. To make your subject even more handsome, use a reflector to *fill-in* dark shadows.

Independent Filmmaking

Outdoor Lighting

In the majority of situations, no additional lighting will be needed for outdoor filmmaking; the filmmaker will probably find the light from the sun and sky, and light reflected from the surroundings, sufficient for his needs. There are occasions, however, in which it may be necessary to use some form of supplementary *fill* lighting. The most usual use for this kind of outdoor illumination is to fill-in shadows on a face when the sun produces harsh light or a high contrast ratio.

The simplest solution to the problem is to use a reflector to lighten the dark portions: the reflector is aimed at the subject to catch the surrounding light and bring it to bear where needed most. A reflector can be a large white card, or a suitable cloth. Reflectors are commercially available in many sizes. Usually, a large sheet of white drawing paper or a canvas will serve very nicely.

An alternative to the reflector is to use some form of artificial illumination. If a standard outlet or 120-volt power supply is available, indoor lights can be used outdoors. Commercial filmmaking units on location often haul in a power supply unit, not only for the lights, but also for the cameras and sound equipment. This is, in all probability, out of the question for the independent. However, there are several battery-operated fully portable lighting units on the market that may serve the purpose.

It is more difficult to use supplementary illumination, provided by a portable halogen lamp for example, than a simple reflector. The reflector will rarely overexpose or wash out what you're trying to fill-in. An electric light however, unless well placed, can produce artificial looking results. Not only is there the danger of overexposing what you intended to fill-in, but there is the danger of casting an additional shadow, at least one extra shadow for every light used. On this planet it rarely happens that there is more than one sun in the sky at a time, even though 'other worldly' effects often appear on motion picture and television screens.

If black and white stock is being used, there is no problem about matching the color temperature of the supplementary illumination and the outdoor light. However, when shooting outdoors with color stock balanced or filtered for daylight, the color temperature of the fill light must approximately match the color temperature of outdoor light. Halogen lighting sources can come equipped with a special filter to transform their normally 3200° K illumination to match outdoor 5500° K to 6000° K.

Night-for-Night

Another use for outdoor illumination is shooting at night. There are at least two possible intentions here. Either the filmmaker is shooting an event, using newsreel technique, or he is shooting at night attempting to create a 'dramatic' nighttime effect. If using color, it's best to use a film balanced for tungsten light, that is for either 3200° K or 3400° K, because there are many portable lighting units with this color illumination.

Shooting

220   Straight newsreel shooting can involve placing the light or lights directly on the camera, or from the direction of the camera. Such head-on lighting is especially unpleasant, and produces unflattering shots of people in most circumstances. It is best to have an assistant holding the light angled to the subject.

Shooting at night for a nighttime effect is a little more difficult than straight newsreel type lighting. It's usually best to light the scene, if it is supposed to be taking place in extreme darkness, for the highlights that might be produced by moonlight or street lamps. Let the rest of the shot take care of itself, and you may have a convincing effect. Depending upon your intention, it is possible to use one light or many. This is one situation in which the Polaroid Land camera may be very helpful in evaluating the lighting setup and exposure.

Day-for-Night

One frequently used technique, called *day-for-night* shooting, simulates a nighttime effect. This is accomplished by shooting a day scene and underexposing it two stops usually. For color, a blue filter can add a bluish cast to the shot. Using indoor balanced film outdoors without the conversion filter will give the same effect.

It is important to choose the setup carefully, so that no bright patches of sky or ground appear in the shot. The sky can be darkened for either color or black and white film with a polarizing filter, but this too has its limitations. The sky will be darkest only when shooting at right angles to the position of the sun. A graduated filter may also be used to darken the sky's color. A deep red filter will also darken the sky for black and white film. Of course, the effectiveness of either the polarizer or a dark red filter depends upon having a blue sky, whereas the graduated filter can be used even with a cloudy overhead. Filters may be used in combination for intensifying the effect.

Infrared film with a dark red filter is sometimes (but not often) used for a day-for-night effect. In this case, since the red filter will tend to wash out skin tones, special makeup has to be used.

Day-for-night shooting is rarely convincing. An uncritical audience may be fooled by the effect, but a filmmaker, technician or hip audience can usually see through the trick. Its use is entirely a matter of taste. A better approach may be to shoot at night, lighting the scene to suit your needs.

If you are planning to shoot day-for-night color, I suggest you discuss the matter with your lab, if printmaking is required. Some labs think they can do a better job adding all the blue to the scene when making the print, and so advise against using color filters at the time of shooting. But bear in mind that the use of this overall blue for a night effect is, after all, a dramatic convention.

Indoor Lighting

The State of the Art

First, some remarks about the state of illumination, and what this will allow you to accomplish when filming interiors. The present technology allows shooting in very low light level situations. Lenses can be very fast, $f/1.4$ in many focal lengths, and even faster. There are many black and white and color films with film speeds in the neighborhood of several hundred, and these films can be pushed to an index of 1000 or more. Furthermore, these films even when pushed a stop or so, can have exceptionally good quality.

This, coupled with the fact that good quality modern high speed lenses are exceptionally sharp and well corrected even wide opened, will allow you to use equipment effectively in very low light level situations with little supplementary lighting. The easiest way to preserve the feeling and character of a room, or any interior location, is very simply, not to tamper with the existing or available lighting. Long ago, the first still photographers learned what wonderful quality can be conveyed with honest lighting. The still photographer has an advantage over the filmmaker, however. He can control the final density of selective portions of the print very greatly. A filmmaker does not deal with a print made from a single negative or frame, but rather with a series of such frames. It is almost impossible to apply such local correction to a motion picture. What the still photographer can accomplish with existing lighting, and control in printing, can only be approached by the filmmaker, principally because the control in printing of selective portions of the frame, through *dodging* and *burning-in,* and variable contrast printing paper, for example, are not part of his arsenal.

For motion picture work, it is possible to make corrections in print timing, that is to say, in the overall exposure given to a shot at the time of printing. This exactly corresponds to the kind of printing service a still photographer can expect to get from a drugstore. The timing may be fine, in other words the correct amount of light may have been given to the print to make a reasonably good exposure, but still it is merely an overall exposure.

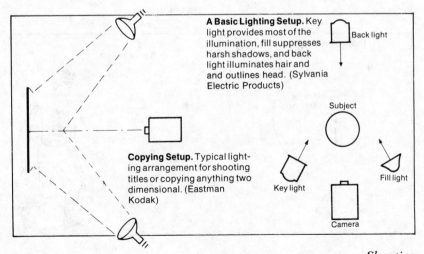

A Basic Lighting Setup. Key light provides most of the illumination, fill suppresses harsh shadows, and back light illuminates hair and and outlines head. (Sylvania Electric Products)

Back light

Subject

Copying Setup. Typical lighting arrangement for shooting titles or copying anything two dimensional. (Eastman Kodak)

Key light

Fill light

Camera

Shooting

Moreover, a still photographer working in black and white has the option of making his print on any one of a number of different grades of printing paper. In fact, the still photographer has had at his disposal, for many years, variable contrast printing stock. Thus, a single piece of printing paper could produce high or low contrast results, depending upon a filter used in the enlarger when making a print.

Consequently, it may be desirable to do as much as possible to help the quality of the final image, at the time of exposure, with some kind of supplementary lighting. However, it's possible to never use, or rarely feel the need for supplementary illumination.

'Location' Shooting

One approach to lighting an interior is to amplify the existing lighting by substituting brighter electric lamps, in existing fixtures, wherever possible. Simply replace the existing light bulb with a flood, or a high wattage lamp. Clear 150-watt lamps, for example, are very bright.

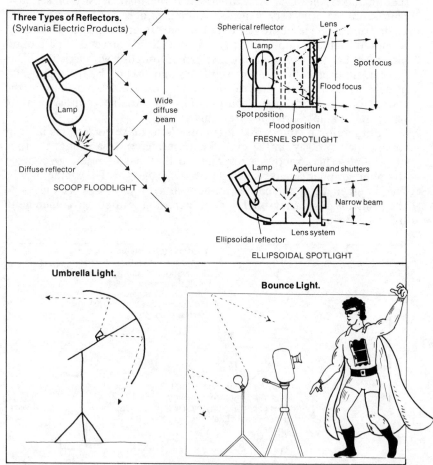

Three Types of Reflectors. (Sylvania Electric Products)

SCOOP FLOODLIGHT

FRESNEL SPOTLIGHT

ELLIPSOIDAL SPOTLIGHT

Umbrella Light.

Bounce Light.

If you are shooting color film with existing tungsten lighting, it is best to use film balanced for 3200° K. Ordinary tungsten lamps generally radiate at less than 3200° K — in the neighborhood of 2900° K — depending upon their power rating, line voltage and age. Using unfiltered 3200° K film with such lighting will tend to warm up the shot, or make it appear somewhat orange. If this is objectionable, a pale blue filter can be used over the lens or light to make the light *cooler,* or color correction can be applied to the print. A color temperature meter can be used to determine necessary color correction filters. Floods rated for 3200° K could be substituted for ordinary electric lamps wherever possible.

Shooting with black and white, in interiors, is a simpler matter than shooting interiors in color. In the first place, the problem of matching color temperature of the illumination to the film, or vice versa, doesn't exist. In the second place, black and white films are somewhat faster than color films. Unfortunately, the faster color films are balanced for daylight.

Bounce Lighting

Bounce lighting, where the lighting source is aimed at a wall or at the ceiling allowing the reflected light to illuminate the scene, can provide natural and even-looking lighting. It's possible to preserve a great deal of the character of the original illumination this way. The technique depends upon having enough reflected light from the walls or ceiling and, in turn, upon having lenses and film fast enough to satisfy the intensity of bounce lighting. You have to be careful to preserve a good balance between the bounce light and other sources of illumination in the room. If you're not careful, bounce light can look very flat.

There are special umbrellas, silver surfaced, with provision for mounting the lighting source, that have the advantage of providing greater illumination off the walls or ceilings than straight bounce light; in addition, they will not discolor the bounced light. However, they are one more piece of equipment to carry around, set up and worry about.

If the walls of the room are not a white or a neutral gray, the reflected light will pick up the color of the walls and ceiling, and color the subject. While this makes no difference when filming with black and white stock, it could cause annoying color shifts with color film. A mixture of bounce lights and substituting high wattage tungsten lamps or photofloods for ordinary electric lamps, can provide adequate lighting in many situations. This approach is very appealing because it requires a minimum of equipment and help to set up.

Types of Lamps

The independent filmmaker, when seeking supplementary illumination, will probably choose either photofloods or halogen lamps (or both). They are available in color temperatures of 3200° K and 3400° K. In addition, the use of special *dichroic* filters with halogen lamps can provide bright light of daylight color temperature, about 5500° K. Dichroic (for two-color) filters are glass which has been coated with a metallic film which, in this case, very efficiently changes color temperature.

Photofloods

Photofloods are very much like household incandescent lamps. Many will screw into ordinary sockets, and a great variety of shapes and sizes of reflectors are available for use with these lamps. Some photofloods have built-in reflectors. The reflectors themselves may be mounted on a stand, or a tripod or taped (with gaffer's tape) to the wall. Some reflectors for photofloods have clamping devices useful for attaching to the back of a chair or the side of a door, for example.

Photofloods are available in various power ratings, from about 100 to 1000 watts and with different bases, in color temperatures from about 2900° K to 3400° K. When mounted in reflectors, they may be used for either direct or bounce lighting. Photofloods have a reasonably long life, are available from many retail outlets and can be powered with the current found in most homes and businesses. The literature is somewhat confused, and the term photoflood is sometimes used to describe lamps rated at 3400° K. I have not been making any distinction between lamps at 3200° K and 3400° K.

If your work demands a lighting source with an accurately controlled color temperature, be advised that photofloods change color temperature with changes in line voltage. The greater the voltage, the colder the light; the less the voltage, the warmer the light. Changes in line voltage, and consequently changes in color temperature, are frequent; but they may not be very noticeable. Photofloods will also change color temperature (the glass envelope will blacken), and they will decrease in intensity with age. This is their most serious disadvantage, because it happens so gradually it may be hard to detect until a radical change has taken place. If you are doing critical work, one solution is to use a color temperature meter, because this takes into account factors such as lamp aging and voltage changes.

Another approach would be to measure the line voltage at the

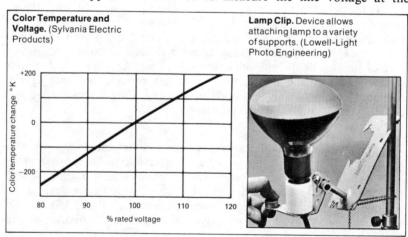

Color Temperature and Voltage. (Sylvania Electric Products)

Color temperature change ° K

+200

0

−200

80 90 100 110 120

% rated voltage

Lamp Clip. Device allows attaching lamp to a variety of supports. (Lowell-Light Photo Engineering)

Independent Filmmaking

lamp, with a voltmeter, or to control it with some kind of a voltage control device. As a rule of thumb, a change of one volt is equal to a change of about 10 degrees Kelvin. Photofloods may be rated to run at from 115 to 120 volts. It's possible to accomplish some amazingly fine effects with just two or three photofloods. The interiors of all of George and Mike Kuchar's films have been lit this way. Good examples of what can be done with such relatively simple lighting with photofloods can be found in George's *Hold Me While I'm Naked* (FMC, CCC) or Mike's *The Secret of Wendel Sampson* (FMC, CCC). Both are in color, and the resulting moods and lighting effects are quite different. The color of George's film is supersaturated Hollywood nightmare, so garish, the mind boggles. The eye is bathed in splendor and strained all at once.

Mike, using the same set of lights produced a weird mood piece, dark and mysterious, shadowy and haunting, like something out of an old Batman comic book. Part of the difference comes from the lighting techniques used, and part comes from the combination of original stock and print stock. Both films are being release printed on Kodachrome (7387) stock. *Hold Me* was shot on lush Ektachrome Commercial, and *Wendel Sampson,* on relatively contrasty projection contrast Kodachrome II. Both of these stocks are comparatively slow, so I want to make the additional point that photofloods are useful even for slow film stock. They are even easier to use, however, with faster stock.

Halogen Lamps

Like photofloods, these are incandescent lamps. Instead of a glass envelope surrounding the filament, the filament is encased in quartz or a similar material in an atmosphere of vaporized halogen gas, such as iodine or chlorine. They are compact, bright, long-lived, and maintain the same color temperature their entire life. They are also known by the names quartz lamps, quartz-iodine lamps and tungsten halogen lamps. They are available in kit form — such as those put out by Lowell and Smith-Victor — with various kinds of mounting and clamping devices and

Gaffer Tape. Lamps may be taped to any surface; barn doors, on the lamp, control light. (Lowell-Light Photo Engineering)

Shooting

stands, and devices which may be mounted in front of the lamp itself, such as barn doors or diffusion screens, to control or contain the light.

They are available on an individual basis, at different brightness levels and color temperatures from about 2900° K to 3400° K. Most lamps are made to work at 3200° K which matches most motion picture camera film. Portable units are also available which operate from rechargeable nickel cadmium or other battery sources. Adapters are available for using halogen lamps in photoflood sockets, and some halogen lamps have the appropriate base for this use without adaptation.

Because they are so bright, it is possible to lose a good deal of light, with an over-the-lamp filter, and still have acceptably bright illumination. For this reason it is practical to convert these lamps, with a suitable dichroic filter, for daylight color temperature. A dichroic filter mounts in front of the lamp and suppresses passage of the red end of the lamp's light out-put. The filtered light may be used with film balanced

Lighting Kit. (Lowell-Light Photo Engineering)

Independent Filmmaking

for daylight use. Some halogen lamps come with a built-in dichroic filter. These lamps would be useful for fill-in illumination outdoors, with daylight balanced film, or for that matter, indoors with daylight balanced film. Halogen lamps may be used for all of the applications of photofloods, but usually they cannot be substituted for ordinary electric lamps since they mount in special sockets. As noted, adapters for this use are available.

Mixing Daylight and Artificial Light for Color

When shooting indoors during the day, the filmmaker may be faced with the problem of filming a mixture of daylight, through the windows, and artificial light. This mixture may be very pleasing, and you may want to leave it just as it is. If, for example, the interior is lit with lamps balanced for $3200°$ K, and the stock is balanced for $3200°$ K, the light passing through the window, or seen through the window, will be recorded on the film as bluish in color, since it is about $5500°$ K.

We have two separate problems here: first, the room essentially lit by the $3200°$ K lamps, with a view out the window included in the shot, and second, the light passing through the window, mixing with the $3200°$ K light in the interior. What to do will depend entirely upon what kind of an effect you want to produce. There is no *right* effect. There's only what you like or want.

You can leave everything the way it is, and hope for the best. You could use film balanced for either $3200°$ K or $5500°$ K, or filter it, perhaps, for some intermediate value. If the light coming through the window is much brighter than the interior illumination, it would probably be best to use daylight balanced film stock. If the subject in the room, faces for example, have warm highlights, this may be perfectly acceptable. It may look natural, in fact. If you want the interior illumination to match daylight, you could use halogen lamps, filtered for daylight with daylight balanced film. Then the light passing through the window and the interior illumination will have the same color temperature.

Another approach would be to filter the light passing through the window. Large sheets of acetate and plexiglas material are available for this purpose. The material is very much like a large 85 filter. Tacked in place, or taped to the interior or exterior, it will filter the light passing through the window so that it may be properly recorded on indoor balanced film. The setup would then be like this: $3200°$ K film and lights, and 85 acetates over the windows. The light seen through, or passing through, the window would now be properly balanced for correct rendering with the indoor balanced film, and it would mix properly with the $3200°$ K lamps. In fact, it would now be outdoor light converted to $3200°$ K.

These 85 filter rolls or sheets are also known as MT-2 sheets. They may have to be used in conjunction with neutral density sheets to hold back more of the light passing through the window. Neutral density sheets would also be useful when filming with black and white stock, in order to bring the outdoor exposure to a level with the indoor exposure. Acetates over the window tend to literally flap in the breeze. The effect is one of shimmering highlights, which can be distracting.

In both cases, black and white or color filmmaking, a certain amount of wash out or bluish cast, or both, through the window, may be perfectly acceptable and look very natural. It's really a matter of taste. Once again, experience is the best guide. I suggest trying such setups with the minimum correction and labor required.

What's Wrong with My Film?
This sheet sent with processed Anscochrome covers many typical areas of trouble. (GAF)

1 Pictures too dark.
Cause: Inadequate light at time of exposure or diaphragm opening too small. This is underexposure.
Correction: Open diaphragm wider. Refer to exposure guide enclosed with film.

2 Pictures too light with highlights lacking in detail and shadows which are too light.
Cause: Diaphragm opening too large. This is overexposure.
Correction: Reduce the lens aperture to allow less light to strike the film.

3 Unsharp pictures.
Cause: The lens of the camera was improperly focused at the time of exposure. Also, lens may be dirty.
Correction: Distances should be more carefully judged or measured and lens carefully inspected for dirt or moisture.

4 Frame line dirty and film scratched.
Cause: Foreign matter in aperture of camera or projector.
Correction: Clean the camera and projector aperture frequently with a soft chamois or brush. Do not use metallic cleaning tools!

5 Pictures unsteady on screen.
Cause: Projection greatly magnifies any movement of the camera while taking pictures.
Correction: Care should be taken to hold the camera steady. A firm support or tripod should be used, especially with long focus lenses.

6 Light areas very thin and shadows very dark, lacking in color.
Cause: Excessive contrast in lighting the subject at the time the picture was made.
Correction: With artificial lighting, reduce the contrast by adjusting lights. In the case of outdoor lighting, use a reflector to lighten the shadows.

7 Orange appearance of subjects exposed outdoors on daylight type film.
Cause: The exposures were made either too early or too late in the day.
Correction: Anscochrome Daylight Type Films should be exposed during the period from two hours after sunrise until two hours before sunset if best color rendition is to be expected.

8 Jumping and blurring of picture usually with vertical streaked appearance.
Cause: This is caused by camera losing the loop when camera is incorrectly threaded. Also, shutter may be out of adjustment.
Correction: More care should be taken in threading the camera or a check of the camera should be made by the manufacturer.

9 Overall yellow, orange, etc., appearance.
Cause: A filter may have been used inadvertently.
Correction: Filters should not be used with color film except for special purposes. See the instruction sheet for information on this point.

10 Overall haziness with circular light area appearing in picture.
Cause: This is lens flare caused by the sun striking the lens while pictures are being made.
Correction: The sun, if possible, should be in back or to the side of the camera. Back lighted pictures should be taken only if the lens is adequately shaded.

11 Picture has overall bluish appearance.
Cause: Exposure of tungsten type film to wrong type of light, such as daylight, without the recommended conversion filter.
Correction: Follow instruction sheet regarding proper film-filter combination under different types of illumination. When exposing Anscochrome Daylight Type Films on a hazy day, the use of a moderate ultraviolet absorbing filter is recommended.

12 Pictures show overall yellowish orange color.
Cause: Exposure of daylight type film to wrong type of light, such as flood or tungsten illumination, without an 80B filter.
Correction: Follow instruction sheet for recommended exposures and filters for use under various conditions of illumination.

13 Clear Film or edges yellow-orange.
Cause: Accidental exposure to white light; light leak in camera.
Correction: Load and unload in subdued light. Have camera thoroughly checked by competent repairman.

14 Opaque.
Cause: No exposure.
Correction: Lens cap not removed, shutter failure. Be sure you have not sent us the wrong film for processing.

15 Poor color rendition and low over-all density.
Cause: Film not processed before expiration date.
Correction: Expose and process before expiration date.

16 Bluish cast.
Cause: Film subjected to high heat and/or humidity or film expired.
Correction: KEEP COOL! Like any high-speed sensitized products, Anscochrome Film should be stored in a cool place, preferably below 50F. An ordinary household refrigerator is suitable for storing unbroken factory-sealed packages. Film should be conditioned to room temperature (about 3 hours) before the package is opened. Avoid leaving loaded camera in such places as automobile glove compartment, or direct sunlight. Expose and process film as soon as possible after purchase, always before expiration date.

Independent Filmmaking

Splicing & Editing

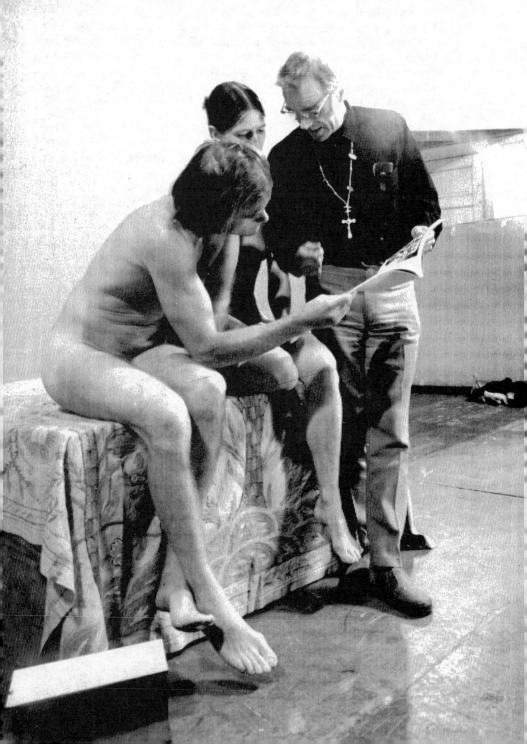

Splices and Splicers

There are two kinds of splices: tape splices and cement splices.

The Tape Splice

In making a *tape splice,* film is cut so that both segments are butted together (the tape splice is sometimes called a *butt splice*). It's exactly like taping two pieces of paper together, joining end to end, without any overlapping. The tape used is transparent polyester tape, consisting of a base or support of polyester, coated with an adhesive material. The adhesive side of the tape is pressed in contact with the base, or emulsion, side of the film, and the splice is made. The adhesive of good splicing tape won't bleed, that is, run out from under the ends of the tape.

The pieces of film must be held together so that they match up frame line to frame line, and the distance between performations, or the *pitch,* is maintained. To accomplish this, the film is usually held in a bedded device that uses registration pins to hold both portions in perfect alignment. Generally speaking, there are two kinds of tape splicers: those that use preperforated tape, and those that use unperforated tape. Preperforated tape machines generally cost around $10. Those using unperforated tape cost about fifteen or twenty times that price.

Machinery

One device that is used for making 16mm tape splices is the *splicing block*. A single-edged razor blade is used to cut the film segments at the frame line. Segments are held in place by registration pins which are also used to position the perforated tape properly. Perforated tape comes in two forms: in rolls and with a paper backing. The paper-backed tape is easier to use and is the only kind you can get for working in 8mm and super 8. Supplied by Kodak and other companies, it is more expensive (per splice) than tape not backed with paper. 3M, Permacel and others supply rolls of single and double perforated 16mm splicing tape.

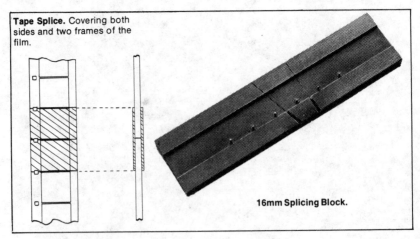

Tape Splice. Covering both sides and two frames of the film.

16mm Splicing Block.

Independent Filmmaking

The paper-backed tape is laid over the film and the backing is peeled off. The tape's perforations are first positioned by eye to align with the film's perforations and then by placement over the registration pins. Tape on rolls, cut for the desired length, and then placed on the film is trickier to use and harder to position properly than backed tape; but it is far less expensive, and if you are going to do a lot of splicing, try it.

Techniques

Depending on your purpose, you can decide to tape splice the film on one or both sides. A somewhat better splice is achieved by taping both sides; at least, it doesn't bend as easily at the joint. But the most important object is to relate the splicing method to its use. If the splice is to function for workprint purposes, and your projector can handle it, you'll save some time, effort and money with one-sided splices.

For making 16mm workprints, tape splices are easier and faster than cement splices and, in general, require less skill. I find them to be more fun to make, a factor to take into account. Also, when making a workprint, you'll probably want to shuffle the pieces of your film around, and this can easily be done with tape splices: simply pull off the tape, and redo the splice. And you won't lose a frame or frames, as you must when remaking a cement splice. When editing the workprint, common practice is to tape just one side of the film, if the projector will easily accept such splices.

The butt for some 8mm and super 8 tape splicers is not a straight line but often an *S* or zigzag shape, weaving in and out of the frame line. The cutting blade of the splicing device is curved. Although such a splice tends to intrude into the picture area, it usually makes the splice less likely to bend at the cut. Such a splice has advantages if you're interested in projecting your original footage.

When making any kind of tape splice, be sure to force all the air bubbles out of the tape. Obviously, if the tape isn't completely held to the film, the splice may part, or it will be unnecessarily visible. If you use two pieces of tape, one on either side of the film, the splice tends to be more visible than those made with one piece of tape.

How noticeable the tape splice will be depends upon the format, how well it is made, how many frames the splice covers and one other factor, the fps rate. It is my impression that the smaller formats show the tape splice more than the 16mm format. This may result from audibility: the smaller format projectors are usually far quieter than 16mm machines, and a splice passing through an 8mm or super 8 projector may be noticeable because it is easier to hear. One of the important factors is how many frames the tape will cover on either side of the join. Usually, paper-backed tape splices extend 2½ frames from either side of the spliced frame line, for a total of five frames.

One thing you can do to make a splice less visible is to make sure that the tape ends at the frame line, whether it covers one frame, two frames or three on either side of the splice. You can get away with a

232 splice that has tape covering only one frame on either side of the frame line: it will be the least visible tape splice you can make, but it will be hard to make with the less expensive splicing machines. The final factor in this survey is easy to understand. The higher the fps rate, all things being equal, the less visible the tape splice.

There are yet other considerations in making splices, but they themselves are problematical, 'iffy.' The first grievous flaw of tape splices is that they tend to spread; that is, both sides of the film tend to pull, increasing the distance between perforations on either side of the splice. One natural thing working to prevent this each time the film is spooled on a reel is that the pressure of the other layers of film forces the tape against the film. At the same time, however, winding the film on spools and the stresses involved in the printing and projection of film with tape splices, tend to make the spliced film draw apart. This may cause difficulties in projection or printing since the film can slip in the projection gate or the printer and be damaged or torn. The problem seems to be less acute in the smaller formats than in 16mm because, I assume, the forces exerted on the smaller films are less than those for the 16mm format.

If a tape splice doesn't cover the film perfectly and it clogs the perforations or extends over the edges of the film, it will cause the film to jam. This defect can only be eliminated by remaking the poorly made splice. If tape splices consistently get fouled up in your projector, you may be able to cure the problem by readjusting the pressure exerted on the film at the aperture, if your projector has an adjustable pressure plate.

Many filmmakers have observed that taped splices tend to bleed or run. That is, after a time, streaks will appear on frames adjoining the splice. These streaks are made up of adhesive material that has oozed out on the film from under the tape and spread around.

If you're going to make a tape splice on film that is mag striped,

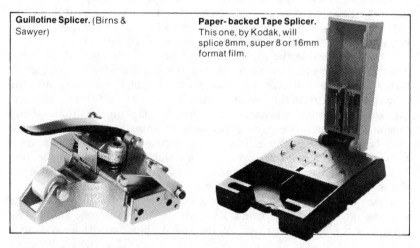

Guillotine Splicer. (Birns & Sawyer)

Paper-backed Tape Splicer. This one, by Kodak, will splice 8mm, super 8 or 16mm format film.

Independent Filmmaking

you can't cover the magnetic oxide material and expect to get good sound from that area. You'll get something, but it will be lower in volume and muffled. An acceptable remedy for this contingency is to tape the film on one side only, away from the mag track.

Also, check with the laboratory to see how they feel about making prints from film spliced with tape. Some don't mind, some give a flat refusal, while others disavow responsibility and will do it only at the customer's risk. The film cleaning technique used by some of these laboratories can cause the film and tape to part company.

One further area needs to be covered: inexpensive splicing machines versus expensive splicing machines. The inexpensive variety use perforated tape, either paper-backed or on rolls. There are two kinds of inexpensive machines (I am dealing in generalizations here—individual pieces of equipment may depart from this classification, but it is *generally* adequate): the simple splicing block, requiring the use of a razor blade to cut the film; the more elaborate machine with a built-in cutter, or blade. The splicing block is offered for 16mm work only, and the smaller format machines use built-in cutting devices. In either case, operation is fairly simple.

The more expensive tape splicer, one designed for professional or industrial applications, is the Guillotine tape splicer, the CIR, or Costruzione Incollarico Rapide made in Italy. Using unperforated rolls of tape, after the film has been trimmed (by the machine), it will apply the tape and perforate it in one operation. It is the easiest-to-use tape splicer, well made, but it's still too expensive, about $160. Whether or not its expense justifies its use depends on the amount of splices you make. Unperforated tape on reels is less expensive than perforated tape, and if you do a lot of splicing it may prove worth your while. From the standpoint of ease of operation, and just plain fun, if you like, the Guillotine beats everything else hands down. However, some filmmakers complain that the Guillotine's cutting blades need frequent readjustment. Actually the cutting blades are likely to need cleaning to work properly.

Tape splicing has been the preferred method with polyester base film. For many applications tape splicing has been the only practical splicing method since conventional cement does not work on this type of material. DuPont offers a cement for polyester base material that can be used with conventional cement splicing equipment. I have been informed that this cement is difficult to work with. Industrial users have resorted to thermal or ultrasonic or dielectric splicing techniques to weld the molecules of polyester film base to film base. These machines make superb splices, but are extremely expensive.

The Cement Splice

A cement splice is made in a machine called a *splicer,* costing anywhere from $10 to $300 or more, depending on the machine's design and workmanship, and the exact purpose to which it will be put. A cement splice is usually made by joining the emulsion side of one piece of film to the base side of the other piece. That is, the picture side of one piece is spliced right over the support side of the other. It is not possible to splice the emulsion itself to the base side. The emulsion has to be removed so that the cement comes in contact with the base beneath the emulsion. Once the emulsion has been removed, and the cement is applied, both pieces of film are held together under pressure for some short length of time.

It is simply not feasible to describe how to work each type of cement splicer, nor would it be desirable. Each machine comes with its own peculiar (weird might be a better description) instructions, piecing together the manufacturer's thoughts on how his machine ought to be used. This is a good enough starting point. That is, follow his advice until you understand how it's supposed to work, and then experiment with your own techniques. There are times when the manufacturer does not know how his machine may be best employed.

Mechanics

Briefly then, here's how to make a splice: the order of these operations may differ from machine to machine. Invariably however, the last steps involve applying the cement and pressing the pieces of film in contact.

Each of the two pieces of film to be spliced are selected. The emulsion side-up portion must be scraped in the splicer to remove the emulsion. This can be accomplished in some machines with the use of a built-in scraper, or in others the scraper is a separate unit. There are many techniques for scraping film (minutely detailed later in this chapter). In any case, you don't want to scrape too far into the base itself, for this will weaken the splice. Once the emulsion has been scraped away cement is applied, usually to the scraped surface. The amount of cement is very critical: too much will make a messy splice; too little will make a splice that won't hold.

Since the purpose of the cement is to dissolve the acetate with which it comes in contact, strictly speaking, it isn't cement at all: it has no

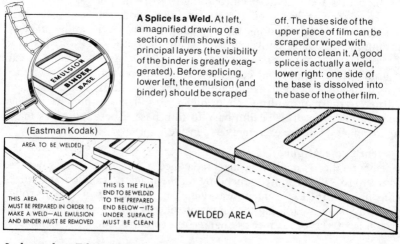

A Splice Is a Weld. At left, a magnified drawing of a section of film shows its principal layers (the visibility of the binder is greatly exaggerated). Before splicing, lower left, the emulsion (and binder) should be scraped off. The base side of the upper piece of film can be scraped or wiped with cement to clean it. A good splice is actually a weld, lower right: one side of the base is dissolved into the base of the other film.

(Eastman Kodak)

AREA TO BE WELDED

THIS AREA MUST BE PREPARED IN ORDER TO MAKE A WELD—ALL EMULSION AND BINDER MUST BE REMOVED

THIS IS THE FILM END TO BE WELDED TO THE PREPARED END BELOW—ITS UNDER SURFACE MUST BE CLEAN

WELDED AREA

Independent Filmmaking

adhesive properties. It's used to make the scraped area and the unscraped base dissolve and rejoin, as it were, welded together. One typical formula for cement (there are many) is to use roughly equal parts of acetone and ether, and about a dash of glacial acetic acid. Film free of emulsion, that is, acetate, is added to this combination of ingredients. Perfectly good ready made cement is also available from a number of manufacturers.

After the cement has been applied, both portions of the film to be spliced are brought together rapidly, and held together under pressure by the splicer. Usually the side which hasn't been scraped, the base side, is brought into contact with the emulsion scraped side by swinging the hinged half of the device holding it through an arc. The film is removed from the splicer, and you've got a splice. Or have you? Alas, there are many factors that will affect the soundness of the splices you make, not the least of which is the splicer itself. A filmmaker might well compare the machine's horoscope with his own, in this way determining mutual compatability.

Hot and Cold Splicers
Most splicers do not have built-in heating elements but rely solely on room temperature and air currents to dry the cement. *Hot splicers* are much more expensive, but they are favored by those who have to make many splices quite rapidly. For this reason, hot splicers are found in most professional editing rooms and laboratories. They are available for splicing all formats; the heating elements use line current and are thermostatically controlled.

In my opinion, hot splicers are overrated. The most important feature of the hot splicer isn't its heating element, but rather its quality design and fabrication. There are two reasons why the heating function of such devices may be of dubious value: in the first place, the introduction of Ethyloid cement (Fisher Manufacturing Co, Rochester, New York) has made it possible to make splices on conventional splicers in the time formerly required by standard cement with a hot splicer.

You can expect to make a good acetone base cement splice with a cold splicer in about thirty seconds, and on a hot splicer in about ten seconds. (Figures are approximate and will vary with technique, the machine used, temperature and, I suspect, relative humidity as well as the vibes.) An Ethyloid splice, on the other hand, will dry in about ten seconds or less with a cold splicer. Since the important factor in using either kind of cement is to bring both pieces of film together quickly, most people have trouble using Ethyloid with a cold splicer, let alone a hot one. Although I have heard of using Ethyloid with a hot splicer, the heating element is usually not turned on. Several filmmakers have told me that Ethyloid splices tend to be less than permanent, coming apart in under a year. My experiences with Ethyloid have been good, on the other hand.

The second reason for not using the heating element of a hot splicer is more controversial. I have been informed by the manager of one fairly large laboratory, that the heating elements have all been disconnected because hot splices, made with conventional cement, tended to 'dry out' and part within six months to a year. Take it for what it's worth.

There are hot and 'cold' splicers available not only for splicing each of the formats, but in all likelihood one which will splice 16mm will also splice 8mm (although the converse may not be true); some machines are even offered which will splice in all three formats.

Bevelled-edge and Film-on-Film.

The diagram will reveal the difference between the bevelled-edge and film-on-film, or normal cement-type splice. The *bevelled-edge splice* is made in a bevelled-edged splicer, of all things, which scrapes both the base and the emulsion side of the film. Once the join is made, there is no raised portion on the spliced film as is the case for the ordinary splice. The most important application of this is for splicing original footage with magnetic stripe. If a normal splice were used, the track will be held away from the sound head for the width of the splice, so that momentary drop-out (loss of sound) would occur.

Is the bevelled-edge splice as strong as the conventional splice? Since it is a more flexible splice, it might tend to last longer. On the other hand, there is less surface area available for the splice itself. However, I am not sure that after a point there is still any correlation between surface area and strength of the splice.

The conventional film-on-film splice with a complete overlap of the two adjoining frames is generally used for the preparation of 16mm splices and is invariably used for A and B printing.

Negative and Positive Splices

Better than these generally used terms might be *printer splice* and *projection splice,* but since these names involve difficulties as well, we'll stick to established nomenclature. The diagram on page 237 shows the difference between these two splices. The *negative splice* gets its name from the fact that at one time only negative material was used for cam-

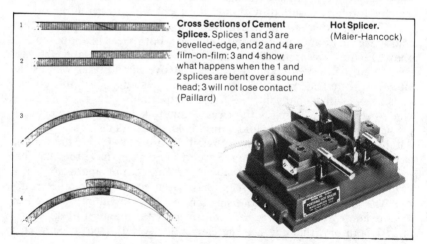

Cross Sections of Cement Splices. Splices 1 and 3 are bevelled-edge, and 2 and 4 are film-on-film: 3 and 4 show what happens when the 1 and 2 splices are bent over a sound head; 3 will not lose contact. (Paillard)

Hot Splicer. (Maier-Hancock)

Independent Filmmaking

era film. Although the same type of splice is presently used for reversal material when it is prepared for some printing procedures, the name remains. As you can see, in a negative splice one frame is completely uncovered, while the overlap is entirely on the adjoining frame.

The positive splice attempts to *split the difference* between adjoining spliced frames by putting some of the overlap on part of the top of one frame, and the bottom of the other. The hope is that upon projection such a splice will go unnoticed. If the filmmaker is going to project original footage, or is planning to make a print from one roll of printing material (instead of two or more as is the case with A and B'ing), he might do well to use a positive splicer; but this statement is open to qualification. Certainly the intention in using a positive splice is to make it difficult to see the splice, as difficult as possible. Instead of covering one frame, it is covering parts of two frames.

Now whether or not this is more visible than the negative splice cannot be settled by reason alone. We should do an experiment. I have not done an experiment. But I do have impressions and opinions, which come all the more easily, unencumbered as I am with precise information. One thing seems apparent though, and that is the visibility of a splice depends heavily on the subject matter of the shot(s). If the splice covers dark tones, it will be masked. If it covers light colored areas of flat masses of color, like sky, it is more likely to be seen.

You may want your splices to show. A splice is part of the filmic medium, after all, and visible splices communicate. For example, a visible splice is associated with home movies or television news footage. It can communicate a feeling of *actuality* or *reality* through these associations. Or, in and of itself, a splice can be punctuation, just like the dissolve or the straight cut.

Be that as it may, the most often used method for getting a *really* invisible splice is in preparation for using the A and B roll technique of printing your film. This requires a negative splicer. If you have any in-

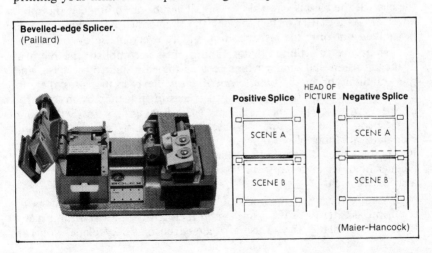

Beveled-edge Splicer. (Paillard)

Positive Splice | HEAD OF PICTURE | Negative Splice

SCENE A / SCENE B

(Maier-Hancock)

Splicing and Editing

tention of using the A and B roll technique, or you have some vague suspicion that you may some day like to use it, you would do well to purchase a negative splicer. Although the A and B roll technique is most generally available for the 16mm filmmaker, there are a growing number of labs that will A and B roll super 8.

In single roll printing, or when projecting original footage, it is possible to use the negative splicer (or positive for that matter) so that the overlap will coincide with subject matter in the adjacent frame that can hide the splice. For example, the overlap could cover the foliage or ground of one frame instead of the sky in an adjoining frame. You have to make a choice. Both types of splicers are available for all formats. If I had to choose one, the negative splicer would probably be my choice.

The Techniques

There are so many possible combinations of little techniques adding to a good splice, that it is impossible to give straightforward advice and say for example, do A, B, C and you'll have made a decent splice. Rather, it's more like, having a choice of A^1, A^2, A^3 . . ., B^1, B^2, B^3 and so on. You are going to have to play with a variety of techniques for each phase of splicemaking. Because so many variables can be encountered, I suggest you keep a record of what you have done. What follows are some suggestions about producing a well made splice.

Scraping

If you scrape your emulsion improperly, you won't get a good splice. The only trouble with this statement, and others like it that follow, is that I am not sure what constitutes the best way to scrape the emulsion from the base. In any case, I can tell you what *not* to do.

Some splicers come with a built-in scraping tool that rides on rails; this tool scrapes a controlled width, if not depth. You must have the right touch, or you can cut too deeply through the emulsion and weaken the base. If the base is scraped too thin, it can begin to hinge at the splice and tear. As a matter of fact, having the right touch for scraping, could be applied not only to this operation but to every phase of the splicer.

There are two things that scraping must accomplish: the removal of the emulsion and binder which secures the emulsion to the base, and the 'roughing-up' of the base. *Roughing-up* the base increases the surface area of contact between the two pieces of film thereby making for a better weld. Remember, splicing isn't glueing; it's really welding. Some people like to scrape the base piece of film as well as the emulsion half. Scraping of the base side is, however, not mandatory. Scraping, besides providing more surface area, will also remove any grease, lacquer or other material from the base side that might have prevented a successful weld.

Among the other methods of making a scrape is to moisten the emulsion — water or saliva is fine — and then scrape it away with a metal tool or razor blade. If you use a single-edged or safety blade, you can

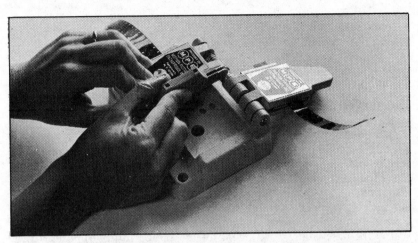

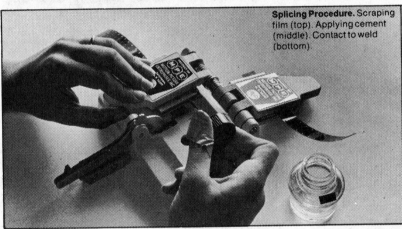

Splicing Procedure. Scraping film (top). Applying cement (middle). Contact to weld (bottom).

Splicing and Editing

use the blade portion or the edge perpendicular to the sharp edge. Such a razor blade should be replaced at the first sign of wear to prevent gouging. Excess material is wiped or brushed away and make sure that the scraped area is perfectly dry and clean before applying the splicing cement.

I have found that this razor-wetting method can leave the film too smooth. Therefore, in order to rough it up a bit, I have passed an emery board a couple of times over the base. Fine sandpaper works equally well. You can use the emery board without resorting to wetting and the use of a blade or metal tool. In such a case, the emery board would be used to rub away the emulsion and to roughen the base. However you do it, the scraping should remove all the emulsion (and binder, which is very thin, and you will probably never see it), and only penetrate far enough into the base to roughen it up a bit. The scrape should have uniform depth if the normal overlap type of splice is being made. Don't scrape the base thinner at the end of the scrape (quite opposite to the way the bevelled-edge scrape is made), for such a splice is especially liable to come apart at these weakened sections. After the scrape, be sure to wipe or brush or blow away all excess material before applying cement.

Applying Cement

There are two advantages to buying cement in pint sizes. First, it turns out to be far less expensive this way; second, cement needs to be replaced quite frequently. After an hour or two of use, the most volatile components of the cement have escaped; the cement *loses its body* and you can no longer make effective splices. Transfer small quantities of cement to glass containers for immediate use. The kind of container used by Craig for their Number 7 cement is practical and can be purchased without cement. The top of the bottle usually comes with an applicator brush which works very well. Every few hours, or before every splicing session, discard the old cement and add fresh cement to the little glass bottle. Rinse the jar with acetone to clean it out before adding fresh splicing cement.

The cement is usually applied to the scraped portion of the film, the side that had held the emulsion (this has been scraped away). Cement is usually applied with a brush, or sometimes with a metal stylus-type instrument. You have to apply just the right amount — if you use too much, the cement will slop over on the frame and may become visible; if you use too little, you won't have enough to make a good weld. My own feeling is that it's better to err on the side of a little too much than too little. As quickly as possible, the other portion of the splice, the second piece of film, should be brought into contact with the cemented area. I cannot stress too strongly the need to perform this operation with all deliberate speed.

Whether you have applied standard acetone base cement (Kodak Professional Film Cement is very good) or Ethyloid cement, both halves of the splicer must be brought together quickly! With quick-drying Ethyloid this is especially important. The time needed for the weld to take place is questionable. I advise at least twenty to thirty seconds for a cold splicer with acetone base cement, and at least ten seconds for Ethyloid. In any case, consult both the instructions on the cement can and those supplied with the splicing device. A hot splicer with standard formula cement dries a splice in from five to ten seconds.

Some machines have been designed so you can lift off half of the holding plate — that on the emulsion side — to promote drying and to wipe excess cement away. Some people like to apply cement to the base side, and then wipe it off immediately. This removes any grease or protective coating which may have been applied to the film during processing or manufacture.

One method that avoids the slopping over of cement to the frame, is to apply the cement directly to the base, not the scraped portion, and to make the splice this way, by rapidly bringing the two halves into contact. So there are many possibilities and you will have to play around until you find which work best for you.

Adjusting the Splicer

Depending on the design of the splicer, and your temperament, it can be very difficult to fix a splicer which has gone out of alignment. If you have trouble repairing or adjusting tiny machines or machine parts, forget it. It's a matter of both manual dexterity and *zeitsfleisch*. You'll have to make small adjustments to the machine, making splices as you go to test your progress. It could easily take a whole day to put even a slightly damaged splicer back into shape. Splicers can go out of alignment through wear and tear, as all splicers will, or you may have damaged it by dropping it (or throwing it).

Usually the splicer arrives well adjusted in all respects. Although it's important to adjust the pressure applied to the splice area, it's best to fiddle with it only if you are convinced that it needs adjustment. If too much pressure is applied, the film can be squashed or deformed; if too little is applied, you won't get splices that hold. Pressure when applied should be even across the splice area. It is possible to modify some splicers to negative from positive design, and vice versa. This is usually a relatively drastic alteration calling for a great deal of precision; and it requires tools like a jeweler's or larger screwdriver, pliers, small wrenches and a file. Such a conversion requires a great deal of skill, patience and trial and error.

I like the super 8 splice because of the distinct advantage of no perforations to worry about. It happens, from time to time, that the perforation in 8mm or 16mm film may be torn while the scrape is being made. This can never happen with super 8 since the perforations are away from the frame line.

If you like, you can use tape over a cement splice wherever you feel that you have made a poor splice. Tape reinforcement shouldn't be necessary (it has been asserted) if you've made a good cement splice. However, tape over a cement splice can be used successfully wherever you plan a laboratory dissolve or fade where the presence of the tape will be concealed.

Base-to-Base Splices and Splicing Different Materials

You may want to splice the base of one film to the base of another with the emulsion sides away from each other. Such footage will be flopped left to right, with respect to the main body of the film, but this may be your purpose in splicing base to base. There is no problem in making such a splice. It may be possible to omit the scraping procedure, but it is best to remove protective coatings and rough up the film. When projecting original material, it is not possible to keep both sections in focus, and you may have to *ride* focus at the projector. If the film is being printed, part of it will get slightly soft, or out of focus. This may or may not be a desirable effect.

There is no trouble in splicing together acetate base films made by different manufacturers. And there's no trouble splicing together nega-

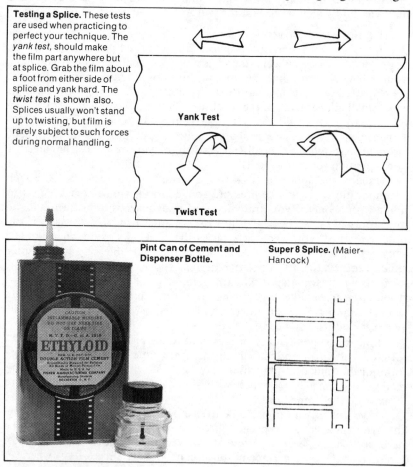

Testing a Splice. These tests are used when practicing to perfect your technique. The *yank test,* should make the film part anywhere but at splice. Grab the film about a foot from either side of splice and yank hard. The *twist test* is shown also. Splices usually won't stand up to twisting, but film is rarely subject to such forces during normal handling.

Yank Test

Twist Test

Pint Can of Cement and Dispenser Bottle.

Super 8 Splice. (Maier-Hancock)

ETHYLOID

Independent Filmmaking

tive and reversal film, or reversal with print, or color with black and   243
white, and so on. Just splice as you usually do. However, you cannot cement splice polyester to acetate.

Splicing Striped Film

If you use a bevelled-edged splicer, you'll remove the magnetic stripe
from the base side of the film as the splicer's scraper works on both the
base and emulsion halves of the splice. If you are splicing with a conventional overlap splicer, remove the iron oxide coating just as you removed
the emulsion from the companion piece of film. You can scrape it away,
but a simpler method is to apply cement to the magnetic stripe and immediately wipe it away.

Repairing a Splice

It happens, all too often, that a splice may part in time, or may have been
improperly made in the first place. The best cure I know of is to carefully
remake the splice, and then make a tape splice over the remade cement
splice since they do have a tendency to part. The tape is insurance that
the new weld will hold.

Editing Tools

The Editing Table

This discussion about setting up your editing table, or editing bench,
as it is often called, will be brief because endless possibilities exist to suit
the individual's needs and tastes. The only guiding principle is that the
setup should be as comfortable as possible since you're going to spend
hours there.

You can buy any sort of table you like, even though there are metal
tables sold specifically for the purpose. I've built my own table, using
a door as the top, with two-by-fours for legs and cross-members for
supports. You can put together a very sturdy table with white glue and
bolts for very little cash. To prevent any wobble which can get pretty vio-
lent when using winds at high speeds, I anchored mine to the wall with
angle irons. You're going to have to figure out the height of your table
and chair for yourself.

About lighting: it ought to be good. The entire room needs good
overhead lighting, and the editing table itself needs additional lighting,
like a high intensity lamp or a desk lamp of some sort. Whatever kind of
work lamp you choose, it shouldn't get in your way. For the lamp and
other electric equipment, you ought to have several nearby electric outlets. You can run a heavy duty extension cord to a set of outlets and
screw it to the top or side of the table, or a nearby molding, window sill
or wall.

The only equipment on the table fixed in place are the winds. Once
the winds are positioned they will determine the layout of everything
used in conjunction with them, like the viewer. The winds should be
clamped, screwed or bolted in place so that they line up; the film must
be able to run in a straight line between them. I've set mine about eight

Splicing and Editing

inches in from the edge of the table. Naturally the spindles should be parallel to each other, and probably will run parallel to the shortest dimension of the table. It's pretty easy to measure where your winds ought to go, using rulers or T squares and the like.

You can mark the table top for the positions you usually use for your editor and synchronizer. They have to be lined up accurately with your winds, and markings take the sweat out of positioning them each time. It's hard to tell you exactly how far apart your winds should be, but from hand to hand with arms outstretched, or a little less, is usually fine. You may want to mount smaller winds, perhaps with an eight hundred-foot capacity or so, near the larger winds. These can be very useful when you're doing matching of workprint and original footage, for example.

You can move around your viewer, synchronizer and splicer in any possible position or combination of positions, as the situation dictates. Often the synchronizer and the viewer are used in conjunction. You may be using your tape splicer or splicing block with the viewer and winds, or the winds with just the cement splicer. If you can move stuff around, and pick and choose what you need when you need it, you'll have a flexible, happy situation.

Light Panel

A built-in light panel is one very useful thing to add to the editing table. It's especially good for finding footage and edge numbers when you're matching footage or A and B'ing. Simply get a piece of heavy opal glass or plate glass backed with tracing paper; a piece roughly a foot and a half wide and two feet long, to suit your needs, would be fine. Cut a hole in the top of your table the shape of the glass. Mount the glass in the top of the table, and illuminate it from the rear with an electric light. You can find a variety of fixtures with built-in reflectors at the hardware store. Although they have been designed for ceiling installation, these

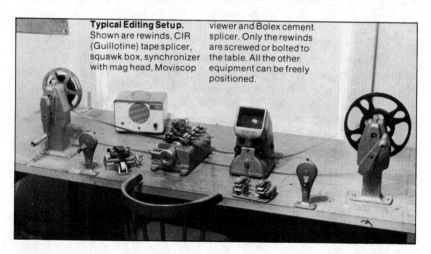

Typical Editing Setup. Shown are rewinds, CIR (Guillotine) tape splicer, squawk box, synchronizer with mag head, Moviscop viewer and Bolex cement splicer. Only the rewinds are screwed or bolted to the table. All the other equipment can be freely positioned.

Independent Filmmaking

reflectors will work well in this application with a 40- to 60-watt lamp.

The Film Winds

Most 8mm and super 8 editing equipment comes in a package that includes *winds* (sometimes called rewinds — rhymes with refined — but why worry about whether you are winding or rewinding?), a viewer (sometimes this is called an editor) and a splicer. It may be possible to obtain this equipment separately for these smaller formats, so that you can compose your own editing bench or table. Some 16mm equipment comes packaged together, but usually it is purchased separately. Film winds are used to transport the film (and sound track) from one reel to another, for viewing, footage counting and other assorted purposes. For example, you might use the winds to help you clean the film. An adequate capacity for 16mm winds is two thousand feet, and usually four hundred feet for 8mm and super 8. Winds are usually bolted or screwed to the editing table.

A wind has a handle turned by the filmmaker to rotate the spindle on which the rolls are mounted. (Some 16mm winds take interchangeable spindles which can hold up to six or more reels or cores of film. This is a necessity for A and B editing procedures, or matching workprint with master material which will be explained in chapter 7.) It is possible to obtain winds with different handle-to-spindle ratios. For example, one popular gearing provides four spindle revolutions for every revolution of the handle. This makes a nice compromise between what is desirable for rapid winding and comfortable for screening action with the viewer. Other ratios are available also.

Most models of winds are also available with adjustable *tension brakes* that prevent accidents occurring when the film on the feed reel overtakes the film on the take-up reel and spills over. This brake is necessary for a viewer like the excellent Zeiss Moviscop which requires back tension on the feed wind. A tension brake is also useful for winding film from reel to reel.

Several accessories are meant to be used with the winds in conjunction with a synchronizer, when several rolls of film are mounted on the spindle at once.

SUPPORTS are available for long spindles which might tend to sag under the weight of many reels of film. The end of the spindle is simply placed in the support where it can freely rotate while it is held.

SPACERS are used to separate reels so that they may be the proper distance apart when used in conjunction with a synchronizer. (Cores are often used in place of spacers.)

REELS, used to store film, are made of metal or plastic which vary greatly in quality. There are some perfectly terrible reels on the market, so bad that they can easily damage film. Some have sharp edges which can cut into film, some warp easily and so on. In my opinion, the best material for reels is metal; however, plastic reels are as good for short lengths, up to about four hundred feet, although they have a decided tendency to crack and warp. You can bend a warped metal reel back into shape, but a warped plastic reel is a total loss, for it invariably cracks if you try to bend it. Cans are used to store reels, and either plastic or metal serve well for this purpose.

Split Reels and Cores

Split reels are sometimes called a split reel set, somewhat like the option one has of calling pants simply pants, or a pair of pants. The *split reel* is made of two metal sides or halves, which screw together at the center. It is used in conjunction with a *core* which is inserted between the halves and held in place between them once they are screwed together. Cores are made of plastic, and laboratories regularly return processed film, workprints, etc. wound on cores.

At first sight, a film wound on a core without any side support, like

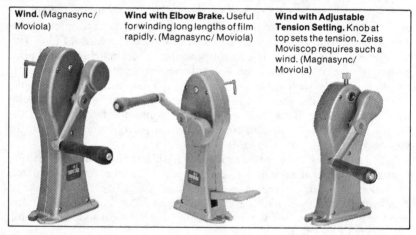

Wind. (Magnasync/ Moviola)

Wind with Elbow Brake. Useful for winding long lengths of film rapidly. (Magnasync/ Moviola)

Wind with Adjustable Tension Setting. Knob at top sets the tension. Zeiss Moviscop requires such a wind. (Magnasync/ Moviola)

Wind with Accessaries. From left to right: support, spring-loaded gripper or reel lock and reel spacers (Magnasync/ Moviola)

Half of a Split Reel. Core wound film shown on reel.

Independent Filmmaking

that provided by a reel, seems a tricky business. But it isn't. If tightly and properly wound, it is perfectly reliable. Film wound on cores takes up less space than film on reels, and cores cost far less than reels, in point of fact, practically nothing if you start accumulating them from your lab.

Film wound on cores is the perfect medium for storage of scenes in the process of editing. Just place the core between the split reel, tighten the halves of the reel together, and you can project your film or screen it on a viewer.

The Viewer

The *viewer* is used for screening the film during editing. It is a rear screen projection device, with a ground glass about 3 x 4 inches or so. The threading path of the film through most viewers is fairly straight-forward. The perforations engage and rotate a sprocket wheel which

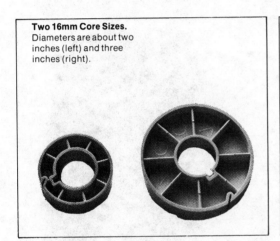

Two 16mm Core Sizes. Diameters are about two inches (left) and three inches (right).

16mm Film on a Plastic Core.

moves a mirror or prism assembly that projects each frame on the rear screen. Viewers do not have a shutter, as do projectors, and conse-quently, the image will flicker until speeds of about 40 fps are reached. However, even at the sound speed of 24 fps, or the slower silent speed, the flicker is not offensive. The editor is able to stop the film wherever he likes, to view the individual frame, or to move the film back and forth to view it in either direction. Some viewers have a built-in marker which can make small notches or grooves on the edge of the film for exact cut-ting point identification.

A good viewer (which has been kept clean) will not scratch or mar film. Many viewers, however, are simply not suited for use with camera film because they will damage it. The winds on your table can be used to drive the film, either forward or backward, through the viewer. With good equipment, winds and viewer, it is possible to study, analyze and absorb your film without damage.

Splicing and Editing

The Synchronizer

A description of what the synchronizer is becomes a list of what it can do: it can count frames and footage, match workprint with camera film, help in the cutting of sound track and prepare multiple rolls for the A and B printing technique which can yield invisible splices, dissolves and multiple imagery. The primary purpose of the synchronizer is to hold two or more rolls of film together, for frame-by-frame correspondence.

The synchronizer is made of metal, and has a number of sprockets, or *gangs* as they are sometimes called, driven together on a single shaft. A synchronizer with just one such sprocket is a footage counter. Film is held in place on each sprocket with a spring-loaded roller bar. The film is threaded on the sprocket so that its perforations engage the sprocket projections or teeth, and the bar with the attached rollers is placed over the film to hold it on the sprocket wheel. The roller bar clamps into place and can be swung out of the way instantly to free the film.

Zeiss Moviscop Viewer.

Precision Four-Sprocket Synchronizer.

Independent Filmmaking

For the 16mm version, each sprocket has forty teeth on its circumference. Since there are forty frames to a foot of 16mm film, the first sprocket wheel has numbers running from 0 to 39 on its edge, allowing frame counting. The revolutions of the synchronizer are geared to a counter which registers footage. After running film through the synchronizer with the winds, it is easy to tell what length has passed through the machine by simply looking at the footage and frame counters. If the footage counter reads 27 feet, and the frame counter reads 21 frames (21 frames in the straight-up position), we know that a shade more than 27½ feet of film has passed through our device.

What can be done for one piece of film, can be done for many. That is, the synchronizer can be used to hold many pieces of film together, frame-for-frame, and the frames and footage may be measured. However, the synchronizer's greatest assets are beyond its simple ability to count footage. Because it can hold a number of pieces of film together in perfect synchronization, it can be used for preparation of camera film so that it matches the edited workprint, for preparation of A and B rolls and editing sound track to match the image. These uses of the synchronizer will be discussed in later chapters.

On the West Coast, the Hollywood Film Company, the J&R Film Company and Magnasync/Moviola, and Precision on the East Coast, supply synchronizers. The West Coast firms provide machines with any number of sprockets on order, and the Precision machine, what the company calls a *unitized* synchronizer, has the ability to add on sprocket wheels as needed.

The most useful synchronizer accessory is the magnetic sound head which is added to the roller bar of your choice. When used in conjunction with just about any tape recorder, or a special amplifier-speaker combination, this head can edit magnetic sound track. Some synchronizers offer a special transmission that can be used between gangs of various formats. For example, it is possible to drive 16mm and 8mm, or 16mm and 35mm film in frame-for-frame synchronization with the proper gear box.

The Projector

You ought to have a projector in or near your editing room. Although with practice you can get a good feel for the rhythm of your edited film, the only way to see it to fullest advantage is at the proper projected speed, and without flicker. Some projectors like the long discontinued RCA 400 16mm will accept short lengths of film without threading on sprocket wheels, eliminating the necessity for splicing leader to segments to be screened. A silent projector is perfectly acceptable for the majority of editing room needs. If you intend to show sound film with mag stripe in 8mm or super 8, or mag or optical in 16mm, it may be foolish to buy two projectors—one for the editing room and one for screenings.

The Seimans, W.A. Palmer, Bauer P6 or Sonorex double 16mm projectors can be used for editing 16mm film in conjunction with magnetic film sound track. One side of the projector shows the film image, and the other side plays back the sound track.

The Moviola

Although this has become a generic name — and I'm sure the company is happy about it — the word Moviola applies to a specific piece of equipment, and not to the ordinary viewer which is often mistakenly called a *moviola*. The Moviola is a rather expensive piece of equipment, so it isn't found in the editing room of many filmmakers who might like to own one. It was introduced for professional 35mm, and the model shown here is essentially the same machine, adapted for 16mm use. The going day rate for renting a Moviola is in the neighborhood of $25, and you can probably find and use one in any large laboratory or film production outfit.

The Moviola is a motor-driven editing device that has a rear projection viewing screen. A rheostat controls a variable fps rate up to 30 fps.

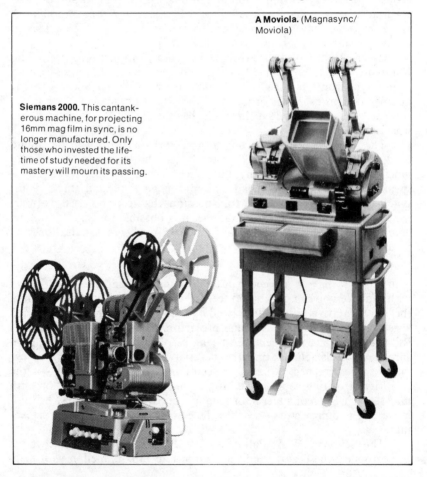

A Moviola. (Magnasync/ Moviola)

Siemans 2000. This cantankerous machine, for projecting 16mm mag film in sync, is no longer manufactured. Only those who invested the lifetime of study needed for its mastery will mourn its passing.

Above 20 fps a shutter comes into operation so that viewing would be flickerless at the sound speed of 24 fps. One major use of the Moviola is for viewing the exact timing or the rhythm of the shot or sequence of shots, as it will appear when projected on the screen. You can't do this with the ordinary hand-driven viewer (but you can make do very nicely with practice with a hand viewer and a pair of winds, if you don't mind using a projector with your editing efforts).

Besides the virtue of flickerless viewing at a constant motor speed, the Moviola has a sound head, or heads, for use with optical or magnetic track; the track can be driven in frame-for-frame synchronization with the picture, at exactly 24 fps for editing lip sync sound. You can watch the image and listen to the track just as it would appear on the screen. However, many filmmakers report that the Moviola is fairly hard on film.

It is possible, and easy, to use the viewer and synchronizer with magnetic sound head and hand-driven winds to approximate the effect of the Moviola. This will be explained in chapter 7. Motor-driven synchronizers are also available. The Moviola is a nice thing to have, if you do a lot of lip sync sound work, and you have the bread.

Horizontal Editing Machines

The latest generation of editing machines are of European origin. Unlike the Moviola, which transports film vertically, these have a horizontal layout. The KEM and Steenbeck (and Moviola horizontal model) offer modular construction which allows rapid interchangeability of viewing screens, sound heads and other components. These motor-driven machines are very expensive.

People who use them claim that these machines, unlike the vertical Moviola, are very easy on film. The KEM Universal will operate forward or backward silently, at from 3 to 120 fps. The machine can play three pictures on three screens and one track at a time, or it can mix

Horizontal Editing Table. Machines like this one are now available for super 8, as well as 16mm. (KEM)

Splicing and Editing

three tracks and show one picture. It is adaptable for use with any format, for 8mm to 70mm, and it can run any combination of format image and track in sync. Controls are electrical, and it is possible with the touch of a button to rewind one thousand feet of film in 45 seconds.

Motorized Viewers

Somewhere between the horizontal editing machines and the simple hand-operated winds, synchronizer and viewer lies the *motorized viewer*. It uses essentially hand-operated equipment that is driven by electric motor. The Precision motorized viewer, which can run precisely at sound speed, is reputed to be a very fine unit.

Odds and Ends

In addition to items like splicing tape and cement there are a number of things that make editing simpler. You'll need safety razor blades, scissors, masking or white paper tape, a stopwatch, grease pencils, white

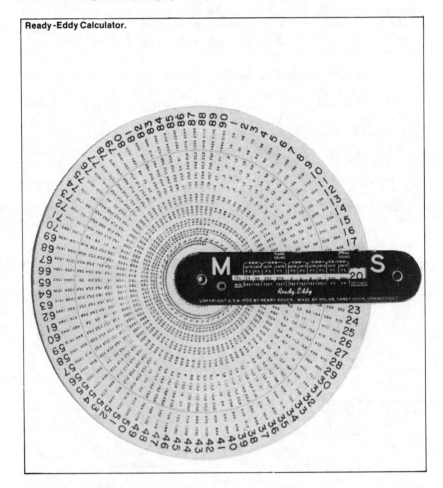

Ready-Eddy Calculator.

and black India ink and appropriate pens. Some filmmakers like to use   253
film bins for storing shots. These use clothespins to hang film, which
usually falls into a cloth sack. You can make such a device yourself, or a
number of firms offer them.

Cotton gloves are an important item. They're an impediment that
interferes with the sense of touch, but I've gotten used to them. For
maximum cleanliness when cement splicing camera original, you'll need
these gloves, which come in a few sizes. You don't need them for editing
the workprint.

The Ready-Eddy circular calculator is a very useful editing tool. It
converts footage into time in minutes and seconds and vice versa. It's
made by Rolab, Sandy Hook, Connecticut.

A cleaning cloth is a good thing to have because workprints, or any
prints you project and handle for that matter, can get terribly dirty.
Prints can be cleaned with cloths especially made for filmmaking, or
those used for phonograph records work well. Run the film by the cloth,
using the winds or projector rewinds, lightly rubbing both sides of the
passing film with the cloth. Eastman makes a cleaning liquid which
may be applied to the cloth if you like.

Cost of Equipment
Editing equipment for 8mm and super 8 is, in general, going to cost quite
a bit less than 16mm editing equipment. You can easily get started for
less than $100 in the 8mm formats. 16mm is something else. With new
equipment, a set of winds, a viewer and splicer (you may need both tape
and cement types) you can spend anywhere from $350 to $600 or much
more. Add a synchronizer and you can up the price by a couple of hundred dollars. I can offer my consolations, but little advice on how to circumvent such costs, except for the obvious ones such as rip-offs or com-
munal use of editing equipment. Equipment can be purchased gradually
as you concentrate more on what you like to do. Good editing equipment
may last as long as you do, but how much consolation is that?

Editing Procedures

So far, in this chapter, I've discussed making splices and basic editing
equipment. Now we're going to go a step further and deal with more
complicated editing procedures such as the preparation of workprints
and A and B rolls.

Single Roll Editing
The Workprint
The basic procedural decision that a filmmaker must make is
whether or not a workprint is justified. This is a decision that can be
made before shooting or after the film has been processed, depending
upon the nature of the film and your intention. A *workprint* is merely a
relatively inexpensive print of original camera footage. Edited in place of
that footage, its main function is to protect the camera original. After
editing of the workprint is completed, the filmmaker matches the cam-

Splicing and Editing

era footage to the edited footage, and is then able to have prints made. If you work in 8mm or super 8 you probably won't be making work-prints, although it's increasingly likely as super 8 becomes a more viable medium of commercial, or *serious,* production. Part of the joy of the 8mm formats is that they're less of a hassle than the 16mm format. Films in 16mm can become rather serious affairs, because relatively large amounts of money are involved. In terms of film stock, at the very least, less is risked when cutting the 8mm formats than the 16mm. Of course this doesn't mean that footage shot in the 8mm formats is any less valuable than footage shot in 16mm, since it's just as precious or irreplaceable to the filmmaker.

Certainly much of the fun of working in 8mm and super 8 is avoiding workprints, sound studios, motion picture labs and all the trouble and expense involved. Stan Brakhage looks upon 8mm as a notebook or a sketchpad. If you have had experience in working with 16mm, 8mm can be a relief. However, even if you are working in 16mm, you may not choose to make a workprint. Editing procedures for each format helps to shape the communication of that format. For some films it simply isn't possible to appreciate what you are doing if you edit a workprint, and for other films it just isn't necessary. Moreover, a workprint although relatively modest as prints go, can be expensive. If you can't afford a workprint, it's obviously better to get your film done any way you can, without one.

There are two alternatives in ordering a workprint from the lab. For example, you can have them make a workprint of the processed footage without your first having seen it (the movie industry calls these *dailies);* or you can view your film to decide what you want workprinted. The first way saves time, the second money.

Suppose you get back your original footage from the lab and look at it with your viewer. If it's a good viewer, and you handle your film carefully, you won't scratch or mar it. It's possible to go through what you have shot, discarding what you obviously don't want — content, exposure, etc. After you have done this pruning, you can assemble the footage, perhaps shot over a period of time, and have a workprint made of this collection of shots. The independent filmmaker, often without deadlines, has the option of working on a film for years.

You can view your footage on some viewers (keep the viewer clean!) without too much danger of damage, although projecting original footage is asking for trouble, if you want to keep it free of scratches. However, under many circumstances it may be worth the risk, depending on your purpose and the capabilities of your projector. I consider scratches to be a perfectly valid part of filmic communication, and like anything else, they should be used when they work.

KINDS OF WORKPRINTS. Several different types of workprint — relating to money and need — are available. Print prices, like processing prices, are based on a rate per foot. The least expensive workprint is a black and white positive print. If your original footage was shot on negative, color or black and white, you can order a positive workprint which will yield normal black and white tones. Some filmmakers order positive prints from reversal footage, color or black and white, and then edit that. Of course, then there's the difficult problem of having to deal with negative tonality. Some people can get used to this quality, however.

If you've shot reversal, you'll probably want a reversal print in black and white stock. Color footage can be printed on reversal color stock, but this is the most expensive workprint you can order.

The least expensive reversal stock for a workprint of a black and white reversal film is color blind stock. There is, however, the option of having your film printed on more expensive ortho or pan stocks that are of great use for making black and white prints from color stock. Ortho will give fairly normal tones from color footage, but pan which is sensitive to all the visible colors will give the best black and white tonality reproduction of color footage.

Another economic consideration is whether or not to order a timed or a *one-light* workprint. During printing it is possible to alter the individual exposure of each shot by controlling the amount of printing light passing through the camera original to expose the raw workprint stock. Timed prints are more expensive than untimed, or one-light, prints. Some people like timed prints because the better quality print makes it easier to appreciate how the finished film will look. Some prefer untimed prints because they give an idea of what exposures were like. In most cases, timed workprints are a superfluous luxury, since you can use an untimed workprint to better evaluate exposures.

Alternately, it is possible to go through your camera footage with a viewer, after studying the workprint, so that you can better understand the nature of the original. This is especially beneficial if you are using a black and white workprint to cut a film shot in color. By looking at the original, you can understand the nature of each individual shot, or sequence or cluster of frames, and relate it better to adjoining shots.

One further consideration when making a workprint is whether or not to have it and the camera film coded or edge numbered to make exact matching easy. Professional 16mm camera film invariably comes with latent image edge numbers (sometimes called *key numbers*). These numbers are visible — with transmitted light, that is, light which must pass through the film — after the film has been processed, and appear at intervals of twenty or forty frames (every six or twelve inches). The numbers progress in a sequence like this: 546890, 546891, 546892 and so on. It is possible to have the laboratory add their own printed edge numbers as well. These are usually yellow and easier to read than the latent image edge numbers because they can be seen with incident light, the way you're reading this book. Cost for edge numbering is usually a cent a foot or less. If you want to save money, latent edge numbers are perfectly adequate.

Here's an example of how you might go about choosing a workprint. Let's suppose your footage is color reversal. You could, for example, choose to order an ortho untimed black and white reversal, without lab printed edge numbers. Or from the same color footage you might order a more expensive print: a panchromatic, timed, black and white, reversal, lab edge numbered. Or you might order an untimed color print without edge numbers, and so on. Keep the lab's price schedule at hand to decide how closely what you want coincides with what you can afford.

Direct Positive Print Film

Direct positive is used for making workprints from reversal camera original or positive prints. It was originally produced by Eastman to be used as microfilm, and it is a very high resolution material. Although it is processed in negative solutions, it yields a reversal image. Its virtue is that it produces adequate workprint quality from reversal material at low cost compared with reversal prints. This black and white film is rather slow, so its use is limited to printmaking. At this time the film is in relatively limited use.

EDITING THE WORKPRINT. After you've chosen a workprint, here are some very general remarks about how to go about editing it: store the camera film on a core (or reel) in a can in some safe place. Since you do not have any immediate reason to look at the camera film, the less you handle it the better—if you want to minimize wear and tear and scratches.

I won't begin to tell you how to edit in terms of placing shots together. I will say, however, that the kind of editing we are accustomed to is extraordinarily simple-minded. It is, in essence, cutting film to match dialogue track. This kind of filmmaking is beautifully boring for me, but if it interests you, turn on your TV, tune to a television series or a feature film and turn off the sound. You can learn practically everything you will need to know about editing melodramas from only one or two of them. All the traditional advice about long shot to medium shot and close-up, or whatever you're suppose to do, is in general, so much bullshit. Such rules are applicable to special cases, and special cases only. A good example of a film that violates these rules, and is a fluid and poetic experience, is Bruce Baillie's *Valentin de las Seiras* (CCC).

Be that as it may, you now have your workprint before you. Project it, probably project it dozens of times before you make your first cut or cuts. Or you can immediately decide, after a cursory examination, which shots are useless. Cut out the footage you think won't be of use. But don't throw it away (or anything else you cut out of the workprint). Save everything, even individual frames! you can wind all of your *out-takes,* as they are called, on a reel or core, splicing them together if you like, so you can easily view them. You can also join out-takes together temporarily with masking tape, as well as segments of your workprint. It's much quicker and easier to make a makeshift masking tape splice than a regular tape splice. If you are making many cuts at once, it may be best to make the first join of the film with masking tape, so that you don't loose your ideas and enthusiasm. Getting hung-up in making splices can sap your strength and make you lose contact with your purpose. You can view what you've done with masking tape splices through your viewer; you can't run this footage through a projector.

I suggest, however, that when editing your workprint you make tape splices. These splices are simpler and faster to make than cement splices, and just as importantly, they are easy to take apart. Also, you don't destroy frames when taking apart tape splices as you must when you separate cement splices. Tape splices allow you to shuffle segments around, add footage to a segment or do any kind of editing with comparative freedom.

Through an assortment of processes like screening the footage with your projector or on the viewer and making cuts as you understand what to do, the edited version of the film gradually emerges. Don't be afraid or inhibited when you cut your film. The best thing about a workprint is that you can mess around with it as freely as you like, working out your ideas with your hands and your eyes.

If you really mess up the workprint, you can always reprint part of the footage or make another complete one. If you get stuck, or reach dry plateaus in your work, put the film away and try to avoid looking at it for as long as you can bear. Time builds a perspective about what you've done. So can other people's impressions. As your cutting progresses, after a while you may become concerned with editing to the frame, that is, removing a frame or two here or there to improve the rhythm of your cutting. On the other hand, you may find yourself totally reworking the film, adding or subtracting segments at what you might have considered to have been the eleventh hour. Although I can make suggestions, I can't tell you how to work. You've got to discover it for yourself.

One of the most tedious parts of editing is filing shots so you can locate them. You'll have to work out a system that best suits your needs and habits; this will develop. You're bound to develop many habits that a time and motion study expert might consider to be wasteful, but there's no way out of it. As long as you edit film, you'll discover better ways to do it.

How do you know when you've finished editing? It's a curious question but it is often asked. The ultimate answer is that you're finished when the film looks the way you'd like it to look. However, I have learned that this never quite happens. The answer that appeals to me at the moment is that you've finished editing a film when you're tired of working on it.

CONFORMING, or matching, involves cutting the camera film to match the workprint. Let us suppose that the workprint is completed. Most independent filmmakers will themselves go on to cut the camera film to match the workprint even though many laboratories offer this service. The price is usually pretty stiff, but when you consider the amount of drudgery involved, perhaps it's not so bad. You did the creative work when you edited the workprint and now that all of the decisions have been made, cutting the camera film is purely a mechanical matter.

There are a series of standard markings that are put on the work-print to tell the *conformer* (or *negative cutter*) where effects are to be placed. These markings are usually made with a yellow grease pencil and are standardized so that any negative cutter will be able to cut any filmmaker's camera film. There is no reason why you need follow these, however, if you are doing the work yourself. You can indicate where effects (fades and/or dissolves) are to go on a sheet of paper, using the

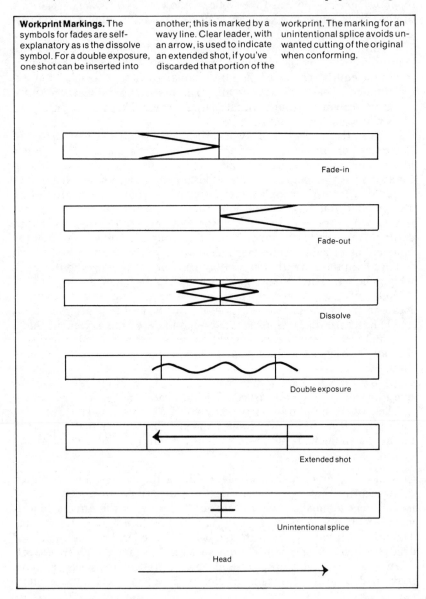

Workprint Markings. The symbols for fades are self-explanatory as is the dissolve symbol. For a double exposure, one shot can be inserted into another; this is marked by a wavy line. Clear leader, with an arrow, is used to indicate an extended shot, if you've discarded that portion of the workprint. The marking for an unintentional splice avoids unwanted cutting of the original when conforming.

Fade-in

Fade-out

Dissolve

Double exposure

Extended shot

Unintentional splice

Head

Independent Filmmaking

counter of the synchronizer to measure footage. Another approach might be to use peel-off labels on the film with instructions written on them.

I will assume that we're now going to prepare a silent film with one picture roll, or what is called an *A roll*. There are two ways of finding corresponding footage from camera film to workprint: by eyematch, and by edge numbers. *Eyematch* is just what it sounds like, you look at the workprint and then by hunting through it try to find the corresponding shot on the camera film roll. You can run the camera roll through your viewer, or if you have a light panel in your editing table or some kind of lamp setup beneath the film, you can use transmitted light to find the proper shot.

The second technique, *matching with edge numbers,* is easier than eyematching. You seek the number on the camera roll that matches the number on the workprint. Remember there are two kinds of edge numbers or coding in use: the latent image numbers found on professional 16mm motion picture stock and the printed edge numbers that can be added by the lab.

Some labs offer printed numbers every twenty frames. Aren't numbers every foot or forty frames apart enough? Most of the time yes, sometimes no. If your shot is less than forty frames you chance missing any edge number completely. In such a case you can always resort to eyematch. As a matter of fact, you can use any printed marks, like the manufacturer's trademark to help you hunt for, and position, footage. If, when editing your workprint, you saw that you were losing an edge number, you could have written the nearest number on the shot with a grease pencil.

Assuming that you have found the matching numbers, how do you proceed? Place the workprint in the synchronizer, and then put the camera film in the synchronizer so that its edge number corresponds with the workprint number. Now with both rolls locked together, measuring off a length of one is like measuring off a length of the other. You can directly cut the camera film, or make marks with a yellow crayon, and then cut it at the beginning and end of a shot. To repeat: match the edge numbers of both rolls when you place them in the synchronizer. You then use the synchronizer as a kind of comparative measuring device.

Some filmmakers find it easier to have the workprint and camera film rolls on separate winds; others get by with just one pair of winds. You have to work out the details for yourself.

Attach the shots of camera film with pieces of masking tape. Some people prefer to make cement splices at this time. I believe it is better if you segregate functions, that is, find the footage before doing the splicing. After you have found all of your shots and attached them in order with temporary joins with masking tape, you can go through the roll of film and make all your cement splices at the same time. This is a generally good rule for editing—segregation of functions. This helps eliminate mistakes despite its assembly line flavor.

Splicing and Editing

Having spliced, you are practically finished with your editing labors. All that remains is to attach head and tail leaders.

Camera Original Editing

If you choose not to edit a workprint, and you decide to directly cut your original—usually the case with 8mm and super 8—there are two things you have to be cautious about: making an unwanted cut and damaging your film.

If you cut too much out of a shot, it is difficult to put back what you've taken out. The splice will show, making things look choppy; also, you may have to lose frames when you attempt to add more footage to a sequence. This may not particularly bother you, and the only way to judge such an effect is in the context of what you are doing. It's probably better to make your initial cuts a bit too long, that is, with a few extra frames, so that you can progressively whittle down or trim your cuts.

As you study your footage, you must handle it quite a bit. Projection and rewinding usually cause most of the damage to film. Many viewers can scratch original footage, and winding your film may also contribute to damage. Wind your footage carefully, and slowly. Clean it occasionally by running it through a soft flannel cloth. Clean your projector and viewer wherever film comes in contact with any part of the machine. Use cotton swabs and soft cloth dipped in denatured alcohol or acetone. Wearing of parts may sometimes dislodge a burr or sharp metal edge which can mutilate film. A machine may come fresh from the factory with such a defect, and so should be carefully checked. In general, 8mm and super 8 editing equipment can't match the professional quality of 16mm equipment; but wear of the smaller gauges, to my estimation, isn't as great as you might suspect. For one thing the forces involved for transporting the smaller gauges through a projector are less than those for 16mm footage. Therefore, they are exposed to less destructive forces. However, any scratch or blemish that does appear in 8mm or super 8 will be magnified about four times greater than a corresponding one on 16mm.

If you definitely plan to make prints from the footage you edit, consider cement splices because labs may have problems printing material with tape splices. If you plan to project your original and never make prints, use either tape or cement.

One trick that will minimize damage to super 8 films in particular is to assemble the footage you plan to edit on a reel and then have it sound striped. The iron oxide coatings on super 8 (and 16mm but not 8mm) can be placed on both sides of the frame—the sprocket side and away from it. One track carries the sound information, and the other which is also of iron oxide composition but thinner, serves as what is called the balance stripe. Together, both stripes produce the *rail effect* which protects the emulsion by keeping it away from the base of the film and abrasive portions of the projector and viewer. Eastman Kodak claims that the rail effect can prolong life of the film three or four times what it would have been without the stripe and balance stripe. Given this information, it makes sense to stripe your super 8 film before editing. Ordinarily, super 8 footage is edited before the stripe is added. By adding the stripe first, you may protect your film and still record your track when you please.

Whether or not you make prints of your footage, if it becomes marred to a point you consider objectionable, you can have the film treated, or rejuvenated, to remove scratches. This process is not inexpensive, usually costing the same for an 8mm, super 8 or 16mm running foot; its success is a function of how bad the film is and the quality of the process.

To eliminate the necessity, expense and effort of a workprint, a few filmmakers have cut their original footage with the intention to rejuvenate it subsequently. The cost of the process cancelled out any savings, and it had other drawbacks: success isn't guaranteed, the film may still be damaged, and unwanted cuts or adding footage are still problems.

Two Kinds of Invisible Splices

Whether you're concerned with printmaking or projecting your original, there are two methods of making *invisible* splices without resorting to the relatively elaborate lab technique, A and B printing. The first is outlandish, and not many people know about it. It was called to my attention several years ago by someone who sent me 8mm and 16mm footage that had been spliced this way. The splices were virtually invisible. What he did was this: he scraped away the emulsion of an entire frame and spliced it to the base of another frame. The part of the splice that had had its emulsion scraped was essentially transparent. The splice was very strong, but it must have taken a lot of scraping. He accomplished this by constructing or modifying a splicer to his own specifications. Anybody who's interested in this might be able to construct such a splicer or modify an existing design. Like the next method, this splice was even less visible when projected at 24 fps than at the silent speed.

The following method is more generally known: you splice one

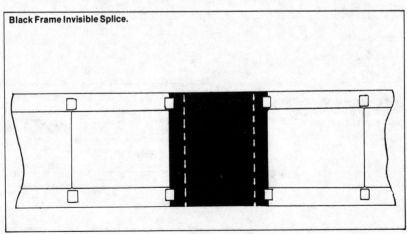

Black Frame Invisible Splice.

262

Head Leader with Mag Film.
A and B rolls, and mag film track. The start mark is indicated by an X in a box. You can also use a punched hole. For double checking sync, a 1000-cycle tone is sometimes used on mag film directly opposite the start of black leader. Work presented to a lab syncked in a straight vertical relationship — as it was edited — is called edit or dead sync. For more information about mag film tracks, see chapter 8.

Tail Leader with Mag Film.
An A roll and mag film. Additional picture rolls would have leader matching that of the A roll. Although this diagram and the one above are standard for 16mm, they'd be OK for super 8. Check with your lab first.

Head Leader with Optical Track. Optical track and picture are prepared in printer sync, with the track displaced 26 frames to maintain separation between image and sound. Unmarked lengths between vertical lines are one frame long. Three dots on the picture roll correspond to the three X's on optical track roll.

Tail Leader with Optical Track.
This diagram, and the one above, are standard for 16mm.

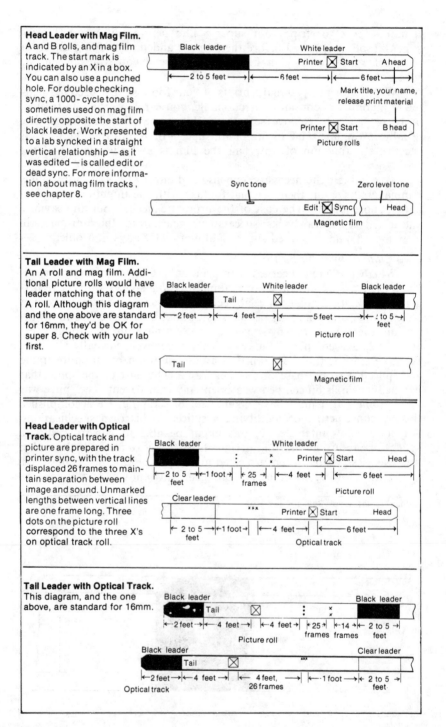

Independent Filmmaking

frame of black leader between the two frames to be joined. You need a negative splicer to use this technique so that none of the picture area is covered. Probably the splicer will have to be turned around (or have the film looped around) to make the second splice on the other side of the black leader. The black leader frame isn't scraped, only the picture frames are scraped to make the splices. It's quite difficult to detect such a splice. I have been told, however, that this method places a great deal of strain on the film, so that splices made this way are likely to part.

Head and Tail Leaders

Head and tail leaders are spliced to the beginning and end of the printing master to serve several purposes: to protect the master; to give the lab ample footage for setting up the film in the printer; to provide sync or start marks so that the printing rolls and track may be printed by the lab in sync; to supply footage for the head and tail of the print so that you can protect these usually manhandled portions of the print; and to identify you and your film.

Standard lengths for the head is about twelve feet of white leader, followed by two feet of black leader and then the picture. For added protection I suggest using four or five feet of black leader instead of just two. Some people like to use a cueing leader, the SMPTE (Society of Motion Picture and Television Engineers) in place of the black leader immediately before the picture starts. The purpose of this leader is to aid cueing up film for TV stations or the *change over* during projection for films longer than one reel. It can be used for focusing the film, but with some difficulty. Somebody might do well to create a standard focusing leader of good quality.

KINDS OF LEADER MATERIAL. Leader material can be purchased from the lab at a few cents a foot. This is usually processed motion picture film with either clear or black emulsion. There are other kinds of leader on the market in opaque and a variety of colors such as yellow, red, white, blue and green. They may be pure acetate through and through and not have an emulsion.

Theoretically, acetate leader is a fine idea. The opaque variety is far blacker than emulsion coated leader, and lacking an emulsion, it does not have to be scraped to make a splice. However, there is some controversy about its quality. It has been reported that the perforations are inaccurately cut, that the material has pin holes which print through on the picture roll, and so on. I have used this material with success for A and B'ing, and have had no trouble with it. The leader I used was made by Neumade Products. However, such plastic leader will not shrink at the same rate as the camera film, and this may lead to complications after several years of print storage.

Instructions to the Lab

The problem of communicating with the lab will be discussed in some detail in chapter 9. For now, let's discuss what's necessary to tell the lab about where you want what effect. You can do this in two ways:

264 either stick peel-off labels on the leader adjacent to the effect, specifying on the label what effect you want; or you can use synchronizer's footage and frame counter to specify where you want what effect. Such footage guides are given from the start mark at the head (front end) of the film. This is an efficient procedure, since you can keep a record of your instructions. Mark the two center frames of a dissolve, on both rolls, with small white India ink X's; these X's should be scribed on the edge of the film, near the perforations.

Use white or black India ink for writing on the emulsion side of your film and leaders. The emulsion side of a processed film is both visibly dull and tactily tacky compared to the base side. Sometimes this is difficult to tell by sight, especially with clear leader. The best test is to moisten your finger and touch both sides of the film to find the stickier emulsion side.

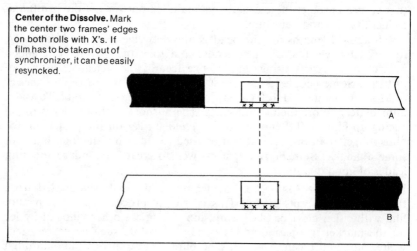

Center of the Dissolve. Mark the center two frames' edges on both rolls with X's. If film has to be taken out of synchronizer, it can be easily resyncked.

Instructions to the Lab Accompanying a Master. This cue sheet is for an answer print; keep a copy.

CUE SHEET for "SHOW & TELL"
from Lenny Lipton   to WA Palmer films
526-0842

~ A & B rolls. Mag film track, in edit sync to be electroprinted. Print on Ektachrome R. Peerless treat print, and return in can. File master.

FOOTAGE	EFFECT	LENGTH	ROLL	NOTES
0009-2	fade-in	20	A	
0017-1	fade-out	20	A	
0038-8	dissolve	48	A	
00132-36			A	Hold the
00145-36			A	same light
0241-17	burn-in			A over B
0244-20	fade-out	64	A	

Independent Filmmaking

Why A and B'ing?

A lot of mystery surrounds the *A and B editing* technique. It is a tedious, time-consuming technique and, when used to match camera footage with a workprint, not any more creative than simple preparation of one printer roll, or *A rolling*. However, the A and B technique can be used as a method of filmic composition, and although previously confined to 16mm, there are a growing number of labs offering this service for the super 8 format.

Here we are concerned with conforming camera film with workprint. When you A and B your camera film, you can expect to achieve invisible splices, fades and dissolves (fades, by the way, are available for A rolled reversal film, but not negative—if you want fades for negative-positive printing you must A and B roll), multiple images, toned sections and burnt-in titles. The list may not be complete, and there is some overlapping in the classifications: for example, burnt-in titles are a special case of multiple images.

Now what is A and B rolling anyway? It involves the preparation of two picture rolls, an A roll and a B roll, each of which consists of a series of images alternated with black leader. When there is an image on the B roll there is usually complementary black leader on the A roll. Black leader is simply processed film with an opaque black emulsion. The best leader sold for this purpose is offered by the lab you use.

Sometimes A and B rolling is described as a *checkerboard* printing technique. Certainly the appearance of A and B rolled material suggests a checkerboard. Before they are printed, the filmmaker places sync marks on the head (and tail) leaders of each roll for the lab to position the A roll precisely in coordination with the B roll and the print film. That is, they all line up with the sync mark. First, let's say, the A roll goes through the printer. Wherever there is picture on the A roll, the print film is exposed. Wherever there is black leader, no exposure is made.

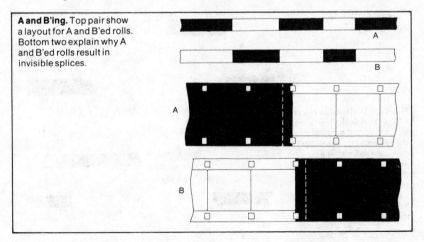

A and B'ing. Top pair show a layout for A and B'ed rolls. Bottom two explain why A and B'ed rolls result in invisible splices.

Now the B roll is printed. The B roll is exposed to light in the printer and the print stock is exposed. Any image on the B roll is printed through on the print film; wherever there was black leader, no image is printed. When the print stock is processed, we find that we have a continuous sequence of images which were alternately contributed by the A roll and the B roll.

Studying the diagram on page 265 will help you to understand the process in general, and the specific points in particular. For example, one diagram shows why the A and B roll technique can yield invisible splices. In preparing the printing rolls, the black leader is never scraped but, rather, the picture rolls are scraped when making the splice. Part of the adjoining picture frame is used to make the scrape. Most splicers would have to be turned around to make the second splice, so that the overlap is on the proper side. A better method might be to loop the ends of the film around the splicer 'pretzel fashion.' When both rolls are printed, no splice overlap shows.

At the risk of belaboring the obvious, where there is image on one roll there is usually corresponding black leader on the other, and vice versa. There is a major exception to this: in the preparation of dissolves, where the pictures overlap, instead of black leader opposite an image, we have picture opposite picture. For the length of the dissolve, we have pictures on both rolls. As the A roll, for example, passes through the printer, a shutter gradually extinguishes the printer light, printing a fade-out. When the B roll is printed on the print stock a fade-in of its shot is made. This superimposed over the fade-out becomes a dissolve.

For printing either negative-positive or reversal-reversal, the technique of making the dissolve is the same. Before preparing your printing rolls, check with your laboratory to find out how they want you to make your dissolves. The length of the dissolve and other important factors are influenced by the printing machine your lab uses. A master prepared for one lab may be difficult to print by another lab.

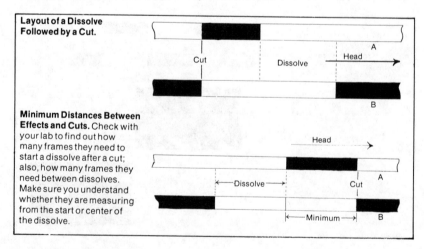

Layout of a Dissolve Followed by a Cut.

Cut — Dissolve — Head — A

B

Minimum Distances Between Effects and Cuts. Check with your lab to find out how many frames they need to start a dissolve after a cut; also, how many frames they need between dissolves. Make sure you understand whether they are measuring from the start or center of the dissolve.

Head

Dissolve — Cut — A

Minimum — B

Independent Filmmaking

Dissolve (and fade) lengths commonly range between 16 and 96 frames, with 16, 24, 32, 48, 64 and 96 frames the most frequently used lengths. With A and B rolling, the length of your dissolve must be a specific length, and not any arbitrary number of frames. When you are making a forty frame dissolve, you overlap forty frames of A roll picture and forty frames of B roll picture. In other words, there will be twenty frames on either side of the center of the dissolve. It often happens, especially for shorter dissolves, that the lab needs more frames to make the dissolve than you thought necessary. For example, a twenty frame dissolve may have to be set up as if it were a forty-eight frame dissolve, with twenty-four frames, not ten, on either side of the center of the dissolve. Mechanical limitations of the printing machines necessitate this weird setup. You will have to check with your lab to find out the minimum number of frames they require for a dissolve.

Some labs are able to mix the lengths of dissolves in any combination. For example, you may be able to follow a twenty frame dissolve with a forty frame dissolve, and then a sixteen frame dissolve, and then a ninety frame dissolve and so on. Some labs offer many dissolve lengths, but only one length of dissolve (or fade) may be chosen for each print. Others may offer limited choices. Once again, before you cut your workprint, or certainly your camera footage, you had better find out what your lab is able to do.

When cutting the workprint, make certain that you have enough frames to make dissolves: it's discouraging to find out you don't have enough frames to make the planned dissolve. Be careful not to cut so close to the end of the shot that you don't have enough frames with which to work. If you discover this while cutting your camera film or when setting up the picture rolls, you may also discover—when you calm down—that you can usually find a way out: turning the dissolve into a straight cut or a fade or shortening the length of the shot to accumulate enough frames to make the dissolve.

Another peculiar restraint that you will encounter is the minimum distance required between dissolves. You usually won't be able to follow a dissolve hard on the heels of the preceding one. There is a minimum length, determined once again by your lab's printing machine, between the center of one dissolve and the next. Suppose you want a forty frame dissolve to follow a forty frame dissolve. Your lab may specify that you must have at least one hundred and twenty frames between the center of the first dissolve and the center of the second. The situation can become more complicated when you intend to mix dissolves of different lengths. You must talk to your lab to find out their tolerances. In this sense, the labs do exert a tremendous amount of creative control, like it or not.

When preparing a fade for reversal film, set up the rolls exactly as you would for a straight cut. With negative film you will need clear leader, not black, opposite the footage to be faded out or in. This makes sense if you think about it. In the case of printing with reversal film, a simple fade of the printer's shutter will result in a fade on the print. A fade of the shutter when printing negative film on positive stock would result in a *white out,* not a fade to black. In order to get a fade to black with the negative-positive system, we must have a reexposure of that portion of the print to white light.

When A and B'ing negative film, black leader is used for the roll without picture just as it is for A and B'ing reversal. A fade-in in the negative-positive system following a fade-out will require clear corresponding leader. Unlike preparation of fades for reversal, which is identical to preparation of a straight cut, negative fade-ins and fade-outs following each other are prepared by splicing the two shots together. A length of clear leader opposite the fades, greater than the length of the fades, is necessary. Exactly how much longer is again determined by your lab. A and B'ing of negative is comparatively uncommon, since reversal dominates 16mm filmmaking. You have to keep clear leader on hand as well as black leader when cutting negative.

The Preparation of A and B Rolls

I want to stress once again that before you begin to cut your camera film, or in point of fact, cut your workprint, you ought to have a conversation with your lab manager or representative about how they would like you to prepare your A and B rolls.

There are many different approaches to the problem. Filmmakers with enough money can turn their camera footage and workprint over to the lab and have them conform the camera footage with the workprint. The lab can then set up A and B printing rolls, following instructions or marks on the workprint for effects, fades and dissolves. This will cost at least several hundred dollars. This amount of money is what a synchronizer costs. Therefore, if you buy one to do your own A and B'ing, as well as other operations, the cost will be paid off the first time you use the synchronizer to conform your camera film to the workprint.

So far the discussion of A and B'ing has been generally theoretical,

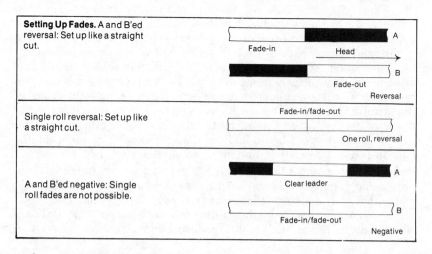

Setting Up Fades. A and B'ed reversal: Set up like a straight cut.

Fade-in Head

Reversal

Fade-out

B

A

Single roll reversal: Set up like a straight cut.

Fade-in/fade-out

One roll, reversal

A and B'ed negative: Single roll fades are not possible.

Clear leader

A

Fade-in/fade-out

B

Negative

Independent Filmmaking

and not from the point of view of how you actually get down to doing it with your hands. Let's suppose you have finished your workprint. Then you've cut your camera film using edge numbers or eyematch to locate the footage; assembled it on a roll temporarily spliced with masking tape —similar to the preparation of an A roll alone. What you have now are the individual shots held together by masking tape on a reel ready to be A and B'ed.

You must use a synchronizer to A and B roll. Once the footage is assembled and taped together, the synchronizer can measure black leader to the proper length and help to retape the shots alternated with black leader. What we wind up with then, are two taped rolls of shots alternating with leader. Then we can go through the rolls, splicing the leader to the shot. Most splicers can achieve the proper overlap (scraping the shot and not the leader) when used in one direction only. For the other end of the shot-to-leader splice reverse the reels, that is switch the right reel with the one on the left wind spindle. After you've reversed the rolls on the winds, go through them again to make the final set of splices. The process is identical for the second printing roll and very mechanical, as you can see.

Any creative endeavor usually has a certain amount of noncreative work. Once we've agreed that conforming camera film is drudgery, we can begin to think about the best way to accomplish our task. I believe one key to A and B'ing is understanding this, and separating or segregating the various tasks. If you can do all the shot hunting at one time, and then the leader measuring and cutting, and then the splicing and so on, you will minimize error, and by setting up a rhythm, minimize effort.

I have suggested one broad working approach to A and B'ing. A good way to get started is to plunge right in and do what you must do. A better way might be to watch somebody who knows what he's doing. The lab you use will probably let you watch one of their people conform A and B rolls. If they don't, consider finding another—friendlier—lab.

Once you've made all of your splices, it's time to put your footage through the synchronizer to check what you've done. Thread your workprint, A roll and B roll in synchronizer, in sync, and wind away. The length of the A and B rolls and the workprint should be the same. The basic test, then, is to wind all three rolls through the synchronizer to see if they are the same length. This same check can be carried out if you've simply A rolled your film.

Then, carefully, virtually frame by frame, check the job you've done. Especially check where you've made cuts. In all likelihood, if there are any mistakes, the mistakes will be in the length of the leaders—too short or too long—and not in the length of the shot. It's easy to add or subtract footage from leader to make it the proper length. If you've cut a shot too long, just trim it to size. If you've cut it too short, time to take a walk for a while. Cutting a shot too short is a disaster than can make even a strong man cry.

Splicing and Editing

In this case, the best way out is simply to admit that a frame will have to be sacrificed, and continue the rest of the shot, minus the lost frame, on the other roll. At least the splice won't show, which will make the loss of the frame less visible. Of course, if you're A rolling only, you don't have this minor blessing, and you are faced with the prospect of remaking the splice. One choice you do have is to make a more or less invisible splice, by inserting one black frame, while maintaining the length of the picture (which also means you don't have to alter the sound track). Depending upon the subject matter of the shot, the omission of one frame may or may not be noticed. In many cases you'll be the only one to see it, which is some comfort, or little comfort, depending upon how you look at life.

When setting up the rolls on your winds to be used in conjunction with your synchronizer, separate each roll the proper distance to match the spacing of the synchronizer sprockets. The manufacturer of your winds or synchronizer can supply spacers, sometimes made out of metal and fiber, to be used between each reel. Some people like to use a plastic core between each reel, but the spacers are inexpensive and work better. The reels and the spacers can be held together tightly with a spring-loaded gripper which fits on the end of the spindle. Sometimes it's best to loosen the gripper so that each reel can turn freely. How much film each reel takes up for one revolution of the spindle depends upon the radius of the film already wound on the reel. For the same number of revolutions, or fraction of a revolution, film wound on a wider radius will take up at a greater rate. This leads to too much tension or slack and spilling over of footage. Often, because of differences in the thickness of the various film stocks you're using, you will find that you must hand-wind the reels, and not the wind handle. That is, you can't operate them very well with the wind's handle, but must jockey all the reels by hand.

Zero-cut Printing

The A and B roll technique makes possible invisible splices. One variation of the standard method, less commonly used, is called *zero-cut printing*. In this method, there can be an overlap of a few frames, say two or three beyond the end of the splice. (You have to find out how many frames your lab needs.) The printer's shutter in effect makes the cut for you by turning on its light when the shot starts on one roll, and turning off the light when the shot ends for the other roll. One advantage of this method is that you don't have to be too careful about the orientation of the overlaps of the splice. In fact, you don't even need a negative splicer. The main advantage of zero-cut printing is that you don't have to cut the shot to add leader. If at some later time you wish to use the complete footage, you may. The disadvantage is that you must have extra frames available at the head and tail of each shot in order to set up your camera film for zero-cut printing. If you wish to reenforce each cement splice with a tape splice, zero-cut printing becomes very interesting. Despite the use of tape here, the splice will be invisible.

Independent Filmmaking

Single or Double Perf Film

Double perf camera film is preferable to single perf film—film perforated on one edge—when preparing film for A and B printing. It's much easier to manipulate film in the synchronizer and to orient your splices with double perf film. If you must mix double and single perf film, you better let the lab know in writing, and by attaching a single perf leader (perfs on the same side as the camera film) to your master to prevent mistakes.

C, D, E, F... Rolls?

There are times when you can't accomplish the effect you want with just two printer rolls. You may need an extra roll, a C roll, or perhaps even a D roll. You might need a C roll if you must have effect following hard upon effect. By using an additional roll, you can circumvent the minimum distance required between effects. By putting the image used in the next effect on the C roll instead of the B roll, for example, you would be able to lessen the footage between dissolves. There are times when extra rolls may be needed with, for example, burnt-in titles, overall tints or multiple images. Each additional printing roll adds a charge of about two cents a foot to the finished print.

Burnt-in Titles

The technique of burning-in titles in printing involves setting up A and B rolls, as described, with the titles on one roll and the background image on the other. The background should be chosen so that the titles clearly appear. When shooting the title, use white letters on a black background, whether or not you are printing with the negative-positive system or the reversal-reversal. With the negative-positive you will get black titles burnt-in over the background; in the case of reversal-reversal, you will get white letters over the background shot. This method can be used for adding subtitles to a foreign language film, for fog effects or snow or rain, for example. It is important that the black background sur-

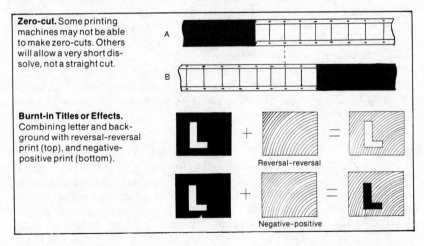

Zero-cut. Some printing machines may not be able to make zero-cuts. Others will allow a very short dissolve, not a straight cut.

Burnt-in Titles or Effects. Combining letter and background with reversal-reversal print (top), and negative-positive print (bottom).

Reversal-reversal

Negative-positive

Splicing and Editing

rounding the white letters (or objects) have a high D-max, or be as dense as possible. Very little tone should be allowed in the letters themselves, but they may depart from perfect white to some small extent, in order to get the surrounding background dense enough. Because of their good maximum density, the following materials are successfully used for title shots: the outstanding material for this purpose is Kodachrome II (outdoor or Type A); Eastman high contrast film or Gevaert high contrast film (either may be processed as a negative or reversal) are also used.

You can specify that the lab, instead of burning-in the title, double expose it so that some of the background shows through the letters. They can accomplish this by choosing the proper printer light level. It is possible to fade the burnt-in title, so that it appears and disappears gradually.

You can burn-in colored titles over your background shot. You can shoot your titles (colored letters on a black background) with color film, or you can tint (see chapter 10) a high contrast black and white title shot for colorful letters.

If you want to have one title dissolve into the next title over one background, you may have to use an additional printing roll. Or you could try making this title dissolve in the camera to avoid having to use another roll for this purpose.

If you have A rolled a film, and would like to have burnt-in titles, you must use a B roll, or if you like, the title section can be optically printed. In the case of using a B roll for a superimposed title on an otherwise A rolled film, all of the footage on either side of the title need not be black leader; you can use scrap footage. The lab is able to do this by closing the printer shutter completely, except when printing the burnt-in title.

Overall Tints

Let's say you're reversal printing black and white film on color stock. If you use a B roll of a solid color, say red, opposite your black and white footage, it will color the print. When the second exposure on the print stock is made through the B roll, the image of the A roll will be colored red. The saturation of the color will depend upon the colored leader used, and the printing light the lab uses for exposing the leader. You can use colored acetate leader, or you can make your own colored leader by shooting a colored card. Shooting it out of focus will eliminate paper or cardboard texture.

Optical Printing

Before the introduction of A and B printing, the only procedure for effects like dissolves was to have the footage printed in an optical printer. More detail will be offered concerning this device in chapter 9 *The Laboratory's Role*. But for now, an optical printer is basically a projector and camera combination, with the projector focusing an image on the film in the camera. The optical printer is used to make fades and dissolves, with the same basic technique as A and B'ing. In fact, printing rolls for the optical printer are prepared in the same manner. Instead of the camera film and the raw stock being in contact, as in the case with release printing machines, the optical printer projects the camera film image on the raw stock.

One practical advantage of the optical printer is that it can make fades and dissolves of practically any length, which can be inserted into the A rolled printing master. An optical printer also has the virtue of yielding a print with the proper orientation. If you think about it, you'll realize that a contact print made of a film must have the image *flopped*, or reversed. But when printed with an optical printer, the image can have the same orientation as it had on the camera film. If we used a contact printer to make the fades and dissolves, and then cut them into the master, we'd wind up with release prints with flopped *opticals*.

The disadvantage of optically printed effects is that they are one additional generation away from the rest of the film. (A print made from the camera film is first generation. A print made from a print is second generation, and so on.) The alteration in quality is usually quite visible. It was this fact that inspired the A and B printing technique for 16mm.

Let us suppose you are preparing a film with just an A roll and wish to have inserts printed with the optical printer. You set up the dissolves using the A and B roll technique. Tell the lab you want an optical print, and be sure to tell them your purpose so they can properly match the emulsion orientation. Suppose your original was shot on color reversal; having the effects printed on low contrast high resolution stock will minimize losses in sharpness and hold down increases in granularity and increases in contrast—intrinsically a part of all photographic copying. The material currently popular for this job is ECO, Ektachrome Commercial film, the camera film stock. (Plus X camera film might make a good choice for printing black and white effects.) Once the effects have been printed, they may be cut into the camera roll.

If you use this technique, I suggest that you print the entire length of both shots going into and out of the dissolve, and not just the dissolved portion. No matter how carefully such an effect is printed, it never seems to match perfectly the camera footage into which it is cut. The effect on the screen is a jarring jump, a tell-tale sign that the dissolve is about to begin. The sudden shift in quality is most visible as an increase in grain and contrast and shifts in color balance. Image quality alterations are less visible if the entire length of the shots making up the dissolve are printed. For reasons of economy, this is not the usual practice. Even though optical printing is expensive, I consider this omission to be false economy.

If we compare what happens when we make a print from A and B rolls with effects inserted into an A roll made with the optical printer, we find that A and B rolling produces better quality prints because the effects are made with the camera film and not from a print of the camera

Splicing and Editing

Number of Frames Separating Sound and Picture.
Figures given are for reel-to-reel projection in which the sound precedes the picture. No optical track standard was ever needed for standard 8. (Eastman Kodak)

	8mm	Super 8	16mm
Magnetic Track	56	18	28
Optical Track	—	22	26

Footage and Running Times of the Formats. (Eastman Kodak)

Film Format	8mm				Super 8				16mm			
Projection Speed in Frames per Second	18		24		18		24		18		24	
Inches per Second	2.7		3.6		3.0		4.0		5.4		7.2	
Film Length and Screen Time	Min	Sec	Min	Sec	Min	Sec	Min	Sec	Min	Sec	Min	Sec
Feet 50	3	42	2	47	3	20	2	30	1	51	1	23
100	7	24	5	33	6	40	5	0	3	42	2	47
150	11	7	8	20	10	0	7	30	5	33	4	10
200	14	49	11	7	13	20	10	0	7	24	5	33
300	22	13	16	40	20	0	15	0	11	7	8	20
400	29	38	22	13	26	40	20	0	14	49	11	7
500	37	2	27	47	33	20	25	0	18	31	13	53
600	44	27	33	20	40	0	30	0	22	13	16	40
700	51	51	38	53	46	40	35	0	25	56	19	27
800	59	16	44	27	53	20	40	0	29	38	22	13
900	66	40	50	0	60	0	45	0	33	20	25	0
1000	74	4	55	33	66	40	50	0	37	2	27	47
1100	81	29	61	7	73	20	55	0	40	44	30	33
1200	88	53	66	40	80	0	60	0	44	27	33	20

film. On the other hand, it may be less expensive to prepare your effects optically and then insert them into an A roll. For example, it may seem very unattractive to A and B roll a thousand foot film with only one or two dissolves.

Composing with the Synchronizer

Eisenstein in *The Film Sense* discussed two kinds of filmic montage: horizontal and vertical montage. By montage he meant the adding together of a shot A plus a shot B to create an effect greater than the sum of the parts. The general idea is the basis of film editing—and other arts like painting, as Eisenstein himself pointed out. In film the predominant form of montage was constructed horizontally, that is, shot following shot in a flow through time. This had the direct musical analogy of a melody with, if you like, each shot considered to be another note. It is also possible to take the position that each frame is another note, and that for example, the shot itself is the melody.

Eisenstein went on to explain that another kind of related montage development was possible, which he called vertical montage. He abstracted and generalized the concept. The musical analogy here, which holds up well, is harmony. If we look at the score of a symphony, we see both horizontal and vertical development of the piece, with each section of the orchestra doing its part in vertical synchronization. Eisenstein conceived of parallel development of another theme, or story, to be intercut with, let us say, the primary story. He is indebted to Griffith (and Griffith to Dickens) for this concept of the parallel development of themes. The kind of *cut-aways* Griffith used in a film like *The Battle of Elderbush Gulch* were only a precursor of his fuller development of the concept of parallel thematic construction in *Intolerance*.

Most of us are familiar with *montage* sequences in which calendar pages tear off a wall, which are double exposed over marching Nazi boots, which are superimposed over a map of Europe. Eisenstein was quite right about the differences between his concept of montage and that of Hollywood. The Hollywood montage was, and as any child could have told him, often the best part of an otherwise dull film. Eisenstein, however, was put off by the content, the bizarre stupidity of these sequences. However, it was Slovko Vorkapich who elevated the montage sequence to a high art. In fact, such a sequence became known, and is still known, as a *Vorkapitch*.

The synchronizer suggests the uses of vertical montage, but like Vorkapitch, or the Hollywood filmmakers (and unlike Eisenstein), the independent filmmaker can show several developing themes simultaneously, by the simple technique of double or multiple imagery. Rows of film set up in a synchronizer immediately suggest the kind of harmonic composition found in an orchestrated piece of music.

Films that use this form of composition extensively are Stan Brakhage's *Dog Star Man*, Bruce Baillie's *Quixote*, John Schofill's *XFILM*, Robert Nelson's *The Great Blondino*, Will Hindel's *FFFTCM* (all CCC & FMC) and many other compositions. You can see examples of this

Splicing and Editing

Running Times and Film Lengths. (Eastman Kodak)

Film Format	8mm (80 Frames per Foot)		Super 8 (72 Frames per Foot)		16mm (40 Frames per Foot)	
Projection Speed in Frames per Second	18	24	18	24	18	24
Running Time and Film Length (Feet + Frames)	Ft + Fr	Ft + Fr	Ft + Fr	Ft + Fr	Ft + Fr	Ft + Fr
Seconds 1	0 18	0 24	0 18	0 24	0 18	0 24
2	0 36	0 48	0 36	0 48	0 36	1 8
3	0 54	0 72	0 54	1 0	1 14	1 32
4	0 72	1 16	1 0	1 24	1 32	2 16
5	1 10	1 40	1 18	1 48	2 10	3 0
6	1 28	1 64	1 36	2 0	2 28	3 24
7	1 46	2 8	1 54	2 24	3 6	4 8
8	1 64	2 32	2 0	2 48	3 24	4 32
9	2 2	2 56	2 18	3 0	4 2	5 16
10	2 20	3 0	2 36	3 24	4 20	6 0
20	4 40	6 0	5 0	6 48	9 0	12 0
30	6 60	9 0	7 36	10 0	13 20	18 0
40	9 0	12 0	10 0	13 24	18 0	24 0
50	11 20	15 0	12 36	16 48	22 20	30 0
minutes 1	13 40	18 0	15 0	20 0	27 0	36 0
2	27 0	36 0	30 0	40 0	54 0	72 0
3	40 40	54 0	45 0	60 0	81 0	108 0
4	54 0	72 0	60 0	80 0	108 0	144 0
5	67 40	90 0	75 0	100 0	135 0	180 0
6	81 0	108 0	90 0	120 0	162 0	216 0
7	94 40	126 0	105 0	140 0	189 0	252 0
8	108 0	144 0	120 0	160 0	216 0	288 0
9	121 40	162 0	135 0	180 0	243 0	324 0
10	135 0	180 0	150 0	200 0	270 0	360 0

technique used in television commercials and the melodramatic cinema, for they have recently come into vogue, apparently being rediscovered by the discoverers.

When composing such a film on the synchronizer, the filmmaker rarely uses a workprint since it cannot show how the combined images would look. The filmmaker must do his best to visualize the resulting composition. The trouble with this method is that you can't see what you've done until a print is made. After receiving the print from the lab, the filmmaker may wish to put the print and the A and B rolls back on the synchronizer to study what happened and, based on this, make corrections.

Sound & Magnetic Recording

In this discussion of sound tracks, we concentrate here on the fundamentals of sound and magnetic recording. Chapter 8, *Preparing the Sound Track,* concentrates on methods of lip synchronized recording, editing and working with a sound studio to produce prints with magnetic or optical sound tracks.

In general, when preparing a sound track, the filmmaker can take one of two courses, even though many of the steps overlap. He can aim toward preparing his track himself—with the use of a magnetic sound projector—or he can concentrate his efforts on sound track prints produced by the laboratory. Although the information here leads to an understanding of laboratory produced sound track prints, this chapter is, by itself, concerned with the first approach.

Recording sound tracks for the formats discussed in this book is usually aimed at the production of monaural and not stereophonic, or two channel, sound. If you are planning to put a sound track on your film in any of the methods described in this chapter, you will probably have to settle for monaural sound, like it or not. I think this is unfortunate, but with the exception of the Heurtier Stereo 42 super 8 projector, the simplest way at present to have stereo sound is to play a tape with your film. But it is far more convenient to have the image and sound together, on one piece of film.

The Nature of Sound

Sounds are produced by vibrating bodies which cause vibrations in the molecules of an elastic medium, usually air. When, for example, a tuning fork is struck, it vibrates and adjacent molecules of air are set in motion causing a wave or signal of sound to propel outward from the point of origin, just like ripples produced by a stone dropped into water. Of course, sound waves aren't visible, and unlike water waves, they don't exhibit hill-and-dale wave motion.

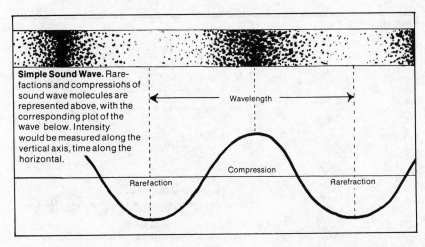

Simple Sound Wave. Rarefactions and compressiohs of sound wave molecules are represented above, with the corresponding plot of the wave below. Intensity would be measured along the vertical axis, time along the horizontal.

Wavelength

Compression

Rarefaction

Rarefraction

Sound and Magnetic Recording

280   Sound waves are made up of regions of *rarefactions* and *compressions* of air of varying pressure. When the air molecules are piled up against one another, the sound wave is under compression; when the pressure is reduced, we have what is called the rarefaction.

Pythagoras, the Greek mathematician who lived during the 6th century B.C. understood and enumerated the fundamental relationship between pitch and wavelength, and the nature of harmonics.

Frequency and Wavelength

The number of rarefactions and compressions which pass a given point in a certain time is known as the *frequency* of the sound wave. For example, one thousand pairs of rarefactions and compressions, or one thousand waves, passing a point in one second has a frequency of 1000 cycles per second, formerly written as 1000 cps, now as 1000 Hz (for Heinrich Rudolph Hertz, the physicist; I prefer cps—I was brought up that way). The figure of the plot of rarefactions and compressions defines the distance between maximum compression (or rarefaction) to the next compression (or rarefaction) as the *wavelength*. Frequency and wavelength are inversely proportional. We'll be more concerned with frequency than wavelength, although the two terms can be suitably interchanged. The human ear can hear a frequency range from about 25 to 15,000 Hz. This range varies with the individual, age and other unrelated factors, such as the reference book you use to look this up. A doubling or halving of a frequency is equivalent to raising or lowering a note of music one octave. For example, middle C is 256 Hz; high C, one octave higher, is 512 Hz.

The physical quantity *frequency* is directly related to the psychological variable *pitch*. Sounds with a high frequency have a high pitch; sounds with low frequency have low pitch.

Harmonics and Waveform

All sounds are not simple, smooth sine waves. They can get to have

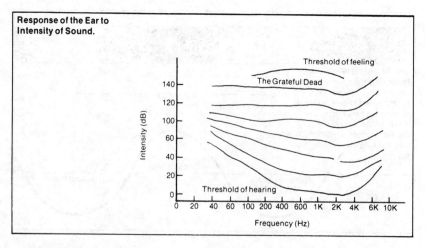
Response of the Ear to Intensity of Sound.

Independent Filmmaking

rather jagged shapes. You may be familiar with this kind of display on an oscilloscope tube. An instrument that plays a note of a certain pitch has what are called *harmonics* which are simple multiples of the frequency of the note.

Moreover, sounds which are recorded will often be the sum of many sources of sound. The *waveform* for such a combination of sounds, like the components of an orchestra playing together, can be extraordinarily complex. Nevertheless, the information necessary to reproduce the most complex sounds can be contained in an accurate record of the waveform.

Amplitude and Loudness

The *amplitude* of a wave is a measure of its maximum displacement. The height of the wave above the axis, in the first graph, is its amplitude. The amplitude of a sound wave is, in psychological terms, its loudness or intensity. Actually, the terms intensity and loudness should not be confused, because doubling the amplitude may double the intensity of the sound, but not double the loudness as perceived by a listener. Intensity of sound is measured in *decibels,* a measure of power per area; a doubling in loudness, as perceived by a listener, is equivalent to a rise of three decibels (dB).

The ear's sensitivity to sound varies with the frequency or pitch of that sound, and it is most sensitive to sounds in the region of 2000 to 4000 Hz. The curves reproduced here give some indication of how this relationship works. Note that the louder the sound, the flatter the curve. For this reason, when playing records softly, people often turn up the base and treble response to compensate for the diminished sensitivity of the ear to respond to both the high and low ends of the audio spectrum.

Dynamic Range, Noise, Overload

The ear is sensitive to an extraordinarily broad range of sound intensities. The range of sound the human ear is capable of hearing covers about 120 dB . Practically speaking, it is very difficult for sound recording techniques to encompass the full *dynamic range* of the human ear. For example, the dynamic range of a symphony orchestra is about 70 dB. Unfortunately, even this range is difficult to record.

In any sound recording there is a certain amount of inherent *system noise.* Such spurious sounds are generated in the electronic equipment itself and also by unwanted sound recorded at the time of the taping. The specific medium of the recording will also limit the dynamic range: magnetic recordings are limited by tape noise, or hiss. Such low level noise in the recording and reproducing systems limit the level at which soft sounds may be recorded.

Similarly, there is an upper loudness range: if sound is recorded at too loud a level, the recording will be *overloaded* — the sound will be distorted. As it turns out, recorded sound is usually limited to a dynamic range from about 30 to 50 dB.

Sound and Magnetic Recording

Acoustics

No matter what generates a sound, once it is in the air, and depending upon the environment, a number of things can happen to it. Just as light waves can be absorbed by pigments or reflected by mirrors, sound waves can be absorbed or reflected by surfaces, floors and walls. The proportion of sound reflected to that absorbed, or vice versa, determines the environment's reverberation qualities. A room can be *dead,* in which case there is too little reverberation, and sound will be muffled; or it can be *live* with rich and full sounds; if it is too live, however, sounds will have too much echo. High frequency sounds may be excessively absorbed by materials like drapes. It seems odd that attempting to make a good sound recording should be as difficult as it is, but the ear and recording part company in some peculiar ways.

Magnetic Recording

Recording for motion picture work—amateur, professional or independent filmmaking—is done on magnetic tape, usually quarter inch magnetic tape, the same used in home tape recorders. Magnetic tape recording has become the universal medium for original recording, for recording phonograph records and for motion picture work because it has some very appealing properties. In the first place, it's capable of making recordings that closely approximate what the ear needs to hear to make sound natural. Magnetic tape recordings easily reproduce the full frequency range of human hearing—about 25 to 15,000 Hz. Even relatively inexpensive tape recorders are capable of this, with limits of plus or minus three decibels, which is quite good. Magnetic tape recording is capable of reproducing a good dynamic range with little distortion. From the standpoint of the filmmaker, a very important feature of magnetic recording is that it can be duplicated or *dubbed* with little degradation. Moreover, magnetic tape may be erased and used over indefinitely; recordings may be played back immediately after recording, as well.

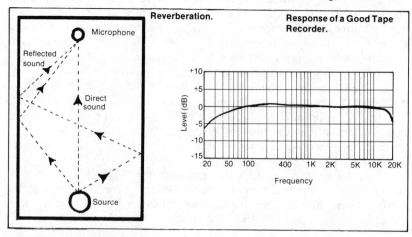

Reverberation.

Response of a Good Tape Recorder.

Independent Filmmaking

Sound Recorded Magnetically

Most of us know how to operate a tape recorder. You place a full reel of magnetic tape on the feed hub or spindle, and thread it by the tape heads to the take-up reel. When the machine is recording, the tape is moved across the record head by the take-up reel. The tape used—a quarter of an inch across and a thickness of 0.002 inch (or 2.0 mil) or less—is made of a plastic material coated with a preparation of iron oxide particles.

What happens to a sound when it is recorded? First, the mechanical energy of sound, deformations of an elastic medium, air, are translated into electric oscillations by a microphone. One type of microphone, the operation of which is fairly easy to understand, is called the moving-coil microphone. It usually consists of a diaphragm of some flexible metal or plastic, to which a coil or coils of current-conducting wire is attached. The coils are adjacent to, or surrounded by, magnets. When the sound waves strike the diaphragm, the coils move. The coils, moving within the magnetic field—the region surrounding the magnet—produce an electric current.

Faraday showed that a wire, or a coil of wire, moving through a magnetic field will produce an electric current. The key word is *moving*. If the wire cuts the lines of the field, a current is produced. Faraday conceived the idea of the magnetic field when he sprinkled iron filings on a piece of paper held directly above a magnet and visibly demonstrated his concept with the resultant pattern of curved lines.

Back to the microphone. The coils are set in motion by the diaphragm moved by the air which was activated by the original vibrating body. The moving coils cut the lines of the magnetic field and generate an electric current. The voltage produced by the coils varies as the pressure of air changes. In fact, we could plot voltage with time to make a graph similar to the first one in this chapter. The electric current is amplified, and other fancy things are done to it; then it is fed to the recording head of the tape recorder.

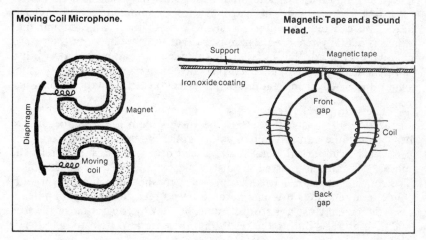

Moving Coil Microphone.

Magnetic Tape and a Sound Head.

Support

Magnetic tape

Iron oxide coating

Diaphragm

Magnet

Moving coil

Front gap

Coil

Back gap

Sound and Magnetic Recording

The recording head is an electromagnet. Just as a moving magnetic field (it doesn't matter whether the wire or the magnet moves) can produce an electric current, varying electric current produces a magnetic field. The tape head resembles two C shapes facing end to end, with a coil of wire wrapped around each. When a varying electric current passes through the coils, a magnetic circuit is set up in the head. At the gaps, or spaces between the C-shaped portions of the head, magnetic fields are produced. When the moving tape passes by the head, or more properly, the front gap, the iron oxide particles are themselves magnetized by the magnetic field of the head. Enough of the iron oxide remains magnetized, and in this way stores or memorizes the original sound which has been converted from mechanical, to electric, to magnetic energy. A sound recording may remain for years in its magnetic potential energy form.

Recording and Playback

Before a signal can be recorded, the tape must be free from any other signal, that is, it must be *clean*. Therefore, located before the record head, is an erase head, similar to the record head, but carrying an inaudible signal. It uses a high frequency signal, on the order of 60,000 to 90,000 Hz, serving to erase the tape in preparation for the audio signal. Separate bulk erasers which can clean an entire tape in seconds are available.

The record head on some machines doubles as the playback head. Most amateur machines use this workable scheme; however, most professional tape recorders use specially designed separate record and playback heads. For one thing, for best results the gap on the playback head should be one tenth of the gap width of the recording head. The *gap width* affects the high frequency response of the recorder—the narrower the gap, the higher the possible record and playback frequency. Another distinct advantage of separate record and playback heads is that the recorded signal may be monitored through the playback head while the recording is being made. In machines with a combined record-playback head, you can only monitor the signal sent to the head, and not that which is actually recorded. There is a slight time lag between the record and playback heads, but by listening to a recording an instant after it has been made, it is possible to correct any errors immediately—loss of signal due to electronic failure or imperfections in the tape *(drop out)*.

The Transport System

In the typical transport system, tape travels from the feed reel to the heads, past the capstan and pressure roller, to the take-up reel. The *capstan* is a cylindrical metal shaft, placed near the heads, driven by the motor. The tape is pressed against the capstan by the pressure roller. The rotating capstan drives the tape past the heads at the proper rate. Some tape recorders use one motor for feed reel, take-up reel and capstan. Others may use a motor for each. Besides the operation of the feed and take-up reels during the recording, they are also used to help locate portions of the tape quickly or to wind tape swiftly from one reel to another. The capstan should be able to drive the tape past the heads at a controlled speed, independent—hopefully—of the varying winding rate of the take-up reel.

Although the top portion of the tape recorder is called the *deck,* this term is usually reserved for tape machines without internal amplifiers and speakers. Such machines, decks that is, are designed to be used as a component of a hi-fi system.

About Heads

The width of the quarter inch tape is often subdivided so that more than one channel of information may be carried on the tape. Professional machines designed for monaural recording usually have a head the full width of the tape, or a quarter of an inch wide.

Another head configuration, besides the full track or monaural version, is the dual track head which can record a signal on half the width

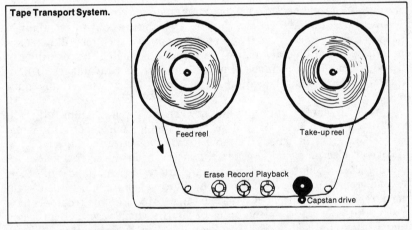

Tape Transport System.

Feed reel   Take-up reel

Erase Record Playback

Capstan drive

Quarter Inch Tape Layouts.
Full track (top), half track (middle) and four track (bottom).

1
2

1
2
3
4

Sound and Magnetic Recording

of the tape. Such machines can record monaurally or stereophonically. Used in the monaural mode, when you come to the end of the tape, flip the reel over, put it on the feed spindle and record on the other half of the tape. Double track tape recording is similar to filming with the 8mm and double super 8 formats.

The most popular head configuration for home recorders is the four track system, introduced essentially for stereo reproduction of pre-recorded tapes. If as we move across the width of the tape, we number the tracks 1, 2, 3 and 4, we'll have some point of reference for the following description. Tracks 1 and 3 carry the stereo signal when the tape is moving in one direction; 2 and 4 in the other. The tape is flipped over and started in the other direction just as it was for half track monaural recordings. Some half track and four track machines will reverse direction at the end of the reel to play the second half automatically.

For the filmmaker there are several disadvantages when using multichannel monaural recordings. It's very, very difficult to locate material on a four channel recording, compared to two channel recording. However, over and above this problem—which turns out to be minor in the long run—using several (two or four) channels when recording makes the editing of one channel impossible without damaging the recording of the other channel or channels. For a filmmaker, the advantages of multiple channel monaural recording are wiped out by the editing difficulties.

As for dynamic range and noise, when we progress from full track to half track to quarter or four track, we reduce our effective dynamic range. The wider the head, the more it can magnetize the tape, and the greater an electric signal is generated in the head during playback, requiring less amplification. If the signal requires less amplification, there will be greater separation from the background noise, consequently the encouragement of a broader dynamic range. Modern tape recorders have a signal-to-noise ratio on the order of 50 dB, which very crudely means that a soft sound will be 50 dB above the system's noise level.

As it turns out after all, half track and quarter track recorders aren't that bad—especially the half track machines which yield good results. If you are planning to have a laboratory or a studio transfer your recordings to magnetic film or optical sound, work in either half or full track because commercial studios may not have quarter track machines. Trying to reproduce a quarter track recording on a half or full track machine will drastically reduce the volume of the recording and increase the noise level. If you are preparing your track for your own transfer to 8mm, super 8 or 16mm mag striped footage, use any system you please.

Bias

It is just not possible to use the simple audio signal to magnetize the record head to produce a good quality recording. It was discovered, however, that by modulating the audio signal, or by combining it with a high frequency signal called the *bias frequency,* high quality recordings

could be achieved. A circuit within the recorder produces this frequency, say from 60,000 to 90,000 Hz, usually used both for the record
bias and erase head signal.

As it turns out, different kinds of tape are recorded best with different values for the bias. Some professional machines have the ability to
alter the bias to match the tape. Find out from the manufacturer or distributor of your tape machine which type of tape he recommends. Using
premium quality tape with your recorder will not help make better recordings if bias and tape are mismatched.

Equalization

In recording the full audio spectrum, it was found that reducing the relative levels of both the low (bass) and high (treble) ends of the spectrum,
and then amplifying these portions upon playback produced best results.
Rolling off, or gradually reducing the bass and treble ends in record, and
then boosting the bass and treble in playback is called *equalization.* The
playback characteristics of equalization must match the record characteristics. Two similar equalization standards exist: in Europe the CCIR
(International Radio Consultive Committee, an agency of the U.N.)
standard is used, in America the NARTB (National Association of Radio
and Television Broadcasters) standard.

Tape Recorder Components

First, a distinction between reel-to-reel and cartridge machines: cartridge tape recorders, like the Norelco Carrycorder, are capable of
making very good recordings. They can be very helpful when you need
a small easily concealed machine. Although they have the advantage of
virtually instantaneous loading, their most serious disadvantage from
the filmmaker's standpoint is the difficulty in editing cartridge recordings. You can rerecord, or dub the cartridge recording to reel-to-reel
tape, and then cut that; but for highest quality, undoubtedly you're

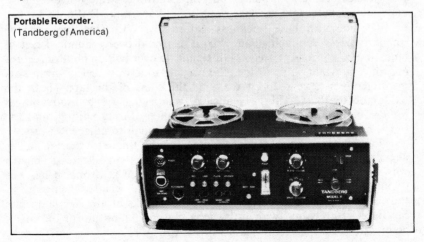

Portable Recorder.
(Tandberg of America)

Sound and Magnetic Recording

better off cutting the original recording. If you are doing your own double system mag tracks or striped footage, you can make your own rerecording directly from the cartridge machine to the sound projector.

Except for tape decks meant as components, manufacturers like to put handles on all tape machines, whatever their size and weight. We are left, after the tape deck, with two kinds of reel-to-reel portables—the portable and the not-so-portable. The not-so-portable portables use line current, while the portables use batteries or rechargeable power cells, even though there are some rather compact machines that use line current. If you make films, and have money for only one recorder, you'll probably be better off with a good battery or rechargeable cell-powered portable machine.

There are some good battery-operated portables which don't cost very much more than a good line current machine. Portables like those made by Tandberg, Stellavox, Uher and Nagra were designed especially for lip sync shooting. These machines can be used anywhere you can bring them, so you can record effectively indoors or outdoors.

Tape

There are many brands, and 'white box,' or unmarked tape brands, on the market. I have had bad luck with white box tape. This very inexpensive tape may have splices, a high background noise level of hiss or low frequency noise that sounds like rumbling; it may have *drop out* (loss of signal) and, because it may not be lubricated properly, it can cause excessive wear of the heads. Having gone through this I can now say that it is possible to find good quality white box tape. One way is to ask someone who knows, someone who works at a radio station using inexpensive but decent quality tape.

The more expensive tapes come in a bewildering variety of oxide coatings and base materials. The information on the box usually states that the base, or support, material is either acetate or polyester. The stuff labeled acetate is probably polyvinyl chloride, while polyester base material is usually sold under various brand names like DuPont's Mylar.

The standard base thickness is 1.5 mils. With this thickness the standard size seven-inch diameter reel can hold twelve hundred feet of tape, or at 7½ inches per second (ips), a little over half an hour of recording time. In an attempt to increase playing time in a reel of given size, manufacturers have reduced the total thickness of the tape—both the oxide and the base. Thin, extended play tapes have two disadvantages for the filmmaker: they are difficult to handle during editing, and the signal recorded on the tape tends to print through to adjacent layers.

Polyester, which is frequently used for the thinner material, but is also used for some 1.5 mil tape, is much stronger than acetate—which is why it can be used in a thinner form. Although it is strong, it has one peculiar disadvantage: it doesn't break clean like acetate when yanked. Polyester will stretch before it breaks, if it breaks at all. While acetate can be easily repaired with little signal loss or alteration at the break point, stretched polyester tape obviously won't.

Independent Filmmaking

In the 1.5 mil thickness, polyester is so strong that it would be a rare circumstance that would cause it to stretch. It has greater dimensional stability than acetate and better keeping qualities. If you're making recordings that are to last for the ages, or desire the best dimensional stability for synchronization, polyester base tape is the choice. But for most purposes, acetate will do nicely.

My observation is that Scotch Brand tape, number 201, a 1.5 mil acetate base tape, is a standard medium for recordings by amateurs and some recording studios. Others use Scotch 131, and I have used the less expensive Scotch 111 with very good results. (201 or 131 may be preferable for music, while 111 is fine for voice recording.) Scotch 206 is reputed to be one of the best tapes available. It is very difficult to saturate 206, that is, record a signal at so loud a level that it distorts. I am unfamiliar with other brands of tape such as Ampex and Sony which, I am told, are very good.

The claims made by manufacturers for their various oxide coatings are very confusing, to me at least. Some coatings are said to have low noise, others better dynamic range, still others high output and yet others great frequency response. And there are yet others that have combinations of qualities that are bound to please. It seems to me that only a very good tape recorder, amplifier and speaker could tell the difference. The recorder's instruction booklet may tell you which type of tape is best to use with the machine.

Filmmakers often have to copy, or dub, their tapes to tape or magnetic film; just as every printing generation degrades film print quality the same principle holds true with tapes. Without question start with the best possible quality recording, so that after the generations of duplication or rerecording you have to go through, you'll still have good quality sound. (The high frequency portion of the audio spectrum suffers most from dubbing.) If you start off with mediocre recording quality, you're bound to wind up with poor sound.

Tape Recording Time. (3M)

TIME CHART	RECORDING ONE DIRECTION			RECORDING BOTH DIRECTIONS		
	Monophonic 1 Track	Stereophonic 2 Tracks		Monophonic 2 Tracks	Stereophonic 4 Tracks*	
	1⅞ ips	3¼ ips	7½ ips	1⅞ ips	3¼ ips	7½ ips
600 Ft.	1 hr.	30 min.	15 min.	2 hrs.	1 hr.	30 min.
900 Ft.	1½ hrs.	45 min.	23 min.	3 hrs.	1½ hrs.	45 min.
1200 Ft.	2 hrs.	1 hr.	30 min.	4 hrs.	2 hrs.	1 hr.
1800 Ft.	3 hrs.	1½ hrs.	45 min.	6 hrs.	3 hrs.	1½ hrs.

*Double these times for 4-track monophonic recording.

Sound and Magnetic Recording

    The faster the speed of the tape past the heads, the better the qual-
ity of the sound because of the broader frequency response, especially
in the high frequencies, and the increased steadiness of the tape speed.
If the tape doesn't pass by the heads at a steady speed, you will hear
changes of pitch. Changes of pitch for high frequencies are called *flutter;*
for the low frequencies, they are called *wow.*

    For music recording, professional tape machines usually run at a
speed of 15 ips. The top speed on many good machines is 7½ ips, and this
speed is capable of delivering excellent recordings too. You may be able
to use a speed of 3¾ for voice recordings. The principal advantage of
using a slower tape speed is economy, or you may want to get more
recording time on a reel, with fewer reel changes and resultant inter-
ruptions.

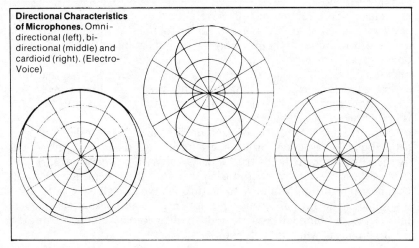

**Directional Characteristics
of Microphones.** Omni-
directional (left), bi-
directional (middle) and
cardioid (right). (Electro-
Voice)

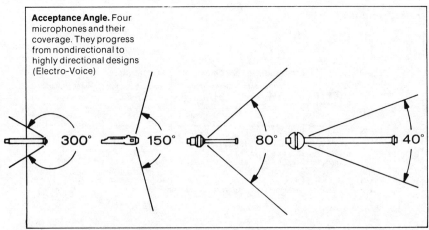

Acceptance Angle. Four
microphones and their
coverage. They progress
from nondirectional to
highly directional designs
(Electro-Voice)

Independent Filmmaking

There are two ways in which microphones can be classified: according to construction or directional pick-up pattern. How they work, or their construction, is generally of less interest to the filmmaker than the pick-up pattern. One type of microphone, the moving coil, or dynamic microphone has already been described. In addition to this dynamic type, there are magnetic, ceramic and crystal microphones.

The directional qualities of microphones can be roughly compared to lenses of wide angle, normal and telephoto focal lengths. There are nondirectional or omnidirectional, bidirectional, cardioid or unidirectional, and ultradirectional or shotgun microphones.

OMNIDIRECTIONAL MICROPHONES are generally supplied with the home tape recorders one is likely to purchase. Their pick-up pattern is circular; that is, they hear equally well in all directions.

BIDIRECTIONAL MICROPHONES hear in a figure-eight pattern. For this reason they are often favored for interviews on radio stations. They are not of very much use to the filmmaker.

CARDIOID MICROPHONES hear in a heart-shaped pattern. Although the microphone will pick up some of the sound outside the pattern, or even behind itself, mostly it hears what's happening directly in front. This microphone is, generally, the most useful type for filmmaking.

A good new cardioid microphone — made by AKG, Shure, Electro-voice and others — will cost in the neighborhood of $100, although used ones can be found for about $50. To improve the quality of your recordings, replace the omnidirectional microphones, if supplied with your recorder, with a good cardioid. In general, microphones supplied with a recorder are of mediocre quality; replacement with a good cardioid will make a dramatic difference.

ULTRADIRECTIONAL OR SHOTGUN MICROPHONES hear within a relatively narrow pick-up pattern. Such devices are often used by people doing *cinéma vérité* type filming because the microphones can pick out speech from background sounds. These microphones, however, are expensive.

Techniques

It is often rather difficult to estimate how well a recording will correspond to what you actually are hearing. The ear has the ability to pick out specific sounds you want to hear or are listening to. It's possible for you to ignore a lot of reverberation or reflected sound that would contribute to making a fuzzy or muffled recording. A microphone and a tape recorder is, in a certain sense, a more objective reporter of sound than your ear and brain working together.

A fortunate thing about magnetic tape recording is that you can immediately play back a test recording to find out if you've found the best position for your microphone. The subject is not that simple, however, and it can be very difficult to place a microphone for some types of recording. It may be extremely complicated to record either a small group

292   or a large orchestra with one microphone; professional practice involves using many microphones placed at various positions. I have read, however, that the Russians use one microphone to record symphony orchestras; and some Russian records I purchased out of curiosity confirm that, if indeed this is the technique they use, the monaural recording produced is at least as good as any American or British recordings I have heard. Mercury Records, before the advent of stereophonic sound, used a single well-placed microphone for recording orchestras, and the results were superb. The point of all of this is that simplicity of technique with microphones can produce good recordings. But it may take a great deal of experience, trial and error and very good equipment to get satisfying results.

The usual guiding principle for indoor recording is that the closer the microphone is to the subject the lower the level of the reflected sound. The more reverberation or reflected sound you want, the farther away the microphone ought to be.

For making voice recordings, you can usually get very good results six inches to two feet from the mouth, depending upon the peculiarities of the microphone you are using. Make test recordings at several distances from the subject and listen to them. Some microphones have a kind of tone control to be used when recording voice at close distances. If you place other microphones too close to the speaker, there is some danger of producing a sibilant recording (the proximity effect).

Although there will usually be less reverberation outdoors, you ought to get close to the subject for voice recording because the ambient or background noise levels may be higher than indoors. A windscreen, if it is not an integral part of the microphone's design, is a useful accessory for suppressing whooshing sounds caused by the wind, or the popping that can be produced by consonant sounds like *p, ch* or *k.*

Mixing Microphones

Since few tape recorders have inputs for several microphones, if you want to use more than one microphone for a monaural recording, you'll need an accessory called a *mixer.* The microphones are connected to the mixer which is connected to the input of the tape recorder. Then it is possible to mix the sound of each microphone, that is, raise or lower its level so that the signal being recorded is the best possible combination of all the microphones' signals. Some mixing units offer more than simple volume control: they may have the ability to alter the high or low portions of the audio signal of any one of the microphones. Attenuation of the low frequencies, for example, from below 200 to 100 Hz, often improves speech recording because low frequency background sounds are suppressed.

It should be pointed out that whether or not you use one microphone or many, one goal is to try for the cleanest possible sound, that is, a recording with as little reverberation as possible. It's always possible to add reverberation in the recording studio, although it might tend to sound artificial.

Independent Filmmaking

Volume Control

The most important control on your tape recorder during recording is the volume, or level, control. One guide to setting the level is actually to listen to the recording by either testing the recording immediately after it has been made or by monitoring the level with the playback head on a three-headed machine. Another method, the one most widely used, is to set the level with the *VU meter,* a galvanometer that monitors the loudness of the recorded sound. The idea is to keep the pointer or needle from peaking into the danger or red zone. It's sort of a game you can play, trying to get the highest possible level without overloading the tape. You have to get a loud enough signal on the tape so that on playback it will be above the noise of the system. If you record at too low a level, you may run into a lot of tape hiss; too high a level, and the sound becomes muddy and distorted. The best recordings are made just on the verge of *overload,* where they will have the least noise and greatest dynamic range. This is somewhat of an oversimplification. Soft sounds, like a tinkling bell, may be recorded at sufficient level even if the VU meter barely budges.

The only way to find out how well your VU meter functions is by testing it with the tape you are using. To use an analogy from film, some tapes are 'faster' than others. Indeed, low level recordings are like underexposing film, and high level recordings like overexposing film.

Some tape recorders use one or two neon glow lamps to help you set the level. You can get good results with this level setting system, but the VU meter is both more accurate and more fun to use.

Your best bet is to fiddle with the recording level setting as little as possible. Unless there are really gross changes in the volume of the sound, you may not have to change the level at all. The initial level that you set, therefore, is very important and should reflect both expectation and an educated guess.

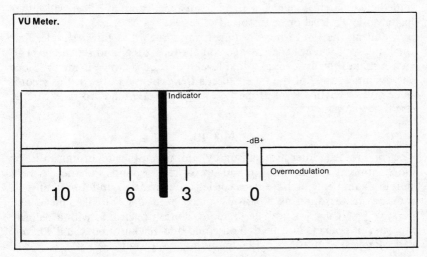

VU Meter.

Indicator

-dB+

Overmodulation

10   6   3   0

Sound and Magnetic Recording

Limiter and AVC

Some recorders offer *limiter* or *AVC* (automatic volume control) circuitry which can be used as the situation dictates. Both techniques try to achieve the proper level for recording. However, AVC doesn't work especially well for music; but both the limiter and AVC can be used for speech recording.

When the volume is set, as usual, for maximum deflection of the VU meter bordering on overload, the limiter clips off those sounds that would have been distorted because of overload. If a sudden exclamation or a shout should be sensed by the limiter, it reduces the excessive intensity to an acceptable level.

AVC, when in operation, makes all the decisions about recorded volume. It has been my experience that microphone placement, say not more than five feet from the subject, is a very important factor when using AVC.

Both the AVC and limiter can produce very good recordings, and if you're working alone or with a small or inexperienced crew, they can be a true blessing.

Recording from Records

Tape recorders have inputs which are suitable for use with different sources such as a microphone or a phonograph cartridge, or the amplified, or perhaps more properly, preamplified signal of the cartridge playing a record. Before taping from a phonograph record, say, the most crucial factor is to choose the proper impedance input from the phonograph cartridge or the associated amplifier.

The *impedance,* or AC resistance (written as Z, and comparable to the DC ohm) of the source must properly match the tape recorder's impedance. (Similarly, the microphone's Z must match the recorder's Z.) Some tape recorders have a control to give different impedance settings, or the input connector itself may determine the impedance. If the wrong impedance match is made, if there is any recording at all, it will either have too low a level or be distorted.

Setting the level for recording from a record is fairly simple: find the loudest portion of the passage you are recording, and set the level so that it makes the maximum signal level indicated by the VU meter. Since the dynamic range of the tape exceeds the dynamic range of the record, once you've set this level properly, everything else tends to take care of itself.

Mixing

You may want to alter a recording by adding another recording to it, or more simply, you may want to add two or more sounds together. A very simple example: you have a recorded conversation indoors that you want to make sound as if it took place outdoors. You'll achieve one possible result if you combine the conversation recording with a recording, say, of crickets in a field. You could add background sounds taken in a cafeteria, or music or, in fact, anything you want.

Independent Filmmaking

Electronic Mix

The most obvious, but not necessarily the easiest approach to mixing two (or any number—for the rest of this discussion I'll assume we're concerned with mixing two) recordings is to add the outputs of two recorders together, and combine the results with a third machine. Unless the third machine which is making the recording, has a built-in mixer, you'll need a separate mixer either commercially available or, if you're an electronic whiz, I'm told it's pretty easy and inexpensive to assemble one yourself.

At any rate, we add the signal from tape recorder A to that of tape recorder B, and adjust the relative volume of each recording so that the resultant composite is the proper mixture of the two input signals. Obviously, you need three tape machines (and a mixer) for this method.

You can use two tape machines and add the signal from a phonograph record, microphone or radio to the recording played back from one of the machines. In other words, you would add the signal of the phonograph record (or any other source) to that of your recording and mix the sounds by dubbing them on the second machine. With this electronic technique, you can mix the signals from a radio and, for example, a phonograph together and record them with simply one tape recorder.

Acoustic Mix

You can avoid any electric connection and mix sound sources with microphone and tape recorder by playing your various sources of sound through loud speakers. If you like, you could turn on the radio, talk and play a phonograph record, and record the whole thing with a microphone and tape recorder. The quality of such a mix, however, is going to be very different from what could be achieved from a purely electrical mix. I suppose you'd call this an acoustic mix. You can get some very interesting sound effects this way, but be aware that the results will be substantially poorer quality, in terms of high fidelity standards, than the electronic mix.

Sound-over-Sound

If you record over a previously made recording, with the erase head switched off, the two signals will mix. That is the basis for the *sound-over-sound* technique offered by some tape recorders and magnetic stripe projectors. It is possible simply to install a switch to disconnect the erase head of any tape recorder. The result of the mix is irreparable however. Once you have recorded over the first recording, you will not be able to change the result. Another bothersome feature is that you can't really control the volume of the first recording. You can control the overrecorded sounds, but the first recording level will have to remain as it is. In addition, the first recording will lose a lot of its high frequency.

Sound-with-Sound

If you have a two, or the more common four track, recorder, you could add a track to that previously recorded. This method hinges on your ability to listen to the first track while you are adding the second. For example, suppose you have recorded something on track 1, and you want to add another track using this method. If your recorder has the sound-with-sound feature you can listen to track 1, while you are recording track 3. Of course, with any stereo recorder you could add track 3 without hearing track 1, using the monaural mode for recording track 3. But if you can hear track 1 while adding track 3, the job will be simpler.

What you will have is not really a conventional mix, since both signals are not melded together on one track; but you do have a flexible kind of a mix, since you can raise or lower the level of either track upon playback.

This method isn't advised if you are planning to make a transfer to 16mm optical track or magnetic film, because professional studios usually don't have four track quarter inch tape machines: they probably have only two track quarter inch and full track quarter inch machines. If you can make an arrangement with the lab to patch in your tape recorder, sound-with-sound may be okay. If you are doing your own dubbing on mag film or mag striped footage, anything goes.

Sound-on-Sound

On a stereo recorder, if we have track 3 recorded, and we plan to mix another source with it using the sound-on-sound technique, we can add track 3 to the new material—a recording, another tape, your voice and a microphone, or whatever—on track 1. In other words, whatever was on track 3 gets added to track 1 with the external source. You can use this method for preparation of tracks for transfer to optical sound or mag film even though the lab may not have a four track quarter inch machine. With a four track machine, a transfer can be made from track 1, for example, providing the adjacent track is clean. The signal will be somewhat lower upon playback, and the level of background noise will be raised, but it may not harm your recording too much. If your goal is to produce your own dubbing on mag striped footage, there is no problem with this method.

Quarter-over-Half

If you have a half track recording and you want to mix another source with it, you can do it by placing the tape on a quarter track machine, and recording on half of the half track. The same kind of thing can be accomplished using a full track recording for the first track and then adding the second source with a half track machine. Whether you use the full or half track machine first, the second recording also erases half of the first recording while it is making the second track. For example, if you use this method, when you run full track tape through the half track machine, half of the full track will be erased while the new signal is laid down. When you play such a recording on a full track machine, both signals will be mixed by the playback head.

Although you are committed to the level of the track which was first

Independent Filmmaking

recorded, you can control the level of the second signal. However, the level of the first signal will be reduced because half of it is being erased. It is possible to make repeated attempts at perfecting the mixed track without harming the half of the original track which has not been erased. The mix can be checked by playing the tape on the machine used to make the first recording.

One difficulty with this method, when making a transfer to mag film or optical track, is the change in relative levels of the tracks by the studio's equipment. If the alignment of the head of the studio machine doesn't exactly correspond to that of your playback head, you'll hear the tracks mixed at some unexpected level.

Editing

There are many reasons to edit tape: you might want to cut out areas that are of no interest, or rearrange material for study or overdubbing (mixing). If you collect discarded tape spliced together on a reel, don't use it for rerecording because of the drastic changes in pitch that might occur wherever there is a splice. Splices made in the recording can sound perfectly natural, but you're taking a chance making recordings on spliced tape.

It's possible to do some interesting things by editing tape. You can cut out awkward pauses in a monologue, or rearrange words so that the speaker says things on tape he never really said. It's even possible to have somebody say words he never said by splicing together syllables. This kind of editing, or any kind of editing, is easier the higher the tape speed, because a greater length of tape represents the same period of time. It is easier to edit tapes recorded at 7½ than 3¾. For fine editing try running the tape at half the recorded speed to get as close to the splice point as possible. Some tape machines will allow you to handwind the tape past the heads so you can move tape at any rate. If your machine

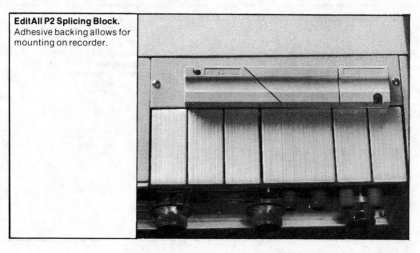

EditAll P2 Splicing Block.
Adhesive backing allows for mounting on recorder.

Sound and Magnetic Recording

has a pause button, you may be able to do handwinding. (By the way, you can get very interesting effects recording while handwinding.)

Editing magnetic tape is technically or mechanically simple, but it does take practice to obtain proficiency and a feeling for what's possible. Tape editing consists of joining sections of tape, end to end, by covering the base side of both sections with special splicing tape. You can't use ordinary cellophane tape because the adhesive will tend to bleed—spread from under the edges of the tape. This can gum up your heads, cause tape to stick to the adjoining layer and encourage the splices to stick to the recorder as they pass by the heads. The translucent white splicing tape, for this purpose, is made of very strong polyester material.

One crude way to make a tape splice requiring minimum equipment but maximum effort is simply to use a scissors to cut two overlapped pieces of tape on the diagonal. Next, cover the cut portions of the

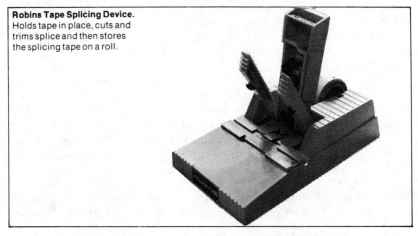

Robins Tape Splicing Device.
Holds tape in place, cuts and trims splice and then stores the splicing tape on a roll.

Chinon DS-300. A rear screen super 8 sound projector that resembles a TV set. Good quality image and sound. (Chinon Corp. of America)

Independent Filmmaking

tape with the adhesive tape, on the diagonal too, in the same direction as you've cut the tape. Press the adhesive tape down on the base side of the magnetic tape which usually is the shiny side (the oxide coating which comes in contact with the heads is, for most tapes, dull), and then trim the edges of the splice, cutting very slightly into the tape.

All methods of making a tape splice involve cutting the tape on a diagonal, and not perpendicular to the length of the tape. The diagonal splice passes by the heads more easily than a perpendicular splice and is perfectly inaudible. Trimming the splice slightly into the tape so that the region of the splice is a little thinner than the rest of the tape also helps the splice make a noiseless pass by the heads.

The scissors method isn't bad for making repairs, but it's troublesome when you are making lots of splices. It just takes too much effort and time to line up the tape and so forth.

Sound studios use a splicing block, usually the EditAll which holds the tape in place and provides for alignment of the adhesive tape as well. In addition, the splicing block has score, or guide, marks for cutting the tape and trimming its edges with a safety razor blade or an X-acto knife. The magnetic tape is laid down on the block, where it is held in place, and then cut with the blade. Next you cut a length of tape, with a scissors, and press it down on the tape.

If you are editing a difficult splice, you can find the desired splice point by a method of successive or diminishing approximations. Try getting closer and closer to the place you want by progressively edging in, perhaps a half or quarter of an inch at a time, until you're down to where you want it. Even the best tape editors have to resort to this technique. It's better to cut too little, so you can cut more out later on, because it's harder to add what you've removed than it is just to keep whittling your cut down to size.

It's important to know which head of your recorder is the playback head so you can exactly find the point at which you want to make your splice. Most two headed machines, or in fact most recorders of any kind, have the feed reel to the left and the take-up to the right. In such a case the erase head is the one on the left, the record-playback on the right. On machines with more than two heads, it may not be easy to locate which head performs what function if there's no information in the instruction book. To find the playback head, make a recording of a continuous sound — you can hum — and splice leader to the end of it. When the leader passes the playback head the sound will cease.

Leader (plastic without oxide coating) is very functional as the head or tail of your reel of tape, or for separating segments. Leader is available in many colors, and it may be inserted into the tape with splicing tape. It's very useful for cueing up segments when you are doing any dubbing or overdubbing.

A final warning of sorts, which applies to cutting magnetic tape or film. If you are getting a pop or a click sound at your splices, your scissors or razor blade are probably magnetized. You can't use mag-

Sound and Magnetic Recording

netized tools when you are cutting magnetic tape or film. Some editors rap or tap their tools against the edge of the table to demagnetize them before using.

Magnetic Striped Track

Preparing Striped Film

As has been said, it is possible to have 8mm, super 8 or 16mm footage striped with an iron oxide coating near the edge or edges of the film. Iron oxide on motion picture film becomes a medium identical in every essential way to magnetic recording tape. It also is possible to obtain prestriped film intended for single system sound on film recording; it can be used for postshooting recording, our concern here.

It's probably to your advantage to have your film striped after it has been shot and processed, since at this time you'll probably know whether or not you want to spend the money. Striping film is inexpensive and services are available from a number of laboratories.

You can, if you like, stripe your own film. A few machines that allow you to do this are on the market. They are advertised in the back pages of the large slick photography magazines.

The usual procedure when you plan to add your own recording to the magnetic stripe is to edit the original footage to finished form, and then have the film striped by the laboratory. Labs usually charge a few cents to do the job. This is the most economical procedure, and some people think it's the best way to do it, since oxide coating applied to the film after it has been spliced—with good bevelled-edge splices (see chapter 6)—will be very difficult to hear. However, it is possible to make inaudible splices with film that has been striped if you make decent bevelled-edge splices.

Both super 8 and 16mm allow a balance stripe to be added to the side of the film opposite the sound or record track. The balance stripe is made of iron oxide and is identical to the record stripe in every way except for its width. This stripe is not used for information, but because of its height, it helps the film wind on the spool evenly. There is no room for such a stripe on 8mm footage.

I have assumed so far that you intend to stripe and project your original footage. Footage which is screened repeatedly has a decidely limited life. It can last one screening or a thousand. After the first screening you could have picked up a tram line, as it is called, running down the length of every frame. If you aren't lucky, you might acquire torn perforations or burnt frames after only a few screenings. If your intention is to preserve your footage, be advised to have a print made from it. You can then, if you like, have the print striped and proceed to add your track as described.

Recording on Striped Film

Let's say that you've had your finished and edited film striped and are ready to record on the mag track. It is difficult, or it may prove impossible, to edit mag striped film *after* it has been recorded. Remember, there is a sound-to-picture separation of 18, 56 and 28 frames for super 8, 8mm and 16mm, respectively. The sound precedes the image in each case. Unless you have planned very carefully, if you record segments separately and attempt to join them together, you will lose either picture or sound. To cut one, means you'll lose the other.

If you are going to make the recording on your edited and striped film, you'll need a magnetic sound projector for this. There are magnetic sound models in all formats that can record as well as play back magnetic sound track. The magnetic sound projector is a mechanically noisy tape recorder. Its operation is comparable to the operation of a monaural tape recorder, with the additional hassle that the machines make a racket recording live sound through a microphone. Some kind of a sound deadening box can surround the projector, or you can use a long microphone cable to keep away from it. Another possible solution is to cut a hole in a wall or a door, fill the hole with glass, and project through that into another room, where the recording can be made in silence. If you dub a tape or a phonograph record to mag stripe, you eliminate this noise problem.

If you work from a recorded tape or phonograph record, you can dub the recording to stripe by plugging in the recorder's output to the proper input in the projector, often called the *line* input, as opposed to the *live* input used for a microphone. Consult the instruction books of both machines to find out how to make the proper connections. You can practice making the tape fit the track, or vice versa, by playing both track and image together. If you decide that the sync is good enough for your purposes, you can then dub the track to the mag stripe. If you don't like the results, you can simply rerecord just as you would rerecord tape.

If part of the recording on the stripe is good and part not, try rerecording just part of the track. Some magnetic sound projectors, like Eumig machines, have a sound-over-sound mixing facility (I don't especially like it). However, it's useful if you do narration dubbed over background music, or things like that. If you make a mistake, you have to start over. Other applications of the magnetic sound projector will be discussed in connection with recording lip sync sound.

Dupes with sound

It is possible to have a mag stripe sound print made from your original mag stripe film. Laboratories offering this service copy your film, say super 8 to super 8, and then add a mag stripe track in sync with your original. You could choose to have your print simply striped, and then record it with your mag stripe projector. By having the lab do the job though, you are assured of maintaining the same image-sound sync.

Some labs can directly blow up super 8 or 8mm mag stripe footage and produce a 16mm optical or mag stripe sound version of the original, without intermediate masters of either picture or track. It is also possible to have super 8 or 8mm reduction prints made from 16mm original (see chapter 9, *The Laboratory's Role*).

Sound and Magnetic Recording

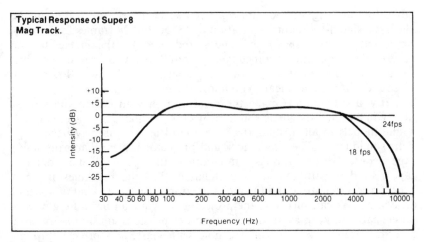

Typical Response of Super 8 Mag Track.

Duping in Sync

If you have two (or more) stripe projectors, you may be able to drive them in sync. The usual method is to run both projectors together using a belt or chain driven by an electric motor. You'll need a projector with what is called an inching knob, like some Kodak or Eumig 8 or super 8 machines. The *inching knob* is used for advancing the film a frame at a time, and it can be used to couple the machines so they run frame for frame in sync. Some labs have such tandem projectors and can do the sync 8mm transfer for you.

Quality

The question arises about how good mag stripe sound is. If we review our requirements for good sound reproduction, we recall that the ear is sensitive to sounds from 25 to 15,000 Hz, having a dynamic range of about 120 dB. From just about the earliest days of magnetic recording, in the middle forties, magnetic reproduction of sound has been able to approach these figures more closely than any other recording medium. Machines of the late forties ran at 30 ips and had a claimed frequency response covering the above range within roughly 2 dB.

Today it is not unusual to find home recorders with pretty much the same specifications running at one quarter or one eighth that speed. Similarly, the dynamic range of magnetic recording is good. Over the years improvements in quality have been steadily made, including perfection of stereophonic sound recording, reduction of distortions in recording, lessening of tape hiss and, most recently, great reduction in noise level, better dynamic range and the ability to make very high quality copies. The Dolby, an electronic compression amplifier, has been responsible for the latest gains in magnetic recording and reproduction. Even without the Dolby, mag sound is extremely good.

How does mag sound on film compare to tape? For 8mm and super 8, the track width is a little narrower than one of the four tracks of a modern quarter inch stereo tape recorder. You'd expect a little higher

background noise and a little less dynamic range. One track of a quarter
track machine is about 1/20 inch, and the mag stripe on 8mm and super
8 is 1/30 inch. Another factor is linear tape speed: home tape enthusiasts
have come to expect good frequency response at 3½ ips. All things being
equal, frequency response is dependent upon tape speed. For 8mm, the
linear speed of the film past the sound head at 24 fps is about 3½ ips,
and for super 8 about 4 ips; for 16mm the speed is 7.2 ips at 24 fps. The
width of the 16mm track, 1/10 inch, is comparable to the width of a half
track tape, 1/8 inch.

Another important factor is the base of the iron oxide coating. It
should be sufficiently flexible so that it can hug the head well. Recording
tape, because it is so much thinner, does a better job of this than motion
picture film, although polyester film as opposed to the thicker acetate
should prove comparable to quarter inch tape.

As it is, the sound quality of the 8mm formats is good, but not up
to the standards of four track machines running at comparable speeds.
Mag tracks of 16mm are capable of what we would normally call hi-
fidelity sound. The response of a good present-day super 8 machine is
claimed to be from about 70 to 7000 Hz which is comparable to 16mm
optical sound.

Putting the Balance Stripe to Work
The balance stripe of super 8 and 16mm films could be used to store
information, which may be interpreted in a variety of ways. The most
straightforward suggestion is to use the balance stripe for a second
sound channel. People have become accustomed to very good quality
sound in their homes, with good stereophonic hi-fidelity components,
and even the best quality monaural sound on film must fall short of the
mark. One argument against using the balance stripe for this purpose is
that it is so much thinner than the record stripe, especially in the case of
16mm, that compared to the record stripe it will have a high noise level
and a poorer dynamic range.

The balance channel could be used to store other kinds of sound
information. For example, it could contain narration or dialogue in
another language. Foreign language versions of films could mix sound
effects and music tracks and record them on the record stripe; and each
version could have its own dialogue on the balance stripe. Both tracks
could be mixed by the projector's amplifier. Other uses for this balance
stripe are possible. At present only the Heurtier Stereo 42 projector can
utilize the balance stripe.

Sound and Magnetic Recording

Preparing The Sound Track

The preceding chapter covered the subject of sound and magnetic

The preceding chapter covered the subject of sound and magnetic sound recording and concluded with a description of dubbing your own tracks on magnetic striped film. We will now go more deeply into preparing the sound track, by first giving methods of lip synchronized sound recording both at the time of and after shooting. Next, the preparation of 16mm or super 8 mag tracks will be described, along with methods for editing magnetic film and synchronizing it to the action of the picture. Finally, we will discuss laboratory produced prints with either magnetic or optical tracks, and how the various optical sound tracks work. Although much of the technology covered applies to the production of 16mm prints, prints in the 8mm formats can be produced, either from a 16mm master or from super 8 master material. In fact, many of the services formerly limited only to 16mm are now available for super 8.

Lip Sync Sound

Much of the information supplied so far can be used for the production of *wild tracks* which are not recorded in synchronization with the picture at the time of filming. The term *wild* has traditionally described sound effects, music, or a recording made at the time of shooting, but not in sync with the camera action. Lately, I have heard the term floating track also used.

A *floating track* does not have to be out of sync with the image: it can be synced to the image at the time of editing. The synchronization can range from rough to tight, depending on your needs or intentions. Sound effects, like a door slamming, can be tightly synced to the image. Often, final editing of a film involves shuffling around track and picture to fit each other.

It seems that the great desire of independent filmmakers has been to make films of people talking. I don't know whether this is a desire to ape Hollywood, or whether present independent filmmakers and Hollywood have been attracted by the same temptation to make *talkies*. It is clear that the entire course of the noncommercial cinema has been influenced, and this has proved a creative impetus, by the technical difficulty of recording sound in sync with the image. Even though a increasing number of techniques have made it easier to record syn sound, barriers remain.

Film historians and scholars are constantly musing about the effe of the introduction of *talkies* in the late twenties. In the long run, th really was no change. Late silent films were filmed plays and until cently most movies have been filmed plays. Initially though, there an impact. Dialogue came to dominate the action totally while the camera mechanism had to be kept in a padded house. Prior to sou rectors had been experimenting with interesting moving camera niques; but at least for sync segments, efforts to move the camer thwarted.

If lip sync had been readily available, the course of rece

making explorations might have been altered. Because filmmakers with limited means have had to explore the relationship between sound and image without the most obvious use of sound—the simple one-to-one relationship existing between lips and speech—many beautiful films have been made. Despite the fact that much remarkable work has been done without lip sync, the freedom of filmmakers is limited if they cannot explore every potential of their medium.

Recording Equipment

Microphones

The most useful microphone for sync recording is the *unidirectional,* or *cardioid microphone.* Its pattern of response may depart from a true cardioid, but it still is essentially dead to sounds behind it and more or less encompasses the hemisphere in front of it. Since the microphone is deaf to what's happening behind it, it won't pick up direct camera noises when used in a room even though it will pick up reflected or reverberated camera sounds—if there are any. The livelier the room—with hard reflecting walls—the greater the noise. The cardioid will give crisper reproduction of voices as well, since it picks up less reverberation than an omni-
rectional microphone. The unidirectional microphone is also less likely
pick up unwanted out-of-shot sounds. Even though there is a reduction
amera noise when shooting outdoors because of the lack of sound
tion from walls, the unidirectional mike still distinctly suppresses
mera mechanism's noise.

radirectional or *shotgun microphones* are especially useful for
reverberation and unwanted noises, since they cover even less
le of view' than unidirectional microphones.

Microphones

microphone—a small dynamic omnidirectional microphone
necklace—may be concealed beneath clothing. Heavy layers

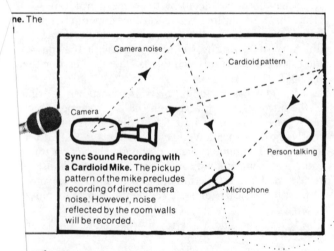

Sync Sound Recording with a Cardioid Mike. The pickup pattern of the mike precludes recording of direct camera noise. However, noise reflected by the room walls will be recorded.

making

of clothing may muffle the sound, but material like light cotton won't. If you use more than one of these, or more than one microphone anytime, you will need a mixer.

Another concealed microphone technique uses the wireless microphone. The microphone might be a lavalier type, or an easily concealed small microphone that can be attached to the clothing. A wireless microphone uses an FM transmitter to broadcast its signal to a receiver, plugged into the tape recorder. Since each wireless microphone must broadcast on its own FM frequency, a receiver for each frequency is necessary. The received signals are then mixed and fed to the tape recorder.

Good quality wireless microphones and receivers are expensive. Also, from what I understand, at this stage, spurious signals such as those produced by citizen's band radio can be received and recorded.

Another approach to recording speech is to conceal both a tape recorder and a microphone within the subject's clothing. It's possible to keep as many of these recorders and suitable cameras in sync as one desires. Nagra offers a high quality miniature recorder designed especially to be kept in sync with a crystal controlled pulse.

Booms

Professional practice, at least for shooting theatrical films, is to use a boom, or a pole, to suspend or hold the microphone as close as possible, usually above the actors without intruding into the picture area. Although a simple boom-type device—a pole on the end of a support—can be constructed easily, a better alternative for the independent might be having an assistant hold the microphone to the side or below the picture, or the microphone may be suspended from a *fish pole,* made of metal tubing or bamboo. The handheld fish pole can be moved to follow the speakers. My inclination here, as it was for lighting, would be to follow *cinéma vérité techniques,* that is, tampering with the environment as little as possible to achieve the best possible effect. Strictly adhered to, *cinéma vérité,* the motion picture analogue of Henri Cartier-Bresson's style of still photography, must necessarily tamper with the environment more than the intrusion of Cartier-Bresson and his Leica.

For the necessary operating room between the camera and the recorder, a long cable between the microphone and the recorder is required. To accomplish this most simply, use a microphone with low impedance.

Camera Silencers

Most cameras must be silenced in some way so that their running noise doesn't interfere with the recording. The problem is much less severe for 8mm and super 8 than 16mm cameras which are much noisier, in general, except for a few self-blimped or specially silenced designs. The farther the camera from the microphone, the lower its mechanism's noise will be recorded. This is especially true outdoors, and indoors in an acoustically dead room. In rooms with normal or excessive amounts of reverberation, moving the camera away from the microphone won't help too much. You can try a simple test of the sound level of the camera by making a recording under normal shooting conditions. Run a test film through the camera, since they often run noisier with film than without.

You can try covering the camera with towels and blankets to help deaden the noise. This method seems useful outdoors, where reverberation is reduced anyway, and with cameras which are relatively quiet in the first place.

Sound barneys are available for many 16mm camera designs. A *barney* is a padded housing covering the camera to reduce the mechanism's noise level. The lens and viewfinder eyepiece remain uncovered by the barney. Like the towels and blankets, barneys are most useful out of doors. To get an idea of how much noise reduction you can get with a manufactured barney, which can cost hundreds of dollars, try wrapping your camera with a pile of blankets and towels. Filmmakers may find it easy to construct their own barney. One design, given by Ernst Wildi in *The Bolex Reporter* calls for layers of velvet, plastic foam, felt, and a waterproof covering. Other suggestions include materials like sheepskin and lead foil. Some barneys have heating elements for use in cold weather conditions.

Another approach to the sound reduction problem is to use a *blimp*, a rigid structure which will produce very good sound reduction; it is possible to use a microphone within three or four feet of a camera operating within a good blimp. Since they must make provision for viewing the image and working the controls, blimps tend to be heavy, clumsy and expensive. (Blimps can cost a few thousand dollars.) The lens of the camera looks out of the blimp from behind an antireflection coated optical quality glass. Newer blimps are less bulky than old designs and use materials like fiberglas. Blimps, like barneys, are available with battery powered heating elements for use in adverse weather.

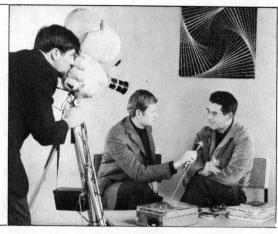

Camera in a Barney. Recording a typical sync sound interview with the camera noise suppressed by a barney. (Paillard)

Yet another approach to noise reduction is to modify the camera to run more quietly. I've heard of attempts to do this by replacing metal gears and bearings with nylon or plastics like Delrin. Results with the Bolex and Beaulieu cameras are said to be fairly good.

Even 'noiseless' camera designs, like the Arriflex and the Eclair NPR, may need some additional sound deadening. Cameras obtained from rental services are especially suspect, and several filmmakers whom I know have complained about noisy rented Eclair magazines.

Recording Technique

Sound cameras, the term always used in books and articles about Hollywood, don't really record sound. A more descriptive word for these machines would be 'silent' cameras, because if they made very much noise, the sound recording would be ruined. For years Hollywood used both cameras and sound recorders driven with synchronous motors. If both camera and recorder have synchronous motors and are driven by the same AC power supply, sync can be guaranteed. Although this system is still in use, it is rapidly being replaced by the sync pulse system.

For years the medium of original recording was optical sound on motion picture film. Although still used for prints, the optical track for original recording has all but disappeared. Magnetic sound recording is now universally used for original recording and dubbing.

Hollywood sound stage technicians are working in ways that independent filmmakers simply cannot emulate, which is just as well since their methods of sound recording are probably not the best for the independent. Recording technicians are primarily concerned with one thing— producing clean recordings. That is, they want crisp, clear, nonsibilant, undistorted, full level recordings without excessive reverberation. If they start with a clean recording they can, they say, do anything they want to it in the dubbing stage by adding the proper *audio perspective*. As the sound engineers watch the screen during mixing, they can change the quality of the recording, matching the acoustical with the visual perspective. For example, if the film has a cut from a close-up to a long shot, the sound engineers can instantly add the proper level of reverberation to match the visual portion of the film. The close-up sound would be crisp, lacking the reverberation added to the long shot. The methods used by studio technicians, or mixers, or engineers, are very clever and often difficult to tell from the real thing. From an economic standpoint, the independent would be in trouble if he had to stick to the commercial studio formula. Studio mixing is one of the most costly procedures a filmmaker can encounter, and most independents avoid it if they can. More important, though, if natural sound quality can be produced, it may be better sound than studio sound. Better is what you like, though.

Single System Sound

When the sound track—optical or magnetic—is recorded on the same piece of film at the same time as the image, we have *single system*

Preparing the Sound Track

sound. Most of the single system sound done by television news crews uses magnetic prestriped film. You can buy prestriped 16mm film from the manufacturers, or you can have the film striped by a laboratory. It may be impossible to fit two hundred feet of some prestriped films on the reel that normally holds two hundred feet, because of the added thickness of the stripe. This is especially true of relatively thick color emulsions.

Because of its better quality sound, single system magnetic sound has more or less superseded optical recording. The Auricon 16mm camera models are the only presently manufactured machines that can record optical sound on film. Even these, however, are often employed with a substitute magnetic sound module. Eclair, Arriflex, Bolex, Scoopic and Beaulieu offer 16mm magnetic sound-on-film recording cameras, or conversion units can be added to their cameras. As for super 8, Wilcam has pioneered with their superb W 1 camera, and Kodak is about to introduce a sound-on-film cartridge and camera system.

After the film passes through the camera gate, where it is exposed, its intermittent motion must be smoothed out before it can pass over the magnetic (or optical) recording head. A loop of film passes by rollers, one of which is attached to a flywheel, changing this stop-and-go motion to the continuous motion that sound recording demands. (This is the way sound projectors work.) The camera then acts just like a tape recorder by adding the sound signal to the iron oxide coating on the film.

The distance between the gate or aperture and head has a standard displacement, so films can be played back and screened on a standard sound projector after processing.

One of the chief disadvantages of the single system recording scheme is its difficulty in editing. For 16mm, for example, sound is twenty-eight frames in front of its corresponding image. What to do? One possibility is to rerecord the sound on 16mm magnetic film, and then cut the picture and track. Another solution is to rerecord the track so that it is adjacent to the picture instead of ahead of it. Magnasync/ Moviola and Amega offer what is called a *displacement recorder* which lifts the track from its fore position and places it opposite the image so that the film can be edited for sound and image simultaneously. Once the editing job is accomplished, the film may be put back into the displacement recorder, and the sound is rerecorded back into the projection sync position.

Sync Pulse-Double System Sound

Double system sound makes use of a camera and usually a quarter inch tape recorder. The cameras used often have DC motors which can be battery powered; the motor may be set for the precise running speed by a tachometer, built into some cameras, while other cameras offer the option of using a precisely running *constant speed* motor; in the United States, that speed is 24 fps; in Europe, for television films, the speed is 25 fps.

Independent Filmmaking

Double system cameras use what is called a *sync pulse generator*— either built-in or as an accessory. This device is an AC dynamo designed to generate a 60-cycle current for every twenty-four frames of exposed film. (For European TV a 50-cycle current is employed.) In the time interval that one frame is exposed, two and a half pulses are generated by the sync pulse unit. The camera is connected to the tape recorder by a cable, and this 60-cycle signal is recorded and used as a reference tone for translation of the tape to magnetic film.

The camera doesn't control the speed of the recorder: it tells the recorder how fast it is going at any given moment: the sync pulse generator simply tells the recorder the rate at which it is running for each exposed frame. If this information is stored on the tape, it is possible to come up with magnetic film having a sound recording with a one-to-one relationship with the film.

The sync signal, recorded on the tape with any one of a few methods, must be present but inaudible. The simplest method uses a dual track or stereo tape recorder: half of the tape width is used for the sound, and the other half for the sync signal. Another method, by Perfectone, rarely used these days, records a signal along the top and bottom edges of the tape. This *push-pull* method of recording requires dual heads to combine the signal into a usable form. The third method, which is the most widely used, is known under the names Pilote, Pilotone or Neo-Pilotone. This uses the full quarter inch track width, but the sync head gap is oriented at right angles to the sound record and playback head gaps. The sync signal is recorded in a narrow track right down the middle of the audio track. A signal recorded on the tape with this method won't interfere with the sound recording.

The most frequently seen machines used for double system recording are the Tandberg II-P, Uher 1000/N, Stellavox, Arrivox-Tandberg, and Nagra models. All can run by rechargeable ni-cad cells. The tape speed most often chosen is 7½ ips, although 3¾ is used as well. Stereo ma-

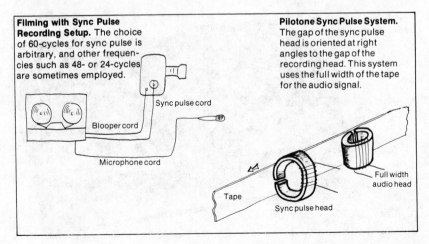

Filming with Sync Pulse Recording Setup. The choice of 60-cycles for sync pulse is arbitrary, and other frequencies such as 48- or 24-cycles are sometimes employed.

Sync pulse cord

Blooper cord

Microphone cord

Pilotone Sync Pulse System. The gap of the sync pulse head is oriented at right angles to the gap of the recording head. This system uses the full width of the tape for the audio signal.

Full width audio head

Tape

Sync pulse head

Preparing the Sound Track

chines may be used, without modification, to record the audio and sync signals on separate channels.

Wireless Sync Systems

There is a way to eliminate the cable connecting the camera and recorder for the sync pulse signal. The solution is elegant, expensive and, for some applications, very useful. The system involves a crystal oscillator controlling the camera motor. In some cases small lightweight AC synchronous motors are used. The most interesting characteristic of this kind of a motor, from our point of view, is that its speed is frequency dependent. That is, the rate at which the motor rotates is determined by the frequency of the current it receives. There are crystal oscillators that can control the current frequency received by the motor to an accuracy of one part per hundred thousand — adequate for all sync applications. A similar crystal oscillator is used at the recorder for generating the 60-cycle sync pulse. This system could also be used to control the speeds of several cameras (and recorders if you like) so that they all run in sync. Such a system is available for the Beaulieu News 16, Eclair NPR and ACL, Arriflex and other brands as well.

Another method of wireless sync uses a radio transmitter at the camera to broadcast the sync pulse signal to the tape recorder.

Double System with Mag Film

Instead of a tape recorder, you can use a magnetic film recorder for the original recording. If the mag film recorder uses the sync pulse to control its speed, you can get synced picture and mag film without resolving from quarter inch tape. A portable 16mm mag film machine for this use is the Amega M-3. Recently, several super 8 mag film recorders have appeared on the market. They have the disadvantage of not leaving the filmmaker with a backup tape in case a mistake is made in editing the transferred mag film, but they have the great advantage of

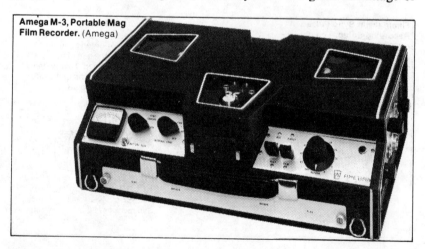

Amega M-3, Portable Mag Film Recorder. (Amega)

eliminating the studio transfer. Moreover, a machine like the Amega can eliminate your need to go to the lab or studio to have any kind of transfer made.

Establishing Sync
It is a good idea to establish sync points on both film and tape at the beginning of each shot. The traditional way of doing this is to use a *clap board,* or *slate,* consisting of a hinged wooden clapper attached to a slate framed in wood. Information identifying the film and shot is chalked on the slate. (It may be useful to identify silent footage this way for later identification. The procedure is called *slating.*) The camera and recorder are turned on, someone calls off the information written on the slate as it is shot, and then the clapper is sounded. The slate is withdrawn, and the shot or action begins.

When it's time to edit, we have the shot identification on both the track and picture, and we have established a sync point on the track (the banging of the clapper) and the corresponding sync point in the picture (when both parts of the clap board are brought together).

Some cameras such as the Eclair, modified Canon Scoopic and Arriflex offer electronic blooping. Blooping works as follows: after the camera and recorder are turned on, a button on the camera is pressed, and a light in the camera either fogs the edge or a frame of the film. At the same instant, a tone, often 1000 cycles, is recorded on the tape. Some cameras do the blooping automatically—no button need be pressed. During editing the fogged film and reference tone establish sync.

Resolving Pulsed Tape to Film
The usual procedure for making a sound track is to have quarter inch tape (sync or silent) transferred, or copied on 16mm magnetic film. The single perforated acetate base film, 16 millimeters wide, is the same as single perf 16mm motion picture film, except that it is coated with the same iron oxide used for quarter inch tape. The advantage of 16mm

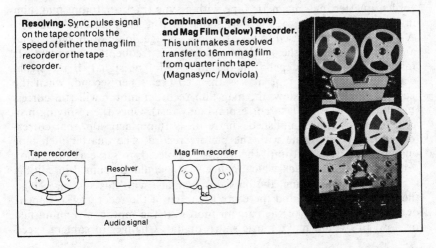

Resolving. Sync pulse signal on the tape controls the speed of either the mag film recorder or the tape recorder.

Combination Tape (above) and Mag Film (below) Recorder. This unit makes a resolved transfer to 16mm mag film from quarter inch tape. (Magnasync/Moviola)

Tape recorder

Resolver

Mag film recorder

Audio signal

Preparing the Sound Track

314 mag film is that a one-to-one relationship exists between a length of mag film and picture. Every perforation of mag film corresponds to a perforation of picture. A simple mechanical system can be used to drive or hold the mag film and picture film in synchronization. When tape with a sync signal is transferred or dubbed to mag film, the process is called *resolving*. (Similar setups now exist for super 8.)

How to resolve the tape to mag film in perfect sync? Remember, the double system tape contains a control track of sync information. The sync pulse generator is designed to produce a 60-cycle signal for every twenty-four frames exposed; two and a half cycles for every frame. Driven by the camera, the generator is attached to a shaft which rotates once for every frame exposed. This means that it will rotate twenty-four times in one second at sound speed. It is designed to generate a 60-cycle current for every twenty-four rotations. If the camera motor slows down, it will generate less than 60 cycles; faster, more than 60 cycles. The signal that it produces, recorded on the magnetic tape, is used in the transfer studio or laboratory to control the rate at which the magnetic film recorder operates.

Magnetic film recorders use AC synchronous motors which are frequency dependent. That is, the only factor that affects the motor's speed is the frequency of the power supply. In the United States, line current is generated at 60 cycles. Therefore, synchronous motors will operate at their rated speed when supplied with a 60 cycle current.

The magnetic film recorder is similar to a tape recorder, except that film is driven by the heads by sprocket drive, rather than capstan drive. A capstan would allow tape or film to slip (if only slightly), but perforated mag film is sprocket driven at 24 fps (7.2 ips) with perfect accuracy.

There are several methods in use, but from the filmmaker's point of view it doesn't make any difference which is used, as long as the studio can do the job. The simplest method (to understand) of resolving the recorded quarter inch magnetic tape with a sync track to 16mm mag film involves amplification of the sync signal to run the mag film recorder. A power amplifier is used to take the low voltage, low power sync signal and amplify it. Since the synchronous motor is frequently dependent, its rate of rotation will depend on the amplified sync signal. If the signal was recorded on the tape at less than 60 cycles per second, when the camera was running slow, the mag film recorder motor will run correspondingly slow (or if fast, correspondingly fast). Once the resolving procedure has been accomplished, the result is 16mm mag film that corresponds frame for frame with the picture record. The quarter inch tape may be saved, at least until the film is completed, to serve as protection for the 16mm mag track which, conceivably, could get ruined in editing.

Practically speaking, the only disadvantage with this system is that the speed of the tape, and therefore the pitch of the recording, is dependent upon the speed of the camera motor. If the motor is running fast or slow, this could make music sharp or flat. Changes in camera speed would be heard as wow or flutter. A good constant speed DC motor will run very nearly at 24 fps, and a variable speed motor may be accurately set by the tachometer to reduce the possibility of sharp or flat recordings (you won't be able to identify small variations in voice recording). Once these motors are running they can run at a constant rate, so wow and flutter probably won't be a problem.

Several manufacturers, such as Tandberg and Nagra, offer resolvers for use in conjunction with their recorders and a mag film recorder. These machines compare the sync track frequency with line frequency and alter the speed of the tape recorder, not the mag film recorder, so that perfect resolving is achieved.

Ivan's Method—Wild Sync

This method described to me by Ivan Watson, columnist for the British magazine, *Movie Maker,* has a decidedly looney flavor to it, perhaps because it is so absurdly simple. Ivan showed me several films shot in lip sync with this method, and the results are astonishingly good. Although Ivan didn't discover it, I have named it after him, and since the shooting is done wild or with a floating track, I've dubbed this method *wild sync.*

The following equipment is involved: an electric-drive camera, a tape recorder and an interlock or a magnetic sound stripe projector. The method will work for any format: use a clap board or similar device, like clapping your hands, to start the shot, just as you would for any double system method. While you're shooting the picture and recording the sound, there is *no* connection of any kind between the camera and recorder. All of the sync work is done during the transfer of the track to stripe or mag film.

When you make the transfer, connect the output of the tape recorder to the input of the projector. Now turn on the projector, and watch for the start mark. As soon as it appears, turn on the *recorder.* It may take a little practice to work this out. The tape has to be positioned just so, and you have to make allowances for your reaction time, and so forth, but establishing initial sync becomes easy with practice.

The projector must run at slightly less than the camera speed: if you shot at 24 fps, you must run the projector at say, 23½ ips. You'll have to hunt to find the proper fps value on a projector with a variable speed control like the Eumig 8mm or super 8 machines, or the Siemans 2000 model with the induction motor (not the constant speed synchronous motor). If you make a transfer to 16mm mag film with the Siemans, you can then use the mag film as if it were double system transfer or resolved track, which, of course, it is. If your magnetic stripe or magnetic film projector won't work at a touch under 24 fps, you can try shooting at 25 fps or thereabouts, if your camera has a variable speed motor.

The point of this method is that any error which occurs must occur in one direction. If you know the projector is running slow, you can slow down the tape speed whenever you lose sync just by rubbing your finger

Preparing the Sound Track

on the feed reel. If the projector wasn't running slow, you wouldn't know in which direction to make your correction. It sounds weird, but it works. You sit there, watching the screen, with your finger hovering over the feed reel of the tape recorder, ready to gently rub the reel at the first sign that you are loosing sync. It takes practice to know just how much you ought to bear down on the feed reel, but your eye will detect lost sync to within a frame. If you make a mistake dubbing, you can, of course, start over. Shorter sequences, say under thirty seconds, are comparatively easy to do. Longer sequences are a bit of a headache, but I saw a five-minute shot, done with an electric-driven Bolex H-8, that was in perfect sync from start to finish.

For short shots, say 15 seconds or less, you may be able to achieve good sync without any of this. A simple transfer to mag stripe or film may do the trick. The success of such wild sync is heavily dependent on the accurate speed of the camera. Tape recorders are usually accurate, with speed variations of less than one percent, but cameras can depart from sound speed by several percent.

Postsynchronized Dubbing

Postsynchronized dubbing is most familiarly known as applied to foreign language films dubbed in English. The best dubbing is that which you don't notice. Foreign language dubbing has at least one strike against it: the actors' lips have a hard time matching their dubbed voices (or rather, vice versa). Dubbing is also a frequently used professional technique whenever a recording might be very noisy, or mike placement impossible. Long shots in theatrical films often require postsync dubbing, because it is very difficult to see the lips in the first place, and the microphone placement might be very difficult.

A tape recording of what the actor says can help postdubbing, especially if there is any departure from a written script. The dubbing technique is not supposed to be very difficult, but it may need dozens of takes before dramatic and sync requirements are fulfilled. Here are some methods for achieving postsync dubbing:

Looping

This method is particularly applicable to an interlocked mag film recorder and projector or a double projector, like the Siemans, Sonorex, Palmer or Bauer. A loop is a piece of film spliced end to end, so that it can pass through the projector continuously without rethreading. Make a loop of the film, say a workprint, and the same length in mag film. Use some kind of leader for the image, so that actors can get set. They watch the screen, 'read' their lines and, immediately after recording, the track and picture can be played back and studied. If the take was not good, the process is repeated.

Forward-Backward

This method is applicable to stripe or dual projectors. Run through the filmed scene or shot, recording voices, then reverse the machine and playback the picture and track. Redo it until you get what you like.

Independent Filmmaking

Kuchar's Method

George Kuchar developed this method in several of his films, notably, *Hold Me While I'm Naked,* and Mike Kuchar made use of it in *The Secret of Wendel Sampson.* Although it defies accepted practice, a fair degree of sync can be achieved with this method. Turn on your projector and have your actors speak into the microphone of the tape recorder, while watching the action. You're recording wild. The particular method that George and Mike used was to play all of the parts, or dub all of the voices, by imitating different voices. Have the quarter inch tape transferred to 16mm mag film, and then fit it to the picture by shuffling it around. How you accomplish this will be detailed in the section dealing with editing magnetic film. You could also record the track at the time of shooting, wild or floating, and then try to match it to the track in editing (short segments, as noted earlier, may be in perfect sync). Either way, if the track is recorded at the time of shooting, or dubbed after, this will work best for very short dialogue segments.

Studio Dubbing

The sound studio or laboratory equipped for dubbing may have any one of a variety of techniques used for syncking image and track. Many labs build their own equipment, or modify existing equipment to suit their needs, or those of their customers. Some studios use conventional sound or silent projectors driven with belts in sync with the mag film recorder; others may use various types of synchronous motors. In any event, what happens is that you and your actors make your recording looking at the screen, while the projector is in the recording booth behind glass, so that its noise won't be picked up. You don't have to use this kind of postsync dubbing just for dialogue. You can use it to add sound effects, which may be created in the studio or added from records or tapes, and so on. What stops more people from using such studio services is that for an independent filmmaker, commercial studio rates are rather high.

Do-It-Yourself Dubbing

If you have a mag stripe or interlock projector, you can do postsynchronized dubbing yourself. Be careful of your projector's mechanical noise when you record. If you don't want the projector's sound on your track (although you might), cover the projector with blankets or, if you have the inclination, construct a padded wooden box or booth. You could cut a hole in a wall, say from a closet or an adjoining room, allowing the projector beam to come through. A glass covering for the hole will further help suppress projector noise. One way of doing postsync dubbing that I have gotten used to is to get right up to the screen, with the projector far enough away, so that its noise is recorded at a very low level. If there is any background noise from the projector (or some other source), one possible way to mask it is to mix in, at some later stage, background sound effects or music to mask any intrusive projector noise. Practically speaking, during the screening of your film, under average

Preparing the Sound Track

conditions, slight background noise will most likely be masked by the projector and audience noises — but I have never felt able to count on this.

One trouble with postsync dubbing of voices is that they tend to have a harsh or studio sound. Studio sound men, or engineers, prefer intelligibility and clarity to anything else. They hope to add the reverb during the mixing steps. This may not be the best way for you to do your dubbing. Even if you can afford future mixes, you might find that natural room acoustics make for better recordings in the first place. Once you've got the natural reverb, though, it is hard or impossible to get rid of it.

Preparing the Magnetic Film

For the benefit of those who have attempted to follow the preceding discussion as a whole, let me tell you a little about where we've been and where we are going. First, tape recordings have been made. Maybe they're in sync, maybe wild or floating. The tapes are edited as tightly as need dictates, with the thought in mind that final editing can take place in the form of 16mm mag film. If you've been working in 8mm or super 8, you may have gone another route, that is, you don't have to turn your tapes into 16mm mag film. You can dub them directly, yourself, using a mag stripe projector, or transfer your tapes to super 8 mag film.

But let us assume that your medium is 16mm, and you are going to have the lab make prints — you may want one print or fifty. Your next step is to make the transfer to 16mm mag film. If you've got an interlock projector, half projector half mag film recorder, or a mag film recorder, you may not have to go to the studio. You then have the option of making your own transfer, dubbing as you would from tape recorder to tape recorder.

Let's assume you have prepared your tapes for transfer to 16mm mag film. Why do this? Because you can edit mag film in frame-for-frame sync with the picture. After you have edited your 16mm mag film so that it fits your 16mm picture, the image and sound track portions of the film are delivered to the laboratory, and a *married* print of the image and track produced. The print's track may be in the form of magnetic stripe or an optical track.

Before the Studio

In general terms, this is how to prepare to go to the sound studio: you've probably fiddled with your quarter inch tape and picture, after listening to the track and screening the picture in rough sync, to get some kind of an idea of how they work together. When I was afraid to mess up the original, I used a *worktape* to help me edit magnetic tape. You've screened your film and listened to the tape in rough sync, knowing that final sync will be achieved when you edit the mag film and picture to match each other. The tape and the image will usually play back in more or less the same relative, although rough, sync each time you play them

Independent Filmmaking

with your equipment. But this may not be the case after transferring the tape to 16mm mag film. Then the mag film may be shorter or longer than you had anticipated. Only rarely will the image and mag film track be the length you had imagined.

Why should the mag film be some other length than your tape? For one thing, the mag film recorder works at 24 fps. If the projector you used worked at 23.5 fps, for example, there is going to be some difference in both sync and overall length of tape dubbed to film. Also, the studio's recorder and your recorder don't run at exactly the same rate. It is not unusual to have a difference—shorter or longer—of five seconds (or more) in a ten-minute transfer. To be safe, you might make some allowance for this by making your tape a little longer than the picture, or you may have to shorten the picture when editing, or return to the transfer studio with a new tape.

If you are dealing with segments of tape that work with segments of image, separate each segment by leader. This will give the engineer in the studio, and you, some reference point so that you can stop the transfer and work out the best possible level, and so on, for transfer of each segment. When you edit the mag film, the portions of the track can be joined together, or separated with silence, if you like. The problem of different lengths of the mag film and the original tape is not so severe for short segments. In a twenty-second segment, you probably won't be off by as much as a second.

You can assemble the tape in segments, if your film is prepared in a segmented form in appropriate order. Have a *cue sheet,* noting the relative volume or level, bass and treble emphasis and so on, of each segment. If you're using records, it may be best to have them directly transferred to mag film and not to tape them first, and then have them transferred to mag film. Remember, each generation will cause degradation of quality. However, if you have a very good recorder, or many records to transfer to mag film, or many portions of records, or mixed record with record, you may find it easier to make your own dub to tape, and have that transferred to mag film. However, before you go into the studio, be prepared, because that will save you money.

Talking to the Engineer
You want to get the engineer to do what you want him to do. Because of his training and experience, he may or may not be able to help you as much as you'd like—remember, he is used to doing things the way the commercial people like them done. Some transfer studios in larger cities do nothing but dub tape to mag film (or optical track). Others were set up initially for magnetic recording to make LP's, 45's and radio commercials. Their desire for television commercial work often inspired them to branch out by getting mag film equipment. These studios are often well equipped and have helpful engineers with experience in many weird techniques. Many laboratories, whose prime business is making prints and processing film, have sound studios and transfer equipment too.

Preparing the Sound Track

There you are, with your tapes and records and cue sheets, and there he is, with his turntables, tape recorders, mag film recorders—and his board. The control board, or console, can be used to adjust the level of the recording—its bass or treble emphasis—or add reverberation or, on occasion, remove unwanted and pervasive noise from your recordings. This collection of processes is called *balancing* or sometimes *equalization(EQ)*.

The engineer threads up your tape or puts your record on the turntable, and sits by his board. He's threaded 16mm mag film onto the mag film recorder. He may ask you if you have a sync recording. If you have quarter inch tape with a sync pulse record on it, you should let him know about it. All recordings for resolving should be placed together so that he can handle them at one time. Previously, you should have determined whether the studio has the equipment necessary to resolve your kind of sync recording. An ordinary transfer costs about $25.00 an hour, resolving about $40.00. You usually pay about 2.5 cents per foot for mag film used. Some studios have a minimum charge based on a full hour or half an hour and others just a rate per foot.

Since you reserve studio time in advance, you have to determine the total time a transfer will take. If you have ten minutes of recording, it could take ten minutes to do the transfer, or five hours. You had better allow yourself at least twice the length of the recording for the time in the studio.

You and the engineer will listen to all or part of your recording. He may ask you to help find the loudest portion of the segment to set his level. If you are dealing with a number of segments, you will be concerned about the relative level of each segment and how they relate to each other. But if you have one recording or segment for your film,

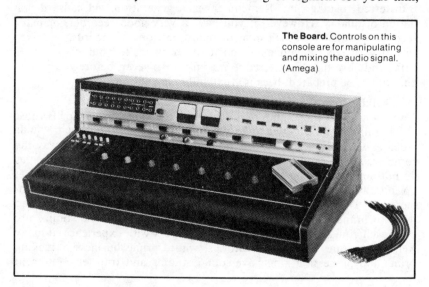

The Board. Controls on this console are for manipulating and mixing the audio signal. (Amega)

Independent Filmmaking

you'll be more concerned, in most cases, with the absolute level of the transfer. You'll probably want the broadest dynamic range and least noise, so the transfer should be made at the maximum level without overloading the mag film.

The first decision is how to set the level. It may be surprisingly difficult for you to tell the engineer what to do. First of all, you are now listening to the recording through very costly equipment. You may be amazed at the hiss, the clinks, the weird sounds coming out of those enormous speakers. The mixes you made may now sound out of balance. Is it the same recording you heard through your equipment? You can ask to hear the recording back through junky speakers. Most studios have auxiliary speakers like those you'd rip out of a table model radio or built-in projector speakers. They more closely approximate how your track will sound on most loud speakers used for 16mm projection.

When you've decided what the level ought to be, there are things to attend to: you may want to boost the bass or lower the treble end of the recording. The controls on the studio's board are an elaboration of the controls on stereo amplifiers. They allow the engineer to carefully adjust or balance the sound. A voice recording, for example, may require some bass roll-off (gradual reduction) in order to make it more intelligible, or the treble can be raised with the same end in mind. Explain what effects you want to the engineer, and let him play the recording back several different ways. A few things may help him to help you. To set the level of a voice recording, for example, you might tell him that it's used with a medium, a close-up or a long shot. You may not have a medium shot or a long shot or a close-up — or a person on screen that moment for that matter — but he's used to getting instructions in these terms. If you try to tell him what kind of a feeling you are trying to communicate, in your own terms, you may or may not get through to him.

The engineer can add reverberation, or echo, during the transfer in two ways. Most studios have a *delay head* for this purpose on one of their tape machines. The amount or degree of reverberation is determined by the distance from the delay head to the record head, and by the tape speed. Some home tape recorders also have this feature. Popular music often adds this electronic reverberation to make the sound fuller or richer.

Another kind of reverberation effect the engineer may have at his disposal is an actual echo chamber, that is, a room with speakers at one end, and a microphone at the other. The recording is played back through the reverberation chamber's speakers and rerecorded by the microphone. Baffles are used to separate one portion of the room from another to control the reverberation effect. You'll probably get more natural effects this way than with a delay head.

The engineer can sometimes eliminate hum or unwanted noise from your recording. One kind of noise he frequently has to deal with is 60-cycle AC hum which is picked up by microphone leads, for example. He can do this by simply cutting off (or rolling off) the bass end of the

Preparing the Sound Track

audio spectrum below 60 cycles. Hiss or high frequency noise may be similarly eliminated. Noise in the mid portion of the audio spectrum may be eliminated with *dip filters,* but often at a great price. You can destroy the recorded sound if you try to eliminate too much 'noise.' There simply are limits to what can be done to salvage a noisy recording.

Other effects are possible: you can change the speed of the recording slightly to restore the best possible pitch for music recordings or grossly alter the speed for weird or comic effect. Most of us are familiar with the chipmunk sounds you can get by playing a 3¾ recording at 7½ ips, for example.

You can have your engineer add sound with sound, or make a simple mix while you do your transfer (you may have to pay an additional charge for a mix). Suppose you have a quarter inch recording of somebody talking, and you want to add sounds of the seashore to it. The engineer can mix the voice tape with a recording of the sea. Some studios provide such background recordings of sound effects, or you can bring them yourself. You could get a mix from several tapes and records. The only limitation is the studio's equipment.

Making Your Own Transfers

Some independent filmmakers have access to quarter-inch-mag film transfer equipment, either through schools, sympathetic professionals or other sources. Possibly the filmmaker may be interested in a straight transfer, one without any added EQ or change in emphasis of the audio spectrum. However you'll often want to alter the low-, high- or mid-range characteristics of the recorded sound at this stage. Here are a few simple guidelines to follow.

Wind noises can be attenuated by rolling off the low frequency response below 100 Hz, 3 dB, 6 dB or even more. Rolling off the lows won't change the properties of recorded voice and will help to reduce the rumbling sound the wind makes.

The human voice can be given added emphasis, or *presence,* as sound engineers call this, to make it sound closer or more live, or present. What's usually needed is a 3 to 6 dB boost in the mid-range or 3000 Hz region. Sibilance, which is often the result of using a cardioid microphone too close to the speaker, can be helped by rolling off the highs, or sounds from about 5000 to 10,000 Hz, although it's questionable that any manipulation of frequencies in the 10,000 Hz region will have any effect on the final optical track—which presently barely responds to 7000 Hz.

Adding EQ to music quite literally has to be played by ear. Commercially available LP phonograph records often have a peculiar balance. Rock music often has a greatly boosted bass, for example.

The nice thing about working a sound console is that you can hear what you're doing while you do it. The hard part is that even a fairly simple console offers such vast possibilities of manipulation that you may be bewildered. Watching a good sound engineer at work, asking him

Editing Magnetic Film

The basic tool used for editing magnetic film is the synchronizer equipped with a magnetic playback head with which the magnetic film recording can be played through an amplifier-speaker combination—sold for the purpose for about $60—or directly through your tape recorder. Plug the lead from the head into the proper impedance input of the tape recorder and then set the recorder for record; most recorders can play the input through their built-in speakers.

Thread the synchronizer with your workprint, if that's what you're using, or your camera film and then thread the mag film on the sprocket that holds the sound reproduction head. Now the picture and the track are locked together. If you want to play back the track, drop or place the sound head on the mag film. With the head's output playing through a tape recorder or amplifier-speaker combination, you can hear the track. Since the synchronizer or the winds are driven by hand, the sound is going to have changes in pitch. It is possible to motor drive the synchronizer, but for most purposes you can do it by hand. As a matter of fact, you can drive the film reasonably steadily with only a little practice. Moreover, driving the film by hand helps locate precise splice points.

If you have trouble understanding what's on your mag track because it is difficult for you to wind film smoothly past the head, play back the original quarter inch tape that corresponds to the passage you are

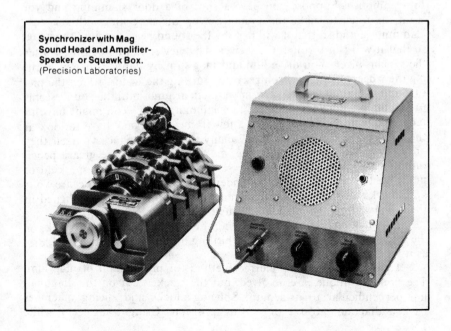

**Synchronizer with Mag
Sound Head and Amplifier-
Speaker or Squawk Box.**
(Precision Laboratories)

Preparing the Sound Track

working on. If you use a tape recorder for your playback amplifier and speaker, it's relatively easy to switch back and forth from mag film to tape.

I've assumed so far that you're using a 16mm synchronizer and editing 16mm mag film. Theoretically there's no reason why you can't work with super 8 this way. You could cut 16mm mag film and synchronize it to the super 8 film. There are synchronizers which will drive super 8 in sync with 16mm mag film when a playback head is mounted on the 16mm sprocket. A far better, simpler, and in the long run, economical approach is to use super 8 full coat mag film in conjunction with super 8 picture. The only good excuse for using 16mm full coat and super 8 picture is that we are in a period in which super 8 recorders and sound editing equipment are being introduced. But more and more labs are tooling up to produce prints from super 8 original and super 8 mag film.

You can observe the picture through a viewer adjacent to the synchronizer. It doesn't matter how far apart the synchronizer and viewer are. Whatever convenient distance enables you to work comfortably is fine. Reference marks can be made on the film with a grease pencil. Once made, these marks can be used to reposition the film in the synchronizer to help you cut the mag film. There are many ways of working with image and track. Your goal is to have the track and image correspond with each other.

Perhaps the simplest kind of track to match is one that doesn't demand precise synchronization like background sounds or music. If you must have your track sync at precise points to the image, that's also easy to accomplish. Suppose you have a shot of a door slamming and you want the track to make the sound. Set up the mag film with the door slamming sound so that it will pass by the sound head; prepare the image so that it will run through the viewer. The viewer can be before or after the synchronizer. You drive film and mag film by hand, either by turning the wheel of the synchronizer or by turning the winds; watch the picture and listen to the track and move them around until the sound seems to be coming from the image of the slamming door. You might have to move the picture ahead or back a few frames. You may have to look at the picture and listen to the track many times to convince yourself they are in sync. Once they seem to be, make a mark with the grease pencil on the frame that is on the viewer screen. Next, make the same kind of mark on the mag film directly under the sound head. Those are your sync marks for that particular segment. Once both marks are aligned in the synchronizer, the image and sound are in sync.

You may find that you are cutting the picture to match the track, or the track to match the picture, or whittling both ends toward the middle, as it were.

Tape splicing is the preferred method for preparation of mag film. The same techniques are involved, but the track is cut on the diagonal, not perpendicular to its length. Splicing blocks and slicing machines have a diagonal groove or cutting position. Using translucent white

Independent Filmmaking

single perforated tape, press it to the base side of the track, not the oxide   325
side, or you'll lose sound or lower its level.

Once the track is prepared, include the appropriate leader and sync
marks so the prints made from the mag film and camera film will be in
track through the synchronizer and viewer to see and hear what you've
done. Place the sync mark for the start of the track under the head of
the synchronizer, and the sync mark for the start of the picture in the
viewer; take up any slack to maintain a constant distance between the
two. Now wind the mag film and workprint, or camera film, and listen
and watch. Multiple tracks are often hard to work with this way, so you
might have to settle for seeing that one roll at a time is in sync. You may
not be able to appreciate the nuances of the track or image this way, but
you can check the sync. You can also check sync using an interlock projector or motor-driven editing console, like a Moviola, or by using a projector and mag film reproducer which are interlocked.

Once the track is prepared, include the appropriate leader and sync
marks so the prints made from the mag film and camera film will be in
sync. If you work with a workprint, use its sync mark (syncked to the
camera film) to make your sync mark on your mag film. There are two
possible positions for sync or start marks: the sound is in line with or
directly opposite the image as set up in the synchronizer, called *edit* or
dead sync; or the sound is out of step or staggered by twenty-six frames,
called *print sync,* corresponding to the position the track and image must
have to produce a properly matched optical track print. Mag film is always positioned with the picture in edit sync, just as you worked with it
during the editing steps. Remember to mark your sync mark on your
track *edit sync* so there's no chance of the lab making a mistake.

In many cases, your next step would be to deliver the picture and
sound track rolls to the lab for a print. (Picture and track should be
delivered wound on cores, not reels.) But you may not be ready to do
that. You may have to return with your mag film to the lab for a mix.

Editing Lip Sync Mag Film

Assuming you've had your quarter inch tape resolved to 16mm mag
film, you can identify the film with the spoken cue at the start of the
track. Your picture will have the cue written on the slate or clap board.
I'll also assume you're working with a workprint, although with slight
alterations and some caution, you could be working with camera original.
If you've done things in an orderly and careful way, you probably won't
have too much trouble matching track with picture. Your problem at
this point is to get the track and image in sync. When you find the sync
point, mark it with ink or grease pencil or a hole puncher on both track
and film.

If you used an electronic blooper, you recorded a tone on the tape
which was transferred with the audio signal to the mag film. Syncking
the picture and track is simple in this case: just use the sound head on the
synchronizer to find the tone, and look at the film to find the fogged
or flashed frame or edge. (Use the last fogged frame as your sync point.)

Preparing the Sound Track

If you used a slate, use the sound head to find the bang of the clapper, and look for the frame where the clap stick is together. There may be some position ambiguity here, because of the difficulty in telling exactly which frame corresponds with the bang on the track. However, you must establish sync to the frame; a lip sync error of one frame can be perceived by a filmmaker, if not a viewer.

If you've made your sync marks, you can assemble all your shots together, picture and corresponding track, and have the lab edge number (sometimes called key, code or printed numbers) both. With these printed yellow numbers on picture and mag film, you can perfectly match one to the other. For some lip sync sequences, you may be able to do without edge numbers if, for example, you're using the entire shot.

Once you've got the mag film and picture edge numbered, cut one and match the other to it. Which one you cut depends on your purpose. After you have edited your sync recorded mag film (or nonsync recorded

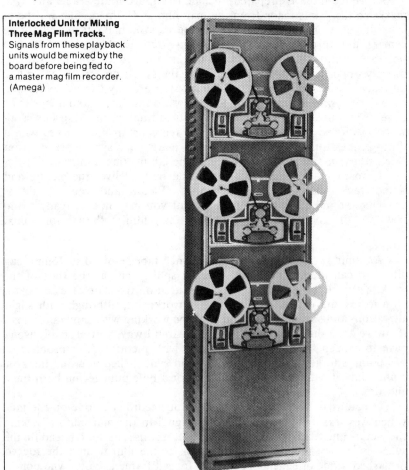

Interlocked Unit for Mixing Three Mag Film Tracks.
Signals from these playback units would be mixed by the board before being fed to a master mag film recorder. (Amega)

Independent Filmmaking

Mag Film Mixing

You can't use magnetic recording tape if you want to mix two sound tracks for a fixed time relationship. If you're mixing the signals from two recorders with a third, you have no guarantee that the two will be properly juxtaposed.

In order to achieve in-sync mixing of this kind, you must prepare two or more rolls of mag film. Studios often have the capability of mixing three or more mag film tracks. The mag film is set up for the mix just as picture rolls are set up for the printing machine: you A and B roll mag film for the mix. You might want sound dissolves, where one sound blends into another, or you might want simply to mix two sounds.

Set up the mag film on the synchronizer, and listen to it on the playback head. Sync the mag film with the image. Even though you don't need more than one head, some people find it convenient to work with more. With one head, sync the second track to the image just as you syncked the first track. Both mag film rolls (or as many as you need) are held in sync by the synchronizer. You can make sync marks at the beginning of each roll, and label them A and B or whatever you like as you will refer to them in your cue sheet.

One practice used for major studios is to use separate tracks for each type of sound. For example, there will be a voice track, a music track, a sound effects track and other tracks. There might be two voice tracks, and so on, that have to be mixed in sync. Sometimes more than twenty tracks are mixed. As a matter of fact, an independent filmmaker will rarely find working with more than, say, three or four tracks necessary.

Prepare the A and B mag film rolls, with leader between the recorded section of mag film. You can use single perf motion picture film stock, or single perf out-takes of discarded footage. If you do use motion picture film as leader, make sure the emulsion — the dull side — is away from the heads in order to prevent clogging them with emulsion.

If you are overlapping mag film for a sound dissolve, use plenty of footage so that the sound won't *pop* out but will fade in and away smoothly.

There's some question whether or not it's wise to have a balanced transfer from tape to mag film if you know you're going to need a mix. Usually the procedure for such a transfer is simply to set the proper level and leave the final balancing for the mixing session. This kind of dubbing is called a *straight transfer*. This may make mixing more difficult, but it does offer greater flexibility.

Usually the filmmaker and sound engineer will watch the workprint projected in interlock with the mag film playback units, getting visual cues for the mix from the film. In addition a thorough cue sheet will greatly aid the engineer in setting the proper level and EQ. The latest generation of mag film mixing equipment can produce a completely mixed and in-sync track, ready for the printer.

If any mistake is made during the mix, the machines are backed up and that portion of the mix is redone. The master mag film recorder is capable of laying in the remixed effort over the prior mix so that it is impossible to hear the point where the new mix has been added to the rest of the track.

Print Volume Level

The technicians who turn your magnetic film track into a print sound track may find it easier to set their level if they are provided with a reference level tone. If the level of the print track is properly set, you will have the best quality recording without distortion of the loudest sounds, the greatest dynamic range and the least background noise.

One way to help them set the level of the print track is to provide them with what is called a *zero level tone*. This tone is recorded on your mag film by the transfer studio at 1000 cycles, so that the studio VU (or VI as it is sometimes called) meter reads zero level. The mark for zero dB, or 0 dB, appears on the meter at the red 'danger zone.' If the studio records the 1000 cycle tone at their meter's zero level, and the people who make your print track do the same for their playback meter, you have a better chance of getting a good level for your track.

An alternative approach to telling the lab how to set the level (and EQ) of your sound track is to give them the position of the loudest portion of the track. For example, you could say: set your EQ and level from 230 to 257 feet (from the sync mark is understood). This is probably superior to simply giving a zero level tone, since the lab's VU meter and the one used during transfer may not closely match; also, by actually listening to a portion of the track the technicians can set a good EQ. Once the level and EQ for a mag film to optical track — be it optical track master, or electro-printing operation — is set, it is held constant for the entire length of the print.

Background Level Tone

Using unrecorded mag film for portions of your track where you want silence will achieve a very *dead* sounding track. Unrecorded tape (or leader) has comparatively little background noise and may sound odd in comparison to the rest of your track. Have the engineer run off as many feet of *background level tone* as you need. Suitable background level tone can be produced by dubbing erased quarter inch tape, at the average level setting, to your 16mm mag film.

Studio Custom-made Tracks

Studios which specialize in making sound tracks for your film may be part of a lab, or they may only do transfers and mixes and custom track work. Provide tapes and records for them and, of course, a print or workprint of your film. They watch the film, listen to you or read your notes, and make up the track using their experience and your intentions to guide them. If the engineers are creative and intelligent, and find them-

selves bored with their usual work, they may give your track more
attention than you might suspect. Then again there's the danger that
they have learned to do things only one way and can't change to meet
your needs. Another danger is that they may get so turned on by something interesting for a change that they may overembellish your track.

When using sound effects from one of the commercially available
records, take care that these same effects have not been used again and
again. My vote for the most overused sound effect, no longer dramatic
but comical, is the "car skid and crash" from Volume 1, *Authentic Sound
Effects,* Electra Records (EKL-251).

Laboratory Magnetic or Optical Track Prints

The filmmaker presents the edited camera film and mag film to the lab.
From this material, the lab makes a print. If you supply the lab with
16mm material, it can produce prints from your master in any format,
that is 8mm, super 8, 16mm and 35mm with optical or magnetic sound
tracks. The possibility of making prints in formats other than that of
camera film will be discussed in the next chapter. For now, essentially,
our concern is with making 16mm sound prints from 16mm camera film
and mag film masters.

Magnetic Tracks

The first print made from the edited footage and mag track is called the
answer print. The answer print is a trial print which may be used as a
basis for making further prints. If more than one answer print has to be
made (this might be required because of additional editing, for example),
the first print made becomes known as the first answer print, the second
will be the second answer print and so on. Hopefully, the first answer
print will match your intention closely enough so that you can use it for
projection purposes. Prints made after this stage are called *release
prints.*

You present your *master material,* whatever is used to print your
film, to the lab. It could be camera original, or an intermediate copy
made for protecting the original and the sound track material. From this
the lab makes a *married* or *composite answer print* that combines both
picture and sound track. If you want to have a mag track recorded on a
stripe, instruct the lab to go ahead and do just that. When you get your
answer print back, watch the image, listen to the track and decide if
things are as they should be. You may decide that the sound, our concern
here, is just fine — no alterations are necessary. If you don't like what
the lab has done, you can have the lab rerecord it. This is much cheaper
than having to pay for a whole new print, as you'd have to if your film
had an optical track. As a matter of fact, at any time during the life of a
mag striped print, you can have it rerecorded: a print with an optical
track can be mag striped over the optical track.

Here's how a print with magnetic sound is made: the lab exposes
and processes your print and then stripes it with magnetic oxide material

Preparing the Sound Track

or uses prestriped print film. In either case, the dubbing from your mag film to the mag stripe is accomplished the same way. The print track is dubbed from your 16mm mag film, just as mag film may be dubbed from mag film (which is, in fact, what is happening). A start mark on the print, sometimes a punched hole, and the start mark you made for edit sync on the mag film are used to cue the two.

A 16mm mag stripe track is capable of giving the highest quality sound and should be virtually indistinguishable from the mag film from which it was dubbed. It should closely duplicate the full range and subtlety of sound the human ear is capable of hearing. Played back with a good projector, through a good amplifier and good speakers, the track should be better than the best LP phonograph record, except that it's not stereophonic.

Here's what's wrong with magnetic sound, practically speaking: in the first place, in this country, there are relatively few 16mm magnetic sound projectors. What good is it to have a print to which nobody can listen? Most magnetic film projectors are found in television studios for playing back single system newsreel footage.

Magnetic track can be inadvertently erased. Of course, if somebody erases your track, you can rerecord it. Magnetic track makes the film slightly thicker, so you may be able to get slightly less footage on a reel. This is a minor complaint. Magnetic tracks are a few cents a foot more expensive than optical tracks, but they're better.

Optical Tracks

At one time, a book like this would have had to devote a full chapter to optical sound tracks. In the past a great deal of research went into perfecting optical sound. Sensitometry, or the study of photographic emulsions, and electronics, as applied to the study of methods of recording and rerecording optical sound tracks were two primary fields of research. Optical track was the medium for original recording and all subsequent mixing and dubbing. Optical track is no longer used, to any sig-

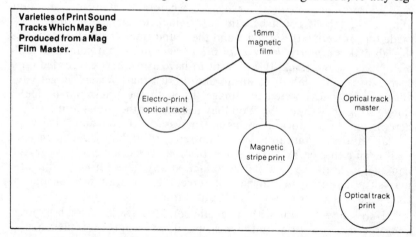

Varieties of Print Sound Tracks Which May Be Produced from a Mag Film Master.

16mm magnetic film

Electro-print optical track

Magnetic stripe print

Optical track master

Optical track print

nificant extent, for original recording, and its use for mixing and dubbing has disappeared.

Magnetic tape and film have replaced it for these functions. Optical track has become essentially a printmaking or distribution medium.

All things considered, optical tracks have reached high levels of quality. Depending on the laboratory, equipment and personnel, expect a fairly good frequency response from about 70 to 7000 cycles, a good dynamic range, inaudible distortion and little background noise. Although the frequency response of optical track is not what we've grown to expect from a good long-playing phonograph record, it's still good sound. We're missing actually just the lower and upper octaves, which are important, but at least the remaining sound is clean and crisp.

Improvements in optical track can be traced to several sources: sophisticated engineering of electronic circuits used for amplification and for the optical recording and playback devices themselves, improvements in film stock, such as high resolution materials, better quality continuous contact printing machines and, most important in recent years, the use of magnetic tape and film for original recording, dubbing and mixing.

Dubbing from optical track to optical track involves a relatively high loss of quality compared to dubbing from magnetic recording to magnetic recording. Magnetic recordings have intrinsically better specifications than optical sound tracks. When used as the medium of original recording, and for subsequent dubbing, magnetic recording makes a heavy contribution to the final quality of the optical track.

Optical sound, its frequency response especially, could be greatly improved. Sadly, if labs were to produce superior prints, the quality would be lost by the majority of antiquated 16mm projectors.

How It Works

Let's say we have some kind of an electric light that is in a circuit carrying an audio signal. The light will fluctuate in brightness, according to variations in intensity or power. The more intense the signal or the greater the amplitude of the sound source, the brighter the light. Such variations in intensity correspond to the waveform of the sound source. Let's suppose the image of the lamp is focused to a small size and beamed on a piece of moving motion picture film. Once the film is processed, we will have a photographic record of the variations of brightness of the electric lamp, which corresponds to the variations of the electric current, which at some point originally came from the vibrations of air we call sound.

If we ran this optical track between a source of light and a photocell — similar to that found in a light meter — the amount of light striking the cell would be controlled by the film, and we could produce an electric current that corresponds to the original sound vibrations. When a lot of light passes through the film, we'd have a lot of current through the photocell; variations in intensity would record the frequency, or actually waveform, of the sound. The current produced by the photocell, whose output is proportional to the light falling on it (the light being modulated by the moving film), is amplified and played back by loud speakers.

This explanation, as simplified as it is, gives you a good idea of how an optical track works. There are two types of optical tracks: variable density and variable area tracks. Briefly, a *variable density track* is a record of changes of sound intensity and frequency in terms of variations in density of the photographic emulsion. A *variable width* or *variable area track* is a record of sound in terms of the width of the track. There are many complicated subcategories of variable density and area tracks. Whether a variable density or area track is used is dictated by the characteristics of the print stock.

In recording, the variable density track uses a source of illumination that changes its overall intensity. This is recorded on film as changes in photographic density.

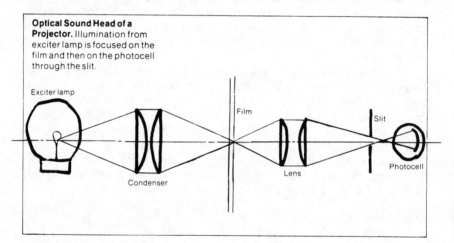

Optical Sound Head of a Projector. Illumination from exciter lamp is focused on the film and then on the photocell through the slit.

Exciter lamp

Film

Slit

Condenser

Lens

Photocell

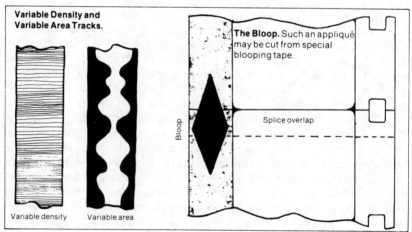

Variable Density and Variable Area Tracks.

Variable density

Variable area

Bloop

The Bloop. Such an appliqué may be cut from special blooping tape.

Splice overlap

Independent Filmmaking

The variable area method uses some kind of device that opens and closes with the changes of intensity and frequency of the sound or, actually, the electric current produced by the sound. For 16mm, the track is placed where one row of perforations would have gone. (That's where the mag stripe is placed too.) Although there are numerous kinds of variable density and variable width tracks, you can usually recognize which is which by examining the print.

Either type of track, variable density or variable area, may be played back through the optical sound projector's photocell or the improved photo diodes (they are less noisy) used on new machines. In other words, the tracks are compatible. The light sensitive cell sees the variation of light intensity that reaches it—whether it was caused by the changing density or area of the track.

Editing

There may be cases in which you find it preferable to have an optical track made directly from your quarter inch tape. Suppose your track requires very little editing, and you are fairly sure you won't need another type of optical track printing master: then have your quarter inch tape transferred directly to the appropriate type of optical track master. Suppose your track is a musical background that doesn't have to sync with the film but simply has to be about the same running time. Then you might choose a direct optical track master.

Let's say you have your optical track master and you want to cut it, for whatever reason. For fine cutting, you'll need what's called an optical sound reader which may be used as part of, or in conjunction with, a synchronizer. You may be able to rent one from a local laboratory or rental supply house. If your editing is not going to be very tight, you can use a projector for playing back your optical track. You could then mark the approximate location of your cut, remove the track from the projector and make the splice. Cement splice optical track just as you would picture. Spliced optical track often makes a popping sound at the splice point. The way to eliminate this is called *blooping*. You make a small oval or wedge shape over the splice with ink. This makes an inaudible sound that covers the sound of the splice. You can use especially formulated *blooping ink,* or you can try metallic blooping tape, cut to the shape of a flat parallelogram, and pressed directly over the splice. Blooping is a good technique when repairing damaged prints at the splice.

Optical vs. Magnetic

Relatively few projectors can play back 16mm magnetic sound tracks. For this reason, you will probably have optical tracks added to your film if you intend any sort of distribution. Optical track prints cost less than magnetic track prints and give fairly good sound, although not as good as that produced by magnetic track. Usually, the conditions under which films are screened are so abominable, that it doesn't really make any difference whether you used a good quality magnetic track, or an old 78 record with your film. Projectors, older models especially,

334

by present hi-fidelity standards, have terrible sound. Many have wow and flutter, hiss and hums, play sharp or flat, and have limited frequency response. Magnetic track can be erased, but optical track cannot. However, as the film gets scratched, optical track gets noisier. If you use a good auxiliary amplifier, and good speakers, you may not improve the sound, but rather make the poor quality of the projector more apparent. Even if you have a good projector, room acoustics will probably defeat you. I don't know why this should be, but the majority of rooms in which I have looked at 16mm sound films demolish what's on the track.

Types of Color Print Tracks
Without any special treatment during processing, color print stock will yield a sound track made up of three layers of dye. Since the picture part of the film is made up of these three layers of dye, this is no surprise. Unfortunately, dye tracks give very poor quality sound.

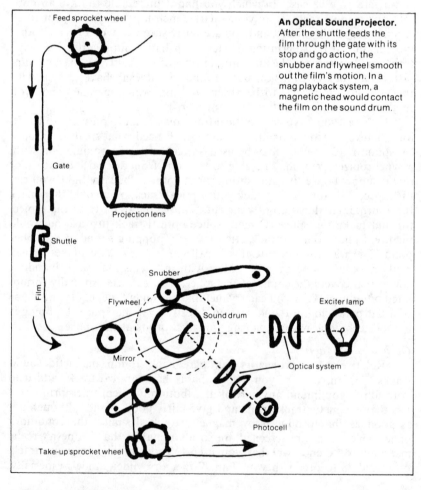

Feed sprocket wheel

An Optical Sound Projector. After the shuttle feeds the film through the gate with its stop and go action, the snubber and flywheel smooth out the film's motion. In a mag playback system, a magnetic head would contact the film on the sound drum.

Gate

Projection lens

Shuttle

Film

Snubber

Flywheel

Sound drum

Exciter lamp

Mirror

Optical system

Photocell

Take-up sprocket wheel

Independent Filmmaking

Here's why: the tungsten electric lamps, exciter lamps, produce much of their radiation in the red and infrared region of the spectrum (see the color temperature curve in chapter 2). For this reason the photocells used in the projector's sound head are chosen for their red and infrared sensitivity.

The sound track of black and white prints are made up of metallic silver, and the varying distribution of silver is what makes up the sound information. A metallic silver track is opaque to red and infrared where it has density, and transparent to red and infrared for the clear gelatin and acetate portions of the track.

This is not the case for a dye track which is substantially transparent to infrared. Although the projector's photocell might see some sound information from a portion of the dye track, most of the sound information will be swamped in background noise produced by a uniform transmission of infrared.

There are two possible ways to make dye tracks work. One would be to alter the sensitivity of the photocell to make it more nearly like the human eye, and able to see the necessary sound information. Although such photocells exist, they have not been adopted. All new projectors could be fitted with blue sensitive or extended sensitivity cells, but what about the tens of thousands of older machines already fitted with red and infrared cells? How could they play dye tracks? They couldn't. So some other solution must be sought.

The second approach would be to find some way to make the sound track of a color print more opaque to the existing photocells. This is the approach that has been sought. Two types of color tracks have been offered: the silver sulfide (usually simply called sulfide for short) and the silver track.

During processing of the film, the edge, where the sound track is to be found, is specially treated with viscous chemicals to produce the sulfide or silver track. A wheel is dipped into a viscous solution and then

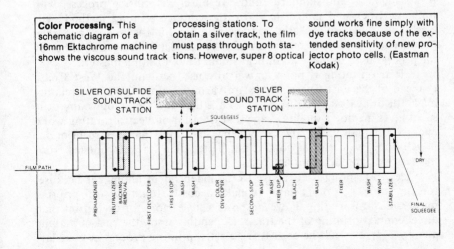

Color Processing. This schematic diagram of a 16mm Ektachrome machine shows the viscous sound track processing stations. To obtain a silver track, the film must pass through both stations. However, super 8 optical sound works fine simply with dye tracks because of the extended sensitivity of new projector photo cells. (Eastman Kodak)

SILVER OR SULFIDE SOUND TRACK STATION

SILVER SOUND TRACK STATION

SQUEEGEES

FILM PATH

PREHARDENER — NEUTRALIZER — BACKING REMOVAL — FIRST DEVELOPER — FIRST STOP — WASH — WASH — COLOR DEVELOPER — SECOND STOP — WASH — WASH — FIXER DIP — BLEACH — WASH — FIXER — WASH — WASH — STABILIZER

DRY

FINAL SQUEEGEE

Preparing the Sound Track

rolled on the sound track portion of the print. The thick solution is used so the chemicals won't run or spread into the picture portion of the print.

In the case of the sulfide track, a sulfide solution is used so that the silver halogen of the track will be turned into silver sulfide which resists being replaced by dye. But the sulfide treatment is not entirely successful and some portion of the silver halogen is replaced by undesirable dyes. This gives the sulfide track its characteristic appearance of brown lines on a yellowish background.

The silver track process requires an additional viscous application to turn the silver halogen in the track into silver metal. The silver track of a color film is substantially the same as that of a black and white print, and looks like a black and white track.

Modern motion picture color print stock, generally speaking, is capable of yielding a silver track. Because of its superiority to a sulfide track, it is preferred. In fact, it is not too much to say that at this state of the art the sulfide track must be considered obsolete because of its distortion, loss of high frequency response and background noise.

Electro-printing

Electro-printing, or *electronic printing,* is the name of the process in which an optical track is produced directly on the print. No optical printing master is used in electro-printing, but rather the optical track is made directly from the magnetic film. After the image part of the film is printed, the electro-printing machine works in conjunction with a 16mm magnetic film reproducer. Both the raw stock and the mag film are cued up and started at their respective sync marks. The signal from the mag film reproducer causes the electro-printer to print an optical sound track, either variable area or density, directly on the raw stock.

The chief advantage of the electro-printing method is that it avoids the traditional intermediate step of producing an optical track on a print: the optical track printing master made from the mag film. Release prints made by the standard route are purely a printing process, with both the track and image made by the contact printing method. The electro-printing process uses contact printing for the image, and then produces a sound track on the film not by contact printing, but rather by the process used to make an optical sound track printing master.

Electro-printing is not a universally used system: the West Coast is ahead of the East Coast. There are various claims and counterclaims made for or against electro-printing. Labs that don't do a lot or any of it say it gives mediocre quality. Labs that do a lot of electro-printing work endorse its quality. My own experience indicates that electro-printing, if well done, is at least as good if not better than tracks produced from masters with contact printing.

Electro-printing is attractive to the independent filmmaker because, for one thing, you don't have to make a costly 16mm optical printing master. Electro-printing, however, costs a little more for each print than direct contact printing of the track. Depending upon the cost of making an optical track, and the cost of the electro-printing process at your lab, there is a break-even point from about three to five prints. That is, if you're going to make more than five prints, you'll start saving money after the fifth with a contact printed master.

Electro-printing is decidedly the preferred method for producing optical track for answer or trial prints. If you want to reedit your track after you get your answer print, it's a relatively simple matter to put the mag film back into the synchronizer and cut it as you please. If you went ahead and made an optical track printing master, you'd have either to cut that, a comparatively difficult procedure, or cut your mag film and then have it turned into a new optical track printing master. And that's going to cost you money.

Another reason for choosing electro-printing is that you may decide to make many prints by using intermediate printing masters with the negative-positive system. If your camera film is reversal and you went ahead and made an optical track master suitable for printing with the reversal-reversal method, it might not be compatible with the negative-positive printing system. So you ought to wait until you're out of the answer print stage before you decide to have a master optical track made from your mag film. You may decide to continue to use electro-printing if you are planning to make a relatively limited number of prints, or if you don't have the cash for a master optical track. Also, you may decide to continue to use electro-printing because you like the quality.

Some labs offering electro-printing will allow the filmmaker to produce his track directly from a magnetic tape recording or phonograph record. Of course, you can't get exact sync, but for some films it may not matter.

Optical Track Masters

Now you have the information you need in order to decide whether to make an optical track printing master. The optical track is printed in a separate operation with the same printer used for the picture. The optical track master has one row of perforations, with the track on the side away from the perforations, corresponding to the position of the track on the print. The master track is held in intimate (the word invariably used) contact with the raw printing stock. At the point where they meet, they are moved by each other smoothly and continuously. A light passes through the master and exposes the raw stock. After processing, the print stock has an image of the optical track.

When you have completed your mag film editing, let us suppose you have decided to have an optical track master made from it. You take your mag film to the lab, and they do it for you. You can have the optical track master made directly from quarter inch tape if you choose. Whether you transfer your optical track master from mag film or magnetic tape, you can use all the audio manipulations available for making a studio transfer from quarter inch tape to mag film. The level of your track, or bass and treble response, for example, can be controlled.

An optical track master (or mag film master) produced without

Preparing the Sound Track

manipulation is called a *straight transfer*. Unlike a transfer to mag film, you can't pick up your optical track at the completion of the recording session. You have to wait for it to be processed. Those labs that are running Eastman Viscomat processing equipment, which can process a superb quality track in a matter of minutes, will enable you to leave the studio with the optical track printing master.

There are several kinds of optical tracks, and the one you pick must be coordinated with your film's printing process.

Positive and Negative Tracks

In order to obtain good sound reproduction with your projector, you must have prints with positive tracks. Without argument, it seems reasonable that just as you want to project a positive image of your film, you need to supply the photocell or photo diode of the sound head with a positive image of the track.

If you start out with a negative track and it gets printed by the negative-positive system, you will wind up with a positive track, which is what you want. If you are making prints with the reversal-reversal system, you'd suspect that you'd want a positive track to print on the reversal print film so you'd wind up with a positive track. But that's not so. It may turn out that you need a negative track to use with reversal color printing stock. This is because of the special viscous processing required for color stock tracks.

A and B Wind

If film is perforated on one edge only, it comes packaged so that the emulsion side is in, the base side out. But the perforations may be on either side. The illustration shows which is called A and which is called B wind. If you made a sound track, let's say A wind, and the lab needed a B wind track, the only way you could get a print out of your track would be to expose it with the base (instead of the emulsion) in contact with the print stock. You want to have the emulsion of the master sound

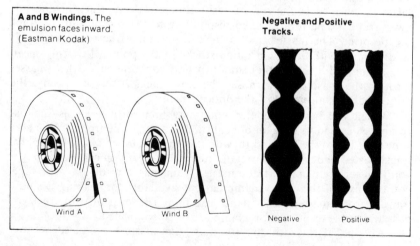

A and B Windings. The emulsion faces inward. (Eastman Kodak)

Wind A   Wind B

Negative and Positive Tracks.

Negative   Positive

track in contact with the emulsion of the print stock. If the base is in contact instead, the track won't print as sharply as it must for good quality sound, and you'll lose high frequency response.

Which Type of Track?

If we let D stand for variable density, W for variable width, A for A wind, B for B wind, N for negative and P for positive, it turns out we can have the following permutations of printing masters for our optical track: DAN, DAP, DBN, DBP, WBP, WBN, WAN, WAP. The hideous part of it all is that we are dealing with terms that are strongly related and easily confused, like area or width and density or A and B wind, or opposites, like negative and positive.

The way out of this mess is to ask the lab what kind of master track they want made from your mag film (or tape). Depending upon the kind of print stock you are going to use, they will tell you what kind of track to make. If the same lab that prints your film makes the track, they know what the specifications are. If you use another lab to make your track, or a studio that specializes in sound work, you'd better write down what kind of track you need. It is very easy to confuse a variable area, B wind, negative track with, say, a variable area, A wind, negative track, or a variable area B wind, positive track, and so on.

Sound for 8mm Prints

There is some question at this time whether the standard for super 8 release prints will be optical or magnetic sound. Both may coexist. The standard for 8mm prints has been magnetic sound. There are collectors who own magnetic sound prints of commercial features and short subjects in the 8mm format. Release printed 8mm and super 8 films are usually in quantities of two or four at a time. If 16mm film is used to release print the films, it is slit after processing; if 35mm stock is used to produce release prints, it is slit into four parts. Eastman offers mag

Married Prints. Variable area (left), and variable density (right) tracks and accompanying images. (Bach Auricon)

striped positive release print stock that has served as an impetus for the adoption of magnetic sound for release printing the super 8 format. Quantity production of 8mm prints on 35mm stock, for example, involves the simultaneous printing of all four pictures from one master negative, and the subsequent recording of all four tracks at one pass through the mag film recorder.

Without having the trouble of striping its release print stock, more labs are inclined to offer super 8 mag sound prints. When super 8 was introduced, Eastman tried to interest the laboratories in mag sound. Moreover, Eastman had to convince the users of super 8 that mag sound was best for them. Those who purchase or rent super 8 prints, and those who distribute or produce super 8 prints must be impressed by the fact that super 8 magnetic sound can be very good. They may be impressed by the *rail effect,* which extends the life of super 8 mag striped films. Lately, Eastman's position seems to be that either magnetic or optical super 8 sound is acceptable.

Technicolor is one of the major labs producing optical super 8 prints, and they are doing this primarily, if not entirely, for use in their super 8 optical sound cartridge.

The Laboratory's Role

The independent filmmaker, at least as I have conceived of him in this book, does all that he can do to make his film. The credits used for feature films — director of cinematography, camera operator, grip, script girl, original story writer, editor and so forth — often get lumped into one credit, the filmmaker. The emergence of the filmmaker as a true *auteur* corresponded with the development of filmmaking technology that allows one person, or a small group of men and women, to do the work formerly done by a large crew. While the new technology has developed to this extent, there are still no shortcuts: everything has to be done; it's just that it's now possible to do it yourself.

The filmmaker doesn't manufacture his film stock, cameras or other hardware, and for these things he is at the mercy of the manufacturers. And after the filmmaker has shot his film, he has to have it processed. After he has edited it, he may need to have prints made. From exposed film with the latent image to projection prints, the filmmaker needs the services of the laboratory.

Labs come in all sizes (and shapes). There are little labs that have a few people printing and working the processing machines; and there are monster labs that do everything from processing, release printing, fancy optical printing and lots more like renting sound stages and equipment for use on the stage such as blimped, or silent, cameras; or renting equipment for film production and editing; providing cutting rooms, screening rooms, sound transfers, television film recording, animation services and so on. Some labs will do titles for your films, including the art work and photography; some will edit tape for you, or mag film. Most labs will store the master printing material for their customers. Labs sell film stock (it's usually cheaper to buy directly from the manufacturer) reels and cans, leader, film mailers, cement, cotton gloves and other odds and ends.

A medium-sized lab may employ a dozen or more people and process both color and black and white. Other labs do not process color and have to farm it out. Practically any lab will process black and white negative and reversal and make black and white and color prints. Many are not yet set up to handle negative-positive color printing, but this is slowly changing; we can expect many more labs to do this.

To get a line on what a lab does, you'll need a copy of their catalogue and price schedule. Cost, however, is not the only good guide to quality. Make a practice of asking local filmmakers their opinions of labs in your area. There may be two local labs with greatly differing processing and print charges. If the processing is of equal quality, obviously, it is wise to use the less expensive lab. If the lab that does good processing does not make good prints, you may have to go to one lab for processing and another for printmaking. You might choose to use an independent sound service to transfer your tape to mag film or optical track. It's possible that you'll be using one lab for color and another for black and white, or one lab for reversal and another for negative. One lab might do

the bulk of your work, and the others might do parts at which you feel
they excel. You may wind up using two or three or more labs or sound
studios for the completion of one film. These situations are quite common.

I have found that it is best to try to stay with your lab and, by sticking it out, achieve some sort of rapport. Since this can take months or
even years, you'll find you do not want to switch for light or transient
reasons.

Talking to the People at the Lab

In a small lab, you may find yourself talking to the owner or his son,
brother or nephew. In larger labs, you may have to talk to the lab manager; in still larger labs, you may have to take your questions to special-
ists in each department, such as printmaking or sound work. There are
no hard and fast rules about who to talk to, but once you find the right
man, it's a good idea to try to interest him in your film, so that he can
give you the benefit of his often considerable experience. Remember,
he will be telling you what he thinks is right from one point of view: how
easy it is for the lab to do what you want. If there is any question on
your mind about how to do something involving lab work, and you think
you might need his help, call him and you may save yourself a lot of
trouble.

For example, if you want film pushed a stop, before you go ahead
and shoot it that way, ask if the lab can do it. If you are going to A and B
roll a film, ask him how to set up your rolls since labs require different
procedures for you to follow in setting up masters for printing.

You can find out how the lab does business in a small lab by asking
anybody in sight; in a larger lab, you may, for example, want to talk to
the people in the bookkeeping department to find out billing procedures.

You can ask for a tour of the lab to see their facilities. Many labs will
take you around and answer any questions. An understanding of the problems that beset the lab personnel may not make you a better filmmaker, but it may make you more considerate.

Getting Credit

Some labs require you to pay for your work as you pick it up at the front
desk; others may extend credit and bill you monthly. Whether or not
you can get credit depends solely upon whether or not you already have
credit. If you don't have credit, you usually can't get credit.

Here's one way to establish credit: save some money and start a
savings account. Now take out a loan for about the same amount, using
your passbook for collateral. Pay it back as specified, never missing or
making a late payment. This is easy since you've already saved the
money. When you've finished paying off the 'loan,' you have credit.
Credit is a good thing to have for several reasons: if you have already
paid cash for work the lab has performed, you are at a psychological disadvantage if you attempt to have them make good on an error. Paying one
bill a month instead of several can help you keep your records straight;

and there are those lean months when the bill is heavy: then you can make a partial payment, deferring the rest, although you may have some interest added to your bill.

Film Processing

The most basic function the laboratory performs is processing film. Much 8mm and super 8 color film is sold with processing included in the cost of the purchase. All you have to do, after the film has been exposed, is to mail it to one of the processing stations the manufacturer has established. Eastman Kodak, as the result of a Justice Department ruling, doesn't sell its film with processing included, but does offer processing mailers for its color films. Film sold PNI (processing not included), as GAF calls it, is probably a good thing: if you don't want an obviously messed up roll processed, you haven't paid for the processing. On the other hand, film sold with processing included is convenient, especially appealing to amateurs. Color film returned to the manufacturer's processing stations can be returned within, say, a week. Film manufacturers often do not maintain processing stations for their black and white products.

The professional motion picture labs we're concerned with do most of their work in 16mm, although many also handle 8mm and super 8 processing. The film is usually dropped off at the lab's reception desk. If you have any problems or questions associated with the film, get the information before the film leaves your hands. Include any special instructions in a note with the film. You may want the film pushed, so your note might read: force develop film one stop; if it's a 200 speed film you might say, develop at 400.

When asking lab personnel about the quality of pushed film, remember they are used to dealing with commercial filmmakers whose concept of what constitutes acceptable quality may be quite different from yours. Great big balls of grain, or weird color shifts may be desir-

Processing Machine. This Ektachrome processor, operated by Highland Labs, San Francisco, was built from Eastman plans. Machines like this can process film at from twenty to one hundred feet per minute, depending on the type of film and design.

Independent Filmmaking

able effects from your point of view. Quality can only be related to purpose; it is not an absolute. You would do well to ignore the lab's advice whenever you think you know better, or they seem incapable of understanding what you want. Of course, if they say they can't push a kind of film four stops, don't shoot it that way, or find a lab that can do that sort of processing.

Most labs charge a surcharge of from 50 to 100 percent for forced development, and they may have a minimum footage rate for billing as well. So check your lab's price schedule for details. If you present them with one hundred feet of film to be forced, you may wind up paying for four hundred feet. Some labs, if they process a lot of forced film, have no surcharge for this service.

In many labs, film dropped off before noon can be picked up by five. Most labs run their own black and white processing machines, but many rely on another specialized lab to do the processing of their color film. If this is the case, you may not be able to get one-day service.

You can, when the film is being processed, have a workprint made from the footage, in which case you get the workprint and camera footage returned to you at the same time. If this is the way you want it, number the cartons in which the film is packed so the rolls can be assembled and printed in order. If you don't want a workprint, don't say anything about it, and you won't get one.

Film is usually returned by the lab on the same reel, in the same can, in the same box, in which it was delivered. You'll want to screen it to see what you've done. At such a time, your attention is likely to be seriously divided. I look at what I've shot to see if the content is what I had imagined, and I look at the technical things, like exposure, focus and quality of the processing. But don't screen your original footage if you want to avoid scratches. If you know by experience that this is not likely to happen with your projector, or if you think scratches won't matter, project the film. Otherwise, have a workprint made, or look at the camera film with a trustworthy, well cleaned viewer. To minimize damage to processed film, some labs treat the film to toughen the emulsion. (Two processes often used are called Peerless and Vacuumate treatment. They're good.) They may do this as a matter of course, or you may have to specify it. Color film, Kodachrome especially, is often lacquered or waxed to protect the emulsion. If the emulsion side does get scratched, unless it's a very deep scratch, it's the coating that's taken the abuse. The coating can be removed, and the film relacquered.

Many labs will process super 8 and double standard 8mm. In the case of double 8mm and double super 8, the lab will also slit the film and spool it on a single reel. Film for the 8mm formats can be pushed as much as the same film for the 16mm format. This usually does not apply to color emulsions without color formers or couplers like Kodachrome II, Fujichrome and Dynachrome.

Processing Errors
I have never used black and white film that was noticeably faster or

slower than its rated speed, and I have never seen film that had characteristics significantly different from other rolls of the same brand and type. One roll of Plus X reversal looks just as granular as another roll of processed Plus X. Manufacturers often improve their product without informing you, and a film can get better over the years without any mention being made of the fact. When big improvements in quality occur, however, there's usually some kind of fanfare to announce the new discovery that will make us all happy.

Color film is something else. The overall color balance of film does vary from roll to roll, even within the same emulsion number. This is usually attributed to the processing. In fact, two rolls processed ten minutes apart can often have noticeable shifts in color balance. I don't know whether this is implicit in the film or attributable to the lab. For most purposes, minor shifts in color are of little or no importance. They can be corrected in printing, if they seem troublesome; but often you're merely asking for trouble when depending on the ordinary lab's skill at color correction.

If there are unusual marks on your film, they come from three sources: film manufacturing, the camera in which it was exposed or the processing operation. Manufacturing errors are very rare.

Since the lab processing machines work continuously, as do the machines that manufacture the film, any mark of an intermittent nature can be attributed to something done at the time of exposure (or if you've projected the film, in the projector). However, you should not rule out the possibility that such defects were caused in processing (or manufacture). A defect which appears on each frame in the same position most likely has been made in the camera. Streaks can also be made in the camera. Dirt, usually from the emulsion, accumulates in the camera and gets stuck on the aperture plate. The film running by the dirt, pressed against it by the pressure plate, is made *developable* by contact with the raised material. One property that photographic emulsions have, and

Plumbing. Equipment used for pumping chemicals from storage tanks to processing machines. One of the great mistakes made by groups of filmmakers is to divert energy to the processing of film. It's a non-creative effort, and usually not worth the trouble.

you may know this from darkroom work, is that the application of pressure can make it developable, as if struck by light. Depending upon the dirt's position relative to the gate, the mark may have either an intermittent or continuous nature. I suspect, without having experimented, that the dirt, if located a frame or so away from the aperture, will produce intermittent marks and continuous marks further away from the aperture. Also, if the camera has a metal burr in the gate region, it can gouge out the emulsion, making a nasty *tram* line running the length of the film.

One curious defect is caused by static electricity. Static electricity marks which look like branched lightning in the night sky usually occur with high speed film at a high fps rate; I have also seen static electricity marks on medium speed film at the normal fps rate. Two important variables are the cameraman and the weather. Some people generate more static electricity than others and when the weather is cold and dry, static electricity is more likely to be a problem.

The lab is not responsible for static electricity marks; they occur at the time of exposure. The manufacturers have done a fair job of treating film so that such marks can be kept to a minimum. At one time, cameramen, the famous cameraman of D.W. Griffith, Billy Bitzer included, grounded their cameras to eliminate static marks.

The lab can make a variety of mistakes as well. A blotched or mottled look, where the film loses density in the blotches, can be caused by improper washing and drying. It may seem strange that a water mark can cause the film to appear less dense, but the areas where marks appear have dried at a different rate from the rest of the film. During drying, a contraction of the emulsion in that region forms a craterlike depression. If the lab washes the film again, and dries it properly, the defect may be diminished.

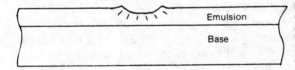

Emulsion

Base

Drying Spot. If drops or beads of water are left on the film after processing, a crater may form as drying takes place. Such a crater will appear as a light blotch on reversal film.

All-over mottling of the processed film is often the result of uneven development, and nothing can cure this. Outdated film which is processed may have the same mottled appearance, and the lab shouldn't be taken to task for this. Similarly, outdated color film may have shifts in color and reduction in contrast.

One of the toughest things you have to do when dealing with a lab is to show them a roll of film that you think has been defectively processed. You are likely to be uptight and the lab man is too. You may want to pin it on him, and he may want to blame it on you. The best attitude to maintain is one of reliance on his experience to help you get to the bottom of the difficulty. If he thinks the defect is not in the processing or your camera, you can take your troubles to the manufacturer's

The Laboratory's Role

representative. If the manufacturer assumes responsibility, about all you can expect is a fresh roll of film. And that's about all you can expect from the lab too if they have made a mistake processing your film.

Now back to facing the lab man with your film. You may be looking at it on the viewer (defects are often hard to see in the viewer) or under a magnifying glass, or best of all because defects are most easily spotted this way, you're projecting the footage. The lab man looks at the defect and tells you what he thinks. Nine times out of ten, he'll tell you it was your camera. You may be looking at blotches, squiggly lines, I don't know what; but no matter how impossible it seems to you, he'll probably tell you it's not his fault. He really knows which defects can be caused by processing. Now it may not be fair to pin it on your camera: it might be something else. It could be that you've had the film in the refrigerator and shot it without waiting long enough for it to get to air temperature. Maybe the film was stored near radioactive material. Maybe it was stored on top of a radiator, or in the trunk or glove compartment of a car on a sunny day. Maybe the manufacturer goofed.

The lab man can disavow blame, but in the process, he may pin the blame on you. Your attitude should be as open as possible, no matter how bad his is. The most important thing to be gained is to find out what went wrong, so that it won't happen again.

Variable Contrast
The contrast of processed film depends upon how long it was developed (first development for reversal emulsions). The longer it remains in the developer, all things (temperature and agitation) being equal, the higher the gamma or contrast. The less time it remains in the developer, the lower the contrast. Still photographers have taken advantage of this to control the contrast of their negatives. This was a simple matter when most workers used sheet film. For a contrasty subject, like a snow scene showing people wearing dark clothes, it was possible to underdevelop the film to reduce the contrast. With flat lighting that, for example, you might find under fluorescent illumination or on an overcast day, the photographer could overdevelop the film to increase the contrast.

Varying the time of development also varies the film's speed or sensitivity. For example, let's say we have a film that is usually rated at 100 E.I. For contrasty subjects, we'd rate the film at 50 E.I. and underdevelop. For flat lighting, we'd call the film 200 E.I. and overdevelop to increase the film's contrast.

Many people recoil at this advice, because it leads to giving greater exposures under some very bright lighting conditions, the snow scene for example. It seems to defy common sense to give a greater exposure when there's more light. But if you want to get film with lower contrast, that's what you do.

Dim lighting conditions, which are often contrasty, are usually shot with pushed film which requires more time in development with a subsequent increase in contrast. That's just what you don't want. This is one of the great difficulties when shooting under reduced light conditions. When some photographers say that a true measure of a film's *pushability* is its ability to record shadow detail, they are saying, in another way, that the film shouldn't pick up too much contrast when pushed.

This relationship between time in the developer and contrast holds true for negative as well as reversal films, color and black and white films. (See chapter 2, under Characteristic Curve.) With the introduction of roll film and the 35mm still camera, it became impossible for the photographer to develop the entire roll for the lighting considerations of one shot.

Then people started to develop their film for a given time and temperature, if they had subjects shot under a variety of lighting conditions. In order to make a decent print, photographers had to use a printing paper with differing grades of contrast. Printing paper for still photography comes in grades from 0 to 6, with grade 2 or 3 used for normal or average subjects. For flat negatives, shot under lighting that wasn't contrasty, they'd use hard paper or paper with a high number. Many years ago *variable contrast* paper was introduced; now many manufacturers make their own variable contrast printing paper. This paper has two emulsions coated on it — contrasty and flat. One emulsion is sensitive to violet, the other to the yellow light of a tungsten lamp. By using appropriate filters, it is possible to vary the contrast grade of the printing paper.

With the introduction of automatic processing machines for motion picture film, film was processed like 35mm still camera film with the *time and temperature* method. That is, for a given time in the developer and temperature of the developer, the film is processed to give negative or reversal of a fixed contrast or gamma. When processing film for higher speed, the object is to get more speed out of the film without excessively raising the contrast. Motion picture film is not developed for contrast. I consider that to be a loss, a surrender to economic factors that limits the potentials of the photographic medium.

One possible solution to the problem for black and white filmmaking would be for manufacturers to offer variable contrast printing stock, either release print material or intermediate master material. There are many printers in use for color correction of prints that could be used to print scene-to-scene contrast correction. As a matter of fact, this isn't a new idea at all. In 1927, Eastman introduced a duplicating stock that could be exposed with yellow or violet filters for variable contrast. It seems unlikely that manufacturers will provide such a variable contrast stock, because so much work is now done in color. I don't know how much interest there is in black and white, but I should think it's still considerable.

Forced Development

Filmmakers frequently rely on the lab to push film one or more stops. This is accomplished by increasing the time of development. In the case of negative film, the meaning of this statement is relatively straightforward, since there's just one development step. For reversal black and white and color emulsions, forced development is accomplished during the first development step. Characteristically, forced development will result in an increase in grain and contrast and, in the case of color film, shifts in color values. Such changes in the film's characteristics may be slight or glaring.

In general, the faster emulsions of a manufacturer's line may be pushed at least one stop with only slight changes in quality. Many film-makers make it a habit of routinely pushing Ektachrome EF or ECO one stop. Usually, the films that are interesting to push are the very fastest available. There are exceptions. Some people would rather push a slower film than use the fastest available film; the argument put forth is that this gives better results than shooting faster film. In my opinion, this practice is probably based on habit. That's what was done before the fastest emulsions were available, and the filmmaker liked the results, so he continues.

The most important factor involved in determining the quality of pushed film, aside from the film's intrinsic ability to be pushed, is the processing technique of the lab. One lab may do a perfectly fine job of pushing one type of film that another lab will mess up. Typical short-comings are excessive contrast, a marked decrease in contrast, blotchy development, excessive grain and weird color shifts. Once again, quality can be judged only by purpose, and one man's poor processing may be just the effect someone else is searching for.

Film is usually pushed in increments of one stop. That is, a fast film like DuPont 933A, rated at 500 daylight, might be pushed to speeds of 1000, 2000 and so on. Departures from expected quality increase the more the film is pushed. After a certain point, reversal may appear to lose contrast, because the D-max is actually decreased. When this happens the blacks lose their fullness, and the image tends to go flat. Some labs are able to push some emulsions one stop (sometime two stops) with very little alteration of quality; Ektachrome EF (in 16mm, but not in super 8!) is a good example of this. The lab will usually be honest with you about their ability to push a specific film.

Censorship
Labs often take it upon themselves to act as censors. This usually takes the form of their refusal to print footage of which they do not approve, such as films of sexual intercourse. The same lab, however, that once refused to print such a scene did not hesitate to print a nude man being whipped by a partially clothed woman.

Many labs will process any footage without any trouble, since they don't know what's on it. If they get up-tight they may call the police, and I know of one case in which the FBI was notified. If the lab gets nasty, they may confiscate the footage, although they are not within their rights to do so.

Whatever excuse the lab may give you, if they refuse to print your film, there's nothing you can do about it. Lawyers reason that there are

Independent Filmmaking

laws against involuntary servitude in this country, and for this reason, it is impossible to force any lab to undertake to do work they have refused. I suggest that you get legal advice if you encounter any censorship problems with your lab. Actually, the lab that refuses to do work for you is engaged in a form of precensorship, and not censorship, if you want to make the distinction.

Printmaking

Making release prints (not workprints or answer prints) is probably the lab's greatest source of income; but the size of a lab is not an indication of the quality of the prints it can produce.

Answer Prints—Print Timing

The first print (after the workprint, if any) made from your camera original is called the *answer print*. Answer prints are prepared with

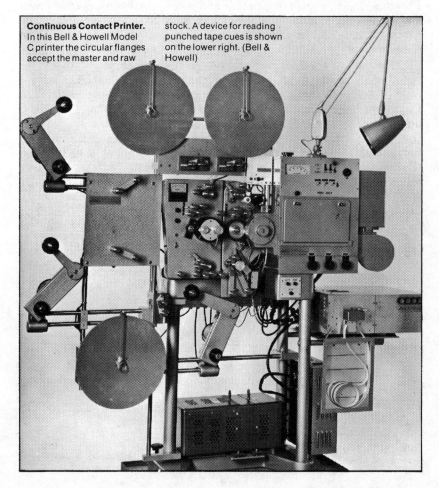

Continuous Contact Printer. In this Bell & Howell Model C printer the circular flanges accept the master and raw stock. A device for reading punched tape cues is shown on the lower right. (Bell & Howell)

The Laboratory's Role

great care in the better labs. A man called the *print timer* or just *timer* looks at every foot of your film and selects the proper exposure for printing each shot. This procedure is called *timing* or *grading.* The exposure at the time the print is made is controlled by any one of a number of means.

In a typical printing machine there may be two shutters, one controlling the amount of light exposing the film and another controlling fades and dissolves. The shutter which controls the printing light may be very much like a camera's variable shutter. The shutter which controls fades and dissolves may accomplish this by varying its rate of rotation.

The printing machine holds the raw stock and camera original (the term often used for processed camera film) in contact at some point. Here a light is passed through the camera original, or printing master, to control the density of the print. It's exactly like the exposure control exercised in the camera by varying the f stop. A dense shot will require a brighter light in reversal printing and a lower light in negative printing. A shot on reversal film which has been underexposed and is too dense will require a brighter light than a shot normally exposed. Negative works just the other way.

The rate of the film through the printing machine is usually not varied, only the level of the printing light. Printing machines have a *scale of lights,* as they are called, in one system ranging from 1 to 21. Every four lights might be equivalent to a stop. For example, two lights brighter are equivalent to an exposure difference of half a stop. Ask, if you want to know more about the system your lab uses. Such information is useful when you get your answer print, if you want further corrections made. It is possible to communicate with your lab like this: make shot (give the footage from the start mark) half a stop lighter or, if you know how the lights work you could say, add two.

The print timer evaluates the proper light by eye. The best light has to be chosen not on the basis of the entire frame, but rather on the

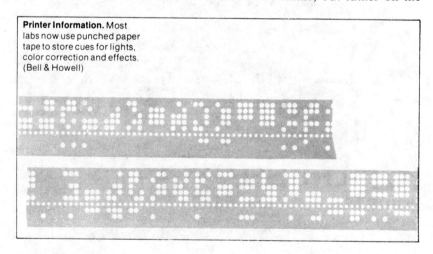

Printer Information. Most labs now use punched paper tape to store cues for lights, color correction and effects. (Bell & Howell)

Independent Filmmaking

most important part of the frame. The timer, in many labs, prepares a punched paper tape to indicate printing lights, fades and dissolves. The tape provides quantitative information about which light and the length of a fade, but not positional information. The film itself must be notched or marked for positioning of the light change or effect. In one system, metal tabs are clipped to the edge of the film. When the tab passes by the sensor in the printing machine, the information on the tape triggers the light or effect. Other systems cut notches into the film itself; these are sensed by rollers or pressure switches.

No two labs seem to use the same system of lights, coding positional information or preparing the punched tapes. Therefore, a film timed by one lab (the term timed here takes in both lights and effects) cannot be run through another lab's printing machine. For this reason, when changing labs, you have to make another answer print of your film.

Some labs will allow you to talk to the timer or even stay by his side while he's working, so that you can try to give him either a feel for what you're trying to do, or so that you can give him specific instructions that might be hard to communicate in writing. It can be very helpful to talk to the technician, if only for your own peace of mind; a lab that understands that is a friendlier lab than one that doesn't. After working on a film, you may not feel right just dropping it off with the receptionist without another word said.

Sometimes a film needs no timing changes at all. I have seen examples of perfectly good films that were printed with the same light from head to tail. Others will require extensive correction. Some films must have light changes within individual shots. For example, suppose you panned from a bright to a dark region. The right light for one region is wrong for the other, and a compromise light may look bad too. One solution is to use a *go-to*, a change in the light while the shot is being printed. A go-to can be a very successfully employed method; if done well, it is not possible to tell that any timing change is taking place.

In addition to timing and effects changes, the timer may also be responsible for *color correction* in the case of color prints. I'll divide such color correction into two categories: gross alterations and corrections. A *gross alteration* would involve an overall tint added to the shot. It might be used to suggest night effects (a deep blue tint) or for sunset effects and so on.

Corrections, as opposed to gross alterations, involve more subtle changes in the shot's color value. They're primarily used to help match one shot against another. If shooting takes place outdoors over a period of hours for example, the effective color temperature of the light will vary. Late in the afternoon, the color of light begins to warm up. Footage shot in the late afternoon may not match footage shot at noon time. The footage shot later in the day may appear to be reddish or orange. Some people like to add correction to the shot with color correction filters as it is being filmed. However, color correction can be done to the shot during printing as well. If you're having reversal-reversal printing done,

one cure would be to print the reddish shots with bluish light. For negative printing, you'd use the same general color.

Color correction is often extremely important when making prints with the negative-positive system. Some labs seem to have a more difficult time making well balanced color prints with the negative-positive system than the reversal-reversal system.

The timer looks at the footage and decides what correction, if any, is necessary. Some larger labs employ elaborate color television devices to decide the color correction to add to each shot. The color TV systems are vastly superior than doing the job simply by eye. The timer observes the film on a TV monitor, selects the best color balance by adjusting a set of knobs, and these adjustments are converted to information that can be used by the printer. However, I feel it's best not to get too carried away with color correction, because it's possible to make many films without it.

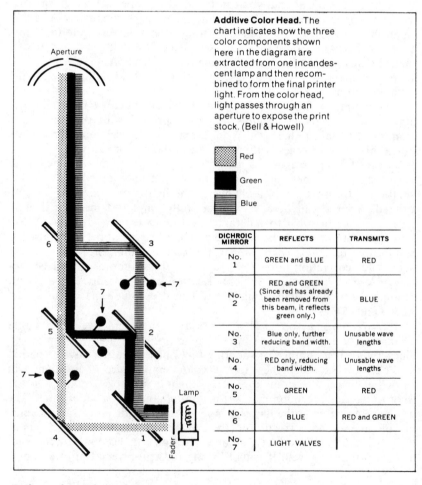

Additive Color Head. The chart indicates how the three color components shown here in the diagram are extracted from one incandescent lamp and then recombined to form the final printer light. From the color head, light passes through an aperture to expose the print stock. (Bell & Howell)

Red

Green

Blue

DICHROIC MIRROR	REFLECTS	TRANSMITS
No. 1	GREEN and BLUE	RED
No. 2	RED and GREEN (Since red has already been removed from this beam, it reflects green only.)	BLUE
No. 3	Blue only, further reducing band width.	Unusable wave lengths
No. 4	RED only, reducing band width.	Unusable wave lengths
No. 5	GREEN	RED
No. 6	BLUE	RED and GREEN
No. 7	LIGHT VALVES	

Independent Filmmaking

Information for color correction is stored on tape and cued by the film, as was timing information. Older printing machines employ color correction filters, if color correction is needed. Newer machines, like late model Bell & Howell printers, have *additive color heads* that mix light from three sources to obtain the final printing light. The color head divides the light from one tungsten lamp into red, green and blue light, then remixes these in any proportion to give a printing light of any desired color. Printing machines using this system are *additive color printers,* since they are adding color to produce the final printer light.

Once all the timing has been done, effects properly placed and color correction, if any, decided upon, the camera film (A roll, A and B rolls, and so forth) is sent to the printing room, along with the sound track (if any), and a married answer print is made.

Print Contrast

When we film a subject and accurately capture its range of brightness, the contrast of the subject and the photographic image should match. If there is an equal change in D (photographic density) for a corresponding change in log E (exposure) we'd have a film with unit contrast, or a gamma of 1.0 (see chapter 2 for a discussion of the characteristic curve). The ideal reproduction of the subject occurs when we have the Goldberg condition, namely when the combination of print and camera film has a gamma equal to 1.0. The gamma of black and white and color negative camera film is 0.65. To obtain Goldberg condition prints made from negatives, we'd need a print stock with a higher gamma. The gamma of a print is given as follows:

negative x positive = print

Because projected motion pictures are surrounded by darkness, it has been necessary to depart from Goldberg's constraint which is intended for paper prints. Goldberg wouldn't mind.

A motion picture looks like it's got the right contrast if its gamma is about 1.4. Black and white reversal and projection contrast color

Color Analyzer. The timer evaluates a television image (left screen) of the master. With this Eastman unit, grading and color correction are achieved by turning the potentiometer knobs. An image of a face on the right screen is used for comparison for correction of skin color. The adjustments are logged and transferred to punched tape. (CFI)

reversal approach this gamma. Prints are made from negative on positive stock with a gamma of 2.5 so that we get a print gamma of:

$$0.65 \times 2.5 = 1.6.$$

In point of fact the final screen gamma will be closer to 1.4 because of contrast losses in all the optical systems involved (camera, printer and projector).

As far as black and white reversal and negative films are concerned, we have a rationalized or consistent system of materials so that camera films used in conjunction with intermediate masters and/or print film will yield a gamma of about 1.4. This is also true for the color negative system. However, for color reversal, probably the most interesting system for readers of this book, things are a mess. Over the years two systems have grown up, one using unit contrast camera original printed on higher contrast print stock, and the other with projection contrast camera original printed on unit contrast print stock; both systems have been designed to produce prints with 1.4 gamma.

It often happens that filmmakers will shoot part of a film on unit contrast or commercial camera stock, like ECO, and part of the film on projection contrast Ektachrome EF or MS. ECO is usually chosen for its very fine photographic quality, and MS or EF for their speed, let's say. All things being equal, these films intercut would yield low and normal contrast images printed on unit contrast stock, or normal and high contrast images when printed on higher contrast stock.

Of course all things are never equal, and gamma is a measure only of potential contrast, the contrast of the subject being a major determining factor of final contrast. Therefore, it can happen that a reasonably good match results. Now this discussion is predicated on the assumption that you desire to intercut film segments that will carefully match. This doesn't have to be the case.

Supposing though that you do want matched segments. What to do? Some solutions suggest themselves. Gevachrome print stock can be processed for variable contrast, but the entire release print must be processed for one gamma. Another approach might be to print portions of the film on both unit and higher contrast stock, to be spliced together. Most of the time this would be out of the question. The approach currently in vogue is to flash (discussed in chapter 5, Flashing) the fast Ektachromes to help them match ECO.

Yet another way out might be to flash the print stock. I've seen good results with a flashed Kodachrome 7387 print. Intercut film could use a B roll of alternating black and clear leader so the lab can flash the portions of the print stock which will be used for projection contrast original. I've never seen such a sequentially flashed print, but I suspect it would work very well.

However, what's really needed for color reversal is an entire changeover to projection contrast original and unit contrast print stock. I think the main hangup is the production of low gamma internegatives from projection contrast camera original. The internegative materials currently available work best in conjunction with ECO.

Color Balance

As a matter of routine, for the formats discussed in this book, labs will make color prints balanced for projection with tungsten lamps. These lamps have a color temperature of about 3200° K, and they are far and away the most commonly employed in projectors that are likely to be encountered. However, it may happen that your film will be screened with an arc projector with a color temperature of from 5000° to 5500° K. If this should occur, such prints will look cool, but usually not objectionably so. A filter, over the projector lens, could be used to warm up the image. If you are making a print that you know will be used essentially for arc projection, it ought to be so balanced.

Answer Print Evaluation

Making films necessitates delay of gratification since, unlike a painter, a filmmaker can't really see what he's done until the answer print is viewed. When you look at the answer print, you are looking at what you may have been working on for months or maybe years, so it's an exciting and dreadful moment.

Besides seeing how your picture and track work together, you'll be looking at a number of technical things (timing, color balance, etc.), which can get in the way of your being able to appreciate anything else. That's a problem you have to work out for yourself, and time may be the only cure. Before ordering more prints, it may be a good thing to wait and ponder as long as possible.

When you look at your answer print and listen to the track, note whether or not the lab made all of the effects you wanted, the quality of the sound, how good a job of timing they did and, if the film is in color, you will naturally be observing the colors.

If the lab has made a mistake, something clearly their fault, like forgetting a fade, they should make all or part of the print over for you. If you have a short film, they may decide to print the entire film. If it's a long film, they may just reprint a section and insert it into the body of the film. The best places to insert footage are where natural breaks occur, such as splice points; and it's probably better to replace an entire head or tail segment than a segment within the central portion of the film. A head or tail segment involves one splice less than footage replaced or inserted within the body of the film.

Here are some mistakes that the lab may make: missing a fade or dissolve or half of the dissolve; entire shots may be dropped out, say from the B roll; the timing may be off by more than you might reasonably expect (the proper timing of a shot can be a matter of individual taste; there are limits though, and some shots can be obviously improperly timed); the print film may have been processed poorly; the track may have been printed with too dim or too bright a light, or it may have been improperly developed. If you have any questions about the print, or what the lab's role may have been, show them the film.

The Laboratory's Role

If there are some segments that require a slightly different light or changes in color correction, that's part of the game; the lab doesn't have to make good for further corrections. Minor changes in prints after the first print are the rule rather than the exception. You're lucky if you can consider your first print suitable.

If alteration is made to the master, and timing changes are to be made, or other effects added (fades or dissolves), these can be incorporated into the next print. If there are many or extensive changes, you may be billed once more at the answer print rate which is higher than the release print rate since initial setup is involved. In this case, you can consider the next print a second answer print. Once you're out of the answer print stage, you can make release prints which cost less than answer prints. In addition, release prints made several at a time are less expensive than prints made one at a time. Labs will usually store the master printing material for you, at little or no cost, so that you can phone in future print orders. You store your master material with the lab at your own risk, so you might consider carrying insurance on films in storage. Labs will not make prints of your film without permission.

Optical Printers

The most frequently used printing machines are *continuous contact* machines. The master material (that from which the print is made is called the master) and the print film raw stock are held in contact and move continuously past a source of illumination which exposes the raw stock. Another kind of contact printer, less frequently employed, is the *step contact* printer, which holds each frame at rest for the moment of exposure. Whether the step contact printer yields better prints than the continuous contact machine is open to question. Contact printers are used for the basic bread-and-butter operation of the lab, the making of release prints.

Optical Printer. An automated machine that can blow up A and B rolled 16mm or super 16mm to 35mm. Its additive color head uses intense illumination for printing on slow, fine grained Eastman 5271, instead of the more commonly used faster and grainier 5254 internegative. (Consolidated Film Industries).

Independent Filmmaking

There is another kind of printer, the optical printer, that comes in the continuous and step varieties as well. The use of continuous optical machines is comparatively rare being confined to special applications.

The optical printer is actually a precision-built camera and a projector combination. The projector portion contains the master (often camera original), and the camera portion has the raw stock to be exposed. A lens projects the image of the film on the raw stock. Such lenses are highly corrected, and the mechanism of the optical printer must carefully position both master and raw stock.

There are one-to-one optical printers, for printing one size format to the same size: such machines will print 16mm to 16mm, or 8mm to 8mm. Reduction and enlargement printers are available for printing from 8mm to 16mm and so forth, from one format to another. Optical printing is the only way to accomplish enlargement or reduction from format to format. The following sections describe other uses for the optical printer. The optical printer is theoretically capable of producing the best possible printing masters. Although this is the favored method for production of intermediate masters (a print from camera film), masters which are made with the finest contact printers produce prints difficult to distinguish from those produced from masters made with the optical printer.

Release Prints

People desiring the highest possible quality prints may order these produced by the optical printer. Because optical printing is so expensive, compared to conventional contact printing, this is usually confined to the production of short prints, such as television commercials.

Effects

Before the introduction of A and B printing, and aside from effects produced within the camera, the optical printer was used for the production of fades and dissolves—especially dissolves. Optical printers, unlike many continuous contact printers in use, can produce dissolves of practically any desired length. However, this advantage is fast disappearing as late model contact printers offer more varied programs of dissolve lengths and dissolve mixes of various lengths. The use of the optical printer for dissolves (and fades) becomes interesting if one is producing a long film with relatively few dissolves. In order to avoid the tedious editing process of A and B rolling, it may be desirable to produce the effects which may then be cut into the master.

Suppose you've shot your film on Ektachrome EF color stock and want to make effects to be inserted into the camera film. Set up the footage to be dissolved in the same way that you'd set up the A and B rolls, and then request an optical print with the appropriate effects. Such a print would probably be made on a low contrast high resolution emulsion like ECO which is the perfect material for this use. The effects would then be cut into the camera film master and release prints would be made in the normal manner.

The Laboratory's Role

Since the footage which is optically printed and cut into the body of the film is first generation, or one generation away from the camera original, we can expect some changes in quality for these sections in the print. Experience shows that color shifts, increased grain and contrast build-up are to be expected. These changes can be minimized if the work is done by a good lab. In order to hide the shift in quality, sometimes registered as an annoying pop, print the entire length of the shots going into and coming out of the dissolve, not just the footage immediately adjacent to the effect.

It is possible to produce effects with a contact printer which can be cut into the master for release printing. The most serious disadvantage of this procedure is that the footage must be flopped, that is, inverted right to left, or a mirror image of the shot. Since film can be inserted into the optical printer with either side of the emulsion facing the raw stock, this flopping of optically printed footage can be avoided. I would say that a good effects insert should be difficult to tell from the camera footage in the final print. This wasn't always the case. The superior ECO material and liquid gate printing (see chapter 2) makes the use of optical effects inserts of interest to 8mm and 16mm format users. For production of reversal black and white inserts of this kind, Plus X or 930A may serve well. I'd even consider the use of ECO here, even though it's a color stock, because of its good grain and low contrast. Special black and white and color internegative materials exist which can be used for the production of negative printing masters from reversal camera footage.

Before you have any optical printing done, discuss the job with the lab. When ordering optical printing, specify what purpose the print will be put to. Like all other instructions to the lab which may be complex or ambiguous, written instructions are preferable when ordering prints. And keep a copy.

Although the optical printer is used most often for the preparation of masters and effects, it has a number of other interesting applications.

Optical Zooms

Some optical printers can be made to enlarge a portion of a frame, with varying magnification, or reduce the size of the image to a rectangle within the frame. In terms of perspective, such optical printer zooms are identical to in-the-camera zooms. Printers used for routine preparation of masters are called one-to-one printers, and the printer which can make optical zooms can naturally be used for this as well as for enlargements and reductions. The printer does not employ a zoom lens, but rather it varies the distance between the projector and camera portions.

A frequent use of this kind of printer in theatrical films is to create a close-up out of a medium shot by cropping the original. The editor may find that he needs the close-up, and instead of reshooting the shot, which may be impossible, he orders an optically printed enlargement of a segment of the shot. Such an enlargement will have an increase in

Independent Filmmaking

grain and decrease in sharpness proportional to the degree of magnification employed.

Frame Line Correction

If two cameras were used to shoot a film, one of which registers the frame at a different position with respect to the perforations, cutting together the footage shot with both cameras will cause an annoying shift of frame line. Frame line correction may be called for. In such a case the master's frame can be shifted in the projector portion's aperture, either up or down, with respect to the position of the camera aperture. The resultant print can have perforations properly juxtaposed with respect to frames (or frame lines, if you prefer this point of reference). The projector crops part of the frame, so it's possible to get away with less than perfect frame line positioning. You may, however, feel that it is necessary to correct gross frame line errors.

Duplicated Shots

You may have occasion to use the same shot in several different portions of your film. One solution is to make a print or prints of the footage with the contact printer, but this will result in the footage being flopped. To avoid this you'll want to use the optical printer. If your original was shot on reversal color stock, ECO is a good choice for your duplicate footage; for black and white, a camera stock like Plus X will give acceptable results. Your lab will probably know the best stock to use for this or any other optical printing requirement.

Hold Frame Printing

Freeze frames, or hold frames, are accomplished this way: one frame is printed over and over again, for as long as required. The effect is to freeze the action. Advice that is often given is to use two adjacent frames printed alternately to suppress grain. If you're alternating rapidly between the two frames, the grain patterns of one cannot be that visible. This isn't good advice if the two frames differ drastically, and you may not mind the grain, or in fact, you may want the grainy effect.

Repeat Frame and Skip Frame Printing

If you've got footage that was shot at the silent speed (nominally 16 fps), and you want the action to appear *normal* at the sound running speed of 24 fps, the solution is to repeat print every third frame. In this case, the sixteen frames of action will take up, or be expanded to twenty-one frames. The method works perfectly for footage shot at today's silent running speed of 18 fps, where printing every third frame will yield 24 fps. Footage which is repeat frame printed may appear to be a little jerky, especially in shots that have a lot of action or camera movement.

Repeat frame printing can be used to create a kind of slow motion effect. For example, if every frame is printed twice, a film shot at 24 fps will now be, in effect, overcranked by a factor of two. Of course, a film that was shot at 48 fps in the camera will have twenty-four new frames projected on the screen every second, whereas a film which has been

The Laboratory's Role

double frame printed will have but twelve new frames in a second of screen time. The effect of such repeat frame printing is jerky and gets jerkier as you go to three, four or more repeat frames. I'm not using jerky in a pejorative sense; only a descriptive one. The peculiar jerky effect may be what you want.

Skip frame printing removes instead of duplicating frames. Film shot at the sound speed can be converted to the silent speed by skipping frames in printing; a reasonably good undercranked effect can be achieved by skip frame printing.

Backward Action

Another obvious use of the optical printer is for the production of backward action footage. The projector portion of the printer simply runs the footage from tails to heads, instead of from heads to tails, making a print on the raw stock as it does.

Other Effects

The optical printer may be used for many other effects, such as wipes, or fancy matte transitions or titles. There are labs that specialize in nothing but optical effects. Liquid gate optical printing is available for suppressing abrasions and scratches on the printing master. It is claimed that the best quality optical prints are made using liquid gate, and some labs recommend its use routinely even if the master film is not worn or scratched. Other optical effects, produced in the printer and elsewhere, are discussed in chapter 10, *Mixed Bag*.

Enlargement and Reduction

When blowing up your 8mm footage—and super 8 and single 8—you have a choice of enlarging it directly to make a projection print, or of making a printing master for subsequent release prints.

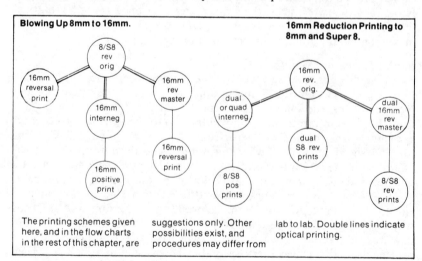

Blowing Up 8mm to 16mm.

16mm Reduction Printing to 8mm and Super 8.

The printing schemes given here, and in the flow charts in the rest of this chapter, are suggestions only. Other possibilities exist, and procedures may differ from lab to lab. Double lines indicate optical printing.

Independent Filmmaking

If projection prints are to be made directly from your 8mm camera film, the footage will be timed and handled like 16mm camera film. Of course, the printing operation will be carried out with the use of an optical and not a contact printer. The answer print can be used as a basis for further corrections. Depending upon your purpose, it may be better to have your footage blown up to a low contrast printing material, like Ektachrome 7399 rather than higher contrast Ektachrome 7390. The Ektachrome 7399 material will yield fuller saturation of colors and less contrast for most subjects, and make more pleasing projection prints. Black and white 8mm can be blown up and printed with fairly good results on any of the available reversal print stocks. If you make your blowup on camera stock like Plus X, you may get good results also.

Some labs (like Hollywood Valley Films) will produce an optical sound 16mm print from your mag striped 8mm footage, with image and track in sync as you had prepared it.

Printing Masters

If you are planning to make several prints from 8mm camera film, in the long run it may be better to make a 16mm printing master than using the 8mm camera original as the printing master. The concern here is not so much preserving the 8mm camera film, but rather, lowering your cost. A print blown up directly from the camera film is more expensive than a print made from a 16mm master made from the camera original. You have to figure in the cost of producing your 16mm master when you compute your break-even point for the master.

Whether your 8mm film is color or black and white, you can make two kinds of masters: negative or reversal. A negative printing master of your camera film, usually called an *internegative,* will produce prints through the negative-positive system, appreciably less expensive than reversal-reversal.

You may choose to have 16mm reversal masters made of your camera footage because you may like the quality of these prints, or you may be cutting the blown-up master into a film with reversal footage or the labs in your area may not be equipped for negative-positive color. Black and white reversal masters work best on a camera film like Plus X, color masters on low contrast Ektachrome 7399 or ECO. Actually black and white camera films have too high a gamma and could stand some overexposure and underdevelopment.

Reduction Printing

You face many of the same problems reducing 16mm footage to the 8mm formats as you do when you go from 8mm to 16mm. But you don't have to worry about the increase in grain and decrease in sharpness that you have when enlarging. If the work is carefully done, reduction printing should result in high quality smaller format prints.

Filmmakers who are making 16mm films with reduction in mind

The Laboratory's Role

would do well to shoot with Eastman Ektachrome Commercial for the best possible traditional standards of color, sharpness, grain and so on.

When reduction printing directly to projection prints, and your 16mm footage is reversal color, of course use reversal print stock; Ektachrome 7399 stock would be a better choice in most cases than the more contrasty 7390 print material. If your 16mm footage is ECO, 7390 print stock would probably be wiser to use. The Ektachrome 7399 stock might be your choice for printing from projection contrast 16mm original, like Ektachrome VNF and Kodachrome.

Ordering two prints at a time is more economical since reduction printing is done on double standard 8, or double super 8, compatible with the rest of the lab's processing operation. Once the print film is processed, it will be slit and returned to you 8 millimeters wide.

You can choose to make reduction masters, having two 8mm master prints side by side on double 8 or super 8 stock. This is called a *double rank master*. For such a master, ECO is a good choice for reversal-reversal prints, or internegative 7272 if you want to have negative-positive color prints. Similar stock can be used for 8mm or super 8 black and white prints, either the reversal-reversal or negative-positive systems.

For larger print orders, some labs are now doing a good deal of volume printing 35 millimeter wide masters. Once the film is processed, it is slit and spooled on rolls for 8mm or super 8 prints. It is possible to obtain 8mm or super 8 prints with magnetic or optical sound tracks.

New Super 8 Reduction Methods
Bell & Howell offers a continuous optical reduction printer, model 6128 CH, for making reduction prints in the super 8 format from a 16mm master: the prints from one 16mm master are made two at a time on 16 millimeter wide film with the super 8 perforations. After the print is processed, the film must be slit. The printer's optical system splits the single 16mm image into the necessary two images of the super 8 dimension. The printer can operate at two hundred feet per minute at the 16mm side. It is an additive color printer and can offer effects using A and B rolls for the master.

With this method, a double rank super 8 master of the 16mm film does not have to be made. The filmmaker need only supply the lab with the 16mm master, which may be in the form of A and B rolls, and a 16mm mag film track just as he would for the production of 16mm prints. In one continuous operation, super 8 prints can be made two at a time (effectively doubling the life of the master), ensuring both low cost and high quality super 8 prints from 16mm master material.

A similar printer, called the Optronics Mark X Quad Printer, developed by John Maurer for Cine Magnetics, Inc. makes four super 8 copies from a 16mm master. The prints are made on 35mm film which is subsequently slit.

Blowing Up to 35mm
In this country and the rest of the world, since Edison and Eastman

Independent Filmmaking

introduced the format, 35mm has been the distribution size of all theatrical motion pictures. Only in recent years have two other formats—70mm and 16mm—begun to rival 35mm; 70mm is used for giant screen and Cinerama films, and 16mm is becoming increasingly popular in small art theaters, usually specializing in revivals of movie classics and screenings of experimental films; lately, small theaters showing 16mm prints of first run films are beginning to appear.

Any of the three formats discussed in this book can be enlarged to 35mm (or 70mm) for distribution to theaters not equipped with small format projection. Although an increasing number of theaters seem to be adding 16mm projectors, there still is a need to distribute 16mm films in the 35mm format.

Extraordinarily high quality duplication of 16mm films to the 35mm format, with the use of optical printers, is possible. Two examples of fine work in this field are the surfing color film, *Endless Summer,* and the black and white *Faces. Endless Summer,* by the way, was shot with a Bolex, *Faces* with an Eclair.

It's a good idea to shoot 16mm reversal, since it can produce clean results. Internegatives may be printed directly from reversal or negative camera original, although Eastman recommends the use of ECO for blowups, even if they are to be in black and white. Positive prints may be made from the internegative. Very good results can be obtained by starting with color negative camera film, in which case you must have a professional cut the camera film. There are laboratories that specialize in optical printing at 16mm to 35mm, and many of the larger labs routinely offer the service. Preparation of the picture master and track in no way departs from printing 16mm to 16mm; for example, the master may be A and B rolled. The work is often done with a liquid gate printer.

One odd problem awaiting the filmmaker seeking 35mm distribution of a film shot in 16mm is that the aspect ratio of 35mm projection rarely matches that of the 16mm frame. At one time, both 16mm and 35mm had a projected aspect ratio of 1.33:1. The advent of Cinema-Scope in the early fifties changed that. At present, most neighborhood theaters project 35mm prints in one of two aspect ratios, either 1.85:1, sometimes called wide screen, or 2.35:1, the *scope* format projected through an anamorphic lens. Some theaters have the diabolical practice of projecting all films in one format, a compromise format of 2:1.

What all of this means to the 16mm filmmaker planning to make a film to be distributed in 35mm, is that he should try to compose his film for an aspect ratio of about 2:1, by cropping the top and bottom of the picture. There are still some theaters that can project 35mm in the 1.33:1 ratio, but these are the exception, rather than the rule.

Super 16
Some people are shooting single perf 16mm in cameras modified so that the aperture covers the additional two millimeters right out to the edge of the film. Such cameras must also have the lens offset by one

366 millimeter to cover the frame properly. Even so, all optics will not work with this scheme, and lenses must be carefully selected. Television (vidicon) lenses, because of their greater covering power, are often used.

By blowing up this elongated 16mm frame to the 35mm wide screen format, complete utilization of the frame is achieved because its new aspect ratio closely matches 1.85:1. This format is called *super 16*. Several companies will modify existing cameras for super 16 use, and some labs have modified their equipment to make its use a viable proposition.

Prints and Printing Masters

Typical Printing Masters

In the simplest possible case, you can have the lab make a print from your reversal camera original on reversal print stock, or if it is negative

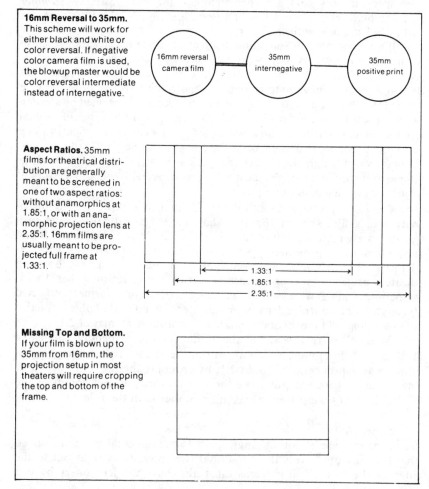

16mm Reversal to 35mm. This scheme will work for either black and white or color reversal. If negative color camera film is used, the blowup master would be color reversal intermediate instead of internegative.

16mm reversal camera film — 35mm internegative — 35mm positive print

Aspect Ratios. 35mm films for theatrical distribution are generally meant to be screened in one of two aspect ratios: without anamorphics at 1.85:1, or with an anamorphic projection lens at 2.35:1. 16mm films are usually meant to be projected full frame at 1.33:1.

1.33:1
1.85:1
2.35:1

Missing Top and Bottom. If your film is blown up to 35mm from 16mm, the projection setup in most theaters will require cropping the top and bottom of the frame.

Independent Filmmaking

film, on positive stock. Positive stock is not reversal stock, it is negative stock which is designed to yield prints of normal (positive) tonality when negative camera film is printed on it.

Returning to our simplest possible case: we hand the lab our processed camera original which in this case becomes our printing master, the film used to make prints. Our simplest case would involve a silent film of one picture roll, which would be called printing an A roll. The lab will time the print, and then make an answer print.

In a slightly more complicated print example, you'd also provide the lab with your sound track which could be in the form of 16mm mag film or the appropriate optical track printing master. One step further in complexity would be a film that has more than one picture roll. A typical situation is having a master in the following form: two rolls of picture (A and B rolls) and a roll of track. Each time a print is made from this material, there is a chance that it will be damaged or destroyed

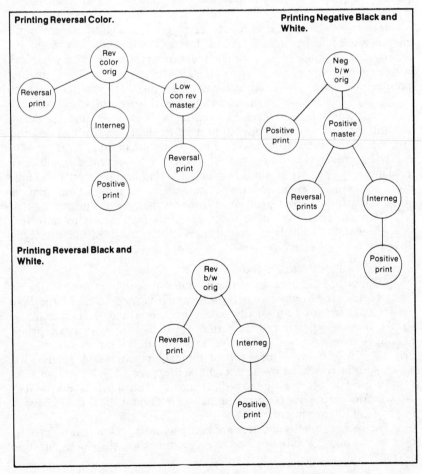

Printing Reversal Color.

Printing Negative Black and White.

Printing Reversal Black and White.

The Laboratory's Role

or that the lab will make a mistake in the print. Some labs use pressure sensitive feelers which drop into a notch cut into the film, sometimes on the side of the film, sometimes between perforations. When the printer's feeler drops into the notched cue, it triggers the next light change or effect.

In older setups, that must now be considered obsolete, a technician had to sit next to the printer and make the light changes whenever the feeler found a cue notch. The man working the printer would occasionally lose cues, or the feeler might sense a thick splice and mistake that for the cue. Every time a mistake of this nature is made, your print is ruined; and your camera film gets more worn out without having contributed to making a print.

The best system employed today (but not universally in operation yet) uses metal tabs attached to the film and punched paper tape which contains information for lights and effects. The tabs serve as radio frequency cues, never coming in physical contact with any portion of the printer.

How many prints can you expect to get from your camera film? The answer could be one or several dozen. The camera film might be destroyed in a single pass through the printer because of mechanical failure, poorly made splices or carelessness. If well maintained, quality equipment is used, and good technicians do the work, you can expect several dozen prints before your camera film is worn out with torn perforations, abrasions, scratches and parting splices. These defects occur not only from the printing operation itself or the film's trip through the printing machine, but from pre- and postprinting handling.

Labs frequently clean the master, necessary to prevent dirt and dust from marring your print. But this is one more additional print handling. Probably as much wear and tear is caused by rewinding your film in preparation for the next print as is done in making the print itself. A better lab procedure would be to make prints from heads to tails and then from tails to heads. Some printers will allow this, and it might double the life of many masters.

Intermediate Printing Masters

Filmmakers often decide to make an *intermediate printing master* in order to save the original camera film, which is used to make the first master and then any additionally needed masters. If the decision to make such a master is postponed until the camera film is worn from printmaking, the master will carry the abrasion and wear marks of the original. Unfortunately, independent filmmakers often lack funds with which such intermediate masters might be prepared.

Before you order an intermediate master, you must have a perfect answer print from your camera original. Don't count on adding changes of any kind to your intermediate.

The highest quality masters are made with optical and contact step printers, although continuous contact machines are also used for this purpose.

Independent Filmmaking

Reversal Original

If you've shot reversal, color or black and white, you can have an internegative printing master made directly from your camera film. *Internegative* (interneg for short) is the name for negative printing masters made from reversal camera film. (Sometimes the term interneg is used for color, and dupe neg for black and white. Here we'll stick to the term interneg for both.) When the internegative has been prepared, it is used to make prints with the negative-positive system, less expensive than reversal-reversal printing. The sequence, to reiterate, has been from camera reversal to internegative which is used to produce positive release prints.

Many laboratories offer another option for an intermediate printing material when reversal color stock has been used in the camera: intermediate printing masters on Ektachrome Commercial or Ektachrome R stock. Prints from the master are made with the reversal-reversal system. Some labs use this system because negative color processing is not available to them. Some people prefer color reversal printing masters to internegative printing masters because the colors are more saturated and contrast more acceptable. This is especially true when the camera original is a projection contrast film.

Black and White Negative Original

You can have prints made from intermediate masters, if you've chosen to use negative camera film. The situation is a bit more complicated than using reversal camera stock.

If you've shot with black and white negative, the release print system you want to use is the negative-positive. The first thing the lab will make is a master positive (fine grain) print from your camera film. Then an internegative (dup neg) will be made from this master positive. This last step is exactly like making an internegative from reversal camera stock. In this case, however, you had to go one additional step (generation) to get to an internegative. From negative camera film, you have

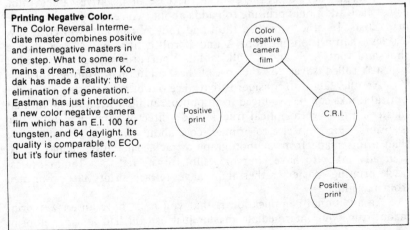

Printing Negative Color.
The Color Reversal Intermediate master combines positive and internegative masters in one step. What to some remains a dream, Eastman Kodak has made a reality: the elimination of a generation. Eastman has just introduced a new color negative camera film which has an E.I. 100 for tungsten, and 64 daylight. Its quality is comparable to ECO, but it's four times faster.

The Laboratory's Role

370   an intermediate high resolution, low granularity positive made, and from this an internegative.

The extra generation here can decide the difference between good or bad release prints, especially if the camera film was exposed less than ideally. Negatives on the thin side will be especially difficult to print after all the generations involved. The extra generation required to get to the internegative stage from negative camera stock is one of the reasons why filmmakers choose reversal camera stock.

One possibility that permits high quality prints is to make reversal-reversal prints from the intermediate positive made from your negative. If the work is well done, they are indistinguishable from original prints. Of course, reversal-reversal release prints are less desirable from an economic point of view than negative-positive.

Color Negative Original

Eastman offers a color reversal intermediate film, 7249, for the production of negative masters printed directly from camera negative. CRI is a reversal material, but something more was needed than just the idea that negative printed on reversal produces negative. Eastman 7249 has built-in color masks, just like those in Eastman color camera stock. CRI has become the standard intermediate material for 35mm and 70mm theatrical productions, but it's primarily of interest to filmmakers working in the larger formats since so little 16mm color negative is shot. Once a 7249 master has been produced, it can be used to make prints with the negative-positive printing system on Eastman color positive stock.

Break-even Point

If you choose to have intermediate masters made from your camera stock, you may actually save money in the long run. Compare the costs of making prints from your reversal camera stock with prints made from internegative: positive prints are less expensive than reversal.

A further consideration, even in the case of negative camera film, is that each additional printing roll adds about two cents a foot to release print costs. In other words, a thousand foot A roll film will cost, say, $20 less than a thousand foot A and B rolled film, or $40 less than a thousand foot A, B and C rolled film. Your printing master, since it is just A rolled, saves you the cost of these additional printing rolls.

Another factor to consider is that once out of the answer print stage, optical tracks can be produced from photographic instead of 16mm mag masters. Prints with optical tracks made directly from mag film, that is, prints which are electro-printed, cost about two cents a foot more than prints made from a photographic track. Therefore, it may be to your advantage to have your mag film transferred to a 16mm optical track printing master, rather than have release prints electro-printed from mag film.

An additional complication is that you must have an answer print made from your intermediate master just as you had an answer print

Independent Filmmaking

made from your camera film. Although all the effects may be incorporated into the master, it may still need timing (and perhaps color correction). If you're lucky, you'll get a good print your first time. But then again it may take several answer prints before you are satisfied.

I don't want to give the wrong impression: release prints made from intermediates are designed to be printed on high speed machines without any effects, light changes or color corrections.

If you take all this into account, it is possible to compute your break-even point, the point after which the intermediate master starts to pay for itself. Suppose you shot reversal camera stock and chose to have an internegative made from it. First you would have had to approve your reversal answer print. Only after approval could you order an internegative from your camera film. The reversal answer print should be perfect before you do this.

If your film was A and B rolled, the internegative will be an A roll. Suppose you choose to transfer your mag film to a master optical track, assuming your answer prints had an electro-printed track. Your film will now be printed from an A roll and a photographic sound track, instead of from the original material which was A and B roll reversal and a mag film track.

The first print made from your interneg and optical track is an answer print, and you'll be billed for it at that rate. Once you've approved the print timing, the sound and so on, you can have about a hundred release prints made from an internegative or ECO master before it's worn out.

Is it worth making an intermediate master of your camera film? For protecting your original? Economically? Obviously an intermediate will protect your camera film. The second question depends on how much money you have, and how many prints you expect to make. Your break-even point is a function of the number of answer prints you have to make from the camera film and from the intermediate material, whether you've shot in negative or reversal, whether your film was A rolled or A and B rolled, whether or not you'll have the track electro-printed or made from a photographic track and so on. Typically, your break-even point may be something like half a dozen prints.

Summing Up

All labs make mistakes. In this respect, they're very much like filmmakers. I'd say, if you can help it, try to stick with a lab that lives up to an acceptable level of quality, at least for printmaking. If the lab makes mistakes, forgive it if it corrects them at its own expense. A lab that is willing to take responsibility for errors is okay.

Once a lab severely damaged my camera film, and in order to make up for it, they made an internegative for me at no cost and repaired the damage to the film as best they could. As a matter of fact, I'm the only person who can see where that missing frame should go. I look at it now as a beauty mark and a milestone in man's search for perfection. I'd

The Laboratory's Role

rather have that frame than the internegative, but I can't go back in time and undo what was done.

If you need a moral, don't live and let live. If the lab makes a mistake, they have to take the responsibility for it. In the same way, you don't want to do business with people whom you feel like taking to court, but if you have to, get an attorney. A threat sometimes does wonders, especially if the going is rough. I've had terrible fights with labs, and we somehow got over it.

Never expect a lab to be able to deliver prints when they say they can. That applies especially to answer prints. Don't schedule screenings until the print is in your hands. Bitter experience has shown this to be a good rule. (I'll probably break it many more times before I'm through, but while I'm giving advice I might as well lay it on thick.)

The general guiding principle then, as I see it, is to continue to use a lab so that you and that lab get to know each other's idiosyncrasies.

Portion of a Typical Lab Catalog. *

Answer Prints • Kodachrome 7387

		silent per foot	sound from photo. track per foot	sound from mag. track per foot
A roll		$.135	$.155	$.17
A-B rolls		.155	.175	.19
Additional rolls, each roll		.02	.02	.02
Minimum Charge	$15.00			

Release Prints • Kodachrome 7387

		silent per foot	sound from photo. track per foot	sound from mag. track per foot
1 print	A roll	.125	.135	.15
	A-B rolls	.145	.155	.17
2 to 10 prints	A roll	.11	.12	.135
	A-B rolls	.13	.14	.155
11 to 25 prints	A roll	.105	.115	.13
	A-B rolls	.12	.13	.145
26 to 50 prints	A roll	.10	.11	.125
	A-B rolls	.115	.125	.14
Additonal rolls, each roll		.02	.02	.02
Minimum Charge	$10.00			

*These prices were current in 1972. To obtain 1982 prices multiply by two.

Mixed Bag

Ingredients

In this chapter, I will treat quite a number of short topics that do not easily fit into any of the chapters. In essence, this is a compilation of digressions.

The Story Board

The story board, first used by animators, has found new applications in filming television commercials and feature films alike. With this method of scripting a film, the director and an artist are able to plan and design the physical appearance of virtually every shot in the film. Through a series of drawings or sketches the story board shows key moments in the film. These could be high points of action, important sets or locations, or anything vital to the flow of the film. Moreover, it can be used to help determine the internal logic in the sequences and elements of the film. The story board closely resembles comic strips, the best of which are more *cinematic* than most filmed melodrama.

Scripts

Scripts can be written in many ways to suit various purposes. As far as I'm concerned, the simplest and most straightforward way to use the written word as an aid in filmmaking is not through a formal script but rather as notes for a memory aid. A great joy in filmmaking is the progressive revelation of the substance of the film itself. If I could totally envision a film, I don't think I would be able to start work on it. Larry Jordan in his program notes for the premier showing of his feature film, *Hildur and the Magician,* said it this way:

The commercial film must know itself beforehand — before from $200,000 to $10,000,000 is spent on it. It must be more or less well defined on paper, budgeted, scripted and organized in order that the element of risk may be minimized. I believe in the future of the 16mm 'feature' film, made organically, outside the safe conventions of commercial cinema. A film like *Hildur* begins on faith and very little budget. It begins and builds, filling its own lee, as a cypress tree grows away from the prevailing wind. *Hildur* is misshapen in this same picturesque manner. The winds of Karmic fortune blew on this project, and you see tonight the result of that growth.

Alfred Hitchcock, unlike Larry Jordan, works out his scripts in the smallest detail before shooting begins. In fact, Hitchcock has said that he considers the film to be completed once the script is finalized. The actual shooting of the film is a mechanical process.

In my own view, a filmmaker writing a script is like a novelist filming an outline of a projected novel. A filmmaker can find himself in the position in which a script is a necessity, but this usually happens only in the case of a sponsored film, or when a filmmaker is trying to get financial support for a project.

Budget

The most important thing about a budget is for whom it is prepared. If it is prepared for people commissioning a film, you'll probably over-

Nick Fury, Agent of S.H.I.E.L.D.
A beautiful story board, edited by Stan Lee, written and illustrated by Jim Steranko and inked by Joe Sinnott, from Vol 1, No. 1 of the comic book.

Mixed Bag

376

Fear not,
Nick wasn't offed — it's his
robot Doppelganger lying
there in the last panel.
(Marvel Comics Group)

Independent Filmmaking

estimate your costs to come up with what engineers call a safety factor. If you're preparing a budget for yourself, try to be more realistic.

I'm not telling you that you have to prepare a budget. However, it certainly isn't a bad idea to estimate how much a film is likely to cost. Some filmmakers I know don't like to do this because they find it depressing. They prefer not to worry about budgets but just go ahead and make the film. If you're working in one of the 8mm formats, the necessity for a budget probably isn't very pressing. If, however, you're involved in a project that demands obtaining outside funds, or if you are working on a commissioned film, you will need a budget for your investors or clients. In preparing this you'll probably need the help of an accountant or someone with business experience.

When preparing your budget take into account the most basic factors involved: aside from equipment costs—which can be added to production costs by amortization—the greatest cost to the independent filmmaker will be film stock and lab work, which are comparatively expendable elements to high overhead theatrical productions. Most of the cost of producing theatrical films is not film stock and processing, usually less than 10 percent of the budget, but expenses such as technicians' and actors' salaries.

If you know the running time of your film, you know roughly how much film you are expecting to expose. Shooting ratios of five-to-one to twenty-to-one are par for theatrical productions. A nature film involving unpredictable wildlife could have a shooting ratio of two hundred-to-one. Andy Warhol shoots about one-to-one. You're probably going to be somewhere in the middle, and only experience can help you estimate how much film you'll shoot.

Then, of course, you should estimate the cost of processing a workprint, if any, recording tape, sound studio time and answer prints. Other considerations might be food and lodging for location shooting, equipment rental and so on.

Income Tax

If it is your inclination to pay income tax, and you spend even a small part of your income on films, obtain the services of a good accountant. People who are *independent operators* pay far less than their share of taxes, compared to white and blue collar workers, since many laws passed for the benefit of corporations are applicable to the filmmaker.

Your car, your home, your utility bills, postage and most certainly motion picture hardware, film stock and processing, are all items that can reduce the base of your income tax providing they are legitimately used in your filmmaking activities. One filmmaker, with several families to support, who grossed at least $15,000 one year, paid taxes on a net of less than $1000. His tax form was honestly filled out and his deductions were entirely legitimate.

Distribution

Besides the theatrical distributors we all know about, like 20th-Century

Fox or Universal, there are many other distributors, essentially non-theatrical in nature, who handle 16mm prints. Although it might be possible to get one of the big theatrical distributors to handle your film, it's unlikely that you will be able to do so, at least in the immediate future. In the first place many firms, for purposes of public relations, distribute reasonably well made shorts free-of-charge to theaters. So there doesn't seem to be any money in it for the big theatrical distributors even though some of them still seem to be making the perennial insipid travelogues.

If you've made a feature film, the chances aren't much better; in fact, they may even be slighter. Despite the success of some films shot in 16mm and blown up to 35mm and though the Disney people were shooting 16mm Kodachrome for their nature films two decades ago, there is still prejudice (albeit diminishing) against 16mm as a production format. Two more areas of trouble might be the Mesozoic tastes of distributors, or hassles with unions about a nonunion made film.

The many distributors handling 16mm feature length and shorter films fall into two categories: commercial distributors and the cooperatives. The commercial distributors are what they sound like, profit making organizations, seeking to accommodate their clientele. The cooperatives (co-ops) are groups of filmmakers banded together to serve their own interests primarily, rather than those of the renter.

The commercial distributors will of course select films carefully. The cooperatives will distribute any film which is the property of the person who places it with them. The commercial distributors usually take at least half the rental of the film, or often the filmmakers' royalty will be based on net rather than gross receipts.

The co-ops, generally speaking, take 25 to 33 percent of the rental, or gross, distributing 64 to 75 percent to the filmmaker. The co-ops' share goes for operating expenses; these organizations have either non-profit status or do not operate at a profit.

Both co-ops and commercial distributors have had success in recent years. Business is good. Besides forcing a greater share of the profits out of the commercial people, the co-ops have also broken the back of exclusive distribution. Commercial distributors have been forced to give filmmakers better deals because of the existence of the co-ops.

Exclusive distribution means exactly what it says: only one distributor can handle the film. Such a situation will severely decrease the earning potential of a film. Co-ops do not have exclusive rights to a film: they usually don't even have a written agreement with the filmmaker.

Aside from whether or not a distributor is commercial or cooperative, a more pressing concern for the filmmaker is whether the films handled are in the same work genre. You may be wasting your time sending a film to a commercial distributor if you haven't found out what kinds of films it seeks. Similarly, your film could rest comfortably on the shelf of a co-op for months or years without getting any rental. Co-ops usually handle films made by people who regard film as an art, and not necessarily as a theatrical experience or a documentary form. The work handled by most co-ops has been variously described as avant garde, underground, experimental, independent and head flicks. The two major sources for these films are cited throughout this book, after film titles. The initials CCC and FMC stand for Canyon Cinema Cooperative and Film-Makers' Cooperative.

Publications

Books and Booklets

American Cinematographer Manual, third edition, 1969 (ASC Holding Corp, 1782 North Orange Drive, Hollywood, California 90028) Aimed at professional 16mm, 35mm and 70mm users, this book features a great deal of information, mostly in the form of charts and tables. It contains a rundown of professional cameras, depth of field tables, filter tables, information about film stock and so on.

Lenses in Photography (Garden City Books, Garden City, New York, 1951) A very basic, useful book by Dr Rudolf Kinglake, formerly Director of Optical Design at Eastman Kodak. Filmmakers who want to know more about lenses will find it has just about everything they might require.

The Focal Encyclopedia of Photography, Desk Edition (The MacMillan Company, New York, New York, 1969, revised) This book contains many pages of information from aberration to zoom lenses. It's an invaluable reference.

The Focal Encyclopedia of Film and Television: Techniques (Communication Arts Books, Hastings House, Publishers, New York, New York, 1970)

Motion Picture Camera Data (Focal/Hastings, New York, 1979) A good guide by David W. Samuelson. Descriptions of cameras, tips and how to load. Well done.

The Technique of Special-effects Cinematography (Communication Arts Books, Hastings House, Publishers, New York, New York, 1969, revised) A fascinating book by Raymond Fielding of Temple University. It covers every special effects technique, with a great deal of information never before in print. There are chapters on mirror-shots, optical printing, traveling mattes, aerial-image printing, miniatures and so on. This is one book in a series that all start with the title *The Technique of* something or other to do with film, like editing and animation.

Kodak Booklets. Eastman Kodak publishes a series of technical booklets that run from simple to sophisticated. They offer many superb publications that are of great interest to filmmakers. By the way, all the booklets are the same size, and can be bound together in looseleaf books the company provides. They're all relatively inexpensive, something like $1.00 or less. Booklets of interest are *Eastman Kodak Motion Picture Films for Professional Use* (H-1), *Basic Titling and Animation* (S-21),

Mixed Bag

Industrial Motion Pictures (P-18), *Storage and Preservation of Motion Picture Film, Kodak Filters and Pola-Screens* (AB-1), and *Color as Seen and Photographed* (E-74). The last booklet is the best, most direct work I've seen on the subject.

Eisenstein's Writings

In the brief history of film there has been but one writer who had a profound understanding of the nature of film. Sergei Eisenstein understood more about the juxtaposition of shot with shot, the relationship between sound and image, and the nature of filmic construction than any of the many writers whose volumes now fill the shelves of book stores and libraries. Although often difficult, either because of Eisenstein's style or the translations from the Russian, his writing on film is so important that there's no way I could overstate it. It's clear to me that the work being done by the most advanced film artists like Brakhage, Baillie and Kubelka, to name just three, takes up where Eisenstein left off decades ago. There are three collections of his writing in paperback: *Film Form* and *The Film Sense* (both from Harvest Books, 757 Third Avenue, New York, New York, $2.45), and *Film Essays and a Lecture by Sergei Eisenstein* (Praeger Publishers, 111 Fourth Avenue, New York, New York, $2.95).

Copyright

The owner of a copyright of a work has the exclusive rights to make copies of it. However, the copyright laws make harsh and unreasonable requirements that discriminate against the creative artist. Organizations like the American Society of Composers, Authors and Publishers, and the American Guild of Authors and Composers are trying to change some of these antiquated laws. Although they are essentially concerned with copyright as it applies to song writing, their efforts will help the filmmaker and all artists seeking copyright protection.

If you want to copyright a film, whether or not you have paid the fee and filed the proper forms with the Copyright Office, you *must* mark your film, on or near the title with the following information: the word Copyright, or Copr, or the symbol ©, your name and the year. For example: © John Doe 1972. If you don't do this for the first public screening you can never properly obtain copyright.

For more information about copyright, what it is and how to get it for your film, write to: Copyright Office, The Library of Congress, Washington, DC 20540. Ask for circular 35 (*General Information on Copyright*), circular 3 (*The Copyright Notice*), circular 7 (*Copyright for Motion Pictures*), and form L-M, which is the proper form for copyrighting a film. None of these publications, by the way, is copyrighted.

Special Mailing Rate

Filmmakers should know that it is often possible to ship prints through the mail at a greatly reduced special fourth class rate for books and films. Films mailed this way will get sent far more speedily if you spend the little extra for Special Handling or Special Delivery. For further details, consult your friendly neighborhood post office.

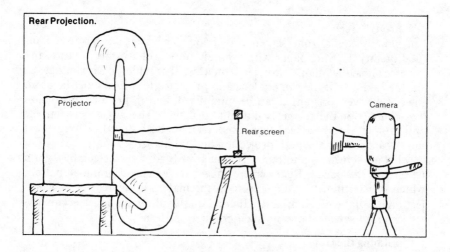

Rear Projection.

Projector

Rear screen

Camera

Rephotography

Many filmmakers have turned to a number of ingenious methods to manipulate their filmed images. The optical printer, one of the most powerful tools for such manipulation, has disadvantages: optical print-ers are expensive to use and require working through an intermediary—a technician. Because of these objections, many filmmakers have devised their own substitutes which often rival the quality and flexibility of the laboratory printer. I've seen quite a few fine quality optical printers built out of projector parts. Short of this, there are other methods.

I have lumped these techniques under the general heading *rephoto-graphy*, because this is the name by which the process is now known and because I can't think of a better name. Rephotography invariably employs the use of a camera and a projector—the projector showing the motion picture image, either continuously or one frame at a time, and the camera filming the projected image, either continuously or one frame at a time. Before discussing the merits of single frame or continuous rephotography, let's look at the setups employed.

Rear Screen

Some filmmakers project the image on a rear screen surface and film from the side opposite the projector. This method allows both the camera lens and projector lens axis to be aligned, with the screen between the two. Usually the projected image is relatively small: it can be measured in inches. There is really no pressing reason to project a large image, and a small image, besides being convenient to work with, is relatively bright. A bright image makes exposure simpler.

Rear screen material is available in several forms: special plastic material which must be stretched on a frame or ground glass screens; replacement viewing screens for sheet film cameras might also work well.

Mixed Bag

Front Screen

I personally favor front screen projection. The image is projected on good quality drawing paper with a barely noticeable surface texture; the camera films the image projected on this. The chief disadvantage of this method is that the camera lens and projector lens axis must be at an angle. However, this angle can be minimized, and in practice, distortion *(keystoning)* of the image is difficult to detect. The angle between the projector lens and camera lens axis can also be reduced if long focal lengths are chosen for both projection and taking lenses.

Front screen rephotography adds little or no detectable grain pattern to the image. Rear screen images have a fixed granular pattern which is determined by the texture of the material, but rear screen projection is usually much brighter. If good quality drawing paper is employed, the front screen shows no such granular pattern.

Filming the Gate

This method bears the closest resemblance to the laboratory optical printer and involves what it sounds like it does: the camera is set up facing the projector and shoots the image in the gate. This can be accomplished by removing the projector lens and photographing the image in the gate as you would a very small object. Usually relatively long lenses are necessary to obtain a comfortable working distance between projector and camera. The configuration of the projector plays an important part in determining how easily and closely the working distance may be approached. Extension tubes or a bellows can be used with the lens to obtain the needed close focusing. A small ground glass screen between the lamp and the gate may help produce even illumination across the frame.

Single Frame or Continuous Run?

Using the single frame technique may warrant modifying the projector since some will not project single frame and others that do may get too

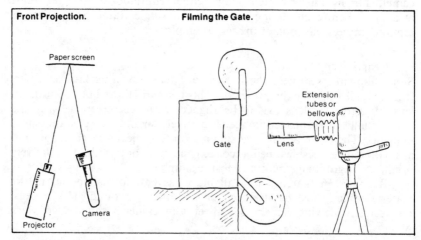

Front Projection.   Filming the Gate.

Paper screen

Extension tubes or bellows

Gate   Lens

Camera

Projector

Independent Filmmaking

hot and burn the frame. Usually, single frame projectors have some kind of heat shield that drops into place to protect the film. This simply works by holding back the light that would have reached the frame. Two types of devices of this sort are employed: the metal screen with punched holes and the heat-absorbing glass screen. The punched metal heat shield, often found on Bell & Howell 16mm projectors, may project a visible pattern when focused at close distances, especially if the projection lens is stopped down. For greater protection, use a resistor in series with the lamp, or a variable rheostat.

When filming single frame, either rear or front screen or in the gate, separately advance each frame with the projector's inching knob and then expose the frame with the camera. This tedious method has decided advantages: the projected frame can be photographed many times to obtain a movement-analyzing slow motion effect, or it can be used to freeze frames.

Continuous filming occurs when both the camera and projector are running normally. Many people balk at this because they know that both the camera and projector shutters must move in synchronization to remove the possibility of an image with oscillating brightness.

I have found that the image may flicker with the continuous approach, but not as badly as expected. In fact, there are techniques that render the flicker hardly noticeable: regulating the camera fps rate slightly under that of the projector's will go a long way toward minimizing flicker. The difference between the two speeds does not have to be very great: for example, the projector might be working at 18 fps and the camera at 16 fps. Experiment with your own equipment: a camera with a moving mirror reflex system will give you some clue about the proper speed to employ. It may be a good idea to reshoot the shot several times because the relationship between the camera and the projector shutters may vary depending upon the starting times.

I have discovered that it is also possible to obtain both undercranked or overcranked effects with continuous filming. If the projector is operating at 24 fps and the camera at 12 fps or 6 fps or 2 fps, there's a good chance of totally eliminating any flickering of the image. Very good undercranked effects from footage shot at the normal fps rate may be obtained with rephotography.

Surprisingly, it is possible to obtain fair overcranked effects. I have run the projector at 5 fps and the camera at 16 fps, achieving a slow motion effect with only some fluctuation of image brightness.

It is possible to interlock the camera and projector so that they are in frame-for-frame sync. For rephotography you'd probably want to remove the projector's shutter as well.

Interlock Systems

The term interlock, in general, refers to any two or more machines which are run in synchronization. The simplest *interlock* system is the double projector, like the Bauer P6, Sonorex or Siemans. These employ mechan-

Mixed Bag

ical means for synchronizing the frame-for-frame operation of a magnetic film recorder and motion picture projector. The most common interlock system employs synchronous and *Selsyn* motors, usually simply called a Selsyn system. To project a picture film and a mag film track in sync, or interlock, the projector and the magnetic film recorder-reproducer usually use a Selsyn system. With synchronous motors the two machines will run in frame-for-frame sync, but only after they have gotten up to speed. The purpose of the Selsyn motors is to keep the machines in sync even when getting up to running speed. In fact, once the machines are up to their normal rate, the synchronous motors will keep them in step, and if desired, the Selsyns can be turned off.

The Selsyn motors are mounted adjacent to the synchronous motors. One of these servo motors watches the other through an electrical connection, and adjusts its rate accordingly. It is possible to synchronize any number of pieces of equipment electrically using Selsyns. One common interlock setup keeps the following pieces of equipment in sync: a magnetic film recorder, magnetic film dubbers or playback units (usually three or more) and a projector. With such a setup it is possible to mix a complex sound track in sync while looking at a projected workprint.

Older 16mm Bell & Howell projectors are frequently converted to Selsyn interlock operation. A number of firms can do such conversions, but you can do a good job yourself, as several filmmakers of my acquaintance have proven.

General Techniques

There are a number of things you can do to improve the rephotographed image, at least in terms of traditional standards. For example, when using a projection lens for rear or front screen rephotography, try stopping it down. Putting a black paper stop in front of the lens can markedly improve the image. Exposure determinations may be difficult, but I have had no trouble using reflected light meters, either hand-held or through-the-camera. As you might imagine, TTL meters are especially useful for rephotography.

Rephotography has many advantages that may not be immediately obvious. For example, good blowups from 8mm or super 8 to 16mm can be accomplished at a small fraction of the cost a lab would charge. Similarly, reductions to the smaller formats may be accomplished, including shooting 8mm to super 8, or super 8 to 8mm. The best results I have seen were obtained by continuous filming with a front screen

Stopping Down a Projection Lens. An idea of the size of the black cardboard stop needed.

projection. Everything had to be carefully done, including stopping down the lenses and so on.

Camera film stock for color shooting ought to be balanced for tungsten illumination say 3200° K — roughly the color temperature of a projection lamp. You can choose a rather slow duplicating stock like Anscochrome 2470. Anscochrome $T/100$ is an especially good stock to use for this purpose because of its very fine grain and well saturated colors. Ektachrome EF tungsten balance, which is a drop faster than the Anscochrome material ($T/100$ is 100 E.I., and EF tungsten is 125 E.I.) would be another good choice. Both of these films are about ten times the speed of duplicating stocks.

Very interesting rephotography has been done by filmmakers: Stan VanDerBeek used rear projection in his film *Skullduggery* (FMC). He added cutouts, moved across the surface of the screen, filming a single frame at a time in order to animate the foreground against the projected background image. His ground glass screen was positioned horizontally.

Michael Stewart used the rear screen single frame approach to great effect in *Freeform* (CCC), originally shot in 8mm and rephotographed to 16mm by the filmmaker. There are examples of front screen continuous rephotography (8mm to 16mm) in my film, *LP* (CCC, FMC). The technique was used in conjunction with a zoom lens moving in and out of an 8mm image, isolating it in black space. In another part of the film the technique was used to split the screen into nine images.

Frame Enlargements

The commercial cinema often employs a still photographer to take pictures during shooting for publicity purposes. Independent filmmakers rarely have the opportunity to employ such an individual; and even if it were possible the additional intrusion of a still photographer might make the filmmaker's shooting under many circumstances next to impossible.

Although there are some custom laboratories that offer such a service, a variety of techniques exist that can yield still photographs directly from the camera original or print. The simplest, and for many applications, entirely adequate technique is to project the film on good quality drawing paper and shoot this screen with a still camera preferably tripod mounted. A 35mm single lens reflex is a good choice — it will produce good 5x7 prints — and many models with their through-the-lens metering simplify determination of exposure. In any case a reflected light meter can be aimed at the screen and accurate readings taken this way. Stop down the projection lens with a black paper stop (see page 382 for the similarities of this technique with front screen rephotography). My experience indicates that a shutter speed of 1/15 second works best. A shorter exposure may miss the projected frame, and a longer exposure may result in too much blur. Black and white or color slides or negatives can be taken. Use color film balanced for tungsten to match the projector's lamp.

Mixed Bag

For better quality other methods are available: the camera original or a print can be placed in the negative holder of an enlarger. (Out-takes can be saved for this purpose.) If you've shot reversal, or are using a positive print of camera negative, a negative can be made on sheet film. The reversal or positive print in the enlarger is projected on the sheet film in a holder taped in position beneath the enlarger in place of the usual paper easel. A good choice for black and white prints from color is a sheet film with panchromatic sensitivity, but color blind stock will do for black and white, and color negative film can also be used. Prints can then be made from your negatives.

Prints can also be made directly from reversal or positive movie film without an intermediate negative if special reversal print paper—usually panchromatic—is used. If you're working from negative original, it can be printed directly on conventional color blind or special panchromatic papers. The major problem with making prints this way is that 8mm, super 8 and 16mm frames are so small you'll have trouble getting a sufficiently large image. There are some enlargers that would work well, like those designed to make prints from ultra-miniature still cameras like the Minox. Other approaches would be mounting a short focal length lens in the enlarger or projecting the image over a great distance. If the enlarger head can be swung to face a wall this is easy to accomplish.

You can also try copying the frame directly with a camera—with a single lens reflex with extension tubes or bellows. There are also a few devices on the market that attach to the standard 35mm single lens reflex. Century Precision Optics offers a $160 device to copy 16mm frames. There are also some inexpensive copying cameras designed especially to blow up the frame to roll film. These devices, in the $20 price range, give really lousy results.

Shooting the TV Screen
It is possible to shoot a TV image with a fair degree of success without the special equipment usually used for *kinescope* recordings. Set up your camera and properly frame or compose the TV image. Turn out the room lights. Take a reflected light meter reading of the screen. If your camera has a built-in meter, use it as the basis for your exposure.

You may be familiar with the bars that roll across the TV image when seen by a motion picture camera. Since the scanned image is on the screen a finite length of time, openings of the camera shutter and 'projection' of the broadcast frame must coincide, or part of the image will be lost. Since the TV image rate is 30 fps in this country, shooting at the sound speed of 24 fps, with a shutter speed of about 1/50 second will lose some image. The best way to avoid this effect, if you find it disturbing, is to lower the fps rate at which you shoot the screen.

If your camera has a variable shutter, open it as much as possible. You'll have to arrive at the maximum fps rate for your TV set and camera empirically, although reflex viewing systems with a moving mirror

may offer a clue even though the mirror is out-of-phase with the image
on the TV screen. You'll probably find that you can eliminate the roll bar
at about 12 or 14 fps.

Bi-packing

An early color process consisted of bi-packing two raw film stocks,
emulsion to emulsion, in the camera gate. Both films were exposed simultaneously, one making a green the other a red record. *Bi-packing*
then, generally, is the sandwiching together of two separate pieces of
film — usually a film with an image with raw stock or two films with
images — to be combined when light passes through. If you could bi-pack
two films in a projector, you'd get an image that was the sum of both,
an effect somewhat similar to a double exposure.

Some filmmakers convert their cameras into a kind of step contact
printing machine by bi-packing film with an image and raw stock, emulsion to emulsion; the raw stock is placed on the pressure plate side of the
gate, the film with the image on the aperture side. Light passing through
the first film will expose its image on the raw stock.

You can try loading your camera with a short segment of bi-packed
material to see if it can handle it. There has to be room between the
sprocket wheels and their guides, and the gate area must also accept the
sandwich. If you can get this far, you can try spooling both the raw stock
and the image film one inside the other on one roll of film. Thin polyester base film might make bi-packing possible in cameras that ordinarily wouldn't accept a double thickness of acetate film.

You can also use two separate rolls for feed and two separate rolls
for take-up with a camera that accepts a magazine. If it accepts an external magazine, and can also hold a one-hundred foot spool of film
within the body, like a Bolex H-5 or an Arri 16S, you may be able to use
feed and take-up spools within the body and magazine sections of the
camera.

Some filmmakers have tried a kind of bi-packing which is actually
tri-packing. They bi-pack two pieces of film with image together and
contact print it on a third piece of raw stock. You can ask the lab you use
if they will try this scheme for you. Bi-packing is a standard commercial
laboratory process in larger labs or houses that specialize in special
effects. Film is bi-packed in an optical printer, and the projected image
is copied on the camera half of the machine.

Traveling Mattes

Mattes are black and white high contrast films used to control the
portions of a frame allowed to print through on raw stock. For example,
if we have a matte of words, say the title of a film, it can be bi-packed
with the background scene to produce a printed image combining both.
This is probably the most frequent use of a lab's bi-packing optical
printer. If the letters were animated and shot on high contrast film, we'd
get animated letters superimposed on the background shot, which brings

us to the subject of traveling mattes. A matte which changes shape or moves from frame to frame is called a traveling matte. Hollywood uses this technique, and rear and front screen projection, to combine a physically unrelated foreground with a background.

For example, we want to photograph actors on the surface of Mars. In such a case, the foreground shot, with the actors working against a solid colored background, might be made with a special camera; while photographing the camera makes both a black and white, or color, film of the actors and the matte which will be used to add them to their background. In one scheme—and there are many—the background is lit with infrared light which is invisible to ordinary camera stock. The camera has a beam-splitter arrangement which allows it to make two images, on say ordinary color stock, and the other on infrared matte stock. The infrared stock will see the background and produce a silhouette with the actors against it. From this two kinds of mattes can be prepared, a matte which is solid where the actors stood and clear where they weren't and one which is clear where the actors were and black where the background was. One matte can be made from another by making a print on high contrast positive stock.

Now the background shot, the Martian landscape, is put into the optical printer, bi-packed with the matte of the actors which has them in solid black. It is printed on the raw stock which is afterward wound back. The shot with the actors next is bi-packed in the printer with the other matte, the matte that has the black background surrounding them. In this way the actors are exposed on the raw stock wherever the first matte held back their silhouette. In this way the actors and their background are combined. Cinema Research and Film Effects of Hollywood offer these techniques for the 16mm worker.

The most important thing to learn from this may not be the Hollywood application, which is almost always given away by telltale blue or black fringes or outlines, but rather applications you can extract for yourself. For example, if you can bi-pack film in your camera, or if your lab can do it in printing, you can make mattes of *wipes*—the transition from one shot to another in which the second one seems to wipe the other off the screen, usually with a vertical edge or a horizontal sweep—or other effects. Mattes of wipes are prepared and animated when shot on high contrast film. The complementary matte can be made by an optical print of the processed animation or by shooting two animated matte sections complementing each other. The subject is complex, allowing for all sorts of variations and, hopefully, innovations.

Aerial Image Printer
The aerial image printer is a special type of optical printer used for combining a drawn foreground with background action. It's most frequently used for adding lettering over a background, although it can be used for a variety of effects, including adding animated characters to a background. The drawing shows the arrangement of such a printer.

Independent Filmmaking

What we have, in effect, is a projector aiming its image directly into a camera. Unlike the standard optical printer, the aerial image printer has two lenses, one for the projector and one for the camera. In addition, an optical coupling device, a condenser lens system, is employed to allow the projector's image to be focused with the camera's lens.

In place of the condenser lens system we might have used a ground glass screen, in which case we'd have a setup that was exactly like that used in rear screen rephotography. The condenser obviates the need for a rear screen, with its attendant difficulties (fixed granular pattern, reduction in contrast, sharpness, etc.) and allows for the direct projection of the image on the film. Now there would be no point to all of this if we couldn't insert foreground subjects. Standard animation cells, known as Acme cells, can be placed with peg registration on a glass plate over the condenser lens system. On these celluloid sheets, titles or any animation can be drawn. The setup is worked out so that the background and the cells can be in focus. The printer uses two passes of film through the camera: the first pass exposes the raw stock to each projected frame. The animation cells are kept in place, or changed sequentially. On the second pass through the camera portion of the printer, the film is exposed to the cell or cells which are lit from the front. The projector portion is inoperative this time. This first pass through, or the first exposure, the cells serve as mattes to prevent exposure of areas of the frame where they will 'fill in' on the second pass. The cells can do this since they are opaque, and they precisely cut off the desired portions of the background frame. In effect, the cells are self-matting. Therefore foreground titles or animation can be added to background material which has been previously shot, with very little loss in background film quality.

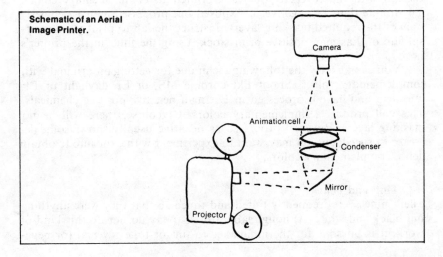

Schematic of an Aerial Image Printer.

Camera

Animation cell

Condenser

Mirror

Projector

Producing Negative Colors

Obtaining more or less pure complementary or negative colors is not as easy as it sounds. You might think you could put negative color camera stock into your camera, shoot, have it processed and that would be that. However, the generally available negative color camera stock is Eastmancolor, which is used to shoot Hollywood theatrical films; it is available in 16mm, but isn't used very much in this format.

This film has two built-in masking layers correcting the deficiencies of presently used dyes. Theoretically, in order to get good color photography from an integral tripack, we must have a material that will have three colored layers, each responding to a third of the visible spectrum. This could be accomplished with pure magenta, cyan and yellow dyes. But such dyes do not exist. Masking for negative color stock is a way of fudging the response of the dyes of two of the layers so they will be more nearly perfect. The masking layers give Eastman negative color original an overall orange cast. When printed on Eastman positive print stock, the orange is eliminated because the print stock is designed to produce natural colors when used with Eastmancolor camera film.

If you have some reversal stock and you want to get a negative, or a print with complementary colors without an orange mask, you cannot just print the reversal on Eastman positive color print stock which is designed to see the orange masking layers of Eastmancolor camera negative film. Without masking, it will print reversal stock with an overall orange tint. In order to *fool* the color print stock, a substitute orange mask must be provided. You can do this by using an unexposed and processed color negative to filter the printer's light. You can obtain the proper filter by processing unexposed 620 or 120 Kodacolor or Ektacolor still camera film. Give the resulting 2¼ x 2¼ square orange negative to the lab with the reversal you want printed to complementary colors. You'll note that the negative, unexposed but processed as it is, consists only of the required masking layers. Instruct the lab to print your reversal film on Eastman positive print stock, using the filter in the printer's head.

You can also try the following technique for getting an original with complementary colors. Shoot Ektachrome MS, or EF daylight or EF tungsten, and have it processed in Eastman negative-positive chemicals. This will produce complementary colors. Of course, there will be no masking layers. Reversal processed as negative usually shows some decrease in speed, so you may want to experiment with exposure to obtain dense complementary colors.

Tints and Tones

Silent films were frequently tinted and toned so that they were anything but black and white. Although laboratories today do not do this kind of work, it is possible for the filmmaker to tint or tone reversal (or nega-

Independent Filmmaking

tive) black and white camera film or prints. Color prints can then be made from these treated black and white originals.

There is a clear difference between tinting and toning which both involve immersing the film in a solution or solutions. What happens to the film in the bath itself becomes the difference between the processes: *tinting* is the use of a dye or a stain to color the gelatin of the emulsion, not the metallic silver itself. The effects you get from tinting are like those gotten from projecting your film through a color filter. A tinted black and white image is no longer black and white; it's black and the color of the tint. The blacks retain their black, and the tint stains or dyes the clear gelatin.

There are commercial tints on the market, but some of the best tinting I have seen was done with vegetable colors, bought in the supermarket. (We are indebted to Emory Menefee, PhD, of the U.S. Department of Agriculture for the work that he did in connection with vegetable dyes.) These inexpensive dyes may be purchased in large quantities from a baker's supply house. Vegetable dye tinting is acceptable for any method of film cleaning your lab may use. The dye becomes part of the emulsion and is impossible to remove, without removing the emulsion itself. For tinting relatively short lengths of film it is possible to apply the dye with a brush. Try using a water wash first, and then when the emulsion is thoroughly wet, brush on the dye.

For longer lengths you can choose among a number of methods. You can wrap the film on an easily constructed wooden cylindrical rack, and dip it into the dye; you also can thread the film on the reels of a processing tank. There are several inexpensive processing tanks available for twenty-five foot lengths (or longer) of double super 8, double 8mm or 16mm film. One is supplied by Superior Bulk Film Co., 442 N. Wells Street, Chicago, Illinois 60610. The reel can be threaded with your film, and then dunked in the tank or some other container filled with vegetable dye. Try a water rinse first, so that the tinting can be as even as possible. Dilute vegetable dye with water to obtain lighter tints, and you can mix the vegetable dyes for any imaginable color. The density of the color may also be regulated by the time the film is left in the dye. Obviously you can produce tints ranging from the subtle to the gross.

Although it is impossible to remove dye from the film once it's there, you can add to, or change, the color through successive dyings. For example, a yellow tint followed by blue would result in a green tint. The colors in *Off-On* (CCC, FMC) were produced with this tinting method.

Toning is something else. *Toning* is the coloring of the black and gray portions of a black and white film, without effect to the clear or lighter portions. What happens when a film is toned is essentially this: the molecules of the toner solution replace the metallic silver of the emulsion. A toned image is no longer black and white, but rather it can be described in terms of the toned color and white. For example, a red toned image is red and white, although the tones of red may run to very dense shades, so dense in fact that they might be described as seeming black in the deeper areas of the image.

There are a number of toners on the market, often available in the form of powders to be mixed with water. GAF (Ansco), Illford, Gevaert, DuPont and Kodak among them offer virtually any color toner you might need. Although these toners were specifically meant to be used with photographic printing paper, there is no reason why most or all of them won't work with your motion picture print or reversal camera film. Experiment before you try either to tint or tone important portions of the film.

Toning, like tinting, may be accomplished by winding the film on the reel of the developing tank, or dunking it into the solution any way you find convenient. Toning, in general, involves a more complex procedure than tinting, and may require second baths for fixing or redevelopment; also it's usually necessary to wash the film as part of the process. The instructions packed with the toner will tell you explicitly how long to leave the film in the bath or baths and so on. If you like to mix your own chemicals from formulas, or you would like to get more information about the processes and effects of individual toners, I suggest you consult the *Pocket Photo Data Book,* published by Morgan & Morgan, Inc, 25 Main Street, Hastings-on-Hudson, New York.

Toners yielding reds, sepia, blues, greens and so on are available. Tints and tones may be used in conjunction with each other. In the silent days this was frequently the case. For example, here's one simple-minded effect to get the idea across: suppose we have a shot of a boat sailing into the sunset. You could tint the shot red, and then tone it blue (it doesn't matter in which order you tint or tone). You'd then have a shot of the boat sailing into a red sunset, on blue water.

One interesting variation is to retone the image. After the first tone has been added, you can, in some cases, add a second tone which will work on the areas of metallic silver remaining in the emulsion.

Drawing on Film

A comprehensive article about drawing on film could run to many pages, more than I can include here. Anybody interested in the subject should be motivated enough to do further research. I'd like to thank Stan Brakhage, Barry Spinello and Emory Menefee for sharing with me many of their *secrets* to in turn share with you.

The Medium

It's necessary to have something on which to draw. A lot of work is done with 16mm, but you can even work in 8mm or super 8. Obviously, you can get greater control the larger the available area. Some people work in 35mm and make 16mm reduction prints. Clear leader, coated on one side with a gelatin emulsion, is a good medium for accepting many types of drawing material. It can be purchased from the lab.

You can draw or paint over already exposed shots, embellishing them as you please. Fine examples of this are Brakhage's *The Art of Vision* (FMC, CCC) and Carolee Schneeman's *Fuses.* You can scrape

away the emulsion of processed film or black leader and paint through
that.

Adding and Subtracting

You can add image, by drawing and painting, or you can subtract image through scraping and bleaching.

The following materials are used to add image — acetate inks, blooping ink, vegetable dyes and whatever you run across you think would be fun. I should say here that materials you can use to draw or paint on film fall into two categories: those which are permanent, and those which will dissolve in the lab's cleaning solutions used before printing. If you are not concerned with making prints, you don't have to worry about your tones and colors coming off in the lab's cleaning solution — usually some organic solvent like inhibited methyl chloroform or Freon-113. Of course you will have to worry about whether or not any material lasts through projection and normal handling. Stay away from India ink, because it cracks and peels, unless you like an interesting cracked and peeling effect.

The simplest way to remove a photographic image from film is to scrape it off. It helps to moisten the film first, or you can chemically remove the image. Preparations for the controlled removal of image, called reducers, are sold in photography stores. If you want to make a clean sweep of it, try a liquid chlorine bleach like Clorox. Once you've removed the image, you can, of course, paint or draw over it.

Frame-by-Frame or Continuous Painting

In general, for these effects you can use two approaches, which are not mutually exclusive. One would be to work each frame and produce a kind of animation not unlike that found in animated cartoons. Another approach would be to paint across many feet of film at a time, in a continuous operation. Both can be very beautiful. Some really fine work using both approaches has been done by the poet Harry Smith (FMC). You can use any sort of drawing instrument that suits your purpose: pens, brushes, cloths, sponges, your fingers or whatever works.

Appliqués

Another class of materials that you can use for adding image to film I'll call appliqués, and consist of tapes, Zip-o-tone shading sheets and Press-apply lettering. Some startling and beautiful images can be derived from using press-apply lettering or a shading sheet. Barry Spinello uses these in his work. Another interesting method for applying an image which I suppose isn't strictly speaking an appliqué, is the use of rubber stamps.

Sound Tracks

It is possible also to draw your own optical sound tracks. Spinello in his film, Sound Track (FMC, CCC), has done some of the most advanced work of this kind using shading sheets to obtain varied sounds. Spinello applies Zip-o-tone sheets to the sound track area of the 16mm format. Different patterns, there are dozens, produce different tones. Sheets with small dots closely spaced give higher frequencies, and those with larger dots lower frequencies.

Projection

Projection is often out of the hands of the filmmaker, but when the film-maker can control projection, he can make sure it is as good as conditions will allow. Ideally, films should be projected in a room with a sloping floor and good acoustics. A sloping floor, one that is higher at the projection end and lower at the screen end, will afford better viewing for almost the whole audience, especially those in the middle and rear. Good acoustics, obviously, will make the sound track seem as full and rich as possible, without adding too much reverberation. The usual problem with projection of sound motion picture films is that the spoken word is rendered unintelligible because of excessive reverberation or poor speaker placement. I'll take up the problems of image and sound separately.

Automatic Projectors

The first requisite toward a good image is having a decent projector. As far as the audience is concerned, wear and tear on film is of no consequence, but since this is a book for filmmakers by a filmmaker let me warn you against an entire class of 16mm projectors. I have nothing against automatic threading, in theory; in fact I like it, when it works well. But automatic threading 16mm projectors are, in general, murder on film. Now there may be a good automatic threading machine on the market, or the machines I am familiar with may have been mavericks, but they all contributed toward any or all of the following problems: torn film if the loop is lost, torn film if operated in reverse and extraordinarily excessive wear and tear on the film.

The 16mm automatic projector craze undoubtedly was motivated by

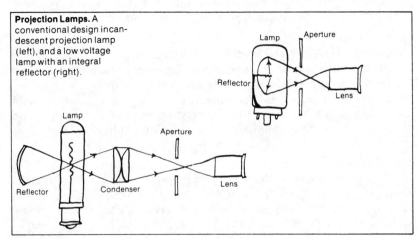

Projection Lamps. A conventional design incandescent projection lamp (left), and a low voltage lamp with an integral reflector (right).

the desire to provide a machine for those considered too incompetent to thread a projector properly. Since the major market for 16mm projectors is probably the audio-visual school field, I'd say that the manufacturers understood the problem correctly, but failed to solve it adequately.

The many available 8mm and super 8 projector models, on the other hand, generally feature good automatic threading schemes.

Brightness and Throw

The first demand on the projected image is that it be bright enough for the screen size. People are often heard talking about how dim an image you get if the *throw* (distance from projector to screen) is long. Distance from the projector to the screen, however, is not the important factor. If the image fills the same size screen, with a lens of any focal length, with the same *f* number, the image will have the same brightness. An $f/2$ fifty millimeter (2 inch) projection lens projecting on a forty-inch wide screen with a throw of about eighteen feet, produces an image which is just as bright as that projected by an $f/2$ one hundred millimeter lens with a throw of about thirty-five feet. Similarly, a three-foot focal length lens, with an $f/2$ aperture, projecting on a forty-inch wide screen at a distance of more than half a mile will be just as bright, assuming the same projector and illumination source in all three cases, and not accounting for intervening haze.

The total brightness of the image is a function not only of the speed of the projection lens, but of the speed of the entire projection optical system. Some projectors will give measurably brighter images if a faster lens is used; in others a lens a full stop faster won't register any more light on the screen.

Illumination sources fall, broadly speaking, into two categories: tungsten and arc lamps. Conventional tungsten lamps, usually cylindrical in shape, come in ratings from about 500 to 1200 watts. The higher

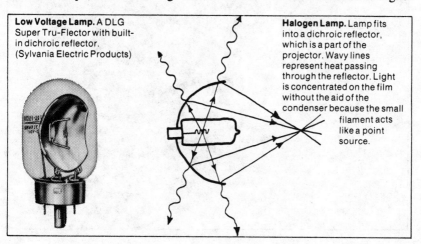

Low Voltage Lamp. A DLG Super Tru-Flector with built-in dichroic reflector. (Sylvania Electric Products)

Halogen Lamp. Lamp fits into a dichroic reflector, which is a part of the projector. Wavy lines represent heat passing through the reflector. Light is concentrated on the film without the aid of the condenser because the small filament acts like a point source.

wattage rated lamps are brighter, but very much hotter. Conventional tungsten lamps require a reflector and a condenser system.

A newer type of tungsten lamp is the *low voltage lamp,* often made with an integral dichroic reflector. The reflector is sometimes part of the back of the lamp envelope itself. These lamps usually do not need a condenser system and while running cooler can produce as much illumination as high wattage conventional tungsten lamps. The dichroic reflector allows passage of heat rays, while reflecting only visible light. Light coming directly from the lamp filament, and not reflected, will still be rich in heat rays; but a dichroic reflector goes a long way toward reducing the amount of heat incident on film.

Because 16mm has about four times the area of the smaller formats, it has a decided brightness advantage. This means, all things being equal, that it can put an image four times as bright on the screen.

Arc Lamp Projector. Bell & Howell Model 566 uses Marc 300 lamp. The projector sits on the power supply for the lamp. If you're interested in arc projection, xenon arc may be a better choice with much lower operating costs per hour. (Bell & Howell)

Independent Filmmaking

Another type of tungsten lamp is the *quartz* or *halogen lamp*. It contains halogen gas which, by keeping metallic ions off the transparent envelope and recirculating them back on the filament, tends to prevent blackening of the lamp. These lamps, giving very good results with relatively long life, are used in a number of 8mm and super 8 machines.

A great jump in brightness occurs when we shift to arc projection systems. Three types, desirable for large screens, are in use: GE Marc 300 lamps, xenon arc lamps and carbon arcs. Although the Marc 300 and xenon arcs are used primarily for 16mm projection (carbon arcs are still most prevalent for 35mm and 70mm projection), I expect that super 8 machines using the Marc 300 or something like it will be soon available.

The *Marc 300* is roughly three to four times brighter than a 1000-watt tungsten lamp and, since it uses only 300 watts, it operates much cooler. Moreover, the image is bluer, more nearly like that of daylight, and this contributes greatly to the apparent brightness and crispness of the image. The Marc 300, however, requires a special power supply to get it going and keep it running.

Xenon arc lamps can be brighter than the Marc 300 with power ratings from about 300 to 2000 watts. Fairly elaborate equipment is necessary to run the xenon arc: each xenon arc lamp requires a special rectifier for its wattage. While many projectors in production were converted to Marc 300 use by the manufacturer—because of the lamp's small size and cool running—xenon projectors usually require special designs to accommodate the lamp.

The *carbon arc*, the first commercially used method of electric illumination (for street lights), is still with us. An electric arc jumps across the short space between two carbon electrodes, producing intense light and heat. Carbon arcs are sometimes found on 16mm projectors designed for theatrical use. They require a special high voltage power supply and a good cooling system. Carbon arc light is about the color temperature of daylight.

The Screen

Any screen receives the same incident illumination from the projector; it's what it does with the light that counts. The narrower the concentration of the reflected rays, the brighter the screen. As the angle of brightness acceptable to the audience narrows, the image brightness within that angle increases. Depending upon brightness requirements and the width of your environment, there are several types of screens you can use.

The *matte* screen reflects light evenly in all directions and is the best choice for very bright projection in a wide screening room. The next choice, and probably the best in most circumstances, is the *lenticular* screen, made up of a series of small cylindrical lenses embossed on the surface of the screen. It is very bright over a fairly broad angle of viewing. The *beaded* screen is coated with glass beads that reflect the light in a tighter angle than the lenticular screen. It may be just right for a narrower hall. It is somewhat less expensive than the lenticular and, before the introduction of the lenticular, it was the screen found in most living rooms.

Next, we have *silver* screens, essentially matte screens coated or painted with metallic aluminum. These screens can only be used for very narrow viewing angles, but they are extremely bright within that angle. This is the preferred screen for stereo projection using polarizing filters, since within the viewing angle the screen will not depolarize the light. Depolarization of the dual images of stereo projection would result in double or ghost images. Another screen, Eastman Kodak's *Ektalight,* makes viewing possible under fairly bright ambient light conditions, within a narrow angle.

Projection Lenses

The most common flaw that projection lenses exhibit is curvature of field which results in fuzzy corners if the central portion of the image is in sharp focus, and vice versa. One cure for a lens with this defect is to stop it down. It really won't cure the curvature of field, but it will increase the depth of field and thereby mask the lens' inadequacy; this, however, results in sacrificing image brightness. In recent years manufacturers have, for the most part, corrected this lens difficulty.

Most projected images will vary half a stop to a full stop from the center to the corner of the image. This fall-off toward the corners of the screen is attributable to the entire optical system of the projector, and not just the lens. A variation of half a stop is entirely unnoticeable.

Zoom lenses for projection are coming into their own, especially for 8mm and super 8 machines. They are very convenient to use, since placement of the screen and projector becomes less critical. Moreover, for super 8-8mm convertible projectors, the zoom lens allows the 8mm image to be zoomed to fill up the screen, without moving the projector

Screen Size. Chart correlates format, focal length, distance and screen size. (Eastman Kodak)

Film Size and Type	Lens Focal Length	Desired Screen-Image Width 40″	50″	60″	70″
		Projection Distance (Feet—to nearest ½ foot)			
8mm	¾ inch	14½	18	21	26
	28mm	21½	26½	32	37½
	zoom (20-32mm)	15½-24½	19-30½	23-37	26½-43
	22mm	17	21	25	29
	zoom (15-25mm)	11½-19	14½-24	17-29	20-33
Super 8	28mm	17½	22	26	30½
	zoom(20-32mm)	12½-20	15½-25	18½-30	21½-35
	22mm	14	17	21	24
16mm	1½ inch	13	16½	20	23
	1⅝ inch	14	17½	21	24½
	2 inch	17½	22	26½	31
	2½ inch	22	27½	33	38½
	3 inch	26½	33	40	46½
	4 inch	35½	44	53	61½

farther back. At this stage of the art, the best fixed focal length lenses have better overall quality than the best zoom lenses, even though there are some good quality zoom lenses on the market.

One question often asked by people who are planning fixed installations, or even those of us who are planning to buy a projector and screen for the home, is: what focal length lens will fill a given screen size at a given distance? There are tables that present this information, but by using a reflex camera with a zoom lens, you will be able to figure out the focal length lens you need for a given size screen and throw. Set up your camera where the projector ought to be, and view the screen, or something representing the proposed screen. Then zoom until the screen fills the viewfinder. Read the required focal length off your lens mount.

Sound

Some sound projectors have a built-in speaker. Such a speaker must be limited in size and, of course, it produces sounds coming from the rear or behind the audience. It's best to use the built-in speaker when nothing else is available. Most films are made by the filmmaker with the thought in mind that sound will come from the same direction as the screen.

Whether or not the projector has a built-in speaker, or a small PA speaker in the cover, you can obtain better sound with different speakers. Some of the best sound track reproduction I have heard has been through home hi-fidelity units — both amplifier and speakers. I have also heard very good sound in fairly large halls, accommodating several hundred people, when these kinds of components are used.

Many projectors have an output for an auxiliary amplifier. This takes the audio signal from some early stage of amplification and makes it available to the auxiliary amplifier. This is preferable to obtaining the signal from the projector's speaker output, since the less the pro-

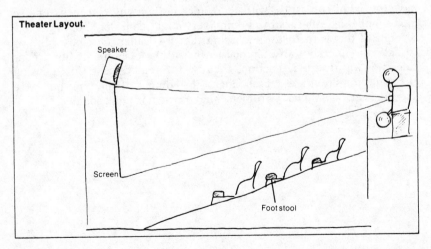

Theater Layout.

Speaker

Screen

Footstool

Mixed Bag

jection amplifier has to do with the sound, the better the final result. You can get good sound in either case, providing your amplifier has the proper impedance input to match the projector's output.

You may want to avoid the use of the low efficiency hi-fidelity speakers which probably will require the use of an external amplifier. In such a case use high efficiency hi-fidelity speakers that can operate comfortably with the projector's amplifier alone.

Besides tone and volume controls found on most projectors, some older models, Kodak machines especially, have one additional control that contributes to quality optical sound. The track, depending upon the master material from which the print was made, might be on the side of the film facing the screen or away from the screen. Prints are distributed with the emulsion in projection position either away from or toward the screen. The projectionist can correctly focus the image for either position simply by focusing the lens. For best sound reproduction, particularly for best high frequency response, the optical system of the sound head should also be focused to accommodate the proper emulsion position. Usually the optical sound system's focus is fixed and set at some intermediate compromise position.

I should say a word about speaker placement. It's important. Get the speakers up from the floor. Just placing the speaker or speakers on a chair will go a long way toward improving overall sound. If you're dealing with installed speakers, you're likely to find they're placed high.

Setting Up

If your temperament allows, it might be nice to set things up before the group arrives to look at the films. You'll want to do such basic things as threading the projector, setting the proper sound level, the tone controls and focusing the image. Setting the sound level and tone controls for an empty room can be tricky. After it's filled with people the acoustical properties may be different. Focusing is often a big drag because the timed leader usually provided is nearly useless for focusing. You have to sort of run a race with the leader hoping you can focus on the next number as it flashes by. Filmmakers might consider shooting a few seconds of the word *focus,* and using that for leader. One possibility is to have the first shot an easy one to focus, like opening credits. I consider this an absurd restriction, because the requirements for focusing the projector should be subservient to the content of the film; but since focusing can be a difficult problem, the idea is not unreasonable.

Video for the Filmmaker

This chapter is written for filmmakers who want to use video. It is not intended as a primer for video production, although portions of earlier chapters in this book, having to do with optics, camera movements and sound, for example, are all directly translatable to video. I intend this to be a basic orientation to the art, so that along with certain fundamental concepts, some practical information about how video cameras work, how film-to-tape transfers work and so on will be given to the film-maker-reader.

The rise of video as a means of creative expression for the independent is clearly linked to the advances in technology in small-format video tape recorders (VTR's). At one time that meant machines using tape less than two inches wide. Now it means tape formats under an inch wide.

Video camera technology has advanced steadily along with advances in microelectronics, and improvements in the efficiency of VTR's and the recording medium itself, magnetic tape. Still, restricted to a specified bandwidth, the video image isn't any better than a good quality super 8 original camera film image projected on the same-size screen. I say this without recourse to calculations of any kind, or any sort of theoretical mumbo jumbo. The literature is filled with scientific-appearing charts telling us that the present video picture is on a par with 16mm imaging technology. This is clear foolishness. A good quality print of a 16mm film can be projected on theater-size screens, producing an exceedingly high quality image. The same cannot be said of a video image restricted to the approximately 4.2 MHz (megahertz) bandwidth standard in this country for broadcast.

However the case may be put by video optimists, the lowliest film technology can equal or exceed video quality when we talk about pictorial image parameters such as color fidelity, sharpness, background noise, gradation, exposure latitude and so forth. This is such an obvious truth that I can only wonder at what inspires people to write off film technology while praising the coming of the video god.

This is not to say that video may not someday equal film's pictorial quality. It probably will. For another thing, there's nothing wrong with well-presented video at this very moment. Video has its own unique qualities, and the medium should be appreciated for these things. The video image stands up on its own. If it weren't for the inferiority complex that hovers over video, it would be possible to appreciate video for what it is, and not simply in terms of comparisons to film.

Lately video paranoia has taken a new turn. To some observers it may seem like the glow of enlightenment. Now video people are talking about *electronic cinematography* and the *film look*. New cameras, particularly by Panavision and Ikegami, have come along boasting of the film look. What could be more difficult for video to live up to? The film look, indeed! Video needs to perfect the *video* look. This is a case in which the medium's friends are doing it more harm than its detractors.

Independent Filmmaking

Camera for Electronic Cinematography. The Ikegami EC-35, designed for tripod or on the shoulder. An outfit will cost about $100,000, about the same price as some 35mm movie cameras. (Cinema Products)

Nevertheless, film does provide certain technical advantages over video-produced footage when transferred to video. It can act as a buffer or kind of filter to interface or modulate the image to make it more suitable for video transmission. Various spurious aspects of video pickup devices, such as image-streaking or comet-tailing, are not present in film, and film has a longer scale of gradation or lower contrast, producing more detail in highlights and shadows. Film has a seven to eight stop scale of luminance, while video has a four or five stop luminance ratio.

Evaluation of whether or not a project should be carried out in film or video can be an interesting voyage into the Twilight Zone. It's possible to argue yourself blue in the face trying to justify one or the other. It's much better to know the answer in advance and then justify your position. Although film stock and processing is more costly than tape, tape hardware can be as costly or more costly than film equipment. Certainly the intended distribution of film or tape is very important. If you're working for a client, what does he want? Usually, that's the most important factor in any commercial project.

Much more could be said in the context of selection of a medium to do a particular job. The human mind, fantastic nit-picking instrument that it is, doesn't need any further comment from me.

The Pickup Tube

The film image is recorded on a single frame in an *integrated* fashion; that is, every portion of the image is recorded simultaneously. The video image is recorded in what might be called a *differentiated*, or *dissected*, fashion, point for point over a period of time. Although film uses fresh emulsion area for each frame, the video pickup device uses the same fixed light-sensitive surface frame after frame. Because of this the history of one frame affects

Video for the Filmmaker

the next, leading to certain defects in the video image which are not present in film. This incomplete erasure of successive frames can, for example, produce comet tails of bright lights if the camera is panned.

The TV camera, schematically represented here, is made up of a lens, a photosensitive surface and an electron gun. An electron beam, located within an evacuated glass envelope, scans the light-sensitive surface. Generally, the light-sensitive surface is either photoconductive or photo-emissive. Some metals, like cesium, silver, potassium and lithium, emit electrons when struck by photons—in other words, light. Other metals, like selenium or tellurium, change their resistance, or ability to conduct current, when struck with photons. The more light, the less resistance.

We can get a feel for how a light-sensitive surface might be made up of metals which are either photoemissive or photoconductive. The scanning electron beam strikes the rear surface of the target of a photosensitive surface. Light projected on the front surface, in the form of an image of objects, then serves to modulate, point for image point, in terms of density, an electrical signal produced by the scanning electron beam.

The electron beam itself is steered by magnetic or electrostatic deflection yokes to form an engraving-like pattern called the raster. We'll discuss the nature of the raster and its relationship to the video image shortly.

The reader will understand that we have presented here a greatly abbreviated account of how a TV imaging device works. Brief and incomplete as it may be, it is better to know a little about a complex subject than nothing, and in this and the forthcoming discussions I hope to at least impart a feeling for what can be an absorbingly complex subject.

The sort of camera, or image-forming system, we've sketched here, is in some ways similar to a motion picture camera. Obviously both cameras use lenses to form images on light-sensitive surfaces. But there the similarity stops. Video cameras don't have shutters, and they don't have a

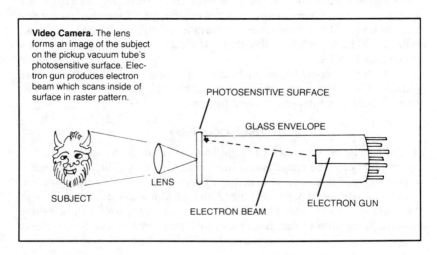

Video Camera. The lens forms an image of the subject on the pickup vacuum tube's photosensitive surface. Electron gun produces electron beam which scans inside of surface in raster pattern.

PHOTOSENSITIVE SURFACE

GLASS ENVELOPE

SUBJECT

LENS

ELECTRON BEAM

ELECTRON GUN

Independent Filmmaking

moving ribbon of film transported through their innards in an intermittent fashion.

The pickup tube we've described here is called the *vidicon*. It is the design basis of all modern CRT pickup devices, such as the Saticon and Plubicon, which have greater sensitivity, color response and other improvements. Most of the tubes in use today have a 2/3-inch picture diagonal, which is about the same size as the diagonal of the 16mm format. Therefore, lenses of approximately the same focal lengths are used for 2/3-inch vidicon-type tubes and 16mm film. In an attempt to scale down the size of the video camera, designers have begun to use new 1/2-inch diagonal tubes. These new low lag Saticon tubes have very high performance, and probably represent the last efforts at pickup tube design innovation, since tubes are bound to be replaced by solid state pickup devices in the next few years.

We will now turn our attention to how a color video camera works. The camera we have described here is monochromatic. It is possible to overlay stripes of color filters, like the additive color Polavision process or the older Dufay or Autocolor systems, on the surface of a single tube's light-sensitive surface. This is the technique that is used for some consumer cameras, and also for some professional cameras, especially those which must be used in tight quarters and for medical or scientific imaging.

As of today, the best quality color video cameras use a different additive color scheme. I should pause for a moment and explain that most modern color processes, like the Ektachrome films or Eastman color negative materials, are classed as subtractive films, and this technology is explained in some detail in chapter 2, under How Color Film Works. Practically speaking, subtractive color in modern color films works by having three layers of color dye sandwiched together, each filtering, or subtracting, a portion of the white light passing through the film for projection.

Additive color, which is the basis for video systems, depends upon, in

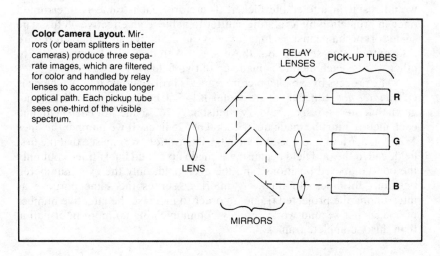

Color Camera Layout. Mirrors (or beam splitters in better cameras) produce three separate images, which are filtered for color and handled by relay lenses to accommodate longer optical path. Each pickup tube sees one-third of the visible spectrum.

RELAY LENSES   PICK-UP TUBES   R   G   B   LENS   MIRRORS

Video for the Filmmaker

the final display device (usually a cathode ray tube), three adjacent glowing phosphor elements: a red, a green and a blue—sometimes called a triad. The final perceived color depends upon the relative brightness of each phosphor of the triad, which are added together by the eye.

The camera pickup device, our concern here, strongly resembles the early Technicolor camera, which was made up of beam splitters and three separate rolls of black and white film. A frame of each roll was simultaneously exposed. The drawing for the video camera shows how a three-tube ensemble can be arranged to produce the red, blue and green signals needed for a color image.

This configuration is the basis for most good quality studio and field cameras. The design is relatively complex, and it requires precision optical alignment and electronic calibration.

The Raster

The rectangle, whose aspect ratio is 1.3:1, scanned by the electron beam in both the camera and (as we shall see) receiver or monitor, is called the *raster*. The beam must be deflected both horizontally and vertically, so that it covers the complete area of the rectangle. In the United States, a protocol for encoding the video signal was developed and codified by the National Television Standard Committee (NTSC). We will discuss aspects of that protocol. In one second there are a total of 15,750 scanned lines. These lines, carrying the density, color and positional information of the image projected by the camera lens onto the light-sensitive surface or surfaces, are ordered into sixty fields per second. (This number was selected to correspond with the 60 Hz AC current used in the United States.)

For motion pictures, twenty-four frames are photographed and projected each second. Upon projection, each frame is broken up into two projected parts by an interrupting shutter, in order to eliminate flicker. Although 24 fps is adequate for smooth motion, projecting only 24 fps would result in intolerable flicker. Therefore, each frame is interrupted once in projection by a rotating shutter to achieve an effective 48 fps. The same sort of thing must be done for television. Thirty complete pictures are transmitted each second, but these are broken down into sixty fields. In other words, each picture is made up of two fields.

The process by which a picture frame is broken down into two fields is called *interlace*. Since there are a total of 15,750 lines scanned each second, given that there are sixty fields, we must have 262½ lines for each field, and each picture must be made up of a total of 525 lines. If we number the lines 1, 2, 3, 4, 5, 6 and so on, as shown in the illustration, we can see that the first field, called the odd field because it is made up of odd lines, traces out only the odd-numbered positions, and the even field, only the even-numbered positions for lines. In this way interlace serves the same purpose as interrupting the projected frame, in order to increase the effective number of images per second while actually communicating no more information than thirty complete frames.

Independent Filmmaking

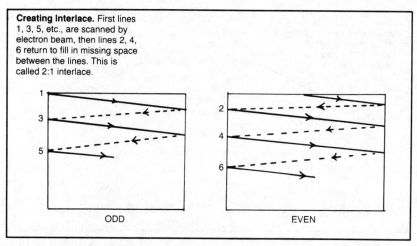

Creating Interlace. First lines 1, 3, 5, etc., are scanned by electron beam, then lines 2, 4, 6 return to fill in missing space between the lines. This is called 2:1 interlace.

ODD   EVEN

The electron beam for the camera is driven by oscillators to follow the carefully controlled interlace scanning pattern. The electron beam writing the raster in the monitor or receiver must follow a similar pattern when creating the image.

The reader will understand that it takes some finite time for the scanned beam to move from the end of one line horizontally to the start of the next. This retrace time is called *horizontal blanking,* because the electron beam's current is reduced to a minimum during retrace to avoid writing a spurious line on the face of the CRT.

The same type of thing must be done in order to move the beam from the bottom of the raster, after the final line of a field has been scanned, back to the top of the raster to begin the scanning of the new field. The time of vertical retrace is called the *vertical blanking* period, and about twenty-one lines are lost from each field while the vertical retrace takes place. You might think of the vertical blanking area as a sort of frame line between fields.

Taking a look at the illustration of a composite video signal, we see three distinct portions: the camera signal, the horizontal blanking area and the vertical blanking area. This schematic representation is what you'd see on a properly adjusted oscilloscope, but there are features left out of the signal for the sake of simplification. For example, I haven't discussed sync pulses, which are added to the horizontal and vertical blanking areas, and serve a function analogous to motion picture film perforations. The sync pulses help keep camera, recorder and monitor video lines and fields in sync. We are also not going to discuss the picture carrier signal as it is modulated by the composite video signal. The composite video signal, or, as it is sometimes known, the direct video signal, can be used for closed-circuit transmission of video; but for broadcast, a radio frequency (RF) signal must be created which can be transmitted and then received.

The video signal as described here is known as an *analog signal.*

Video for the Filmmaker

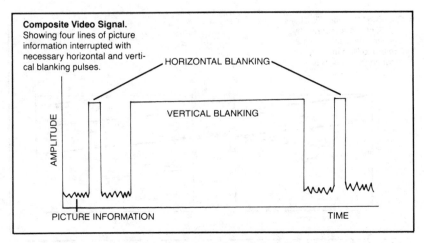

Composite Video Signal. Showing four lines of picture information interrupted with necessary horizontal and vertical blanking pulses.

HORIZONTAL BLANKING

VERTICAL BLANKING

AMPLITUDE

PICTURE INFORMATION   TIME

Voltage in the picture information portion of the signal is proportional to, point for point or line by line, density of picture information. But as we shall see, this technique using voltage analogous to picture density is not the only way the video signal can be treated or encoded.

The Monitor or Receiver

In video parlance a receiver has a tuner, and is used for receiving television images broadcast from a station. Receivers are found in people's homes. Monitors, on the other hand, are used for closed-circuit operation, and are generally of higher quality than receivers. There is a marketing trend these days in the direction of video components, using a sales approach similar to high-fidelity equipment marketing. You can buy a monitor, a separate tuner, separate speakers and so forth.

People who are involved with video often purchase a good quality monitor so they can easily play back and observe their work originating in composite video form. Receivers are usually designed to accept only a radio frequency (broadcast) signal rather than a direct or composite signal. But recorders, cameras and disk players all put out direct or composite video, which has to be turned into radio frequency or a modulated picture carrier signal so that the receiver can display the image.

That's not the way to go if you can help it. You'll get a better quality image, with less noise, that's sharper and more pleasing, if you can avoid turning your composite video into RF—if you can use straight composite video instead. One less step of signal processing can add quality.

The heart of the monitor, or maybe the eye, is the *cathode ray tube,* or *CRT.* CRT's are a well-developed technology, and have remained the dominant video display technique. Although it is bound to be replaced by flat panel-type displays, using low voltage, low power and solid state components of one sort or another, the millenium has not arrived and we still have the CRT, alive, well and living all over the world in hundreds of

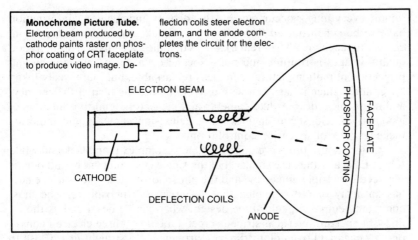

Monochrome Picture Tube. Electron beam produced by cathode paints raster on phosphor coating of CRT faceplate to produce video image. De-flection coils steer electron beam, and the anode completes the circuit for the electrons.

ELECTRON BEAM

PHOSPHOR COATING

FACEPLATE

CATHODE

DEFLECTION COILS

ANODE

millions of television sets. A replacement for it in the marketplace has yet to be seen, and remains a glimmer in the eye of the inventor.

The drawing shows a schematic cross-section of a CRT picture tube display device used for monochrome, as they say in videoland, or black and white, as they say in movieland. The picture tube performs the inverse function of the camera pickup tube, by turning the action of electrons into light. The cathode produces a beam of electrons which scans the inner surface of an evacuated glass bottle. The wall of the bottle on the side directly opposite the cathode is coated with phosphors which, when excited or hit by the electrons, emit light. The more energy the electrons have, the more light. The electron beam paints the image, line for line, creating the interlaced raster. The position of the beam is in synchronization with the beam within the pickup tube CRT.

Point by point, line by line, the image is written across the phosphor face of the picture tube. It's a remarkable process, when you consider how

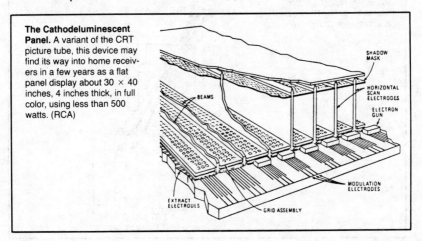

The Cathodeluminescent Panel. A variant of the CRT picture tube, this device may find its way into home receivers in a few years as a flat panel display about 30 × 40 inches, 4 inches thick, in full color, using less than 500 watts. (RCA)

SHADOW MASK

HORIZONTAL SCAN ELECTRODES

ELECTRON GUN

BEAMS

MODULATION ELECTRODES

EXTRACT ELECTRODES

GRID ASSEMBLY

Video for the Filmmaker

rapidly everything is occurring, and that density and positional information have to be synchronized throughout a complex transmission chain from camera to receiver. What's remarkable is that the transmission of such good quality images is routine, and not a special event. The photography and projection of motion pictures is no less remarkable, but more easily taken for granted, since it has been with us from before the turn of the century, and mechanical devices like cameras and projectors tend to remind us of locomotives and steam engines while television cameras and monitors make us think of spaceship control rooms.

Color picture tubes are quite a bit more complex than black and white tubes. Basically they are similar, but the single electron gun, or cathode, is replaced by a triple-gun array, and the phosphor-coated inner surface now has an array of red (R), blue (B) and green (G) phosphors. The most commonly employed color tube design, what can be described as the in-line, slit aperture, vertical-striped screen tube, uses three electron guns— one for each additive color primary—arranged in a straight line. Close to the striped phosphor screen is a thin metal mask with slits cut in it. These slits serve to aim the red gun beam at the red phosphor stripes, the blue gun at the blue stripes and the green gun at the green stripes.

If all three stripes are excited in a specified manner, the result is a white light. If none are excited, the result is black. Excite green and red in the proper proportions and you'll get yellow.

The idea of using an aperture to mask the unwanted electron beams and properly aim the wanted one was first used by RCA in their shadow mask tube, in which round holes are cut into the aperture mask and the guns (the delta gun design) are aligned 120 degrees apart on the circumference of a circle. The screen has circles of RGB phosphor, and one unit—made up of an R, a G and a B phosphor—is called a triad.

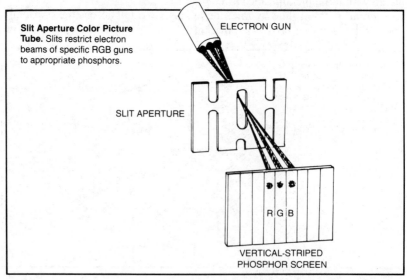

Slit Aperture Color Picture Tube. Slits restrict electron beams of specific RGB guns to appropriate phosphors.

ELECTRON GUN

SLIT APERTURE

R G B

VERTICAL-STRIPED PHOSPHOR SCREEN

Independent Filmmaking

Another popular type of tube was developed by Sony from a basic idea by Lawrence, the inventor of the cyclotron. It's very similar to the slit aperture tube and also uses a vertical-striped screen.

The Video Projector

The most widely used video projector designs are possible because of an ingenious projection scheme based on telescope optics and a high-gain screen originally perfected by Kodak for slides and movies. The drawing shows the design of the projection tube, which closely resembles the Schmidt mirror telescope. The CRT faceplate is at the focus of the mirror, shown in cross section here. The light reflected by the mirror passes through a correction lens, and then through a color filter. An ensemble of three tubes is used, projecting images in coincidence. These are black and white tubes, with red, green and blue filters mounted over each. The resultant additive color mixture gives the desired result.

A necessary ingredient in the system is a high-gain screen. Originally many of these were made under license of Kodak, who invented the first successful form of a modern super-bright screen. Now various other manufacturers make improved versions of high-gain screens for video projection.

Video projectors, with screens running from something like three feet to seven feet (or more) wide, are now a commonplace consumer item, and a standard means for displaying video works shown to audiences. Really large screen projection, based on technologies developed by General Electric and others, is also available.

The front screen projection-type consumer display has an interesting variant, the rear screen projector. Housed in a cabinet, the image is projected onto a rear screen. These rear screen materials have been greatly improved in recent years, and both front and rear screen devices are free from annoying hot spots, while both types have a relatively limited, although adequate, viewing zone.

From my observation the front screen projectors still have a quality edge, and are available in larger screen sizes.

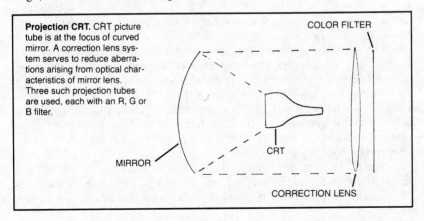

Projection CRT. CRT picture tube is at the focus of curved mirror. A correction lens system serves to reduce aberrations arising from optical characteristics of mirror lens. Three such projection tubes are used, each with an R, G or B filter.

COLOR FILTER

MIRROR

CRT

CORRECTION LENS

Video for the Filmmaker

Good quality color television was introduced in the United States in the early fifties in its modern form, an invention of RCA known as NTSC (National Television Standard Committee) color. The other systems in use, PAL (Phase Alternation Line) and SECAM (Sequential Color with Memory), in various parts of the world are variations on the basic NTSC concept and have been chosen as much for political as technical reasons. Unfortunately there is no worldwide television standard either for color encoding or field rate, or number of lines per field.

Color video broadcast systems are compatible with black and white transmission. In order to do this a good deal of work on the nature of color perception had to be undertaken. It was discovered that for two out of the three primary colors it was acceptable to transmit low resolution signals. This additional color, or *chrominance,* information is transmitted along with the *luminance* signal, which is essentially the black and white signal combined with the green signal.

Simply put, the low resolution chrominance signal modulates a portion of the video signal, called the *color subcarrier,* and a higher resolution luminance signal is broadcast as usual. These signals are then decoded in the receiver and displayed on the picture tube.

Color film uses three separate channels, one for each primary color. Color film uses the subtractive system, and the primaries are magenta, cyan and yellow—unlike additive color video, which uses red, green and blue for primaries. Nevertheless, three primaries would usually require the use of three separate channels. For color film these channels are layered, or sandwiched, one on top of the other in integral tripack films. But color video cannot be broadcast this way since certain specific frequencies were allotted for the transmission of television. Each channel has a bandwidth of about 6 MHz. (Picture information is restricted to about 4 MHz, but additional room is required for sound and to help isolate one channel from another to avoid interference.) To transmit a full RGB signal would cut the available channels to one-third of the present number. Hence, the motivation to develop a system like the NTSC system, which would take advantage of perceptual and electronic tricks to produce a pleasing image within the existing bandwidth.

The system of encoding the color information for broadcast is sometimes called colorplexing, an abridgement of the words *color multiplexing.* The chrominance information (the limited resolution B and R) is encoded as phase information at 3.58 MHz in the picture signal. The relative proportions of the colors encoded in the luminance and chrominance signals are determined by algebraic formula, and then separated out at the receiver so that each electron gun—the R, the G and the B—will be driven by its appropriate color signal.

The NTSC system of color, like the PAL and SECAM systems, is a fantastically complicated method for encoding color information. It's beyond the scope of this book to discuss these systems in any detail;

however, a few more comments ought to be made before passing on to other
topics.

While the NTSC system used in North America and other countries uses phase information to encode color, the PAL and SECAM systems do not. Phase distortion, because of difficulties in transmission, is fairly common. Therefore, color errors can occur in NTSC color more frequently than in the other color systems, which have stable color by comparison. Nevertheless, NTSC color has been improved to the point where I believe, given the choice today, it would be more difficult to support the virtues of the other systems against the disadvantage of not having a worldwide standard.

Video Standards

As we have discussed, there are three major worldwide standards for encoding color information. Conceptually they are very similar, but very different in terms of implementation. As it turns out, the problems of color standards are relatively trivial compared with the more basic field and line rate standards. An inexpensive convertor box can turn PAL color into NTSC color, and so forth. However, the difficulties encountered when attempting to turn NTSC line and field rate into PAL line and field rate, for example, are relatively complex and do not yield to a simple solution; but, as we shall see, there are solutions.

In some parts of the world 60 Hz alternating current is used, and in other parts 50 Hz alternating current is used. When video was introduced, it was decided to tie in the field rate with the alternating current frequency. Given the perspective of the video engineers at the time, it's easy to see why they made the choice they did. However, we now have several standards for various parts of the world. In some countries, like those in Western Europe, a field frequency of fifty was selected, and 625 lines per picture (two fields make up a picture) used for a total of 15,625 video lines per second. The video channel bandwidth used is between 5 and 6 MHz, and for the PAL system of color encoding, a color subcarrier at 4.43 MHz is employed.

France and the USSR employ SECAM encoding, with a color subcarrier at 4.43 MHz, with the same number of fields and lines as Western Europe. In North America and most of South America and Japan, 525 lines per frame are used with a field frequency of 60 Hz, with 15,750 lines per second transmitted. The video bandwidth is 4.2 MHz, with NTSC color encoded with a subcarrier at 3.58 MHz. Then there are exceptions, like Brazil, which uses basic NTSC for line and field rate, but PAL for color encoding. This system, unique to Brazil, is called PAL-M. I've seen it at work, and it's a good system.

It's a pity that all these standards exist. It simply makes video less of a universal medium for the diffusion of information. Perhaps the introduction of high-definition video systems will lead to the adoption of a new universal standard.

Right now the only universal standards that exist for the transmission of moving images are motion picture standards. A super 8, 16mm, 35mm or 70mm projector can play the same film in Casablanca or Pocatello.

Although there are standards for the various formats, these standards are quite rational, and help the user. What I'm getting at is this: Super 8 is meant for small screen, say three or five feet across, and 70mm for large screen, say fifty or seventy feet wide. But video, whether it's PAL or NTSC, or one inch or quarter inch tape, usually plays on the same relatively small screens.

Digital Video

The kind of video signal we are most familiar with is called an analog signal, using voltages corresponding to variations in picture density. The cathode ray tube is an analog transducer, which serves to photograph or display an image. The signal as it is transmitted or stored is also treated in an analog fashion. However, in recent years there has been a great deal of interest in digitization of video information, and a number of devices have been put into service using this principle. A *digital video signal* assigns numbers to density and color. These discrete numbers, or digital words, resemble the computer processing of information. A number of procedures which require circuits of great complexity in analog form become trivial in digital form, partly because digital circuitry can take advantage of the latest advances in integrated circuitry and computer techniques.

One major advantage of the digitized image is that it can be copied many times, without any perceptible signal loss. Analog signals lose appreciable quality every generation of duplication. After a few dubs, the image will show losses in sharpness, increased background noise, increased contrast, color shifts and so on. At this moment digital recorders have been shown, but none to my knowledge are on the market.

The digitization of video has made possible relatively high quality standards conversion. NTSC to PAL or vice versa, for example, is now commonplace.

Digital effects boxes are responsible for the various 'opticals' that have proliferated in broadcast video. Wipes, zooms and effects that I can barely describe in under a page are now commonplace.

Whether or not video will become entirely digital remains to be seen. There are difficulties. A digitized signal of the same information content as an analog signal can require appreciably more bandwidth, making it quite a bit less attractive for broadcast and for recording. Digital transducers for photography and display need to be perfected as well. These are major challenges that have prevented a stampede to digitization of the video signal, whatever the advantages. It may well be that digital and analog video will live together comfortably for quite some time, each doing the job it does best.

Solid State Sensors

The Hitachi VK-C1000 camera introduced in 1982 uses the first solid state imaging sensor for color videography. This simple but interesting camera is

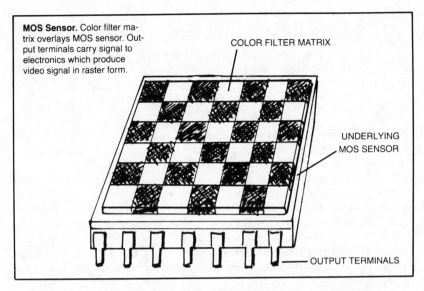

MOS Sensor. Color filter matrix overlays MOS sensor. Output terminals carry signal to electronics which produce video signal in raster form.

COLOR FILTER MATRIX

UNDERLYING MOS SENSOR

OUTPUT TERMINALS

aimed at the consumer, and it uses a single MOS (metal-oxide semiconductor) chip, overlaid with a mosaic of color filters.

Several months after the introduction of this product, Hitachi demonstrated at trade shows its similar SR-1 and SR-10 cameras, which use an array of three MOS sensors to produce the RGB information. These new solid state sensors use less power, requiring no high voltage like the CRT. They take up less room, weigh less, use less backup circuitry, and in this, their first generation as color pickup devices to reach the marketplace, clearly rival the quality of tube cameras and in some respects exceed their quality. The handwriting is on the wall for CRT pickup tubes.

The sensor used in the VK-C1000 is well matched to the needs of the consumer marketplace. It produces good color and a sharp image, but it has some problems which remain to be solved. Before we get to the problems, however, let me add that the sensor exhibits no lag, or smearing of image or color with motion, and it cannot be damaged by pointing the lens at the sun or other bright light. CRT devices can have an image of a bright light source burnt into their light-sensitive surface, which may or may not fade in time.

Most of the problems of the current single-chip sensor arise from its use of an additive color grid overlaying the light-sensitive surface. This leads to higher background noise levels than tube models. Also perceptible is an effect that looks like halation for motion picture film when shooting under bright lights. For video it's called *blooming*.

Apparently the three-sensor professional camera has none of these defects and produces a splendid image, in most ways on a par with the best quality ENG equipment.

The Hitachi professional cameras, meant for ENG applications, use MOS sensors—one for R, one for G and one for B. A beam splitter assembly produces the necessary RGB components, and it and the MOS chips are epoxied together to form one unit which cannot get out of alignment.

Other similar products have worked their way onto dealers' shelves. These cameras, manufactured by various Japanese firms, use related solid-state technologies to bypass the pickup tube of prior art cameras.

The Telecine

The term *telecine* is used to describe a device which translates motion pictures into video signals. Telecines have been an important part of the video infrastructure from its very inception.

The most widely used telecine is essentially nothing more than a motion picture projector and a video camera. Since there are twenty-four motion picture frames and thirty video frames per second, there must be some way to translate the twenty-four frames of motion picture into thirty frames of video. One solution is to use an intermittent movement which can produce alternately three TV fields from one film frame and then two fields from the next. In this way twenty-four frames can be turned into sixty fields.

This technique can provide very good results. For one thing, the motion picture image has a far greater contrast range than the video image produced by a video camera. There will be more detail in highlight and shadow areas of a film frame than in a corresponding video-originated frame. Therefore, the combination of film and telecine serves to produce an image which is generally pictorially superior to a video-originated image in many circumstances.

Lately a new generation of telecines has been introduced, and these have characteristics superior to the intermittent telecine. These new machines, using continuous motion, have either *flying spot scanners* or *charged-coupled devices* to generate the video image. Since the motion of the telecine is continuous, the machines are suitable for handling camera original, which can be damaged when transported by intermittent techniques. The new telecines also give noticeably superior images.

The Rank Cinetel uses a flying spot scanner, and the Robert Bosch telecine uses charged-coupled device sensors and a semiconductor frame store to create the appropriate interlace video signal. The drawing shows the operation of the flying spot scanner. A CRT generates a raster which is projected through the motion picture frame while it is in continuous motion. An optical system, similar to that which is used within a three-tube camera, separates the light passing through the film into red, green and blue images. The raster projected on the film is the flying spot which dissects the image. As you can see from the drawing, three photomultiplier tubes sense the instantaneous signal strength of the RGB components of the video signal. Processing circuitry is then used to create the desired video standard: NTSC, PAL or SECAM.

The charged-coupled device manufactured by Bosch eliminates the CRT, and instead uses solid state sensors to image a single video line at a

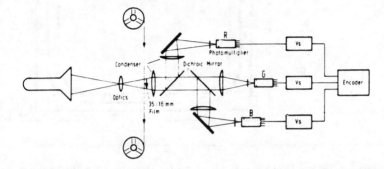

time. These lines of image are stored and processed to produce the needed video output.

Both of these devices produce fantastically good video images from well-shot film. Many transfer houses use these machines in conjunction with other techniques to process or enhance the video signal. In particular, negative camera film, when transferred to video tape using these techniques, produces superb images.

Many filmmakers and production companies are transferring their original camera film to tape to take advantage of video postproduction facilities, especially when a film involves lots of opticals, which can be produced in real time during editing. If a film is bound to be shown on the tube, and it must be cut in a hurry, video postproduction may be the way for those who have the bucks.

Something very interesting is happening with video. The new electronic cinematography cameras from Panavision and Ikegami produce video images that look like film, and the new flying spot telecines produce video from film which looks like it was originated on video. Someday it may be difficult to tell whether a television program was originated on video or film.

Film Shot for Video

People who are shooting theatrical films for the television screen don't need my advice. They know what they're doing. They can control the lighting precisely and accommodate their efforts to the display medium. The general approach is to use lower ratios of key to fill light when shooting for video.

The rest of us, who may be shooting documentaries or who knows what, may not be able to light what we shoot. Terrifically good transfers to tape

Video for the Filmmaker

418

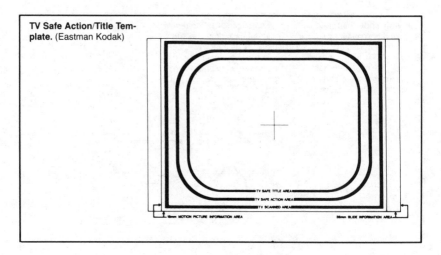

TV Safe Action/Title Template. (Eastman Kodak)

are still possible. There have been great strides in transfer techniques, including flying spot and CCD continuous telecine machines, image enhancement techniques, and more sophisticated kinds of color and gamma control than are possible for the production of release prints. As a general rule, based on my work and what I've seen, if it looks good as a projected film image, it is possible to make a successful transfer to video.

The most important thing to keep in mind is that the video image is cropped to different extents by sets made by various manufacturers, and there is absolutely nothing you or anybody can do about all those weirdly adjusted receivers out there. Study the television graphics production template I've reproduced here. You'll see that there is within the normal film rectangle provision for safe action and safe title areas. You can count on losing quite a bit of your composition when transfers to video occur. You'll have to concentrate your compositions in the central portion of the frame. Some film cameras provide reticules within the finder image so that you can see the outline of the safe action area.

Tape to Film

Transferring film to video is relatively easy and inexpensive, and can produce beautiful results. Transferring video to film is relatively difficult, expensive and very often produces indifferent results.

From its earliest days it has been desirable to record video images, but in those days there was no electronic video recording medium. Therefore, film was used as a storage medium. Early film recordings made by directly shooting the face of a picture tube were called *kinescopes,* which is taken from the name of the picture tube itself. These early kinescope recordings were relatively crude. Today many video-to-film transfers are made in basically the same way. A camera, with intermittent locked to field rate, shoots the face of a CRT. However, new electronic enhancement tech-

Independent Filmmaking

niques are used; and for color, some sophisticated techniques use a black and white CRT photographed in three successive passes through red, blue and then green filters.

Higher tech methods have been shown involving electron beam recoding of photographic emulsions and laser-scanned emulsions, but the old standby, basically the kinescope technique, remains with us and is used more often than not.

RGB Color

We've discussed how NTSC and similar electronic color encoding schemes eliminate the need to triple the video bandwidth. But these techniques substantially reduce the quality of the image. If recording is not required—if we're getting a video signal out of a camera, or a computer, and displaying it directly on the monitor—RGB may be the way to go. In this case three separate channels, one for each primary, are transmitted to the monitor. The result is substantially superior pictorial quality, with a sharper-appearing image and better color.

RGB recorders are just appearing on the market, and, as we shall see, more advanced recording techniques now separate the chrominance information from the luminance, to give a sharper color image.

Each receiver or monitor finally shows an RGB signal, since the three electron guns in the CRT excite, respectively, RGB phosphors. However, the signal sent to each gun has had its potential color information diluted if the source was NTSC (or PAL or SECAM). There are now available special monitors which can show RGB (and NTSC also) with prices starting at about $600 list.

High-Definition TV

There is a great yearning for better quality video images which are on a par with good quality motion picture images. Such a system would use more lines per field, use a superior method for encoding color, and might also have a wider aspect ratio to reflect the trend set in the movies in the early fifties.

It's one thing to specify the characteristics of such a system, and another to actualize such a suggestion. NHK, the Japanese television network, has for a decade been researching such a system, and they have shown their efforts in this country. I haven't seen a demonstration of it yet, but all the reports I've read (and there have been many) and the eyewitnesses who've talked to me say it looks great. CBS has championed the system, and has been using whatever clout it has to make the FCC take notice.

The present system we are discussing (others have been shown, and others are possible) uses 1125 video lines, with a picture aspect ratio of 1.67:1, a 2:1 interlace, and a 60 Hz refresh rate. Proposed is a 20 MHz bandwidth for luminance and 7 MHz for chrominance.

Sony has demonstrated a special modification of its one inch Type C format recorder which can record the necessary 30 MHz bandwidth (approximately) for this high-definition format.

Color encoding is not RGB, as has been falsely reported, but rather a variation of the PAL system.

High-definition cameras, recorders, peripherals and, obviously, displays need to be perfected. Many questions spring to mind. Is this not an excellent opportunity to provide a worldwide video standard? Will 50 Hz field rate countries feel left out, or will they simply opt for 50 Hz high-definition systems of their own? To my eyes the fifty field rate European TV flickers, but Europeans can't see it, so they say. But I'm afraid that for large screen display, which goes along with high-definition video, the flicker will be worse. Europeans think our color system is for the birds (Never The Same Color twice), and I say PAL and SECAM also leave a great deal to be desired.

Proponents of high-definition video think it might make its greatest impact initially for the production of feature films. Maybe, but 35mm film still has a far, far greater bandwidth.

High-definition TV will also breathe new life into film as a source of video production. Film is intrinsically high definition. All those 35mm films sitting on the shelf exceed the NHK high-definition system's quality. But what to do about 525 line tape-originated shows? Film ought to do very well in the high-definition era.

Questions remain about the compatibility of high-definition and present video standards. Can you make one receiver to pick up both standards? Can you convert programs shot in one standard to the other?

Transmission Shortcomings

In the United States system, based on 525 lines per picture, there are certain shortcomings inherent in the system that prevent maximum image quality. If the most were made of the present video system, if it were maximized, there could be an appreciable increase in the quality of the image.

In the first place, 42 of the 525 lines must be used for vertical blanking, as discussed earlier (21 for each field). That reduces the number of lines per image to 483. Unfortunately, the losses don't end there. There is what is known as the *utilization ratio,* a way of explaining that some detail will fall between the scanning lines and not be transmitted. Moreover, the typical receiver crops a good deal of the top and bottom and sides of the picture, resulting in even more picture information being lost. The image as transmitted is rectangular, with a 4:3 aspect ratio. The CRT in your home probably has rounded sides, contributing to the image cropping.

In addition, the field interlace may not be properly adjusted in your set. Lines may be scanning on top of each other, a condition known as *line pairing*. The result is a loss of picture information.

Although the video signal has a bandwidth of 4.2 MHz, the majority of receivers only process information to about 3 MHz. By filtering out the higher frequencies, the set manufacturers hope to eliminate unpleasant background noise especially visible in color images; but they are also eliminating all the higher spatial frequencies, or fine detail, from the image.

There are other factors that also prevent all the possible image information from making a contribution. It's probably fair to say that the TV image is only about half as good as it could be. You'll notice some improvement from many closed-circuit sources, such as disks, compared with broadcast images, because interference can be eliminated when we don't have to deal with the spurious reflection and other losses in the transmission of radio waves.

A new high-definition TV standard is not the cure-all for the video image problem, and we ought to consider standards which could make the most of the system we've already got.

Tape Formats

Modern video tape recorders all use *helical scan* geometry. The tape itself is wrapped around a cylindrical post, which rotates rapidly. The cylinder incorporates one, or often two or more, heads which wipe a diagonal pattern of recorded tracks on the moving tape. This ingenious method allows for the tape transport itself to move tape at a rate of only a few inches per second, while the actual writing speed of the recording, measured by the tape-to-head speed, can be more like several hundreds of inches per second.

The writing speed for video must be many times faster than that for audio recording. For recording audio we need a tape and recorder combination that will produce a bandwidth of about 20,000 cycles. For video recording we are talking about being able to cover a 4,200,000 cycle bandwidth, some two hundred times the audio bandwidth.

However, the half inch amateur formats, the similar Beta (for magnetic

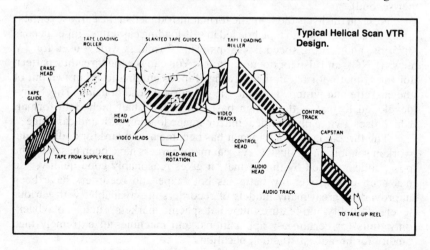

Typical Helical Scan VTR Design.

Video for the Filmmaker

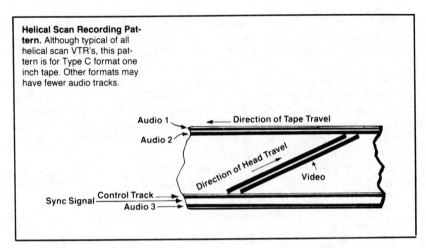

flux) and VHS (Video Home System) systems, settle for a bandwidth that's less than half the full bandwidth. This compromise is made to cut costs and extend playing time. Even the professionally oriented three-quarter inch format does not record the full video bandwidth, but it does do a better job than the half inch formats. Of the formats on the market, only the one inch Type C (and similar Type B) covers the full video bandwidth.

The one inch Type C format was developed jointly by Sony and Ampex to suit the needs of broadcasters. It provides the highest broadcast quality video signal, and it is frequently used for mastering programs which are intended for distribution in the smaller formats, since duplication losses are kept to a minimum. No cassette or cartridge is available for handling the tape. There is an alternative one inch format, developed by Bosch, which is of similar quality, known as Type B, which is not used to any great extent in North America. The writing speed for these formats is about 950 ips (inches per second).

Next on the list is the U-matic format introduced in the early seventies, using three-quarter inch tape housed in self-loading cassettes. Tape speed is 3.75 ips, and writing speed is 438 ips. This format is widely used for TV news (ENG), and also for documentaries. You can see the threading pattern for the U-matic format in the drawing. Tape is automatically drawn out of the cassette and wrapped around the cylindrical head housing. This Sony-developed format is the design basis for Sony's half inch Beta format, which uses a virtually identical mirror-image loading path and cartridge.

The three-quarter inch format has become a standard for audio-visual work in schools and industry. A great many careers have been based on the possibilities opened by this format. It gives reasonably good quality, and has been getting steadily better as both tape and recorders have been improved. A great many models of recorders are available, with various levels of quality and features aimed at specific markets, such as playback-only units for certain a-v applications, and machines of extremely high quality for broadcast studio applications.

Independent Filmmaking

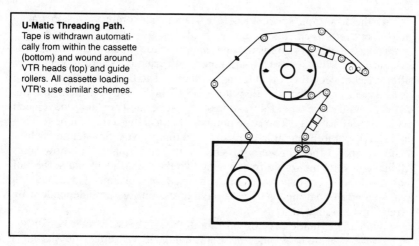

U-Matic Threading Path.
Tape is withdrawn automatically from within the cassette (bottom) and wound around VTR heads (top) and guide rollers. All cassette loading VTR's use similar schemes.

The U-matic format may have been responsible, to a large extent, for preventing the possible expansion of super 8 into audio-visual and video applications. The fact that you don't have to set up a screen and douse the lights to look at video has been a strong selling point. Low duplicating costs per copy have also helped. Nevertheless, 16mm has remained a strong audio-visual contender, undoubtedly because of the large number of 16mm projectors in place and the large commitment that has been made to 16mm software—prints, for those of you who grew up before the rise of video.

The Beta and VHS formats were designed to help consumers get more out of TV by allowing them to record their favorite programs when they were out playing golf, or maybe even going to the movies. Many of these units contain their own tuners and programmable clock mechanisms.

The existence of the technology has opened the door to creative possibilities for the independent, since there are a number of nifty half inch machines with which to work, and many interesting cameras and peripherals are now aimed at the home video market for people seeking to make home movies on tape. And there is a large and flourishing market for feature films using the half inch cassette formats, which has created a climate and a distribution system which could possibly help the independent.

The Beta and VHS cassette formats are very similar, and both are based on the three-fourth inch U-matic format. They use much slower tape speeds, and there is even a selection of two or three speeds for longer running times. The Beta speeds are 1.58, 0.79 and 0.53 ips, with writing speeds of about 275 ips. The fastest speed, 1.58 ips, is reserved for Beta I industrial products. Home Beta machines, Types II and III, use the slow speeds. VHS has three speeds: 1.31, 0.67 and 0.44 ips—known as SP, LP and EP, respectively—and a writing speed of about 229 ips for SP and LP, and 221.4 for EP. The VHS outsells the Beta format by a factor of three or four, primarily because longer playing times are available for the TV freak. You can have up to eight hours of junk recorded on a single VHS cassette, as opposed to five hours of foolishness on a Beta cassette.

Video for the Filmmaker

At the low tape speed there are significant compromises in image quality, but improvements have been made.

The existence of two formats has simply made things inconvenient for the consumer who seeks to trade tapes with friends. There is very little difference between the two in terms of quality. The Beta cartridge (6 × 3.5 × 1 inch) is slightly smaller than the VHS (7.38 × 4.06 × 1 inch), but the VHS can hold more tape. Interesting battery-operated portables have been made for both formats. The large number of consumer units that have been made have inspired manufacturers to outdo themselves. Smaller and lighter machines than I thought were possible, with better quality, are now here. All in all, despite the stupidity of having two Ike and Mike formats, the half inch machines have ushered us into a new era of consumer video, making available additional means of creative expression for the independent by extending the range of tools.

While the U-matic cassettes are about the size of an average book (8.68 × 5.31 × 1.25 inches), and the Beta and VHS cassettes the size of a paperback, the CVC cassette (4.13 × 2.63 × 0.44 inches) is about the size of an audio cassette. The CVC cassette, introduced by Funai and offered at this time in the United States on a nonexclusive basis by Technicolor, may well be the basis for future home tape formats.

Design for Home Movie Camera/VTR. Shown here in this 1980 Kodak patent, we see a solid state imaging array used in place of a CRT. The inboard cassette (64, to the right) uses longitudinal recording scheme with fixed (not rotating) heads to record multiple tracks for chrominance and luminance. Other Kodak disclosures call for prerecorded sync pulses, unlike other tape formats which have the recorder produce sync pulses. It would take a film manufacturer to think of prerecording the pulses like prepunched perforations.

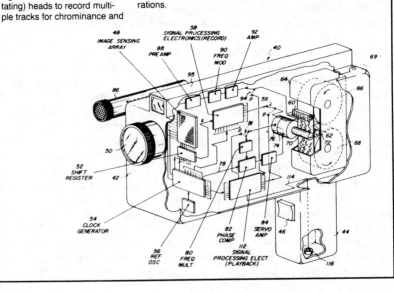

Super 8 was caught in a squeeze. People who might want to make home movies were scared off by the mere existence of half inch equipment. Although too bulky to really compete, it does offer instant playback and lower software costs. The half inch equipment hasn't been accepted as a home movie medium because of its bulk, despite the fact that the equipment has gotten smaller. It was the threat of video, rather than the existence of any actual equipment, that helped put the whammy on super 8. The CVC format, or similar formats, would certainly be a more appropriate tool.

European and Japanese manufacturers met in Japan early in 1982 to set standards for a new tape format to be used by home movie makers. Although they may deny it, there's little doubt that such a format would also be a likely candidate to replace the present half inch formats. The new format, it has been reported by leaks in the trades, will use tape 8mm wide, a cassette designed by Matsushita (Panasonic) and a system for dynamic track following invented by Philips.

Kodak may well be going it alone with their own tape format, as we can see from the patent drawing reproduced here. The European-Japanese manufacturers plan to use the usual helical scan head system, but Kodak has chosen a multiple-channel longitudinal (fixed-head) system similar to that used for audio recording.

Time Base Correction

All video recorders can need *time base correction*. This is a process whereby the sync pulses of the video output of the recorder are synchronized with the sync pulses of another recorder, or a broadcast system. (If we tried to feed the signal from a recorder into a video system, and the video coming out of the recorder was not in sync with the system, the picture would tend to break up or roll, or in general become quite unwatchable.)

Time base correction is analogous to driving two rolls of film in perfect sync, say one roll of mag film on a mag film recorder and a roll of picture on an interlocked projector. For motion picture film, synchronization may be achieved by mechanical, electrical or electronic means. For video, synchronization of two video signals can only be achieved electronically.

Time base correctors usually work by delaying the signal, often using digital techniques, from the video recorder so that it interfaces with the rest of the video network. Time base correction is not needed when feeding the video output from a recorder to a monitor for display, or to another recorder for duplication.

New Tape Formats

In 1982 dramatic developments took place in VTR technology. Present ENG equipment uses a separate VTR and camera. This is cumbersome for the operator, who must strap on a recorder backpack; or the recorder is pushed around on a little cart with cables run to the camera. In some cases the video signal is transmitted to a remote recorder by radio. How much

Video for the Filmmaker

simpler to incorporate the recorder and the camera into a single unit.

Bosch, Hitachi, Ikegami, Panasonic, RCA and Sony showed various camera/recorder configurations based on half inch and quarter inch tape cassettes. The three-fourth inch cassette was too large to turn into a portable inboard recorder, so the smaller Beta, VHS and CVC cassettes were used with tape running at higher speeds than used in the consumer versions. For example, the M format of Panasonic, which is identical to the Chroma Track format of RCA, uses the Panasonic-developed VHS cassette, but with tape running at 8 ips and with a writing speed of 225 ips. Most interesting is that the chrominance and luminance information is separated and recorded on two channels with two heads. This eliminates many of the problems associated with small format color quality by increasing chrominance information to a full 1 MHz bandwidth compared with a 0.3 MHz bandwidth for three-quarter U-matic format. Sony has shown a similar format based on their Beta technology.

These formats have quality that in most ways equals, and in some ways exceeds, one inch quality. We could confidently predict the imminent demise of one inch Type C, but I'll hedge my bet because of high-definition video, which may be the only good reason for hanging on to the costly one inch format. Sony has demonstrated, in prototype form using a modified Type C deck, a 30 MHz deck suitable for the NHK-proposed high-definition system.

For my money, the most astounding and interesting format to be shown was developed by Bosch, and is called the Lineplex system. It uses the CVC cassette, which holds quarter inch tape in a package about audio cassette size. The tape speed is 5 ips, and it records a full 4 MHz video signal with 3 MHz for luminance and 1 MHz for chrominance, using a recording scheme similar to that employed by the new half inch equipment. The Bosch format is very provocative and appealing since it matches the new half inch efforts in quality, thereby upstaging these formats.

Video Disks

After years of waiting, the video disk finally made its appearance in the early 1980s, as a consumer product. While initial sales of players were not up to manufacturers' expectations, video disk technology has made a place for itself not only as a consumer entertainment medium, but also as an important industrial and educational a-v medium. Unlike the cassette tape medium which can record programs, disks are prerecorded only—like phonograph records, which they strongly resemble.

The two systems, which are also suitable for a-v applications, are the Philips and MCA–developed technology, variously known as Disco-Vision, LV (laser vision) and by the generic name of *optical disk;* the SelectaVision disk, also known as CED (Capacitance Electronic Disk), was developed by RCA.

The LV disk appears in two versions: one, suitable for special functions, called *constant angular velocity,* which stores half an hour on a side; and the other, called *constant linear velocity,* which stores an hour on a side and cannot be used for special functions. The former runs at 1800 rpm, and the latter from 1800 to 600 rpm.

The LV disk is laser scanned in the player, and, because there is no physical contact between the sensor and the software, it is possible to index and find any one of the 54,000 frames encoded on a single constant linear velocity disk. Moreover, slow motion, still frame, backward motion and random access are possible. The random access feature is particularly provocative since the laser sensor needs only to track inward along the disk's radius to find appropriate material. This is much speedier to do than for the serially recorded tape formats, and creates the possibility of interactive disks, which can respond instantly to, for example, a student's answers to program questions.

Laser disks can be handled directly without being incorporated in a special caddy or sleeve, as is the case for the RCA disk. Fingerprints don't hurt them. One would also expect indefinite longevity since the laser disk does not come into physical contact with, and is not worn out by, a stylus, as is the case for the RCA capacitive disk, whose technology more closely resembles LP audio disks. Both the RCA and Philips-MCA disks are about the size of an LP. The Philips-MCA disk, however, uses microscopic pits to reflect light to a sensor. This is purely an optical process. The RCA disk must be scanned by being in physical contact with a diamond stylus, and the action of the stylus tracts capacitance and creates the variations in electrical signal which are turned into the video output.

The RCA disk rotates at a constant 450 rpm, and until now did not allow for the interactive and other special functions of the laser disk. However, RCA has shown that such applications are possible.

There are other disks which might be of interest to the filmmaker, but these products will probably never be offered in the marketplace to any significant extent. I'm thinking of technologies such as the Thomson optical disks and the VHD disks developed by Matsushita.

Disks maintain a substantial quality margin above the half inch tape technology in the consumer marketplace. Movies distributed on the laser disk can look as good as one inch dubs, and have high-fidelity stereo sound. Most half inch dubs of features distributed even by reputable majors have loathsome quality, suitable only for visual illiterates who don't give a damn about quality. Nevertheless, I have seen recent examples of better quality Beta and VHS feature films. But the fact remains that the laser disk has the ability to record the full 4 MHz bandwidth, while the ½ inch tape formats usually do less than half that. (The RCA CED disks are limited to a 3 MHz bandwidth.) Prerecorded disks also cost about half or a third of their tape format competitors. While they have the quality and the price, they don't have the ability to record, and this lack seems to be the major strike against the disk as far as consumers have been concerned.

However, technology marches on, and disks will someday be able to be recorded by the user—and systems that can do this have been shown. More taxing on the designers is a system which can not only record, but which is also erasable.

Video for the Filmmaker

The video disk is a marvelous invention, but it's not new. John Logie Baird, the indefatigable British tinkerer, showed video disks that actually worked—but had very low resolution—half a century ago.

Video Postproduction of Film Projects

Cameras with a video-assist viewfinder, commonly called a *video tap*, take a portion of the image-forming light from the camera optical system and use it for a video camera. The use of the video viewfinder is somewhat controversial for the theatrical film industry, since it can lead to production slowdowns because the image can be taped and then studied.

The cinematographer and director are dependent upon the camera operator to report to them the quality of the camera work immediately following every shot. The camera operator is clearly in a hotseat, since he must literally call the shot, either pinpointing his own mistakes or mistakes of other crew members. Sometimes errors will get past him. The video-assist finder would tend to prevent that from happening.

It is also possible to use the tape produced through the video finder for editing the film. (Or tape could be transferred from the camera negative.) The director can take half inch cassette versions of the shots home and make paper cuts in his living room. These practice sessions could aid in the final edit of the film. If there were some way to exactly link the film shot in the camera with the video record being made, a way to index both frame for frame, then the job of cutting a feature film might in some ways be simplified.

As of this writing, Kodak has published a feasibility study to inform the film industry that it possesses a portion of such a technology. By coating a thin and nearly transparent magnetic layer across the entire surface area of the base of camera negative, film can be converted into magnetic tape suitable for storing time code information. Such a time code has been standardized by SMPTE (Society of Motion Picture and Television Engi-

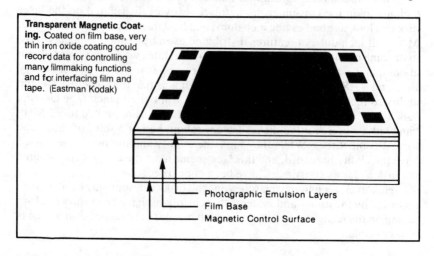

Transparent Magnetic Coating. Coated on film base, very thin iron oxide coating could record data for controlling many filmmaking functions and for interfacing film and tape. (Eastman Kodak)

Photographic Emulsion Layers
Film Base
Magnetic Control Surface

Independent Filmmaking

Tape Editing Suite.

neers), and is a binary code which can be read out as frame information.

At the time of shooting, both the negative being exposed and tape in the video-assist system could be coded to correspond on a frame-by-frame basis. The resultant tapes could be edited using standard video techniques. Workprints, or dailies, in the scheme discussed here, would not have to be made.

After the tape has been edited, its time code could be used to drive a computer controlled printing machine that could produce an answer print from the camera film without the camera film ever having been cut. A number of advantages might accrue from such a high-technology approach. For one thing, many versions of the same film could be produced for various markets or purposes.

I've outlined briefly some of the possibilities of linking video and film technology. Film editing is not highly automated and requires physical cutting of the print. Video is highly automated, less precise than film editing (accuracy to a frame or two), and tape cannot be physically cut. Film editing equipment is relatively inexpensive, and an editor can afford to work long unscheduled hours since film editing suites are rented by the day or week or month. Video editing suite rentals are too expensive to lease and use in the same way. Video cutting is a hands-off computer-assisted affair, and film editing is just the same old down-home affair it has been for decades.

For some productions the possible interrelationship of film and video makes sense. It depends on budget and time considerations that are beyond the scope of this book. Although it's a promising field, it's possible to be led astray. Witness the ballyhoo associated with Francis Coppola's video-assisted disaster, *One From the Heart*. When all is said and done, the play's the thing.

Video for the Filmmaker

Index

Note: numbers in italics indicate illustrations

Index

Index

Index

443

Photographic Credits

Title page: Robert Nelson shooting *The Great Blondino*
page 6: Frame from the computer animated film *Poem: Fields* by Stan VanDerBeek and Ken Knowlton
page 10: Stan Brakhage (Photo by Michael Chikiris)
page 21: Layout of strips of hand-drawn film from Barry Spinello's *Sound Track*
page 49: From *THX 1138*, directed by George Lucas (Pacific Film Archive)
page 50: From Bruce Baillie's *Quick Billie*

page 86: Gunvor Nelson shooting a work in progress
page 137: Ed Emshwiller (Photo by Carol Emshwiller)
page 186: Lenny Lipton shooting *Far Out, Star Route* (Photo by Diane Julie Lipton)
page 229: James Broughton directing *The Golden Positions*
page 277: From *Barbarella*, directed by Roger Vadim (Pacific Film Archive)
page 278: Federico Fellini directing *Satyricon*
page 304: Donna Kerness during the filming of *The Sins of*

the Fleshapoids, directed by Mike Kuchar (Photo by Lenny Lipton)
page 341: From *Christ of the Rooftops*, directed by Herbert Jean deGrasse
page 373: From *Metropolis*, directed by Fritz Lang
page 431: Mick Jagger in the 'Memo to Turner' sequence from *Performance*, directed by Donald Cammell and Nicholas Roeg
page 401: From a piece by Denise Gallant of Synopsis Video

Index

444 List of Illustrations

Index

Lenny Lipton was born in Brooklyn, New York, in 1940. Later at Cornell University, where he studied physics, he wrote the song, "Puff, the Magic Dragon." He worked for Time Inc., and then edited the movie section of *Popular Photography* magazine. In 1965 he began to devote himself entirely to film and filmmaking; he was the film columnist for *The Berkeley Barb* during its first four years of publication; has been a director of Canyon Cinema; and has taught filmmaking at San Francisco Art Institute. His films have been screened on NET, and at the San Francisco and New York Film Festivals, the Whitney Museum of American Art, the Pacific Film Archive and the Cinèmathèque Francaise. Lenny Lipton's films are available through Canyon Cinema, San Francisco, and Filmmakers' Coop, New York.

Anne Liggette

Index